SOLARIS
PERFORMANCE
ADMINISTRATION

Solaris
Performance
Administration

Performance Measurement, Fine Tuning, and Capacity Planning for Releases 2.5.1 and 2.6

H. Frank Cervone

McGraw-Hill

New York   San Francisco   Washington, D.C.,   Auckland   Bogotá
Caracas   Lisbon   London   Madrid   Mexico City   Milan
Montreal   New Delhi   San Juan   Singapore
Sydney   Tokyo   Toronto

Library of Congress catalog card number: 98-65523

McGraw-Hill

A Division of The McGraw-Hill Companies

2 3 4 5 6 7 8 9 0   DOC/DOC   9 0 3 2 1 0 9 8

ISBN 0-07-011768-3

The sponsoring editor for this book was Judy Brief, the editing supervisor was Paul R. Sobel, and the production supervisor was Clare B. Stanley. It was set in New Century Schoolbook by Donald A. Feldman of McGraw-Hill's Professional Book Group composition unit.

Printed and bound by R. R. Donnelley & Sons Company.

McGraw-Hill books are available at special quantity discounts to use as premiums and sales promotions, or for use in corporate training programs. For more information, please write to the Director of Special Sales, McGraw-Hill, 11 West 19th Street, New York, NY 10011. Or contact your local bookstore.

This book is printed on recycled, acid-free paper containing a minimum of 50% recycled, de-inked fiber.

To my Father

CONTENTS

INTRODUCTION

What is the purpose of an introduction to a book? Primarily it is used as a marketing tool. A good introduction contains a brief explanation of what the book is about and why someone should buy it. So, here goes.

This book is a comprehensive guide to performance management and capacity planning in the Solaris environment. Unlike other books on this subject, this one is written from the perspective of a real user of the Solaris operating system—not someone employed by Sun Microsystems, Inc. Because of this, I believe the treatment is more neutral, objective, and balanced than that found in other books on this subject.

This book contains four sections that are divided into 18 chapters. The first section is a general introduction performance analysis and capacity planning.

- Chapter 1 is an introduction to performance tuning and capacity planning. It explores the meaning of both performance tuning and capacity planning and looks at the tools and methods used in both.

- Chapter 2 focuses on some of the issues related to running Solaris on both uniprocessor and multiprocessor systems. It starts with a discussion of the various types of processors that may be used; the rest of the chapter discusses Solaris implements and uses main memory, cache, virtual storage, and sway space.

- Chapter 3 defines performance and describes how to select metrics for performance measurement.

- Chapter 4 focuses on queueing models, which are essential components of performance analysis. After exploring the laws of queueing theory, the rest of the chapter examines processes: the differences (similarities) between discrete- and continuous-state processes, the properties of Markov processes, and the unique properties of Poisson processes.

The second section provides an overview of the structure of Solaris.

- Chapter 5 is devoted to understanding the architecture of the kernel. This chapter discusses how the kernel divides up the total physical memory of the computing system into logical address spaces.

- Chapter 6 focuses on virtual memory and how it is implemented on the physical memory of the machine, primarily as a mechanism for extending the capability of the system to support additional processes.

- Chapter 7 describes how Solaris implements processes and uses threads as a means to do so. In order to understand this, lightweight processes (LWPs), multiprocessing, preemption, interrupts, scheduling and scheduling classes, and priorities are investigated in this chapter.

- Chapter 8 discusses the implementation of file systems on Solaris:

  - The types of file systems in general
  - The physical media upon which file systems are implemented
  - Network based file systems
  - Pseudo file systems

Although the majority of the chapter is dedicated to discussion of the UNIX file system (UFS), the chapter concludes with a discussion of NFS—the network file system—and DFS—the distributed file system.

- Chapter 9 explores networking and intersystem communication. This chapter focuses on the physical implementation of networks, both in the local enterprise and in the larger global scheme. Beginning with a discussion of basic input and output and network protocols, the topics expand to include various network topologies such as Ethernet, Switched Enternet, Asynchronow transfer mode (ATM), Fiber Distributed Data Interface (FDDI), and token-ring.

This third section is about system performance tuning.

- Chapter 10 investigates the basic procedures and commands for monitoring activity, and workloads are investigated.

- Chapter 11 is related to memory management. This chapter examines the major indications of memory problem and how to resolve and avoid them. The concluding part of the chapter discusses the memory issues related to program development, end-user application execution, and system configuration.

- Chapter 12 focuses on I/O performance management. Disk performance tuning basics, computing maximum throughput, disk controllers and interfaces, Redundant Arrays of Inexpensive Disk (RAID) configurations, and file system implementation and optimization are all explored in depth.

- Chapter 13 relates to the physical implementation of networking. As such, this chapter focuses on understanding latency, bandwidth, and utilization, which are all critical to network performance management. Identification of performance problems and understanding the utilization characteristics of the network are also topics in this chapter.

- Chapter 14 follows up on Chapter 13 by exploring the issues involved in tuning network services such as (NFS), Network Information Service Plus (NIS+), and Domain Name Service (DNS). The concluding part of the chapter gives tips and hints for optimizing the performance of World Wide Web (WWW) servers.

- Chapter 15, the final chapter of this section, is concerned primarily with tuning system parameters in the **/etc/system** file.

The fourth, and final, section is related to the capacity planning function.

- Chapter 16 discusses the system activity data collector and reporter, which are used for gathering and interpreting system performance data.

- Chapter 17 complements the preceding chapter with a discussion of the System Accounting subsystem. Both tools are used together to gain an accurate picture of the activity on the system.

- Chapter 18, the concluding chapter, is devoted to capacity planning management. In this chapter, the major aspects of capacity planning management are disected:

  - Predicting capacity requirements
  - Characterization of the workload
  - Development of a workload model
  - Forecasting expected needs
  - Developing recommendations for action

This book is a comprehensive treatment of performance management in the Solaris environment, therefore, readers, whether novice or advanced, should find it a useful addition to their bookshelf.

Whether you have bought or borrowed this book, I hope you enjoy it and find it useful as you explore the Solaris operating system.

H. FRANK CERVONE

ACKNOWLEDGMENTS

Special thanks must go to:

Jay Ranade, Alice Tung, Judy Brief, and Paul Sobel at McGraw-Hill for their patience, suggestions and help;

Doris Brown, Catherine Marienau, Slawek Chorazy, John Neufeld, everyone else at DePaul University, and in particular in the Libraries, for their input and assistance in ways they may not even have imagined;

Christine Cervone, Brian Nielsen, Jeff Graubart, Bob Miller, John Feldman, and Steve Cooper for their assistance, in various ways, in putting this together, and finally, to Michael Dale—WOOF!

SOLARIS
PERFORMANCE
ADMINISTRATION

1

Preliminaries

This first section addresses some of the basic issues in performance tuning and capacity planning management:

- What is performance tuning?
- What is capacity planning?
- What are the major components of the system?
- What are major factors in evaluating and measuring performance?
- What are the theories and formulas used when measuring performance?

People new to the performance tuning or capacity planning function should review this section in its entirety because it defines many of the terms used throughout the remainder of the book. Experienced system administrators will probably want to skim through this section, only stopping at those sections with information that may be new to them.

1

Introduction to Performance Tuning and Capacity Planning

In this chapter, the terms *performance tuning* and *capacity planning* will be defined and the basic concepts and vocabulary of these activities will be introduced.

What Is Performance Tuning?

Since the beginning of time, people have been observing the operations of activities, both human and mechanical. Although some people engage in these observational activities simply because they enjoy the observational process, most people engage in observational activities specifically to try to predict what will happen the next time an activity is performed. This is no difference when the activities are related to a computer or a computing system. It has been said that the first performance check procedure for a computer was introduced after only two computer programs had been written. This check was designed to let the operator of the computer know how far a program had progressed in the calculations it was performing. Considering the instability of the hardware in those days, this was very valuable information; it lets the operator know where execution could be restarted if there were a failure of some sort.

With the degree of complication in today's computer systems, it is no mystery why performance observation and measurement are so important. Performance is a key criterion in the design and operation of a computer system. Obviously, people want their information processed as quickly and efficiently as possible. But what is performance tuning?

For the purposes of this book, performance tuning is the process of observing the operation of an entire computing system and then based on those observations, making adjustments to the various components of the system. The end result is that the overall system is more efficient. This definition differs somewhat from more traditional views in that we are not saying we are trying to make a particular component (or indeed even all components) more efficient; we are making the entire system more efficient. In general, this means making all components more efficient, but this is not necessarily a given. An example will clarify this point.

Consider the case where a system is already in a bad state. Access to disk drives is slow and memory is significantly overcommitted. Therefore, because memory is overcommitted, the system pages quite a bit and it does so very slowly due to the problems with the disk drives. Will increasing the speed or number of the disk drives help? Probably, but possibly not. It could be that by increasing the speed at which the system is able to page, the system automatically increases the amount of multitasking. This, in turn, ends up bringing the paging rate to a new, higher level that makes the system again come to its knees. So, even though there are more processes running and the performance of the disk drive subsystem has been improved, because of the increase in paging, no more real work is being accomplished in a given time quantum. Consequently, the performance of the system has not really been improved.

The above scenario is extremely undesirable. After spending a great deal of money on improving the disk system, one would expect a quantifiable increase in overall system performance. The end result of performance tuning should give the system administrator just that: a quantifiable and demonstrable increase in overall system performance.

What Is Capacity Planning?

Capacity planning complements performance tuning. Whereas performance tuning is used to alleviate some type of bottleneck or slowdown in the system, capacity planning is an ongoing process designed to ensure that there is adequate computing capacity for an enterprise. By definition, then, performance tuning is one of the components of capacity planning.

The desired end result of capacity planning is a situation where the users of the system never experience degraded service. Of course, this is a theoretical goal, and under most circumstances it is not possible to guarantee adequate service at all times under all situations. However, it is the goal toward which the capacity planner strives. If adequate service can be guaranteed to most users the majority of the time, one can usually say that the capacity plan is successful.*

One of the primary components of the capacity planning process is the regular reporting of the current status of the system and its capacity. Included as part of the reporting mechanism are details of anticipated changes or shifts in the use of the system. If the various people involved in the system's use and operation (management, end users, system administrators, system operators) are not kept informed, the capacity planning effort is a purposeless exercise. One of the primary goals of the capacity planning effort is to react to anticipated changes *before* problems arise. If people are not kept informed, there is no way for this to occur.

As would be expected, the end result of capacity planning is similar in many respects to the end result related to performance tuning. Capacity

---

*Of course, there are situations where reliability and availability must be 100 percent, such as in air-traffic control or life-support systems. However, for most business and academic use, 100 percent availability is a desirable goal as opposed to an absolute requirement.

planning should give the system administrator a quantifiable and demonstrable methodology for maintaining overall system performance on an ongoing basis.

Tools and Methods

Performance tuning and capacity planning require the involvement of a wide range of technical and managerial areas (Fig. 1-1). Performance problems can result from a number of different sources. No one tool or technique can locate the problem source in every instance. Likewise, no one tool or technique can correct the problem.

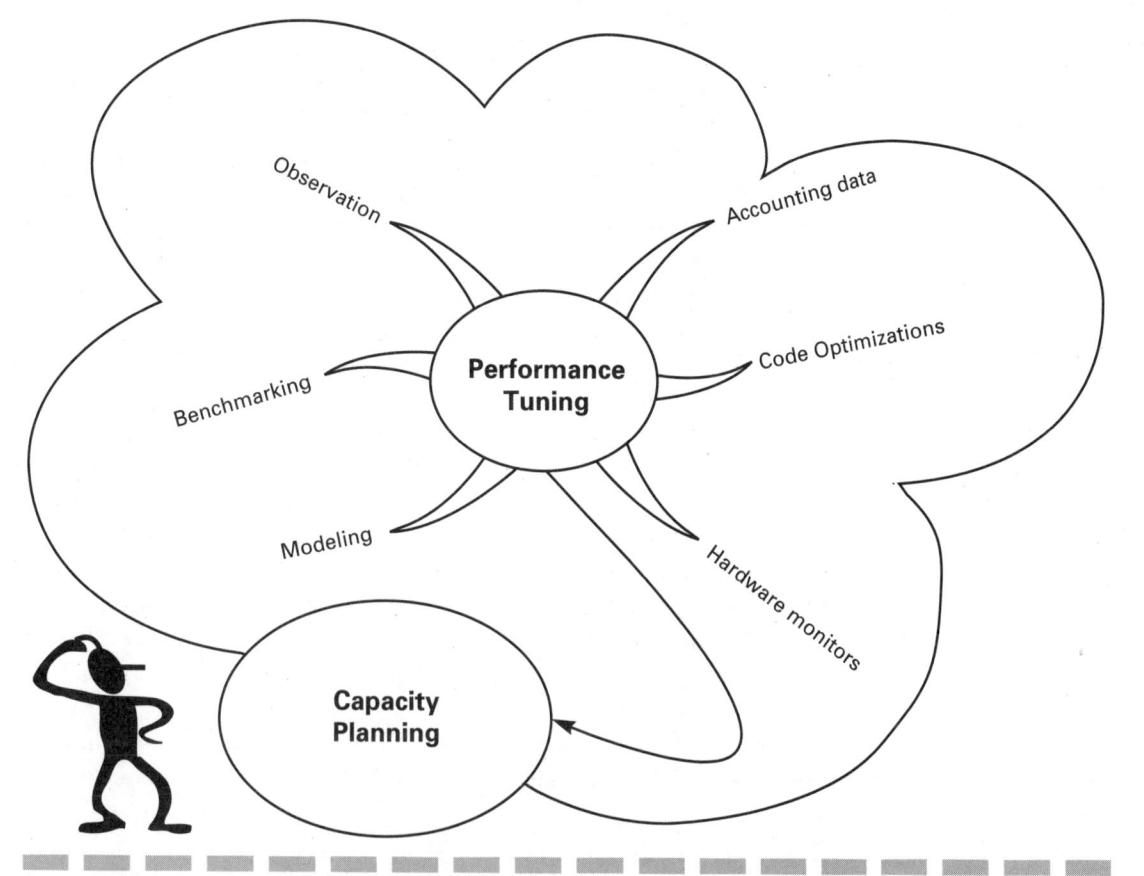

Figure 1-1
Capacity planning requires multiple tools and methods.

Performance tuning and capacity planing are both an art and a science. Certainly there are standard procedures and mathematical formulas that may be used to determine many aspects of system performance, but like fine art, successful evaluation of a system cannot be arrived at mechanistically. Every project or system evaluation requires a detailed knowledge of the system under investigation and a careful selection of the tools, methodologies, and approaches to be used for determining the source of the problem.

Perhaps the most important tools used in performance tuning are *observation* and *common sense*. Before any other analysis occurs, the entire computing system should be inspected to see what is really happening. Most often, performance problems are brought to the attention of the system administrator or other responsible party by an end user. Although it is certainly important to get a reliable and complete description of the problem incident from the user, the performance analyst must look beyond the user's description to see what else is happening and could be contributing to or causing the problem.

As an example, a user from accounting reports to the performance analyst that with the introduction of a new closing program, it now consistently takes 10 minutes (min) to close the books for the day whereas before the new program it only took a minute or two. The user has reached the conclusion that the new closing program has some type of coding error. What the user did not, and cannot, tell the performance analyst is that a few days before the new closing problem was implemented, an entirely new customer reporting system was introduced. The marketing department is now running several computationally intensive reports at the same time the accounting department is trying to close. It is quite possible that there is absolutely nothing wrong with the new closing program; the problem is that the system load is now much greater than it had been previously. Although the closing program should be investigated for potential problems, the performance analyst should also take a look at the customer reporting system.

Of course, with a good capacity planning program in place, the above would not have taken place in the first place.

Accounting Data Reduction Programs

Accounting data, in the context of this book, is information collected regarding the use of computing resources. In the Solaris environment, this information is collected and reported on by various programs in the `/usr/lib/acct` subdirectory.

Accounting data reduction programs trace their beginnings back to the check flags that were inserted into programs in the earlier days of computing. Eventually, these check flags evolved into *trace routines* that allowed the programmer to record the execution of individual instructions as a program ran. By inserting these trace routines into programs at appropriate points, it is possible to gather extensive information on how a program is executing and what factors are influencing its execution. However, this method places additional demands on the computing system and therefore has the potential of significantly influencing the resulting accounting data.

Software Monitors

Another descendant of check flags and trace routines is the *software monitor,* which is the `sar` program in Solaris. The major difference between software monitors and accounting data reduction packages is the level of detail in the collected data. Software monitors generally perform closer examination of the execution of instructions than do accounting data reduction packages. Because of the way software monitors gather information, this method is the most detailed and complete method of all of those to be discussed. However, as with accounting data reduction packages, this method places additional demands on the computing system and therefore has the potential of significantly influencing the statistical validity of the collected data.

Program Optimization and Program Optimizers

Most programming languages provide options in the compiler to *optimize* the executable code. Various levels of optimization are usually offered, but the basic functions of optimization revolve around several common issues (Fig. 1-2):

Removing constant operations from inside loops

Computing common subexpressions only once

Optimizing the use of registers and memory

Optimizing the access of elements in an array

Removing code that can never be executed

Unoptimized Code

```
int process(int factor)

{
  float values[i][j]
  for (j = 0; j<n; j++);            Array is referenced incorrectly in row/column order
  do
    {
     for ( i=0; i<n; i++);
       do
         {
          multiplier = i*factor;    This can be computed once outside of the loop
          avg(values[i][j], j*multiplier);
          median(values[i][j], j*multiplier);   The expression j*multiplier should be computed once before calling
          mode(values[i][j], j*multiplier);       these functions
         }
  return TRUE;
  printf("Function process complete");    This statement will never be executed
}
```

Optimized Code

```
int process(int factor)

{
  float values[i][j]
  for ( i= 0; i<n; i++);            Array is referenced correctly in column/row order
  do
    {
     multiplier = i*factor;          This is now correctly computed outside of the loop
     for ( j=0; j<n; j++);
       do
         {
          int j_multiplier = j*multiplier;
          avg(values[i][j], j_multiplier);   The expression j_multiplier is correctly computed once before calling
          median(values[i][j], j_multiplier);   these functions
          mode(values[i][j], j_multiplier);
         }
  return TRUE;
}
```

Figure 1-2
Code optimization.

Moving subroutine code inline

In addition to optimization of code by the compiler, separate programs are available that observe the operation of a program while it is executing. These programs may stand alone, or they may be compiled into the program that is to be observed. They output reports that detail the execution characteristics of the observed program. With these reports, the program can focus attention on the areas of the program that are most frequently used.

Hardware Monitors

Hardware monitors are electronic devices that are attached to the internal circuitry of the computer system. By monitoring changes in the circuitry of the system, the monitor is able to detect system use patterns and problem areas therein. Hardware monitors are generally only used in specialized areas, most frequently in monitoring network traffic. As a general tool for monitoring computing systems, they tend not to be useful to the majority of performance analysts. This is because the use of a hardware monitor presupposes formal training and practice in use of the monitor, a detailed knowledge of the architecture of the monitored computing system, and a thorough understanding of the computing system's workload. Furthermore, hardware monitors tend to be very expensive to both purchase (or rent) and use.

Benchmarks

Benchmarks are usually used to establish a base level for the comparison of different computing systems or alternate configurations of the same type of system.

Benchmarks are typically implemented as programs (or sets of programs) that represent a "standard" or "typical" workload to be used on the system user study.

As such, benchmarks differ from the prior tools in that they are used in a *predictive* manner rather than as a measurement tool. The tools discussed previously only measure an existing workload; they do not and cannot predict future usage patterns. Benchmarks, however, are most often used to predict what will happen given a set of circumstances on a particular configuration.

A set of standard benchmark programs is a very valuable tool in the capacity planning process. By running these benchmarks at regular intervals, the performance analyst can assess the ongoing effectiveness of the system configuration. By tracking the performance of these benchmarks, the performance analyst is able to better predict when system changes or upgrades may be needed.

Modeling

Modeling uses simulation to predict the performance of a computing system. By creating mathematical models of the target system, it is possible to predict what the effect of a given action will be upon the system being studied or built. Modeling is used in those cases where it is too expensive, time-consuming, or dangerous to perform monitoring on the target system itself.

The power of modeling is that it allows the performance of a system to be examined before the system is constructed or purchased. Therefore, unlike the previously discussed methods that are tools for solving problems, modeling can be used to solve problems before they develop.

Summary of Tools and Methods

Generally, the tools used most frequently in performance monitoring are accounting data reduction packages, software monitors, and program optimization. When analyzing networks, hardware monitors may also be thrown into this equation. In capacity planning projects, benchmarks and modeling are used to take the information gathered from performance monitoring and create a long-range plan.

Capacity Management

The complete task of ensuring that an organization has adequate computing capacity is often referred to as *capacity management*. This process takes into account performance tuning and capacity planning (Fig. 1-3). Although performance tuning is a necessary prerequisite to capacity planning, performance tuning is a discipline and function unto itself. Performance tuning is concerned primarily with short-term results and benefits. Capacity planning is predictive and concerned primarily with longer-term results and benefits. Capacity management, therefore, is the combination of these elements. Specifically, capacity management is concerned with ensuring that the organization provides acceptable service to existing users while providing adequate capacity for future workloads.

Successful capacity management programs consist of several interrelated components (Fig. 1-4):

Management commitment (for both personnel and equipment)

Recognition that the capacity planning task is a necessary function

Use of appropriate tools

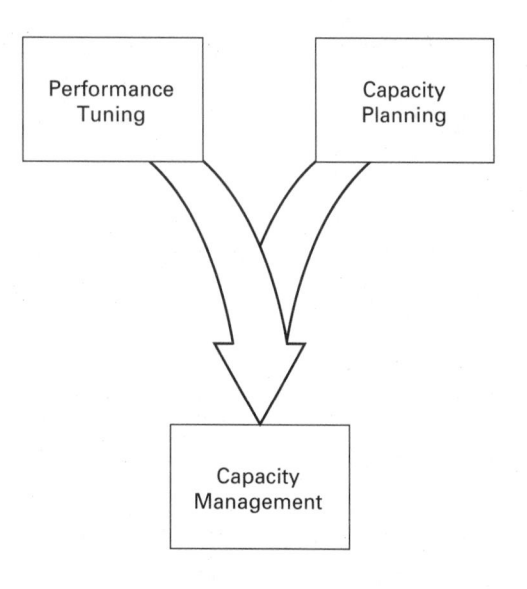

Figure 1-3
Capacity management is the combination of performance tuning and capacity planning.

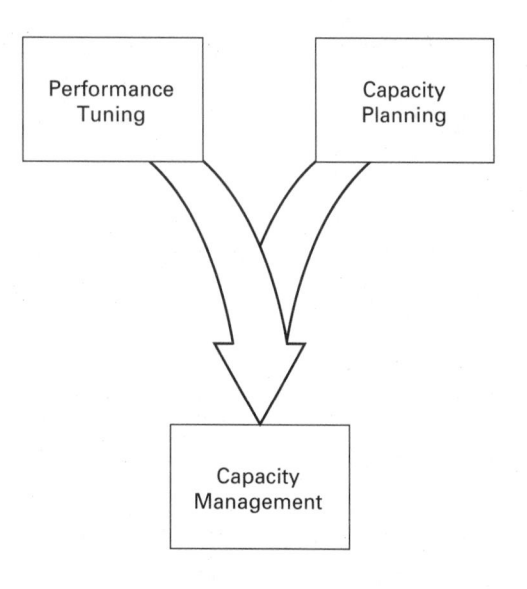

User involvement

Skilled personnel

Capacity management is an extremely important element in the satisfaction of an organization's computing needs. If one of the components listed above is missing from the capacity management program, the program will eventually fail. Ultimately, this will have a detrimental impact on the organization's entire computing environment. Therefore, it is essential to any organization's long-term well being that a capacity management program be in place and that it have the complete support of the organization.

Capacity Management Life Cycle

Capacity management is a cyclical process. It is a never ending process. No matter how well tuned a system may be today, tomorrow will bring some new variable to the equation to upset the balance. It is of utmost importance to realize that the process will always be in motion and, depending on the complexity of the system, will be in various stages at any one time. But what are the major stages of the capacity management life cycle? Although several delineations are possible, this discussion will focus on four stages (Fig. 1-5):

Existing system analysis

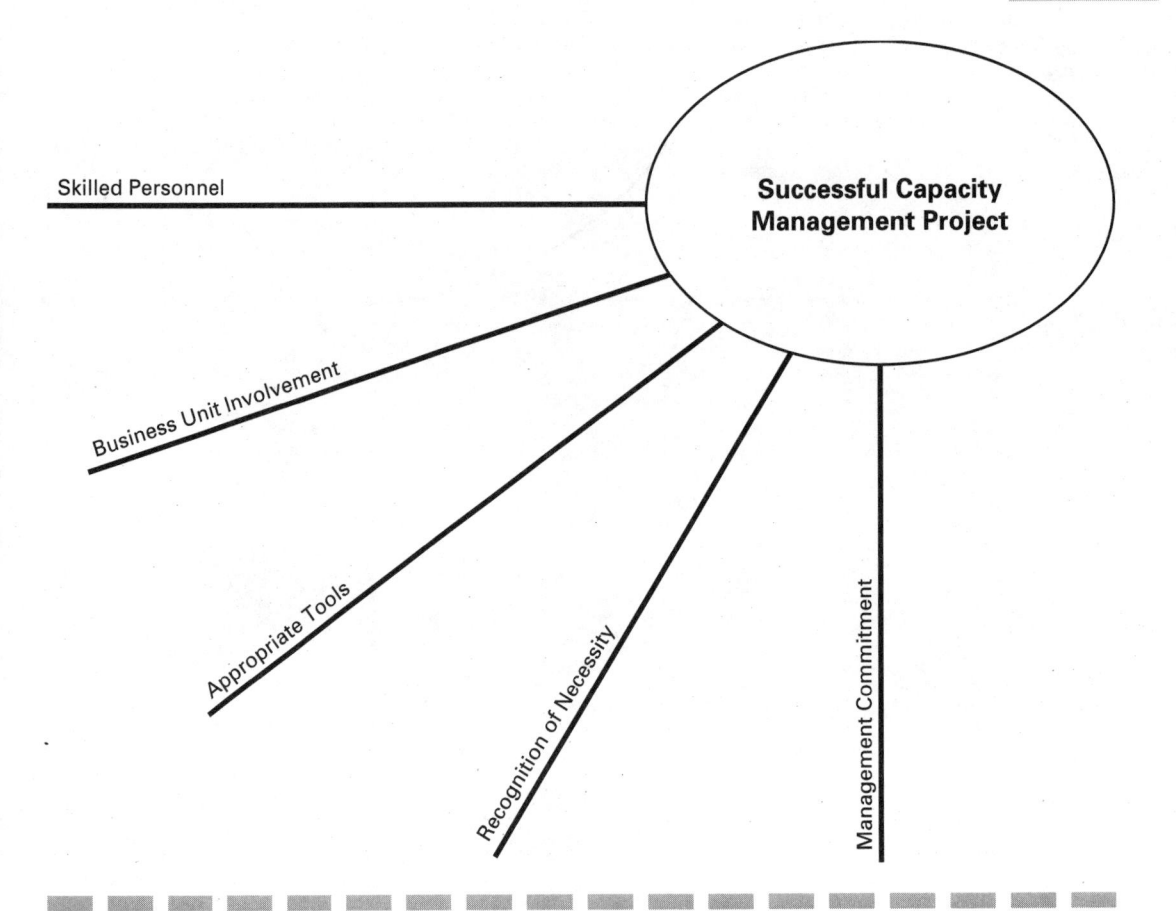

Skilled Personnel

Successful Capacity
Management Project

Business Unit Involvement

Appropriate Tools

Recognition of Necessity

Management Commitment

Figure 1-4
Successful capacity management involves comprehensive involvement at multiple levels.

Determination of future requirements

Ensuring requirements are met

Ongoing activities

Existing System Analysis. During this stage, the preliminary goals of the capacity management plan are set. The responsible parties are selected and trained, if necessary, in the areas in which they need to become more knowledgeable.

On the actual system, the existing workload is analyzed. If it has not already been done, the system configuration, both hardware and software, is documented. This is the stage where users are consulted about

Figure 1-5
The capacity man-
agement life cycle.

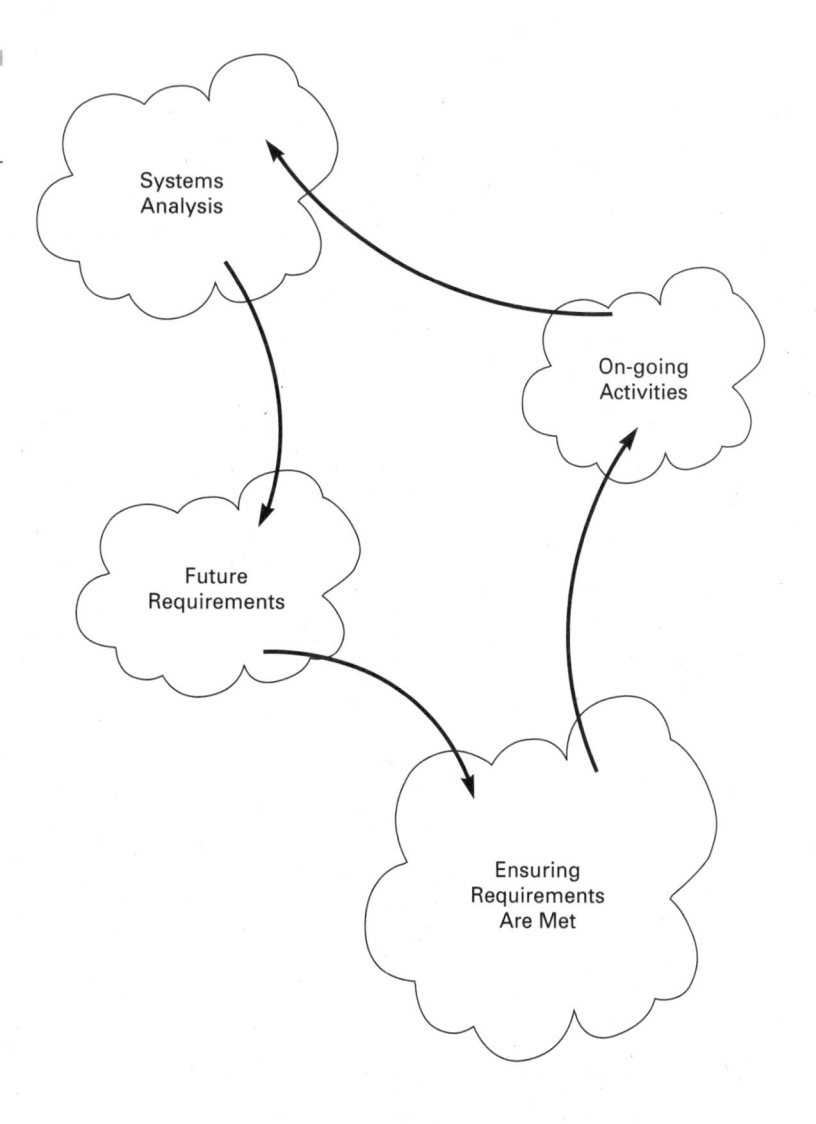

their *service-level* requirements. These service-level agreements typically include

Requirements for availability, such as 24 hours (h) a day, 7-days a week
uptime

Transaction response times, such as receiving requested data within 10-
seconds (s) of clicking OK

Problem-handling procedures, such as a person will be on call to handle
system outages from 6 A.M. to 12 midnight Monday through Saturday.

Determination of Future Requirements. In this stage, the performance analyst evaluates the plans of the organization in relationship to future computing needs. This process is called *workload forecasting*. The analyst is trying to predict what the computing workload will be in the future based on the system plans of the individual departments of the organization. Often, these plans are given to the analyst in "user terms," and so they must be translated into a measurable quantity. For example, the analyst may take an estimate of future customer orders and break this down into processing categories based on anticipated transaction complexity. This will allow the analyst to derive the anticipated capacity recommendations; which, along with the analysis of cost, is then presented to management.

During this stage, the performance analyst also compares the actual workloads to what had been previously predicted. When discrepancies arise, these should be investigated to see what factors are at work to make the estimates inaccurate.

Ensuring Requirements Are Met. In this phase, the analyst oversees the installation of the capacity improvements and measures the capacity increment that is due to the installed equipment. Although the actual responsibility for installing the improvements may belong to another individual or group, it is the performance analyst's job to ensure that the installation does take place.

Measuring the capacity increment is critical at this stage. It is vitally important to ensure that the anticipated increase was obtained. Furthermore, the performance analyst needs to check that the methods used to arrive at the capacity improvement recommendations are reasonably valid. If the anticipated results are not achieved, it will be necessary to go back and find out why the recommendations did not deliver the anticipated results. It is at this stage that benchmarks, run before and after the capacity improvements, will be most beneficial and enlightening.

Ongoing Activities. The performance analyst should be in constant communication with the application development group. It is easier to design good performance into an application right from the start than it is to retrofit code changes after a program has gone into production.

Historical workload and service information should be continually collected and organized into meaningful data. Additionally, system configuration history and workload forecasts should be saved for future reference. All of these information sources are needed for the proper analysis and control of system capacity.

In addition, the performance analyst must constantly stay current on technological developments and how these will influence future plans.

Other Considerations

A great deal of the work of a performance analyst is not technical but is of a "political" nature. The performance analyst must be able to negotiate with users and management and be able to persuade people to accept a particular point of view. The performance analyst must be willing to accept ideas and suggestions from outside sources. A reluctance to try new ideas can defeat the entire capacity management process.

Finally, the performance analyst function ideally should be independent of other functions within the organization's computing structure. For example, if the capacity management effort is directed by the application development group, too much effort may be expended in application program tuning, to the detriment of other performance tuning functions. Similar reporting structures to operations or system administration can lead to similar results. In those cases where a separate function is not possible, the capacity management function is best placed reporting to the system administration (or equivalent) function. This is based somewhat on traditional information system department organization, but it is also chosen because the system administration group typically has the most global involvement with the complete computing environment.

Summary

This chapter has served as an introduction to performance tuning and capacity planning. We have explored the meaning of both performance tuning and capacity planning and looked at the tools and methods used in both. Some of these tools and methods include:

- Accounting data reduction programs
- Software monitors
- Program optimization and program optimizers
- Hardware monitors
- Benchmarks

■ Modeling

Finally, the chapter concluded with a discussion of how performance tuning and capacity planning combine to form capacity management.

In the next chapter, the components of a computing system will be reviewed.

Computer Component Overview

This purpose of this chapter is to review the concepts and vocabulary related to the hardware and software components commonly found on a Solaris system.

When analyzing and diagnosing performance problems, the problem hardware component can generally be categorized into one of four major areas (Fig. 2-1):

Processor (central processing unit) subsystem

Memory subsystem

I/O (input/output) subsystem

Networking subsystem

These categories will form the basis of further discussion related to hardware performance issues.

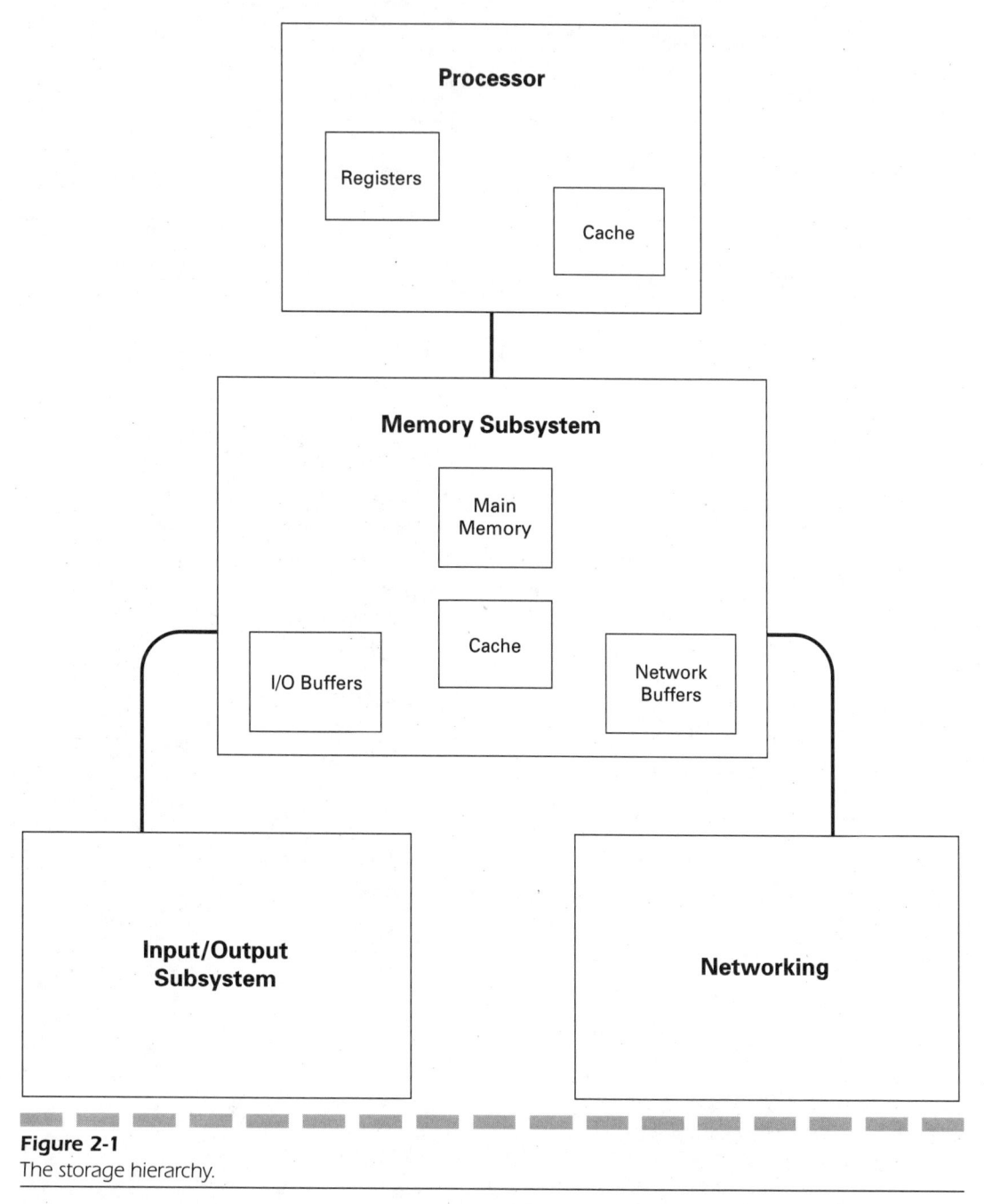

Figure 2-1
The storage hierarchy.

Performance problems, however, are not limited strictly to hardware or the lack thereof. The operating system (or modules related to it) and application programs have a significant impact on the overall performance of the system. In many cases where performance is less than optimal, the hardware is functioning as designed, and it is the configuration of the operation system or application program that is in error. All too frequently, additional hardware is thrown at these types of problems in the hope that that will solve the problem. In some cases this works, at least for a while. In many other cases, no amount of additional hardware will alleviate a software-based problem. The problem in the software must be found and corrected in order to bring performance up to acceptable levels.

The Processor Subsystem

The primary function of the processor subsystem is to execute instructions that "process" data. Probably in the majority of commercial sites and educational institutions, most processing functions in a computing system are related to the transformation of data from one form to another and moving data from one place to another. At most scientific and engineering sites, the majority of work in the computing system is related to performing calculations on data.

The workload characteristics of these two environments are very different. In the first environment, the emphasis will most likely be on the input and display of large, varied amounts of data. In the second, the emphasis will be on the manipulation of smaller, more cohesive data. Therefore, the majority of performance problems in the first environment will probably be related to I/O functions. In the second environment, the processing power of the system will probably be the most significant issue. It is because of the great degree of variation in functionality possible in various computing systems that generalizations must be interpreted carefully in the context of the individual situation.

Uniprocessor Systems

Uniprocessor systems are computers with only one processing unit. Workstations and small to medium-size servers usually fall into this group. This, therefore, includes the majority of Solaris systems.

Architecturally, uniprocessor systems are simpler than *multiprocessor systems,* which contain two or more processors. This level of simplicity is true both at the hardware and software levels.* At the hardware level, the components and interconnections are less complex. At the software level, the operating system does not need to bother with such things as keeping accesses to memory synchronized among the various CPUs and coordinating the execution of programs on separate processors.

The processor itself is constructed from a silicon chip that has tiny circuits etched upon it. The processor is mounted in a square ceramic case that has electrical contact pins radiating from the bottom. These pins are arranged to fit into the processor socket on the main system board (*motherboard*) in a specific manner. When placed into the socket correctly, the processor completes an electrical circuit that connects the processor to the motherboard. Through the motherboard, the processor can access the *system bus,* which is used to transfer data within the system to various components of the I/O subsystem.

Processors are differentiated from one another by several criteria:

Architecture

Size of the data elements manipulated at one time within the processor

Width of the data path to devices

Amount of memory addressable by the processor

Clock frequency, or speed at which the processor executes instructions

The processing of instructions in a processor can be divided into several discrete stages or components.† The *prefetch* unit gets instructions from memory and puts the instructions in the instruction *queue,* or pipeline. The interpretation (or decoding) unit translates the instructions in the queue into a format the *control unit* can understand. The control unit oversees the execution of instructions, with its major function being to ensure that memory accesses are valid and that memory conflicts don't occur. If the instruction is a floating-point instruction, it is passed to the floating-point math unit (FPU) for execution; otherwise the instruction is passed to the arithmetic/logic unit (ALU), which executes all logic and mathematical operations not handled by the FPU.

---

*The complexities inherent in multiprocessor systems are discussed in the following section.

†This describes an Intel-based processor. However, the basic process is the same for SPARC processors.

Paging and segmentation units translate relative (logical) addresses in the program into physical memory addresses.

Two additional components include the bus interface unit and cache memory. The bus interface unit manages the data and instruction transfers from the processor to the system bus. Cache memory is used by the prefetch unit to preload instructions from main memory. Because cache memory is much faster than main memory and the cache memory controller tries to predict which data and instructions will be required next, instructions can be passed to the instruction queue from cache memory far more quickly than they can from main memory.

One of the most difficult problems in predicting performance is the variability of execution time for a given sequence of instructions. This is particularly true in a uniprocessor system because a single processor is responsible for managing everything that occurs on the system. I/O, which is usually not thought of as being a great drain on CPU resources, can be a large burden on the processor in a uniprocessor system if there is a high I/O level. This is because the processor is burdened by the constant interrupts the I/O devices are generating.

Multiprocessor Systems

A multiprocessor system has two or more processors. In a *tightly coupled* environment, the processors work together, controlled by a single copy of the operating system and sharing the memory and other devices on the system. All Solaris systems run in this tightly coupled model. In a *loosely coupled* environment, the processors do not share memory or devices.

In addition to the aforementioned dichotomy, operating systems either run *symmetrically* or *asymmetrically*. In an asymmetric system, one of the processors (referred to as the *main processor*) is dedicated to running the operating system kernel. This processor handles all kernel functions: I/O, scheduling, virtual memory operation, and management of the system. The other processors are used to run user programs only. The problem with this arrangement is that performance degrades significantly when there are a large number of system requests. Because the requests cannot be parceled out to multiple processors, the processors running user programs often spend a significant amount of time waiting for the main processor.

In a symmetric system, the operating system kernel is divided into pieces, referred to as *threads* in Solaris 2. Each thread is an independent function that can run on any available processor. Because of this, requests to the kernel can be parceled out to any available processor, which alleviates the amount of time user processes must wait for kernel functions to complete. Solaris 2 is called *highly symmetric* because not all kernel functions are symmetric, but most are.

Multiprocessor systems do not achieve linear increments of performance improvement with the addition of new processors because of the inherent overhead in managing additional processors. For example, it is not possible to double the performance of a system simply by adding an additional processor. In fact, there is a point at which the addition of more processors will actually *decrease* the performance of a system. This is because the amount of overhead expended in managing the processor is greater than the additional processing power added.

Coprocessors

On Intel-based machines, certain processor models do not have a floating-point unit built into the processor. For these units, performance can be enhanced by adding a *coprocessor* that handles the floating-point operations. Without a coprocessor, the main processor must perform any floating-point instruction via simulation, which can significantly slow down overall processing speed. When a floating-point coprocessor is used in conjunction with the main processor, the floating-point instructions are executed in parallel with the main processor.

The only Intel-based processors for which external coprocessors are necessary are the 386SX and 486SX processors. The 386DX, 486DX, Pentium, and Pentium Pro, and Pentium II processors incorporate the floating-point unit into the same unit that houses the main processor.

The Memory Subsystem

The memory subsystem can be divided into four general classes:

External, such as disks and tapes

Swap space or virtual storage

Cache

Main memory

The discussion in this section will focus on the last three items because the first item is discussed as part of the I/O subsystem.

Main Memory

All computers, regardless of make, model, or operating system, have main memory. This type of storage is also known as real storage or core memory. When instructions from programs are executed by the processor, the instructions will have first been read from a location in main storage. The same is true with data elements; they are always brought into main memory before they are accessed by the processor.

Main memory, however, is not as fast as the processor. Because of this, the processor can spend inordinate amounts of time waiting for instructions and data from main memory. To alleviate this, cache memory is used in most systems as an intermediate step to speed up the processor's access to main memory.

Cache Memory

Cache memory is used to *prefetch* instructions and data from memory. As the main processor executes programs, an additional logic unit of the main processor tries to predict what instructions the main processor will need for the next several steps. Based on these predictions, instructions and data are loaded from main memory into the cache. If the predictions are correct, the main processor can access the instructions and data directly from the cache at a savings of approximately 3 to 4 times the access time compared to accessing them from main memory. This is because main memory typically has an access time of 60 to 70 nanoseconds (ns), whereas cache memory usually has an access time of 15 to 20 ns.

Because cache memory has traditionally been significantly more expensive than main memory, the relationship of cache memory to main memory is usually disproportionate. Another factor in the amount of cache on a given system is that every processor has an optimum cache size. Above this point, additional cache does not substantially increase processor speed.

In many newer processors, cache is further divided into two layers (Fig. 2-2): Cache built into the processor chip acts as intermediary with the cache memory located on the motherboard.

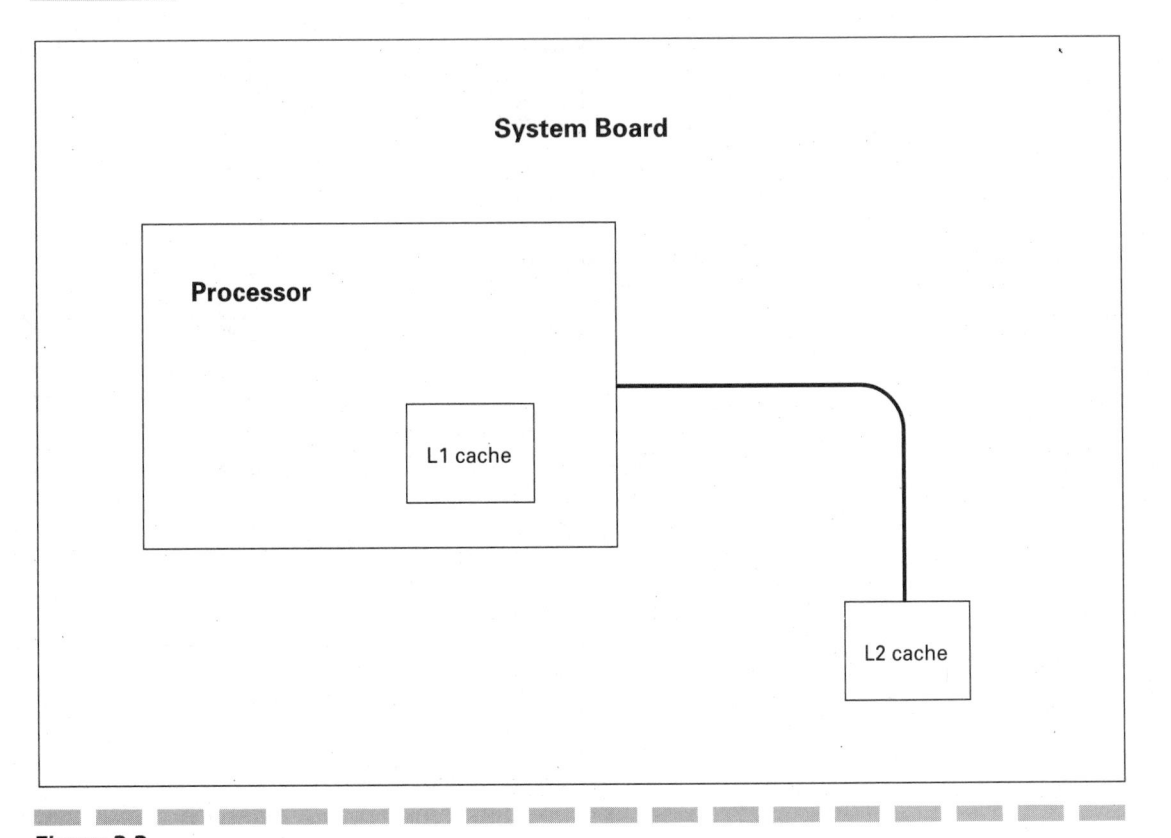

Figure 2-2
Cache interaction.

Virtual Storage and Swap Space

Virtual storage, or swap space,* allows the memory requirements of processes on the system to exceed the physical memory available. For example, virtual storage is the mechanism that allows 64-megabyte (MB) programs to execute in 32 MB of real storage. This is implemented through *paging* and *swapping*.

Paging is the process by which inactive portions of currently executing programs are temporarily moved from main memory into *swap space*

---

*In the Solaris environment, these two terms are often used interchangeably, although they *are* different. *Virtual storage* is implemented on the part of the disk designated as *swap space.*

on disk storage. The main memory evacuated can then be used by another program that needs the space. When, and if, the portion of the program moved to the swap space is needed again, some other program's inactive space will be moved to the swap space, and the original program's swapped-out portion will be returned to main memory from the swap space.

Swapping differs from paging in that swapping occurs when an entire process is removed from main memory and placed in the swap space. The operating system performs this more drastic operation to make room in main memory for another, higher-priority process.

Neither of these two functions, paging or swapping, is inherently bad or an indication of major system problems. Almost all systems page and swap at times. The problem with paging and swapping is when the amount of time the system spends in paging or swapping becomes excessive and prevents the execution of other, productive work.

There are basically only two ways of solving main memory problems: reduce the amount of memory required or add additional memory. In subsequent discussions of performance tuning, various ways of reducing the amount of memory required will be investigated.

The Input/Output Subsystem

In solving I/O subsystem problems there are two concerns: maximizing the throughput of individual processes and maximizing the overall throughput of the system. In some cases, these two issues can work against each other. By maximizing the performance of one process, other processes may suffer. Conversely, by making the entire system perform at maximum levels, individual processes can suffer.

Although many different devices are part of the I/O subsystem, the most consequential to overall performance is the disk subsystem.

The Disk Subsystem

As seen in Fig. 2-3, the process of sending data to or receiving data from a disk drive is not simple. The disk subsystem consists of two distinct parts that may or may not be separate physical entities. The *disk controller* interprets the instructions the *CPU* sends to retrieve or store data. These instructions include requests to position the heads of the

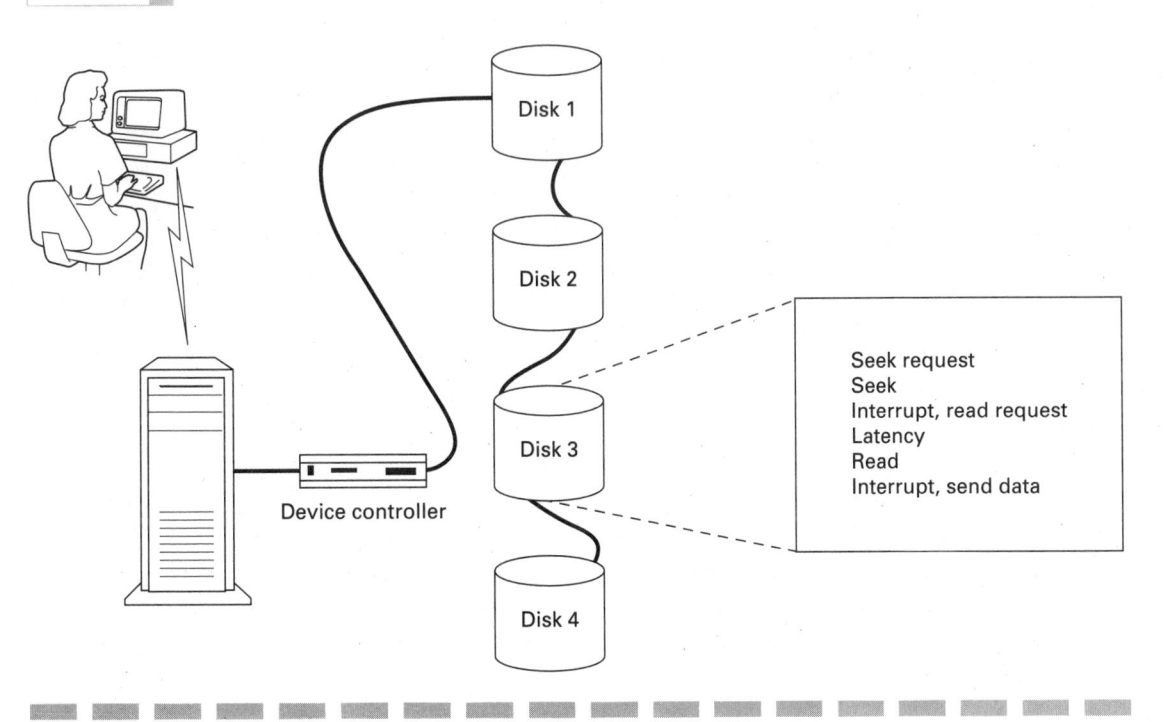

Seek request
Seek
Interrupt, read request
Latency
Read
Interrupt, send data

Figure 2-3
The disk I/O process.

disk over a particular track (*seeking*), select a particular disk platter, and find a particular *sector,* or area, on a track. The controller reads and writes data from main memory and applies error correction and detection algorithms as necessary. When an error is detected, it must signal the processor that something has gone wrong. The disk drive performs the physical operations requested by the processor.

With this scheme, there are several areas where problems can occur. During data transfers, the processor and the disk controller can compete for access to main memory locations during data transfer operations. When this occurs, the transfer fails and must be retried. In almost all disk transfers a seek must be performed. The amount of time it takes for the requested sector to arrive underneath the read/write heads is called *rotational delay*. When several processes are requesting information from the same device, rotational delay can become quite high, especially as the read/write heads are moved from one track to another. The delay incurred by the movement of the heads back and forth is called *seek latency.*

The I/O Bus

The *I/O bus* significantly affects the overall performance of the I/O devices. This is not as important in SPARC-based systems as it is in Intel-based systems where several different bus architectures (and combinations thereof) are possible. If the I/O bus is slower than the I/O devices, the I/O devices will never run at their maximum rate.

Tape Subsystems

Tapes are primarily used to back up data that is located on disk drives. Although not common in the Solaris environment, tape drives may also be used for the long-term storage of extremely large data files. The primary concerns with tape drives are related to the data transfer rate and the volume of data that can be stored on a tape device. Both are generally increased by grouping records together into larger units of data transfer, that is, *blocking* data.

Printers

Depending on the requirements of the site, printer performance may never be an issue. However, sites with high-volume printing needs must pay close attention to the performance characteristics of printers. There really is little that can be done to make a slow printer print fast. However, in many environments, users do not have printers directly attached to their local workstation. Instead, printers are shared via the local area network. In these cases, the performance of both the network and the disk subsystem can have a significant impact on the overall performance of printing, and both areas must be investigated whenever a printing performance problem arises.

The Networking Subsystem

Perhaps the most complex, and in many ways most difficult, subsystem is the networking subsystem. This is especially true when dealing with network connections to the Internet. In addition to the network interface card (NIC), its software, and configuration, the performance analyst must take into consideration the intermediary devices in the local network (routers, hubs, and other types of interconnection devices), the network protocol(s) and architecture used, the connections to external networks, and the performance of the external network itself.

The volume of data transmitted over the network is, obviously, the largest factor affecting its performance. The volume of data moving from one machine to another may be as few as a couple of characters that acknowledge receipt of some transmitted data to several hundred megabytes when a file transfer is performed.

A network becomes overloaded when the amount of data transferred is too great. When this occurs, every process on the system slows down. This is something that can happen as the natural result of network growth, but it can also occur transiently because of user error or thoughtlessness. For example, if a user were to start several very large file transfers simultaneously, the network could easily become overloaded, especially if it was at a high utilization level to begin with. However, network overload can also be created by network hardware errors. Integrity problems are the result of network errors; these cause intermittent data transfer problems. Because data transferred incorrectly must be resent, integrity problems can cause slowdowns due to repeated and excessive retransmissions.

The performance analyst can do several things to improve the performance of the local network and the NICs on the system. There is very little that can be done with the network outside of the performance analysts domain without the assistance of the administrator of the outside network. That is, it is unrealistic to expect that tuning of the NIC will solve all (or even most) Internet access problems.

The Operating System

Obviously, how the operating system (in this case, Solaris) is used and how it is configured plays a major part in the overall performance of the system. Solaris provides all of the basic functions a typical operating system provides:

Processor scheduling

Process scheduling

I/O services

File services

Clock functions

System security

User interfaces

The scheduling functions allocate a processor to a process and allocate a specific amount of time to the process in which it may run (Fig. 2-4). The performance of individual processes can be influenced by assigning and

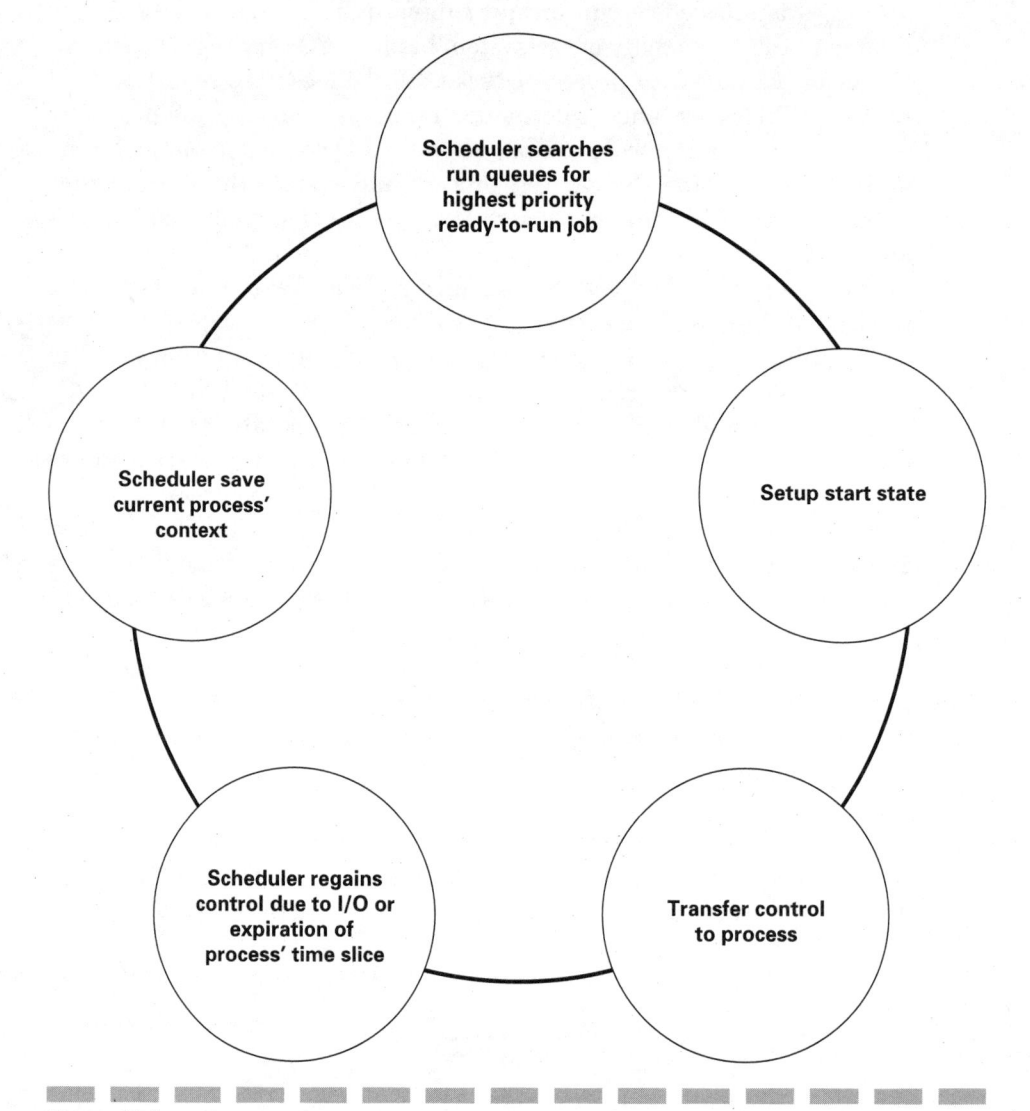

Figure 2-4
The scheduler loop.

changing the *priorities* of the processes. Higher-priority processes are allowed to run more frequently than lower-priority processes.

When too many processes are running at one time, it is possible that the operating system may spend the majority of its time managing processes rather than actually running them. The scheduler can be tuned to minimize the possibility of this occurring.

Another factor that influences performance is the optimum time that a process is allowed to run uninterrupted (*time slice*). Time slices are related to the I/O activity of the system because I/O services are generally run in parallel with processor tasks. Most processing sequences end with an I/O request, and while the I/O request is pending, the processor may select another process to run. When the I/O request is complete, the processor must stop the current process and restart the process that requested the I/O in the first place. This process of stopping one process and starting another is an example of a *context switch*. Context switches are very "expensive" in that they require a great deal of intervention on the part of the operating system.

Changing the maximum time of a time slice influences what types of processes end up favored for execution. A short time slice favors I/O-intensive jobs and on-line users but creates more operating system overhead due to the context switches. Long time slices favor processor-intensive jobs but can have a great negative impact on on-line users.

File services are responsible for creating and retrieving files on disk. These services also influence system performance. For example, when a file is created in a contiguous area, there is little seek latency and usually little rotational delay. As a file becomes fragmented and dispersed through a file system, both seek latency and rotational delay increase, thereby decreasing the performance of the system overall. The solution to this type of problem is to reorganize the file system and make the files contiguous again.

The effects of the operating system cannot be underestimated. Because Solaris needs system resources to execute its functions, any problem on the system in general will affect the ability of Solaris to do its job, thus creating a vicious circle of degenerating performance.

Application Programs

Finally, the design of application programs and their implementation cannot be underestimated. Because the majority of the processes on the system are application programs, it seems obvious that this is a great area for investigation. However, in many cases, this area is often overlooked.

Although certain general programming recommendations can be given, it is very difficult to provide specific programming guidelines that are applicable in all cases. Because languages, and their implementations, vary so much, hard and fast rules are hard to come by.

However, the time to do performance evaluation of applications is not after they have been written, but during the design stage. During the design stage, the performance analyst must try to gain an understanding of the processing time and I/O characteristics of the application system and make recommendations based on this analysis. If analysis and recommendations are not made at this time, the likelihood of implementation of performance-related recommendations later on in the development cycle is usually fairly remote.

Summary

In this chapter, some of the issues related to running Solaris on both uniprocessor and multiprocessor systems were explored. The chapter started with a discussion of the various types of processors that may be used and moved on to how Solaris implements and uses main memory, cache, virtual storage, and swap space.

Additional component considerations include how the I/O subsystem performs. This includes the disk subsystem, the I/O bus, tape devices, printers, the network, Solaris itself, and application programs.

In the next chapter the focus will be on how performance is defined and what metrics are used to measure it.

Defining Performance and Selecting Metrics

Before one can determine if there is a performance problem with a system, a definition of acceptable performance must be made. At first glance, this may seem to be simple; however, it is not as straightforward as it may seem.

Data input operators on the system would probably define performance as how fast the system responds to their input. Application programmers would probably define performance in terms of how fast their program finishes execution. Performance analysts or system managers must look at performance from a higher-level perspective than either of the other two.

A performance analyst must optimize performance for all users of the system. Although the optimization of individual programs and operations may increase overall system performance, it is the study of the interaction of all components on the system, and the optimization of the whole, that is the domain of the performance analyst. It is this complex interaction that makes fixing performance problems difficult.

There are four major elements that influence and affect system performance:

Workload placed upon the system

Service level expected by the users of the system

Actual, maximum capacity of the system

Efficiency of the current operations

The workload of the system is simply the number of tasks the system is expected to perform at a given point in time.

The service level of a system is a measure of the satisfaction and expectations of the users in relationship to the work they are performing on the system. Most commonly these service levels are measured in terms of *response time,* that is, how long it takes the system to process input and produce meaningful output, and *system availability,* which is a measure of how often the system is unavailable.

System capacity is a measure of the total system processing power. This would include (among other things) processor speed, disk data transfer rates, and network throughput rate.

Operational efficiency, in this context, is typically thought of in terms of how efficiently the computer system handles the demands made of it. However, operational efficiency should also consider the manual and human-computer interactions that may affect performance. Computer systems that are not operationally efficient waste capacity on the machine and, more importantly, also waste human resources.

All four of these factors are part of the considerations in performance tuning, which is, for the most part, a process focused on short-term benefits. Capacity planning and management, on the other hand, are concerned with long-term effects and results and are very dependent on performance tuning processes. Capacity planning uses the results of performance tuning exercises as objects of study. It is only possible to project future requirements if current needs are understood.

Performance Variables

In most traditional analyses of the factors affecting performance, performance variables have been divided into two camps. *External variables* are those factors that are visible in some meaningful and tangible way to the end users of the system. An example of this type of factor would be response time. *Internal variables* are those factors that are not seen by the end user—processor utilization, for example.

External Performance Variables

The most common and well-known external performance variable is *response time*. Response time has many definitions, but for our purposes we will use the following one: *the elapsed time between the point where the user enters data upon which the processor acts and returns a meaningful result*. For example, a data input operator would measure response time in terms of how fast the screen is refreshed after data has been entered.

Response time is the most important, and visible, factor to end users of the system. As such, it is also one of the most important considerations during performance tuning.

Related to response time is *think time*, which is a human process. Think time is *the elapsed time between the point where the user receives data from the system and decides upon the next input and request to the system*. Picking up from the prior example, think time would be the amount of time it takes the data input operator to enter a new screenful of data after the system has successfully processed the prior screen of input.

Think time (Fig. 3-1) is an important factor because, although it does not affect processor utilization directly, it greatly influences the performance of the system. For example, if it takes a data input operator 10 min to enter a screenful of data, one could estimate that, on the average, there will be six transactions per hour per operator. This is very important information in the overall performance tuning process.

Throughput is another measure of response time, but for a different type of process. Response time is used as a measure for interactive

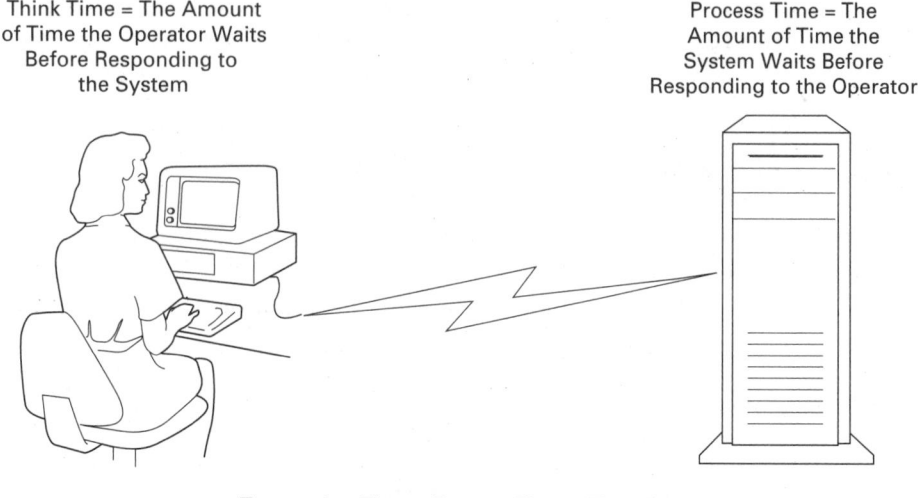

Think Time = The Amount
of Time the Operator Waits
Before Responding to
the System

Process Time = The
Amount of Time the
System Waits Before
Responding to the Operator

Transaction Time = Process Time + Think Time

Figure 3-1
Think time versus process time.

processes, that is, those processes that request input from an operator and then display some type of result based on the prior input. Throughput is used as a measure for all other types of processes that do not directly interact with a user. In UNIX-based systems, *daemons,* or *background processes,* are the best example of this type of process. Throughput measures the rate at which processes are completed.

Internal Performance Variables

Service time is the measure of performance used for the devices on the system. The service time of a disk drive would be the amount of time it takes for an input or output operation to complete. The *base service time* assumes that the device is able to complete its operations in the minimum amount of time. This assumes the device runs unimpeded as other operations are occurring on the system at the same time. This does not reflect reality for the most part. Because of this, the *mean service time* is the measure actually used for performance analysis. The base service time is a desired goal but is rarely, if ever, achieved. Devices are interrupted or preempted while performing their operations because the processor dispatches other tasks while waiting for the device to complete its operation. These additional tasks most often, in turn, request additional I/O functions that can interfere with the original request. Therefore, the mean service time is a far more accurate indicator of the true time it takes a device to perform an operation.

Along with service time, the performance analyst observes the *distribution* of requests and service times. This type of analysis is used to determine if there are specific times or actions on the system that cause larger than normal numbers of requests or processing requirements to occur. This can greatly affect the *utilization* of a device. Utilization measures the amount of time a device is busy.

Device utilization is also affected by the *arrival rate of requests* (Fig. 3-2). If requests arrive in a regular pattern, where the arrival rate is spaced out of a period that is longer than the mean service time, the device may become very busy but will not become a bottleneck. Devices become bottlenecks only when the arrival rate of requests is faster than the mean service time of the device.

Workloads

Processes on the system are divided into types that are based on common features of the processes. There are several ways of making these divisions. This book will present one method; other categorizations are certainly possible.

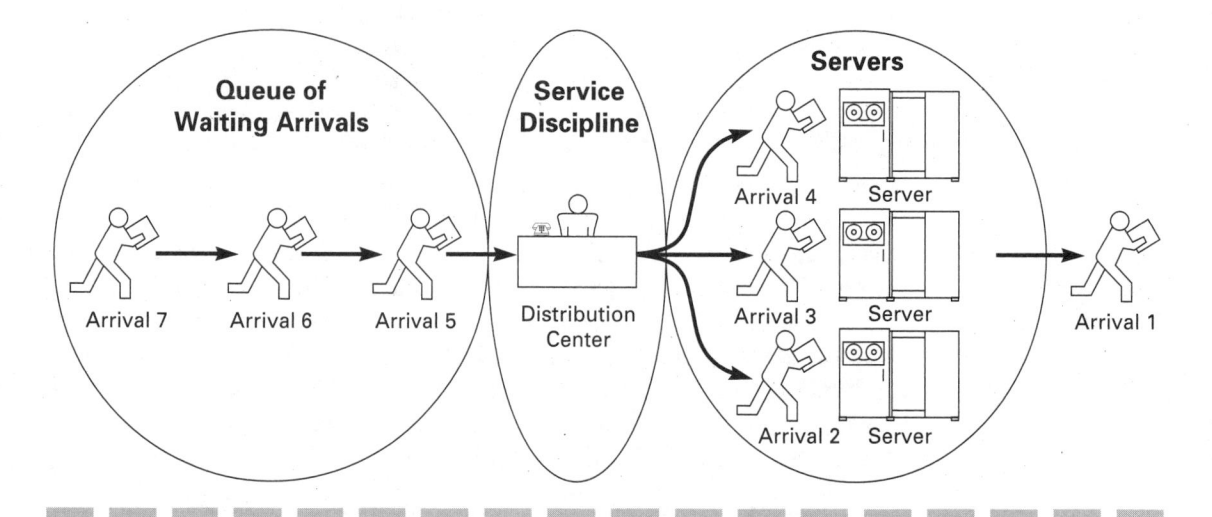

Figure 3-2
Mean service time, utilization, and queuing all interact as distinct parts of a continuous process.

Transactional processes are characterized by their unpredictability, frequent usage, and diverse user base. The arrival rate of new transactions is independent of other processes on the system or the capabilities of the system. A characteristic example of this type of transaction would be an automated teller machine (ATM) withdrawal. The transaction starts when a customer wants to withdraw money and ends when the money has been delivered. The duration of the transaction has no influence at all on the number of other customers who start ATM transactions or when a given customer may start a transaction.

Interactive processes are less prevalent than transactional processes. These processes are somewhat dependent on the current state of the system; the arrival rate of new processes and the continuation of existing processes are loosely based on what else is occurring on the system. An example of an interactive process is using the **vi** editor. The user receives immediate and continuous feedback on the state of the system based on the *response time*. If the response time becomes too great, the user will terminate the process. When enough other users terminate their processes, response times will return to acceptable rates, and users will begin running interactive processes.

Background processes and **cron*** jobs are examples of what traditionally have been known as *batch jobs*. The arrival rate of batch jobs is (supposed to be) directly related to the state of the system. Ideally, additional jobs are dispatched by the system only if the system is able to run the new jobs effectively. That is, additional jobs are run only if there will be no detrimental effect to the existing transactional and interactive processes.

Daemons are most characteristic of the fourth type: the *service* process workload. Service workloads do not directly interact with a user; however, transactional and interactive processes can be extremely dependent on the operations of a service process. For example, processes that provide for the network file system (NFS) are daemons, that is, service processes. They primarily provide services for interactive and transactional processes. As such, it is important that these service processes be given high priority in order to service the interactive and transactional processes that depend upon them. On the other hand, it is also important that a background process not monopolize the system by making inordinate requests of one of these service processes.

---

*A **cron** is process (i.e., job) schedule. These processes are run based on schedules that are defined in files known as **crontabs.**

Service Levels

Service levels are measurements that indicate how well, how fast, or how often a function is performed. The two most common service-level indicators are related to how fast a function is performed:

Turnaround time is the amount of time between the start of a process and its finish.

Response time is the amount of elapsed time between when the user enters input and when a meaningful response is received.

The above two measurements are predicated on *system availability,* which is a measure of when the system is scheduled to be available to the user community. If a system is not available when the user community expects it to be, the importance of any other indicator diminishes greatly. For example, a system available 24 h a day with a transaction rate of 5 s is probably more useful in the majority of cases than a system that goes down eight or nine times a day but has a transaction rate consistently less than 1 s. In addition, system availability may also be affected by operational tasks such as backup operations or preventative maintenance.

To define what is important to the user, the data center may enter into a *service level agreement* (SLA) with the user department. SLAs are the end result of negotiations between user departments and the data center. These negotiations define what an acceptable level of service means to the end-user department and how the acceptable level of service will be measured. In most cases, service level agreements are formally documented, but this is not mandatory.

Performance Evaluation Techniques

There are three basic techniques for analyzing the performance of a system: modeling, simulation, and measurement. Choosing which method to use depends greatly upon what is to be analyzed.*

Analyzing the performance of an existing system lends itself most readily and simply to measurement. All the performance analyst need

---

*This would seem to be self-evident, but in many cases, it is not.

do is crank the system up and observe what happens. Of course, it is a bit more complicated than that, but that is the basic gist of measurement.

Predicting the performance of new hardware on the system is frequently based on modeling. Using present measurements, assumptions are made about the new hardware and then applied to create a *model* of what the performance of the new hardware will be like. When the new equipment is installed, the model can be compared to the actual performance. When deviations from the model are noted, they are captured and factored into future modeling exercises.

Simulation is often used to test new software. A test workload is generated and applied to the software. The results are then analyzed in relationship to the expected changes in the system. If the simulation does not generate the expected results, the deviations are noted and analyzed in relationship to the system.

None of these three methods is perfect, however, and there are many factors that affect their effectiveness and applicability. Both simulation and measurement generally take longer to perform than modeling; however, simulation and measurement are generally more accurate than modeling. Modeling usually involves a number of generalizations, simplifications, and assumptions that diminish the validity of the end result of the model. Simulations can mollify the simplifications and assumptions of modeling, but the extra effort and consumption of resources, both human and machine, must be balanced against the end result. If a quick report or test is necessary, modeling is the most effective route to take.

Measurements are often taken to be absolute fact because they are based on observed occurrences of behavior. Yet measurements can be very poor indicators of "reality." If the measurement data of an event cannot be compared to other events under equivalent circumstances (i.e., system configuration and workload), the measurement data may not be of any use. Furthermore, measurement data may not take into account all possible combinations of factors that may be possible, that is, unusual or extraordinary circumstances.

Because of these problems, and to alleviate the negative effects of a technique, in most cases a combination of techniques is used. In fact, the results of a technique are validated by comparing them to those of another technique:

Modeling is verified either through measurement or simulation.

Simulation is verified through either measurement or modeling.

Measurement is verified through either modeling or simulation.

When the results of the technique used to verify the primary technique contradict the primary technique, a problem exists and must be uncovered. However, the opposite case does not mean the results are in the clear. It is possible for correct analysis to be misunderstood or misinterpreted. This is why it is so important to select good performance metrics, ones that will alleviate the probability of misunderstanding.

Performance Metrics

The three metrics most often associated with performance tuning and capacity planning are *speed, reliability,* and *availability.* These are related to the three possible outcomes of a request for system service:

The service request is completed successfully, in which case a primary concern is how long it takes for the service to be completed (speed).

An error occurs during the service request, in which case the concern is why the error occurred (reliability).

The service request is not performed, in which case the concern is what system resource is not available or functioning (availability).

When the service request is completed successfully, four aspects of performance may be investigated: *responsiveness, productivity, utilization,* and *efficiency.* Each of these can be represented by a measurement technique. User response time is a classic example of the responsiveness metric. *Throughput,* or the rate at which a device can service requests, is an example of the productivity metric. The utilization metric is represented by the measurement of the percentage of time a resource is busy servicing requests. Closely related to this is the efficiency metric, which is a measurement of the ratio of the maximum usable capacity of the device and its nominal capacity.

Measurements are also made for the two metrics that relate to errors and lack of service. For the reliability metric, the likelihood of further errors (probability of error) or the estimated amount of time before another error occurs (the mean time between failures, or MTBF) may be measured.

Availability is measured by mean time to failure (MTTF). This is different from MTBF because MTTF measures the amount of time the system is up (uptime) before the system comes down (downtime).

Obviously, not all metrics are measured the same way, nor are all results interpreted the same way. For example, a low response time is desirable; however, a low resource utilization may not be desirable. A high throughput rate is desirable, as is a high MTTF. However, a low throughput rate is very undesirable.

Avoiding Mistakes

Most mistakes in performance monitoring and capacity planning efforts are related to poor planning at the onset. If the performance analyst does not understand the goals to be met, or has defined them too broadly, it will be impossible to take useful measurements or come to meaningful conclusions.

Goals that are biased, either intentionally or unintentionally, can also create problems. Preconceived notions and assumptions may influence the choice of metrics that, in turn, may skew results and lead to incorrect interpretation of measurements.

A systematic approach is critical to the success of any performance tuning or capacity planning project. Without a clear plan and understanding of the problem, it is impossible to correctly identify those items that must be measured, modeled, or simulated. A disorganized or incomplete plan can lead to the measurement, modeling, or simulation of an unrepresentative workload. Also, without an organized plan, it is possible that important parameters or factors may be overlooked or ignored.

Once the modeling, simulation, and measurement have been performed, it is important that correct analysis be performed. If the level of detail in the analysis is inappropriate, either too detailed or too vague, conclusions may be erroneous. If the amount of data is too great, the analyst may be overwhelmed by the sheer volume of the data.

At this point in the process, it is important to yet again verify that the workload is representative of the system and that any biases have been identified and resolved. This includes identifying data that does not seem to fit the general scheme (the *outliers*). Outliers may be the result of an anomaly (in which case they may be ignored); however, they may be representative of an unusual, but repeatable, system event. In this case, the outliers must be included as part of the data to be evaluated. Averages (or the mean) have a tendency to obscure outlier values, and vice versa, outliers skew average results. Therefore, analysis should usually include treatment of the median and mode values of the individual measurements to verify the correctness and influencing factors in the mean measurements.

Finally, it is important that the results be presented in a professional and appropriate manner. Improper presentation of results can do more damage to a report than anything else. The conveyance of results is an extremely important part of the capacity planning and performance tuning process and should not be underestimated. Trust between the audience of the report and the performance analyst is critical, as is an understanding on the part of the performance analyst of the needs of the audience. The performance analyst must be careful that enough detail and background are given in the report to make the audience feel comfortable that the analysis was performed thoroughly, and yet the report should not deluge the audience with what it may consider to be useless details.

So what are the critical components of a good plan and report? Clear goals to be attained; clearly defined system services or components to be tested; correct metrics and factors to study; valid workloads and evaluation techniques to use; unbiased, valid analysis and interpretation of measurement, modeling, and simulation results; and a clear and effective report are all critical components to a successful capacity planning and performance tuning effort.

Summary

Defining performance and selecting metrics for performance measurement have been the focus of this chapter. Examples of performance variables, both internal and external, were given. Definitions and examples of workloads and service levels were also discussed. The latter part of the chapter concentrated on performance evaluation techniques, selecting performance metrics, and how to avoid mistakes when performing both activities.

The next chapter, and last chapter in the first section, introduces some basic concepts of queuing theory.

4

Queuing Models

Queuing models are important tools in performance management and capacity planning because they provide the framework for predicting system performance in given situations. An understanding of queuing theory is also helpful in understanding why certain system behaviors occur. This chapter does not attempt to be a complete discussion of queuing theory but is instead a fairly simple, general introduction to the basic concepts of queuing models that will be useful in later chapters.

Everyday Queuing Models

Queuing models are all around us. Two everyday examples are found in the grocery store and the bank. In the grocery store, the customers select a checkout line and then wait for other customers in the line to check out before they can themselves check out. In this model, the customer makes an initial decision about which line to join. This is usually based on the number of customers already in line but can be influenced by what those existing customers have in their carts and any constraints that may be placed upon the checkout line—cash only, ten items or less, etc. In this model, once the customers have made a decision, they generally must wait to be serviced, regardless of what may be going on in other checkout lines.

In a bank, typically all customers are in a single line. The customer who reaches the head of the line goes to the first teller who happens to be free. In this model, the customer does not need to make a decision because all tellers are equally capable of delivering the services the customer may need.

Although simplified, these two examples represent the majority of queuing situations found in computer systems. In the first example of the grocery store, the queuing model assumes that not all potential service points (cashiers) are capable of delivering all services to all customers. In the second model, the potential service points (tellers) are capable of delivering all services to all customers.

In a computer system that has swap space on one disk, the first queuing model would be applicable. The system can only send requests for new swap pages to one specific disk drive, so all requests for new swap space pages must be organized in a single queue and wait for service. If, however, the swap space were distributed over several disk drives, the system could use the second model, which would allow the request for a new page to be serviced from any of the disk drives that were available and had space.

Basic Concepts

In order to predict the behavior of a queuing system, six factors must be analyzed:

Interarrival time

Service time distribution

Number of servers

System capacity

Population size

Service discipline

Using the grocery store as an example, the interarrival time is how often and how many customers get into the lines. This is a classic example of a *Poisson distribution,* which means that the interarrival times are independent, identically distributed random variables that are exponentially distributed.

The service time distribution is the amount of time each customer spends with the cashier. The number of servers is the number of cashiers. The system capacity is the number of customers that can reasonably wait in line given the space constraints within the store. The population size is the number of potential customers who might ever come to the store. And finally, the service discipline is the order in which the customers are served. In this example, the order is first in, first out (FIFO). Another order is last in, first out (LIFO).

Using the swap space example, the interarrival time is how often and how many requests for swap space are made. The service time distribution is the amount of time it takes for each request to the disk to be serviced. The number of servers is the number of disks that can service swap space requests. The system capacity is the number of waiting requests that can be queued. The population size is the number of potential requests that might be made. Note that in many cases, both system capacity and population size are assumed to be infinite capacities because it makes analysis simpler. The service discipline is the order in which the requests are serviced. Most likely, in this example, the order will not be FIFO.

Service Orders

As stated earlier, FIFO stands for first in, first out. However, several other orders are possible:

LIFO—last in, first out

RR—round robin

SPTF—shortest processing time first

SRPTF—shortest remaining processing time first

SEPT—shortest expected processing time

BIFO—biggest in, first out

HPFO—highest priority, first out

Each of these has its place in queuing models. LIFO is the classic implementation of a stack; the last item in is the first item to leave.

Round robin (RR) is primarily used in scheduling algorithms. Each process is allocated a specific amount of time to perform operations. If the operation is not complete within the time frame, the process is suspended and scheduled to resume after all of the other waiting processes have had a chance to execute.

Shortest processing time first (SPTF), shortest remaining processing time first (SRPTF), and shortest expected processing time (SEPT) are self-explanatory. However, note that somewhere a determination must be made as to what the "shortest" item in the queue is. Typically, these algorithms are used to give higher priority to interactive processes.

Biggest in, first out (BIFO) is an example of the opposite approach. Here, short requests are given lower priority than those that will take up more system resources. This tends to favor batch or noninteractive processes. Highest priority, first out (HPFO) is also self-explanatory and is used to allow the operating system to take precedence over user processes.

The various service orders are not mutually exclusive and are usually used in various combinations with different resources to make the most effective use of the system.

Workloads

Different job types influence the system in different ways. For example, a batch process is going to place different demands on the system than is an interactive or a transactional process. This was discussed in some detail in Chap. 3. When looking at queuing models, it is often more convenient to look at these demands another way—open and closed.

In an open system, where the bulk of requests are transactional processes, requests arrive at the system at a rate that is independent of the system response rate. Requests to a World Wide Web (WWW) server are a prime example of this. The queue lengths and the response time of these requests can grow without any limit. This can lead to system instability.

In closed systems, where the majority of requests are either batch or interactive processes, there is a direct relationship between the arrival of new requests and the system response rate. If the response rate is bad, users will simply stop making requests until the response rate improves.* The system is "automatically" self-regulating. Generally, this self-regulation prevents the instability that is possible in an open system.

The differences between the systems are demonstrated in Fig. 4-1. With transactional processes, there is a point at which the system reaches a critical value for the interarrival time. When the system hits the interarrival time critical value, the response time increases without limit and the system becomes unstable. The system stops doing productive work on behalf of the user and is completely consumed with the overhead of managing the system. With interactive and batch processes, as the number of processes increases, it also generally limits the number of additional processes. This, in turn, tends to regulate against reaching the interarrival time critical value. Note, though, that if the terminal users, or operators submitting batch jobs, ignore the ever-increasing

---

*Of course, this is also true of requests to a WWW server. However, with a WWW server request, the relationship is not as direct.

Figure 4-1
Response time
characteristics.

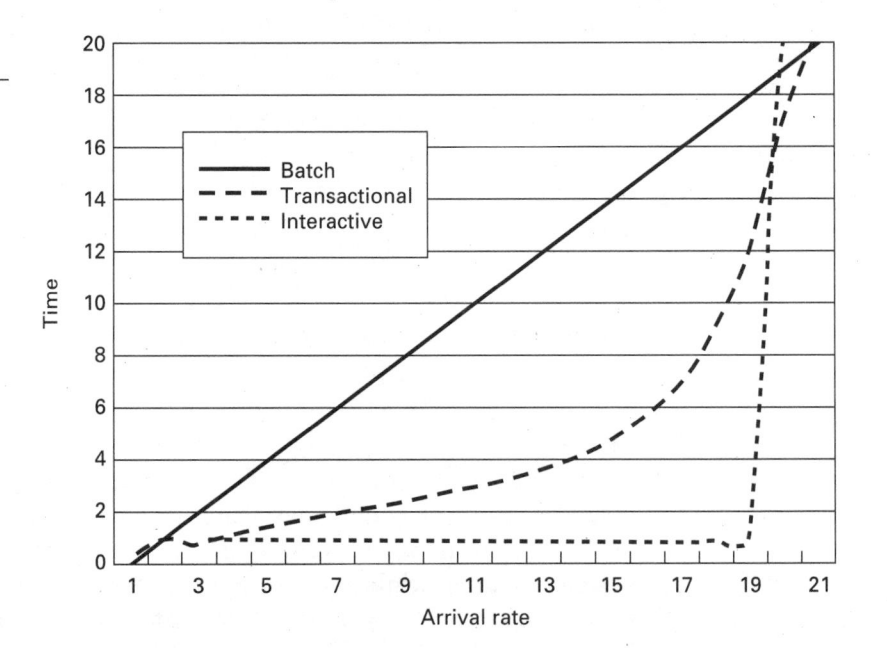

Response Time Characteristics

response time, the system will eventually reach its interarrival critical time and become unstable.

Queuing Notation

Several quantities are obtained by direct measurement of a computer system. These include

T Length of *time* the system was measured

A Number of jobs that *arrive*

C Number of jobs that *complete* execution

C_d Number of *completed* service requests from device d

B_d Amount of time device x was *busy*

N *Number* of servers

With these observed variables, several variables may be derived:

λ Mean arrival rate $= A/T$

X System throughput rate $= C/T$

S_d Service time of device $d = B_d/C_d$

X_d Throughput rate of device $d = C_d/T$

U_d Utilization rate of device $d = B_d/T$

V_d Visit ratio of device $d = C_d/C$

Using observation and derivation, the additional factors in performance analysis are arrived at:

s Service time

n Number of jobs in the system

n_q Number of jobs in queue waiting to be serviced

n_s Number of jobs in queue being serviced

r Response time

w Waiting time

μ Mean service rate

Several basic rules and relationships among these variables may be observed. For example, reiterating a point from the previous discussion, a system is stable while $\lambda < \mu$. That is, while the mean arrival rate is less than the mean service rate, the system will be stable.

The second relationship is that the total number of jobs in the system is equal to the number of jobs waiting for service plus the number of jobs being serviced:

$$n = n_q + n_s$$

The third relationship is that the time a job spends in the system is equal to the amount of time spent waiting in the queue and the amount of time receiving service:

$$r = w + s$$

These relationships are of interest because they are useful in determining the *steady state behavior* of the system, that is, the behavior of the system during "normal" operation. During most normal periods of operation, a system exhibits a characteristic called *job flow balance*. This is when the number of inputs (or arrivals) to the system is equal to the number of outputs (or departures) from the system. The implication of this is that whenever observing the behavior of a system, it is desirable to choose a period long enough such that the system can be shown to exhibit job flow balance.

Almost all analysis of systems is performed on a system in its steady state. Transient state analysis, such as when the system is first starting or when a job load is tapering off, is extremely difficult. Furthermore, for most applications, it is not particularly useful.

Queuing Laws

There are a number of laws in queuing theory. In this section, only the most common laws will be presented.

Little's Law

This law is named after J. D. C. Little, who first proved it in 1961. It is used to determine the mean number of processes in the system as a function of the arrival rate of processes and their mean response time. It can be used to measure any part of the system in which the number of entering activities is equal to the number of exiting activities.

The first step in defining Little's Law is defining the arrival rate in the system. This is simple: The arrival rate in the system (λ) is equal to

the total number of arrivals (A) divided by the total amount of time (T):
$\lambda = A/T$.

Figure 4-2 demonstrates three different ways to plot the equation. In the first frame, the number of arrivals and number of departures are shown separately as functions of time. In the second frame, the number of departures is subtracted from the number of arrivals, resulting in a graph of the number of processes in the system at a given point in time. In the third frame, the number of arrivals is subtracted from the number of departures, which shows the amount of time spent in the system. In all three cases though, the area under the graph represents the total time spent in the system by all processes. All three areas under the

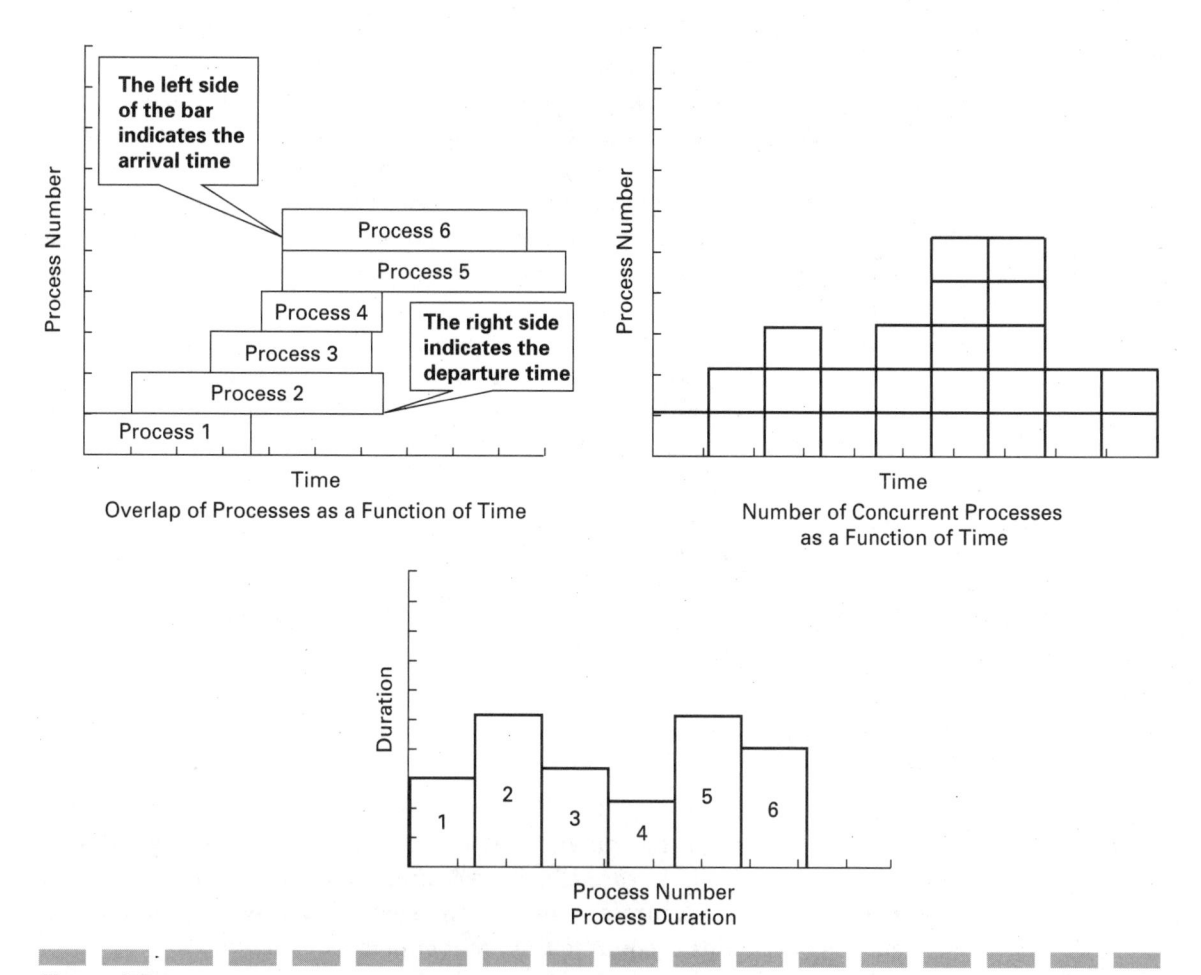

Figure 4-2
Various methods of graphing arrival and departure time data.

graph are equal. If we call this area J, the mean time spent in the system $= J/A$.

Similarly, the mean number of processes in the system can be represented as J/T. This is because it is equivalent to

$$\frac{A}{T} \frac{J}{A}$$

which is the same as arrival rate multiplied by the mean time spent in the system.

In application, Little's Law can be used to determine the number of processes waiting in a queue. The formula would be stated as

Mean number in queue = arrival rate * mean wait time

Additionally, to determine the number of processes being serviced, the formula can be stated as

Mean number in service = arrival rate * mean service time

As demonstrated, Little's Law can be applied to most systems or subsystems and is most useful in helping to prove other laws that are commonly used.

The Utilization Law

The Utilization Law is a special case of Little's Law. It is used to prove that the utilization of a device d is equal to the service time of device d multiplied by the throughput rate of device d. This is often a more convenient way of measuring device utilization compared to the definition of utilization, which was previously stated as $U_d = B_d/T$.

By multiplying both the top and bottom of the right-hand side by C_d, the formula becomes

$$U_d = \frac{B_d}{C_d} \frac{C_d}{T}$$

The two fractions on the right-hand side of the equation are equivalent to S_d and X_d, respectively. Therefore, the equation can be expressed as $U_d = S_d * X_d$, which states that the utilization of a device is equal to its service time multiplied by its throughput rate.

The Utilization Law is applicable in many situations. For example, if a disk is known to be handling 30 transfers per second and the transfer rate of the disk is 10 milliseconds (ms), the average utilization rate is 30 percent. The formula is applied as follows:

$$U_d = S_d * X_d$$

$$= 10 \text{ ms} * 30 \text{ transfers}$$

$$= .01 \text{ s} * 300 \text{ (convert from mx to seconds) transfers}$$

$$= .30 \text{ s/s}$$

$$= 30\% \text{ utilization}$$

Terminal Response Time Law

The Terminal Response Time Law is also a special case of Little's Law. The formula for the law is

$$r = \frac{N}{X} - Z$$

where r = the response time minus the time from when a process starts to the time when it ends*
X = the rate at which jobs leave the computer system
N = the number of active terminals
Z = the average "think time" of the user at the terminal

To demonstrate, if processes are executing in the system at a rate of two per second, there are 90 interactive users, each of which is using 30 s think time, the calculation would be

$$r = \frac{90}{2} - 30$$

which means that the average transaction takes 15 s from start to finish.

Rearranging the terms into the equation

$$X = \frac{N}{r + Z}$$

---

*This is not the "processor time." It is the complete transaction time.

results in a formula that is useful in determining what the throughput rate must be in order to achieve a response rate of R. In this case, X represents the number of processes that must be processed per second in order to achieve the desired response time.

To increase the response time to 10 s, the calculation would be

$$X = \frac{90}{10 + 30}$$

which means that the system must execute 2.25 processes per second to achieve the desired response time.

Forced Flow Law

The Forced Flow Law is used to relate system throughput to the throughput rates of individual devices. Simply stated the throughput rate of a device is equal to the number of accesses to the device multiplied by the system throughput rate, that is, $X_d = V_d X$. This equation can be manipulated to calculate the system throughput rate based on device throughput rate and number of accesses to the device. The equation for this is

$$X = \frac{X_d}{V_d}$$

For example, if a process is making 10 accesses to a disk drive and the disk can perform 30 transfers per second, the system throughput rate would be 3 processes per second.

Process Models

In addition to the random variables discussed so far, sequences of random variables are also used in queuing models. Although we will not go into a detailed discussion of these variables and models, a basic understanding is useful.

Such random functions of time or sequences are called *stochastic processes* and are particularly useful in representing the state of queuing systems. Be careful not to confuse the use of the word *process* in this context with use of the term *process* as it relates to the tasks of the system.

Discrete-State and Continuous-State Processes

If the number of values a process can take during its states is finite, the process is called a *discrete-state process*. However, if the number of values is infinite, the process is called a *continuous-state process*. An example of a discrete-state process is keeping track of the number of processes (tasks) in a system. Starting at 1, the sequence continues up to the maximum number allowed. Because this value is finite and countable, the process is a discrete-state process.

On the other hand, the amount of time a process (task) spends waiting for a system resource is not a finite number. It could be any amount of time, which mathematically could be any point on the real number line. Therefore, the process is a continuous-state process.

Markov Processes

Markov processes are independent of their past state and rely only on the present state to determine what the future state should be. Simply put, they cannot and do not rely on the past to predict the future. How long the process has been active is irrelevant to predicting future behavior. When a Markov process is also a discrete-state process, it is called a *Markov chain*.

Birth-Death Processes

Discrete-state Markov processes in which the transition from one state to another can only be to the neighboring states are called birth-death processes. In the processes, it is only possible for a process to go back to its prior state or the next state in the chain; it cannot jump over intermediate steps in the chain. The name of this type of process comes from one of its most common applications: a single server queue with individual arrivals. As each new process arrives at the queue, a birth occurs and the state changes to $+1$. When a process departs the queue after service, a death occurs and the state changes to -1.

Poisson Processes

The term *Poisson* was used earlier in Poisson distribution. The meaning in this context is similar. When the arrival times of processes are independent and identically distributed, the number of arrivals over the given interval of time has a Poisson distribution. Therefore, the process is called a Poisson process or Poisson stream.

Performance Bounds and Bottleneck Analysis

In open systems, as the input rate increases, so does the throughput rate until some device in the system becomes *saturated*. When a device becomes saturated (that is, its utilization is at 100 percent), no further increase in throughput rate can occur. As a result, inputs begin to queue and eventually the system will become unstable.

Utilization in an open system is proportional to the product of $V_d S_d$ for all devices on the system. The device with the largest $V_d S_d$ is the device that will become the bottleneck as the utilization of the system increases. If the bottleneck device is denoted as

$$V_b S_b = \frac{\max}{d} (V_d S_d)$$

we can say that the system is stable as long as the mean arrival rate remains less than the mean throughput rate. That is,

$$X = \lambda \le \frac{1}{V_b S_b}$$

This value represents the upper performance bound on the mean throughput rate in an open system. Values higher than X denote an unstable system. The lower bound on the mean response time rate* (on a stable, nonsaturated system) is calculated through the summation of the response times of the devices on the system. The formula for this is

$$R = \sum_{d=1}^{D} V_d S_d$$

---

*That is, the best possible response time.

where D is the total number of devices. Taken together, these are the *asymptotic bounds* of an open system. These are the two factors that limit the performance of the system—the upper bound on mean throughput rate and the lower bound on mean response time.

The application of this formula is demonstrated in the following. Assume a system with three devices: a CPU, a disk with a mean service time of 10 ms, and a tape drive with a mean service time of 50 ms. The process under examination makes an average of 10 visits to the disk, 5 visits to the tape drive, and 20 visits to the CPU. During each CPU visit, the process spends 15 ms. Calculation of the $V_d S_d$ results in the following values:

$$V_1 S_1 = 20 * 0.15 = 3.0 \text{ s}$$
$$V_2 S_2 = 10 * 0.10 = 1.0 \text{ s}$$
$$V_3 S_3 = 5 * 0.50 = 2.5 \text{ s}$$

Because it is the device with the highest utilization, the CPU is the device that will become the bottleneck as utilization increases. The lower bound on response time (the best possible response time) is calculated with the formula

$$R = \sum_{d=1}^{3} V_d S_d \quad = 3.0 + 1.0 + 2.5$$
$$= 6.5 \text{ s}$$

The arrival rate (the maximum number of possible processes per second before the system becomes unstable) is computed with the formula

$$\frac{1}{V_b S_b} = \frac{1}{3}$$
$$= 0.333...\text{processes per second}$$

In closed systems, the rate of submission of new requests is inherently regulated by the response time of the system. In this case, the consideration is not, therefore, when the system will become unstable but only what the upper performance bound is. As was the case with a nonsaturated open system, the lower bound on mean response time on a nonsaturated closed system is calculated by the formula

$$R_{unsat} = \sum_{d=1}^{D} V_d S_d$$

The maximum throughput rate can be calculated by taking this value and using the terminal response time law

$$X_{unsat} = \frac{N}{R_{unsat} + Z}$$

with the caveat that Z is equal to zero for a batch workload.

In a closed system where a device is saturated, the formula for computing the lower bound on the mean response time changes to $r_{sat} = NV_bS_b - Z$. This makes sense because the saturated device must be factored into the equation because it is going to be the object that slows down response time. The formula for computing the upper bound on the mean throughput rate is

$$\frac{1}{V_bS_b}.$$

In a closed system, the asymptotic bounds are taken as the worst case of the saturated and unsaturated calculations. That is, the lower bound of the response time is represented by the formula

$$R = \max\left(\sum_{d=1}^{D} V_dS_d,\, NV_dS_d - Z\right)$$

and the upper bound of the mean throughput rate is represented by the formula

$$X = \min\left(\frac{N}{\sum_{d=1}^{D} V_dS_d + Z},\, \frac{1}{V_bS_b}\right)$$

Of course, in the real world, it is rare to find a system that is either completely open or completely closed. In most cases, one of the first questions the performance analyst must ask is which model the system under observation is most like. Then based upon this answer, the performance analyst can choose the appropriate modeling technique. It should also be noted that in calculating the performance bounds in the prior examples, assumptions were made regarding the interference between different processes on the system. Basically, it was assumed that there was no interference. In the real world, this is not the case. Furthermore, some assumptions were made about the workload on the system. These assumptions, related to the distribution of service times and the interarrival times of jobs on an open system, are that the system is "memoryless"—past behavior does not influence future decisions.

Two assumptions are made to implement a memoryless system:

1. If a job is using a device, the expected time until the job releases the device has the same value regardless of how long the process has been using the device.

2. In an open system, the expected time of the next arrival to the system is a constant value sometime in the future, regardless of how recently an arrival actually occurred.

These two assumptions define a probability distribution known as the *exponential distribution*. Even though the actual devices of a system rarely exhibit exponential distribution, the assumption of exponential distribution in estimation formulas leads to accurate results in most cases and is used in most performance analysis exercises.

Summary

Queuing models are essential components of performance analysis. Although we may not immediately recognize them, queuing situations occur frequently in everyday life. Once the basic concepts of queuing theory (such as service order, workloads, and queuing notation) are understood, it is easy to move into the laws that govern the performance of computer systems. These laws include

- Little's Law
- Utilization Law
- Terminal Response Time Law
- Forced Flow Law

After exploring the laws of queuing theory, the chapter concluded with an examination of processes: the differences (and similarities) between discrete-state and continuous-state processes, the properties of Markov processes, and the unique properties of Poisson processes. To conclude, performance bounds and bottleneck analysis were considered.

In the next section, the chapters take detailed looks at particular aspects of Solaris:

- Kernel architecture
- Memory
- Process and thread management
- File systems
- Networking and communications

Operating System Structure

In this section, the basic components that make up Solaris are discussed in detail. Understanding the structure of the operating system is a critical component of understanding the issues related to performance tuning. The five chapters of this section discuss the following:

- Kernel architecture
- Details of the memory subsystem and its implementation
- How processes are structured and run
- What types of file systems are supported in Solaris and how they are implemented
- Networking subsystem

Kernel Architecture

In order to understand the architectural organization upon which UNIX-based operating systems such as Solaris are built, it is important to remember that the original UNIX system was designed as a reaction to a very large and cumbersome operating system, MULTICS. The overriding factor in all design decisions was a desire to keep things small and efficient, sometimes at the expense of clarity and usability.

As seen in Fig. 5-1, Solaris is a layered operating system; each layer depends upon a lower layer for services and provides the higher layer with enhanced services. Most discussions of UNIX-based operating systems divide the operating system into five components:

Kernel (or the base operating system)

User command interface (the shells)

Commands and utilities

System services

Programming interface

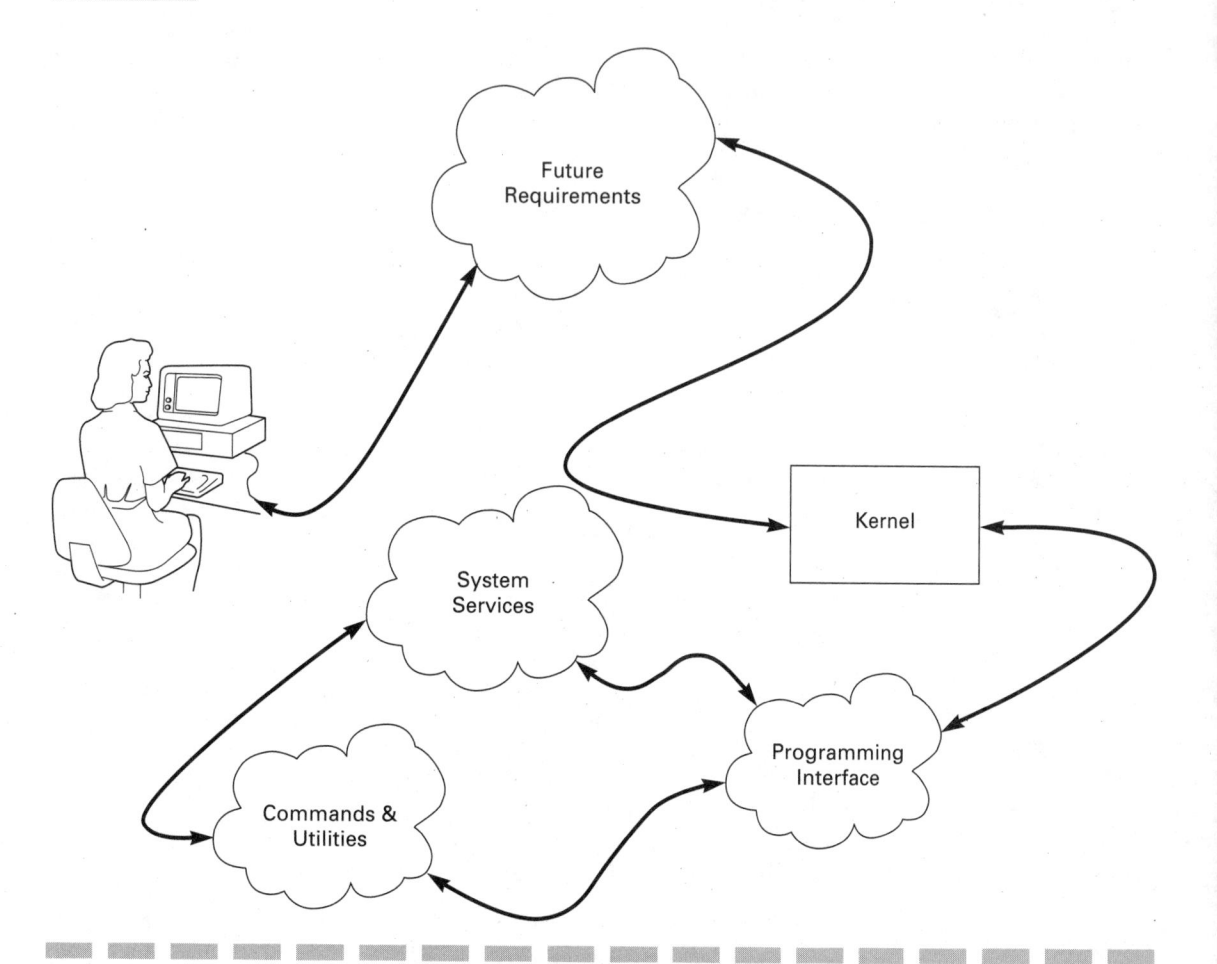

Figure 5-1
The user interface and its interaction with system services.

Before delving into the specifics of the kernel, a quick discussion of the other items is in order.

As discussed above, shell programs implement the user command interface in Solaris. First-time users often find the user interface of UNIX-based operating systems to be extremely unfriendly and cryptic. For the nonprogrammer, this is, for the most part, true. Because of this, several different interfaces are available, each geared to slightly different audiences: the C shell is popular with C programmers, whereas the Korn shell is more popular with general users of the system. In addition, public-domain shells are available for those users who desire different functionality, and many third-party vendors supply shells that are specifically designed for use with their products. For users of graphics workstations, a shell that is designed to work with graphics terminals using Windows is available.

The commands and utilities of Solaris provide operating system functionality that is not provided by the kernel directly. Examples are the commands to copy files, stop a task, or print a report. Solaris commands and utilities are implemented in two ways: as built-in shell functions or as distinct programs. Commands built into a shell are only available as part of that specific shell, whereas programs can be invoked from any shell. Although part of the Solaris distribution, these commands and utilities are not a part of the kernel.

Solaris system services provide several different areas of functionality: system administration, system configuration, file system maintenance, networking services, etc. These are implemented as separate programs or subsystems.

The programming interface provides the mechanism for user programs to access system functions. By calling the routines defined in the *run-time library,* the user program can request services of the kernel that include management of system resources such as memory, disk storage, and peripherals. The run-time library maps the system calls in the program to the kernel routines that perform the specified function.

Introduction to the Kernel

The heart of the Solaris operating system is the kernel. In the nomenclature of other operating systems, the kernel performs the same function that a nucleus or supervisor does. Regardless of name, it provides the services that user and utility programs depend upon to function.

The kernel is the program that manages the resources of the system. Most of this management is concerned with control—who currently has control of a specific resource and who is going to get it next. In a perfectly tuned system, every process will obtain access to the resources it needs when it needs them, will be able to use these resources for as long as necessary, and will not be interfered with by other processes. This, of course, almost never happens in the real world, so the kernel provides the management mechanism to ensure that resources are shared equitably and safely among processes.

The kernel is the lowest level of the Solaris operating system structure, and as such, it provides the layer that interfaces directly with the hardware. The kernel, through various modules, manages and schedules processes, allocates and deallocates memory, starts and stops devices, checks and resets device status codes, and reads and writes data from or to devices.

The kernel protects the resources of the system from unauthorized or inappropriate use. It can do this because it owns the shared resources of the system: disk drives, file system, network cards, internal clocks, the CPU. In order for a process to gain access to these devices, the process must make a *system call* to the operating system. The system call is simply a request for a service. The kernel receives these requests, evaluates them, executes them on behalf of the requesting process, and returns the result to the process that requested it. When the kernel is running on behalf of a process that has made a system call, the process making the system call is said to be in *kernel,* or *system,* mode. In its "regular" state, the process is said to be in *user* mode. The major difference between the two modes is that the protected resources of the system cannot be accessed while in user mode; they can only be access while in system mode. The transition from user mode to system mode, and then back again to user mode, is an inherent part of the system call function. That is, when a process makes a system call, the kernel takes care of switching the mode back and forth as appropriate. As we will see later, although this setup provides for good security and generally equitable use of system resources, it generates a lot of overhead, which can slow a system down.

The kernel has several layers. In addition to the hardware layer, there is the kernel services layer, which provides the support for mapping user-level system calls to kernel-level actions. User-level system calls include requests for general input/output services, file system access, terminal handling, process creation and termination, and transmission and receipt of data. This level also handles switching a process from user mode to kernel mode so that protected kernel mode functions can be performed.

User processes run outside of the kernel layers. This includes shells, commands, and utility and application programs. This level has no direct access to kernel routines or functions; all access to kernel functions must be transmitted through system calls.

In addition to this layering of services, the kernel divides the physical memory of the system into two distinct areas, or *spaces:* user space and kernel space.

User space occupies all of the physical memory that is not used by kernel processes and data. All user processes are loaded into this storage area. The storage in the user space is protected; it is not possible for one user process to interfere with another. The only processes that can access an individual user space, except for the user process itself and other user processes with special permission, are kernel processes. While executing code in the user space, a process runs in user mode.

Kernel space is the part of physical memory in which the kernel resides and kernel processes execute. Kernel space is *privileged*; it cannot be accessed by a user process except through system calls. A user process enters kernel mode when it executes a system call that invokes kernel code on behalf of the user process. User processes also enter kernel mode when I/O completes. Upon completion of an input or output operation, the I/O device sends a completion signal, or *hardware interrupt,* to the kernel *device handler,* which is responsible for translating the I/O stream into and from the format the device understands. Each type of device on the system has its own device handler. System error conditions, as opposed to application error conditions, are *trapped* by the kernel. The user process enters kernel mode to allow the kernel to either correct the condition, signal the application of the error, or, in severe cases, terminate the process.

As we shall see, the kernel is not a monolithic, static structure. It is made up of a number of separate parts, or *modules,* each of which provides a unique service or facility. If kernel modules are no longer needed, they may be removed from the kernel space; if new or additional kernel modules are needed during the course of the run, they may be loaded into kernel space dynamically.

Address Spaces

Each process on the system has its own unique view of the memory of the system. The addresses start at address 0 and continue to the high end of the virtual address space, which is generally 0xFFFFFFFF,* or 4 gigabytes (GB).

This view, though, is a view of the *virtual storage* of the process. That is, the addresses the process uses do not have a formal linear relationship to the underlying physical storage addresses. This is because Solaris is a virtual storage operating system.

---

*This is assuming the use of 32-bit addresses, which is what will be used throughout the rest of the book; as this book is being written, 64-bit addressing is still not common.

In order to facilitate throughput on the system, the parts of a process' address space that are not currently being used are moved out of physical storage (that is, they are *paged out*) and held in a temporary *swap space* on disk. This way, the underlying physical storage occupied by the vacated space can be reused by other processes that now are using a previously unused portion of their address space. These processes are *paged in* to the available physical address space.

A process that has been paged out can still use the paged out area though. Basically, the process described above is repeated for the paged out process. When the process makes a request for an area of its storage that is paged out, the kernel finds an empty (or infrequently used) area of physical storage and moves the paged out area of the paged out process to the new physical location. The kernel then adjusts *paging tables* so that the process will be able to use its virtual addresses and have them point to the correct physical location.

Layout of the Address Space

The layout of a virtual storage for a process is standardized and divided into three *segments,* or areas: text, stack, and data (Fig. 5-2). All Solaris processes, including the kernel, have these segments laid out in the same order. The *process address space* is the combination of all of the segments. Each segment has its own purpose and function.

The Text Segment.   The segment loaded at the load end of the process address space is the text segment. The text segment contains the executable program code. It has several important properties; it is

Read-only

Sharable

Backed up by the file system

Read-only means that the process cannot modify the contents of this segment; the program cannot modify itself. If the program were to attempt this, either intentionally or accidentally, a SIGSEGV (segmentation violation) is raised and the process is terminated.

The text segment is sharable, which means that it can be used by more than one process. For example, a WWW server usually has several different processes available to serve incoming requests. Each of these processes runs the exact same program; only the requests and data

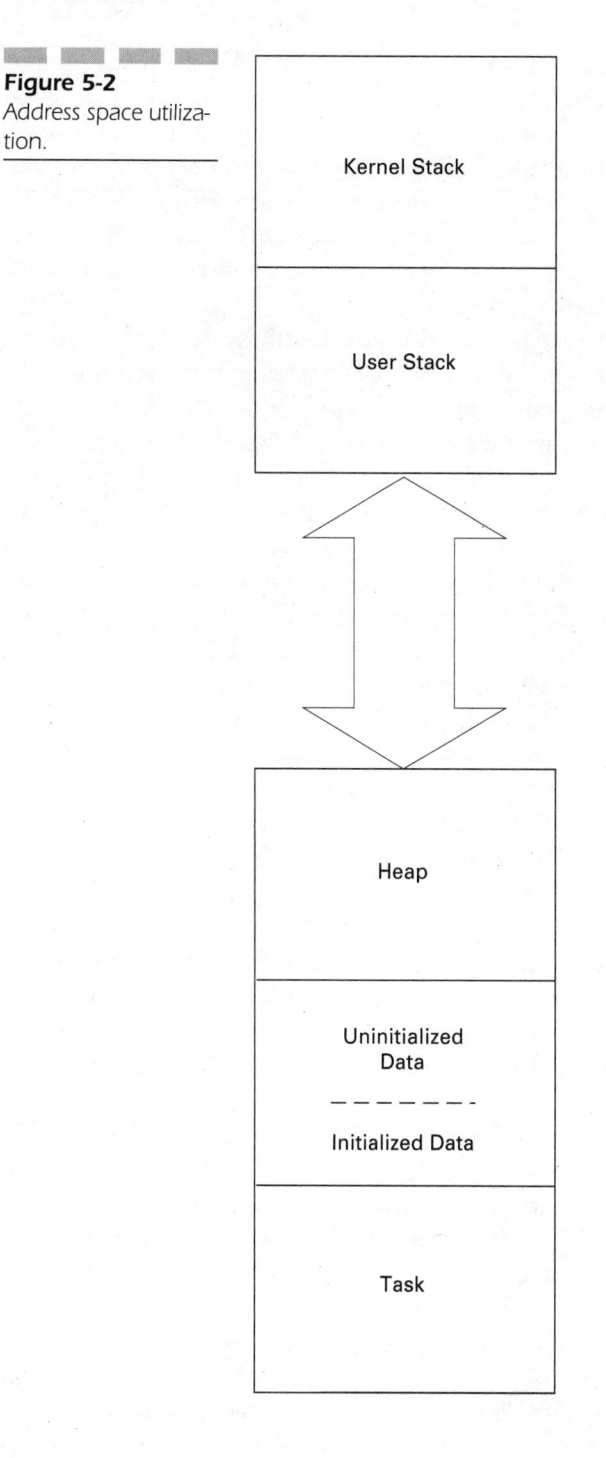

Figure 5-2
Address space utilization.

Kernel Stack

User Stack

Heap

Uninitialized Data

Initialized Data

Task

being served are different. There is no reason, because the text segment is read-only, to load individual copies of the program for each process. Each process would contain exactly the same thing, which could be a potentially large waste of physical memory space. Therefore, the text segment in processes using the same program are all mapped to the same physical memory location. In the process address space, it appears that each process has its own copy, but this underlying physical storage contains just a single copy.

Finally, the text segment is backed up by the file system. When physical memory resources become scarce, the system pages out unused or infrequently used portions of process address spaces. This could include the text segment. However, because the text segment is read-only, the executable program is not modified during execution. Additionally, the program is already located in a file system. Because the text segment has not been modified, there is no reason why it could not be paged in from the file system. And indeed, that is exactly what happens, because it is much more efficient. When a text segment is paged out, it is not copied to the swap file. The kernel simply modifies the page table of the process to indicate that the text segment is not in physical storage. If the paged out area is referenced, the kernel reads the text segment in from the file system and places the needed parts into physical storage, just as if they had been read directly from the swap space.

The Data Segment.   The data segment is where all of the data the program uses is stored. It is divided into two sections, *initialized* and *uninitialized* data.

The initialized area contains global variables that were assigned a value at compilation time. The area is writable, private, and initially backed up by the file system.

A process can modify the area; therefore, each process must have its own copy. This is what is meant by the area being private and writable. If the area has not been modified and it is paged out, the kernel will not write this area out to the swap file but instead will reload it, as with the data segment, from the file system. Once the area has been modified, though, the kernel must write the area to the swap file if it is paged out.

The uninitialized data area has the same properties as the initialized area, except that the initial value is 0x00.

The data segment is located immediately after the text segment and can grow toward the top of the process address space. This expansion area is known as the *heap area*. The heap area grows and shrinks throughout the course of the process. When a call to allocate memory (malloc()) is made, the allocated memory comes from the heap. If the area is returned, via a free() call, the memory is returned to the heap.

The User Stack. The user stack is located at the high end of the process address space at address 0xE0000000 in 32-bit systems. The user stack contains the *user context*.

The user context is all of the information needed by the system to keep a process running. This includes

Contents of the hardware registers

Program location counter

Arguments to current function calls

Arguments to current system calls

Local data for the current function

Return values for the system call

It is necessary to keep all of this information because a process can be swapped out or stopped at any time. When the process is swapped back in or restarted, the information above is used to continue execution at the correct place and with the correct parameters.

The user stack area is writable, private, created in virtual memory, and allocated as needed. There is no area in the original executable file that corresponds to the user stack area; it is built when the process first starts and expands as needed throughout the execution of the process.

For example, when a process written in C is started, after pushing the system information onto the user stack, the arguments passed to the main() function (argc(), argv(), and envp()) are pushed onto the user stack. Then, local variable declarations in main() are pushed onto the user stack. Subsequently, any functions called from main() are pushed onto the user stack, and they in turn push their local variables onto the user stack. When the function returns, the arguments and local variables are popped from the user stack, and the return value of the function is pushed onto the user stack. Similarly, when main() exits, the return value (from the exit() function call) is pushed onto the stack for the shell to use as it determines.

Unlike the heap in the data area, the user stack area is allocated from the top of virtual storage and works its way down. The address space between the top of the heap and the bottom of the user stack is known as the *hole*. If the top of the heap and the bottom of the stack meet, there is no space left for new memory or stack allocations. In this case, an attempt to allocate more stack space will result in a "Stack

Overflow" error, and an attempt to allocate more memory will result in a "Malloc failed" error.

The Kernel Stack.   The kernel stack is not a stack; it is the area reserved for the executing kernel program.* It occupies the highest segment of the process address space: the space from the top of the user stack to the top of the process address space. All of the kernel parts (text, data, user stack, and other kernel stacks) are mapped into this area.

The functions of the kernel segments are the same as the functions found in a user process except that the kernel stack keeps track of system activities.

The virtual storage address space of each process maps to the kernel stack area as accessibility to the kernel portion of the address space is required when a process enters kernel mode.

Execution Modes

In most cases, the majority of time a process spends in execution is spent in user mode. This means the process is using data and resources that are not shared with other processes. All of these resources will be stored or referenced from addresses below where the user stack begins.

Access to local resources is much faster than access to system resources, in some cases up to 100 times as fast. For example, a file that has been mapped into the process address space will be accessed much faster than a file in a file system. This is mainly because access to a locally mapped file does not require the use of system calls in order to gain access to the data in the file. Every time a system call is made, the user enters kernel mode.

When a process enters kernel mode, it starts running on the shared copy of the kernel. Because there is only one physical copy of the kernel, each process in kernel mode must queue and wait to use the resources of the kernel. This slows access down.

Additionally, all resources in kernel mode are assumed to be sharable; therefore, the kernel must mediate access to all resources that are used

---

*Generally stored in /kernel/unix.

while in kernel mode. These resources are not necessarily physical hardware, such as tape or disk drives, but they can be shared memory segments, sockets, or a process data structure that is being shared.*

Part of the overhead of kernel mode is the saving and restoration of process data that must take place before the mode can be changed. For example, when entering kernel mode, all of the arguments to the system call must be transferred from the user stack to the kernel stack. Similarly, when the function returns, the results that must be transferred from the kernel stack must be copied to the user stack.

Kernel Functions

The kernel is divided into two portions, each dealing with different types of activities. These activity types are divided between those that are synchronous and those that are asynchronous (Fig. 5-3). The use of the terms in this context is somewhat different from standard use.

A synchronous kernel function is requested directly by a process via a system call. A request to read a file from disk or send data to a terminal or modem is an example of synchronous kernel activity.

An asynchronous kernel function occurs without a user context; it occurs outside of a specific process. Most commonly, an asynchronous kernel function is an *interrupt,* which is a request from a device for service from the operating system. When a process request a service from a shared device, the device may not be ready to service the process at that time. When this occurs, the request is queued by the kernel and sent to the device when it is ready. When the device has completed the request, it sends an interrupt to the kernel to let the kernel know the function is complete. Interrupts do not know the source of the original request for their service; therefore, they do not occur within the context of a specific user or process. It is the responsibility of the kernel to associate the interrupt with the correct process.

Asynchronous functions are not strictly limited to hardware. The signals SIGKILL and SIGINT are asynchronous functions because these signals can be sent to a process from outside its user context.

---

*In this case, even the process that created the data structure would have to enter kernel mode to access it.

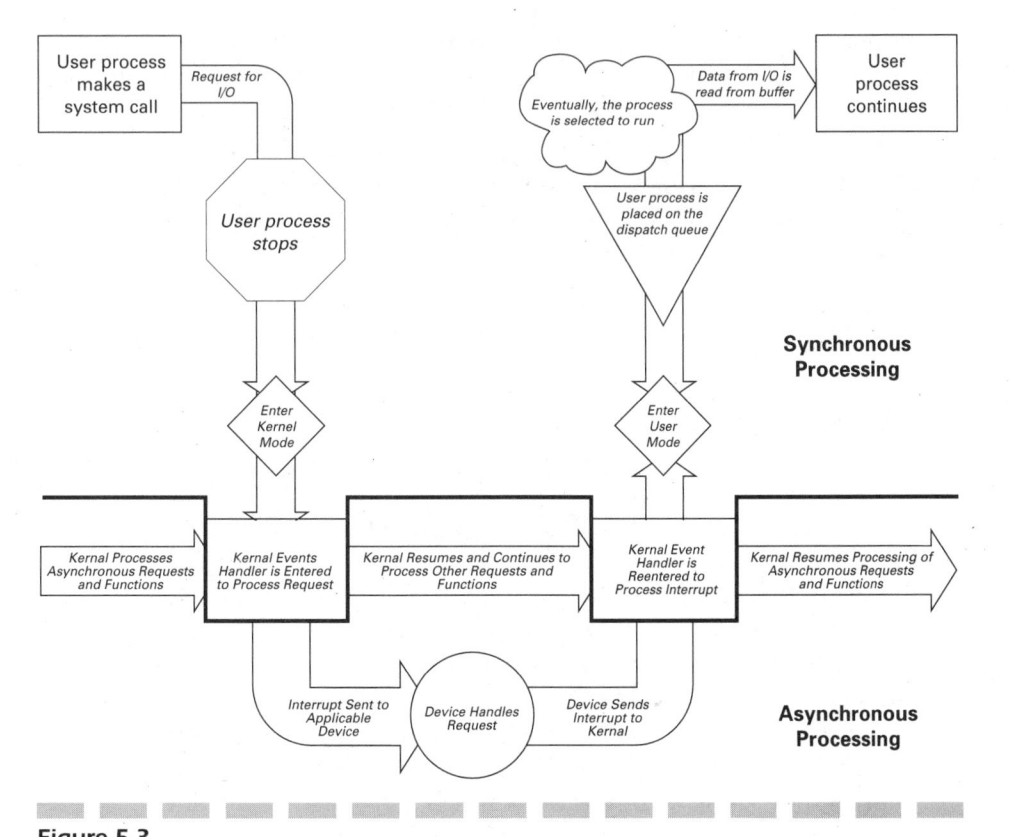

Figure 5-3
Transfer of control between synchronous and asynchronous routines in the kernel.

Kernel Structure

In Solaris, the traditional monolithic kernel has been abandoned in favor of a static core kernel program and a large number of loadable modules including device drivers, streams modules, scheduling modules, and file system modules. Using this model, the base kernel is slightly less than 1024K.* This is particularly advantageous because only the amount of storage required for the static core is allocated and locked down† at boot time; this is a substantial improvement compared to other UNIX implementations that lock down the kernel and all possible device drivers.

---

*This applies to Solaris 2.5 and 2.6. In Solaris 2.4 the size is ,900K.

†Locked storage is never paged out, regardless of how little it may be used.

In order to effectively implement the loadable device driver module concept, Solaris uses *dynamic linking*. With dynamic linking, the compiler does not bind libraries into the executable program but instead loads the library routines at run time as they are requested. There are several advantages to dynamic linking:

1. Compiled programs are smaller because the library routines are not part of the executable. This also saves disk space for program storage.

2. Overall memory requirements are reduced because unused library routines are not loaded.

3. All processes can share the same copy of the library, thereby reducing physical memory requirements.*

These advantages apply both to the kernel and to regular user processes.

A side effect of this implementation is that there is no need to rebuild the kernel, ever. The static core is the minimum configuration; all device drivers and system software modules are implemented as separate entities. To effect the same types of changes that typically require a kernel rebuild in other types of UNIX, the system administrator simply places the new driver or module in the appropriate directory and reboots the system.

The kernel can be customized, however. The **/etc/system** file is for specifying the configurable parameters of the kernel. The **/etc/system** file is discussed more fully in Chap. 14.

The /kernel Directory

Given the implementation of the static core, a directory structure that allows the kernel to find specific types of modules easily must be in place. This directory structure is the **/kernel** directory. The directory contains several subdirectories, each of which contains modules of a similar type. The basic elements in the directory are

/drv   Device driver subdirectory; contains all of the kernel level code that allows communication with I/O devices

---

*The primary disadvantage with dynamic linking occurs when a routine that is not currently loaded is called. The system must resolve the reference and load it from disk, which causes a delay. For some processes, primarily those dealing with real-time data collection, this may not be acceptable. For those cases, regular static linking is still available.

/exec	Executable file formats subdirectory; defines the various formats executable program files may have*
/fs	File system formats subdirectory; allows for the implementation of various types of files systems
/misc	Miscellaneous modules (DES, ipc, swap, etc.)
/sched	Scheduling classes subdirectory; includes time-sharing, real-time, and system classes
/strmod	Streams modules subdirectory
/sys	System calls subdirectory
/unix	The static kernel; an executable file

This directory structure reflects the structure of the kernel (Fig. 5-4). Each subdirectory contains modules that implement a particular part of the functionality of the kernel.

User-Kernel Interface

At the highest level of the diagram in Fig. 5-4, the interface between user mode and kernel mode is implemented through system calls. A process can only change mode through a valid system call. Because of the actions it performs, the system call itself is a kernel mode function.

When a system call occurs, several actions occur:

1. The system call number is placed into a global register.
2. The `trap` instruction is executed; this changes the state from user to kernel mode.
3. The `trap` handler is invoked to handle the `trap` instruction.
4. The trap handler invokes the `syscall()` routine to perform the system call.
5. The system call executes.
6. The system call returns.
7. The results of the system call are placed into the user stack area.
8. The state is changed back to user mode.
9. Control returns to the user program.

---

*One example is the differences between an executable Solaris program for SPARC and a Solaris program for x86.

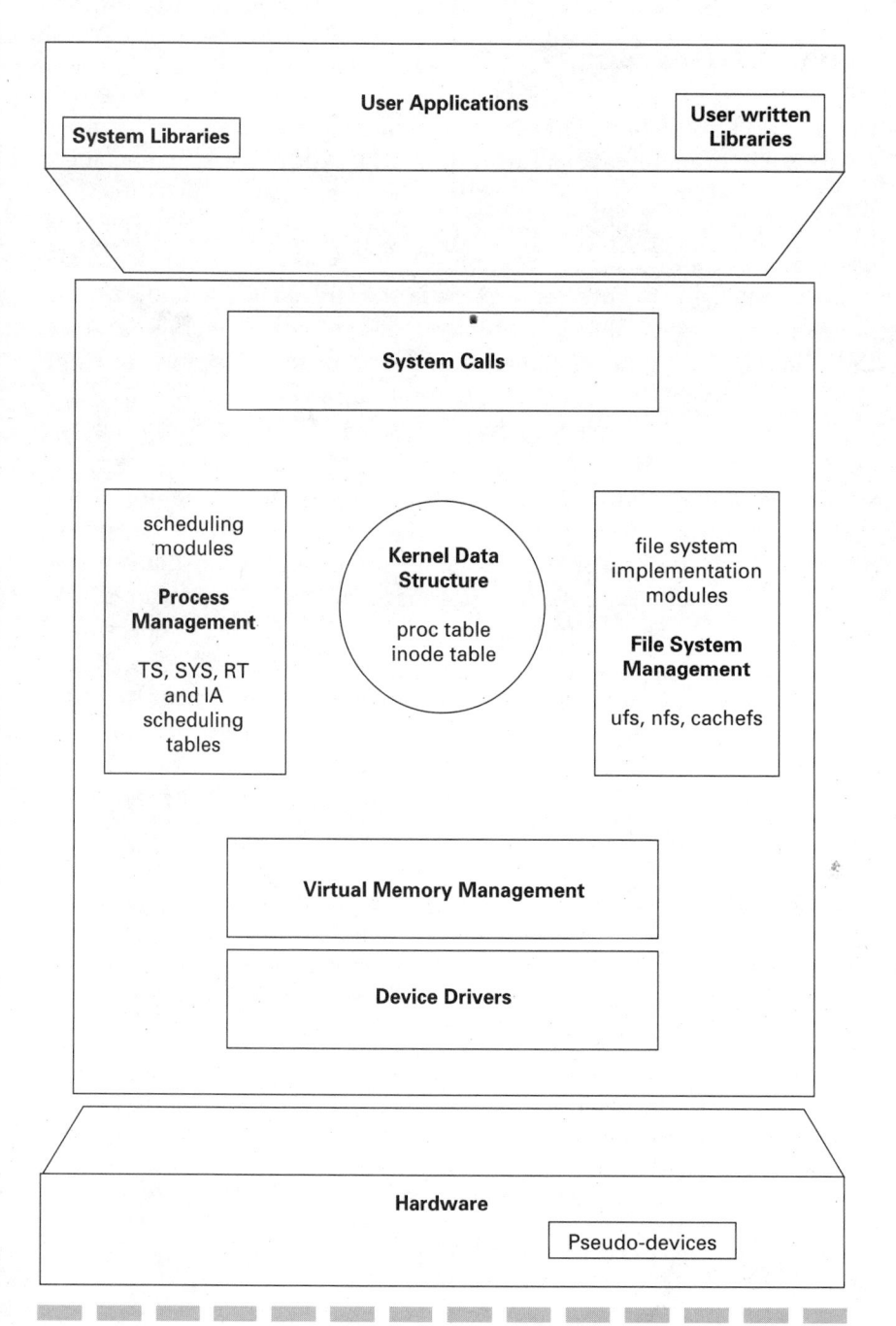

Figure 5-4
The kernel structure.

Kernel Interfaces

Inside the kernel level, interaction among functions is much more diverse. The system calls interface directly with process management and file system management functions. Process management functions include all of the scheduling functions, interprocess communication, signal handling, and process creation. Typically, the only hardware the process management functions access is the CPU. The file management functions are responsible for mediating access to data storage sources. Because the implementation details of the data storage sources are usually irrelevant to the requester of the data, access to the underlying hardware devices is further mediated via device drivers. Using this two-level architecture, the implementation details of the underlying hardware need only be known to the module responsible for communicating with the physical device—the device driver. The device driver returns a non-device-specific data stream to the file management functions.

It is also possible to have a device driver that is not associated with any "real" device. Output from an executing program that is not wanted is often directed to /dev/nul, which is the null *pseudodevice*. It is a pseudodevice because there is no underlying physical device. However, the process using the pseudodevice does not know that. It uses the pseudodevice just as it would any real device of the same type.

Completing the picture, both the process management functions and the file system management functions interact directly with the kernel data structures and virtual memory management. Process management functions use virtual memory to allocate memory for the user processes on the system, whereas file system management functions interact with virtual memory to load data (perhaps even an entire file) into the process address space. Both types of functions are constantly changing the state of the kernel data structures to indicate what is going on in the system.

The kernel data structures includes the inode, superblock, and vnode tables for the file systems, proc structures, and address space translation tables, just to name a few. All of the kernel data structures are defined in two files: /usr/include and /usr/include/sys.

Summary

Understanding the architecture of the kernel is critical to understanding the issues involved in tuning Solaris. This chapter discussed how the kernel divides up the total physical memory of the computing system into logical address spaces. In addition, the two modes of the kernel (user and system), and the interfaces used to pass between the two, were explored in detail.

The next chapter looks at the memory subsystem in detail.

6

Memory

Current SPARC and Intel architectures can address up to 4 GB of real storage on a machine.* Access to this memory is performed via 4-Kt segments, called *pages*.† Every page of memory is assigned a *page number* by which it is addressed. The kernel keeps a *memory free list* that indicates whether or not a particular page of real storage is used, and if used, by whom.

---

*Whether the hardware can actually support this is another question.

†The UltraSPARC models use an 8K page size.

On a Solaris system, many programs run at the same time. These programs support the multiple users and many processes that perform functions for the system overall. At any one time, only a portion of each of these programs is actually being used; the rest of the program is dormant. There is no reason for the dormant routines of these programs to reside in memory unless they are needed. Because of this, virtual memory is used by almost all modern-day operating systems* because it allows for the implementation of more efficient systems overall.

An Overview of Virtual Memory and Paging

Virtual memory is a set of algorithms the operating system uses to allow the execution of user programs that are not completely loaded into physical memory. Therefore, virtual memory allows Solaris to load more programs into real storage than will actually fit into the available real storage. The user program is unaware of what part of the program is actually loaded into the physical memory of the machine. Furthermore, the user program is not aware of where the parts of the program that are loaded reside in the physical memory. In both cases, neither point is relevant to the user program. It is the role of the kernel and hardware to keep track of these things.

Virtual memory allows the operating system to write those portions of the program not currently needed out to a special file on disk, the *paging space,* where the pages are stored until needed. This process of writing a program out to disk is referred to as *paging out.* As long as a page is not modified, it is only necessary to write the page to the paging file once, regardless of the number of times the page is actually removed from real storage. However, once a page has been modified, it must be written to the paging file if the page is removed from physical memory.

The opposite process occurs when the operating system detects that a portion of the program not currently in real storage is needed (a *page fault*); it *pages in* the necessary portion of the program from disk (Fig. 6-1).

This paging architecture, *demand paging,* differs from the original UNIX implementations, which used *swapping.* Conceptually swapping

---

*MS-DOS is the most notable exception.

1) A program is read from a file on disk and loaded into the user's address space

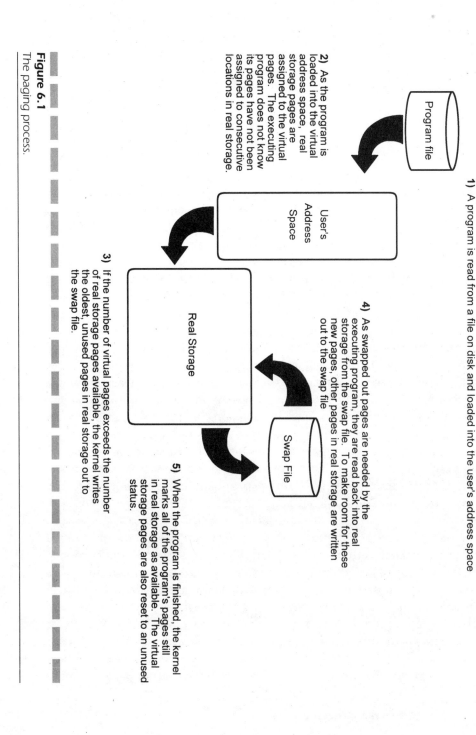

2) As the program is loaded into the virtual address space, real storage pages are assigned to the virtual pages. The executing program does not know its pages have not been assigned to consecutive locations in real storage.

Program file

User's Address Space

Real Storage

Swap File

4) As swapped out pages are needed by the executing program, they are read back into real storage from the swap file. To make room for these new pages, other pages in real storage are written out to the swap file

3) If the number of virtual pages exceeds the number of real storage pages available, the kernel writes the oldest, unused pages in real storage out to the swap file.

5) When the program is finished, the kernel marks all of the program's pages still in real storage as available. The virtual storage pages are also reset to an unused status.

Figure 6.1
The paging process.

is not much different from paging; however, instead of transferring a single page, multiple pages are transferred. Originally, UNIX systems did not implement virtual memory, and the only way to provide for multiple, concurrent users was to take a user's *entire* address space and write it out to disk while, at the same time, bringing into storage another user's address space. Most recent UNIX systems only use swapping when the paging rate reaches a critical point. In these situations, the operating system will swap out entire processes until the overall system paging rate returns to a reasonable level. Gradually, these swapped out processes are reintroduced into the system.

Demand paging relies on the ability of the operating system to determine how often, or if, a page in real storage has been referenced. Obviously, pages that have not been recently used are the best choice to be paged out when paging is necessary. In traditional UNIX systems, a software mechanism is used to determine the age of pages in real storage. This process, the *pagedaemon,* periodically scans all real storage and maintains tables that track which pages are being used and by whom. Software processes are necessary because some computer architectures do not have a way to indicate this information in the hardware. This is not the case in Solaris; page use information is available directly from the hardware (the memory management unit, or MMU), and therefore the pagedaemon process is not necessary on Solaris.

Virtual memory also allows the operating system to present an application program that has a linear memory space. As discussed in Chap. 5, this *process address space* always starts at the same location and is unique to each process. For all practical purposes, the user process does not know that the storage it "sees" is not real. Each process on the system believes that it has exclusive access to up to 4 GB of real storage. The user process accesses data and instructions via the *virtual addresses* of the address space. When the user process accesses these virtual addresses, the hardware (via the MMU) translates them to the real address at which the information is actually loaded.

Within the virtual address space of each process, memory is divided into three segments: text, data, and user stack.

The text segment is where the program code is loaded, and it cannot be modified by the executing program. In addition to providing for greater code reliability, this permits the operating system to skip the page-out process for all text segments of programs, which can result in better performance on systems that are deficient in available real storage.

The data segment contains *all* of the static data areas used by the program. Even if data definitions are interspersed throughout the program source code, the compilation and link editing process moves all data definitions to the data area (Fig. 6-2).

The stack segment has two major uses. Primarily, the stack area is used to store information when transferring control between programs or parts of programs. Secondarily, the stack area is used as an area in which to create dynamic data structures.

The term *segment* has a slightly different meaning when referring to hardware. The hardware definition of a segment is a contiguous collection of physical memory pages that are referenced as a single group. They can be referenced this way because they all share a single segment entry in the virtual address. This facility is used by the kernel to move groups of pages at a time, which is much more efficient than paging just one page at a time.

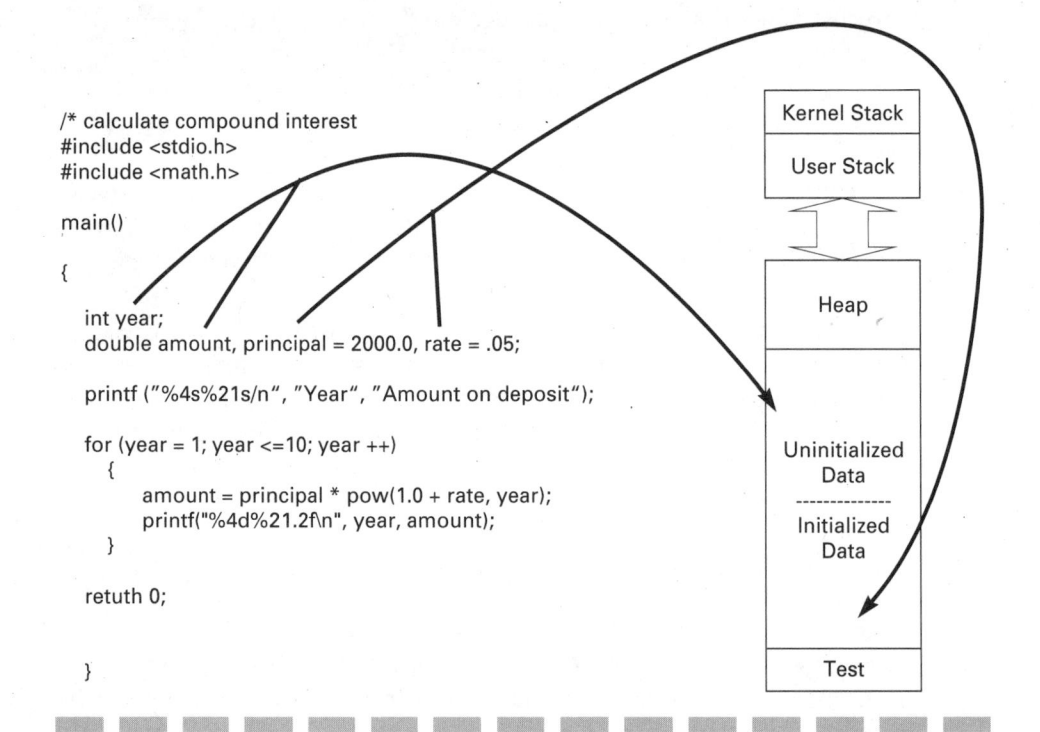

Figure 6-2

Allocation of data in the process address space. (*Code Sample adapted from* C how to program, *Deitel and Deital, Prentice Hall, 1994.*)

User Contexts and Hardware Contexts

The text, data, and user stack areas, along with the process address space and the registers used by the process, constitute the *context* of the process. That is, all of the resources a process is using at any given instant constitute its context.

Every process on the system has its own unique context. As discussed in Chap. 5, most of this information is stored in the user stack segment of the process. It is not stored in a kernel stack for two reasons:

1. It would be very inefficient due to all of the system calls that would be necessary.

2. It is irrelevant to the kernel.

The kernel only needs to know specific information about the context of a process when the process requests a specific service from the kernel.

At the hardware level, referring to the MMU, the term *context* is used in a slightly different way. The MMU views the context of a process as the translations that must be done to derive a physical address from a virtual address for the given process. The MMU can support more than one context at a time, which allows more than one process to run without having to have an MMU context switch. However, the MMU does have a finite number of process contexts that it can support. When an MMU context process switch occurs, the current contexts must be unloaded and stored and the new context must be loaded and restored. In general, the number of contexts the MMU supports is not something a performance analyst can do anything about; however, it may be a point to consider when choosing between different processor architectures.

Physical Memory Types and Cache

In most systems, there are (at least) two different types of real memory: main storage and cache. They are used in combination to allow the processor to gain access to data and instructions as quickly as possible.

In general, the average access time for main memory is 50 to 60 ns. This is because of physical limitations in the type of memory that is most commonly used—dynamic random access memory (DRAM). When you consider that a 40-megahertz (MHz) SPARCstation 2* requires a 25-ns access time to keep the processor running at maximum speed, it becomes evident that there is a problem if the processor is being fed data and instructions directly from regular DRAM main memory.

Cache memory is generally faster, with an access time of 5 to 20 ns. This is because it is implemented with static random access memory (SRAM). It would seem self-evident that the solution to the problem is to just use SRAM for main memory. However, this is not possible for three reasons:

1. SRAM is very expensive compared to DRAM.
2. SRAM uses much larger amounts of electrical power compared to DRAM.
3. SRAM requires many more chips to implement the same amount of storage as implemented in DRAM.

In many cases, two caches are used—one on-chip with the processor and another off-chip in SRAM. The cache closest to the processor is referred to as the *Level-1* cache (L1), or primary cache; the off-chip cache is the *Level-2* (L2), or secondary cache. Depending on the clock speed of the central processor, it nominally takes 5 to 10 ns to access data in an on-chip cache and 15 to 20 ns to access data in SRAM cache. On a 200-MHz Pentium processor, it may take only 1 cycle to access data in a L1 cache but as many as 20 cycles to access data in an L2 cache. Compare this to the 200 cycles it would take to access the data from main memory.

Several different types of cache memory are used in Intel-based workstations and servers. Newer processors, like the Pentium Pro, use a two-level cache—16K on-chip primary cache and 256K secondary code or more. The 486 and Pentium processors generally use eight 32k × 8 asynchronous RAMs. At 66 MHz, the clock period is 15 ns. The speed of the cache, which is the number of clock cycles it takes to bring something in from cache (the 3:2:2:2 time), depends on the speed of these processors. The first access requires three cycles, 45 ns, to match a cache address, and every cache access after that takes 30 ns, every write takes 30 ns, and every read cycle takes 30 ns (i.e., 3:2:2:2 relative to the 15 ns of the SRAM chips). Alternately, some processors and chip sets can use four 32k × 18 synchronous RAMs. (The 18-bit organization includes a parity bit, which is actually two 8-bit bytes with 1 parity bit for each byte.) The synchronous RAMs allow internally self-timed writes. The

---

*This is an old machine that is not even a particularly fast machine by today's standards.

speed of memory accesses changes to 2:1:1:1; that is, the first access takes 30 ns, but every successive access and every read and write after that takes 15 ns. Every wait state saved increases system performance by about 2 percent.

SPARC-based machines also use a multilevel cache scheme. The first level cache is on-chip: 16K for data and 20K for instructions. The second level cache is 1 or 2 MB SRAM chips.

The importance of having enough physical memory in a machine cannot be underestimated. In a report by Samsung Inc.,* the performance of systems was increased by as much as 63 percent simply by adding more physical memory. In fact, the data indicated that the performance of a 100-MHz Pentium could exceed a 200-MHz Pentium Pro that was starved for physical memory. Much of the decreased performance of the Pentium Pro in this example can be attributed to the excessive paging that occurs when a machine does not have sufficient physical storage.

The Paging Process in Uniprocessor Machines

Given a uniprocessor machine, the following sequence of events can be described as a typical instance of what occurs when data is requested from storage by a program (Fig. 6-3).

First, the program issues an instruction that references the location in virtual memory where the data is located. Before anything else, the cache (all levels if there is more than one level) is checked to see if the data has been referenced recently. If so, the request will be satisfied from the cache.

If the data is not in the cache, the virtual address of the data is passed to the MMU. The MMU looks up the virtual address of the translation tables it keeps to find the real physical location. If there is a valid translation, the data is read from main storage into the cache and then is passed to the requesting program.

If the translation was not valid, a *page fault* occurs. This means that the requested page was not in memory. The swapper daemon is called to retrieve the page from the backing store (in this case, the swap file) and place it somewhere in physical memory. Once the page has been

---

*http://www.more.memory.samsung.com/.

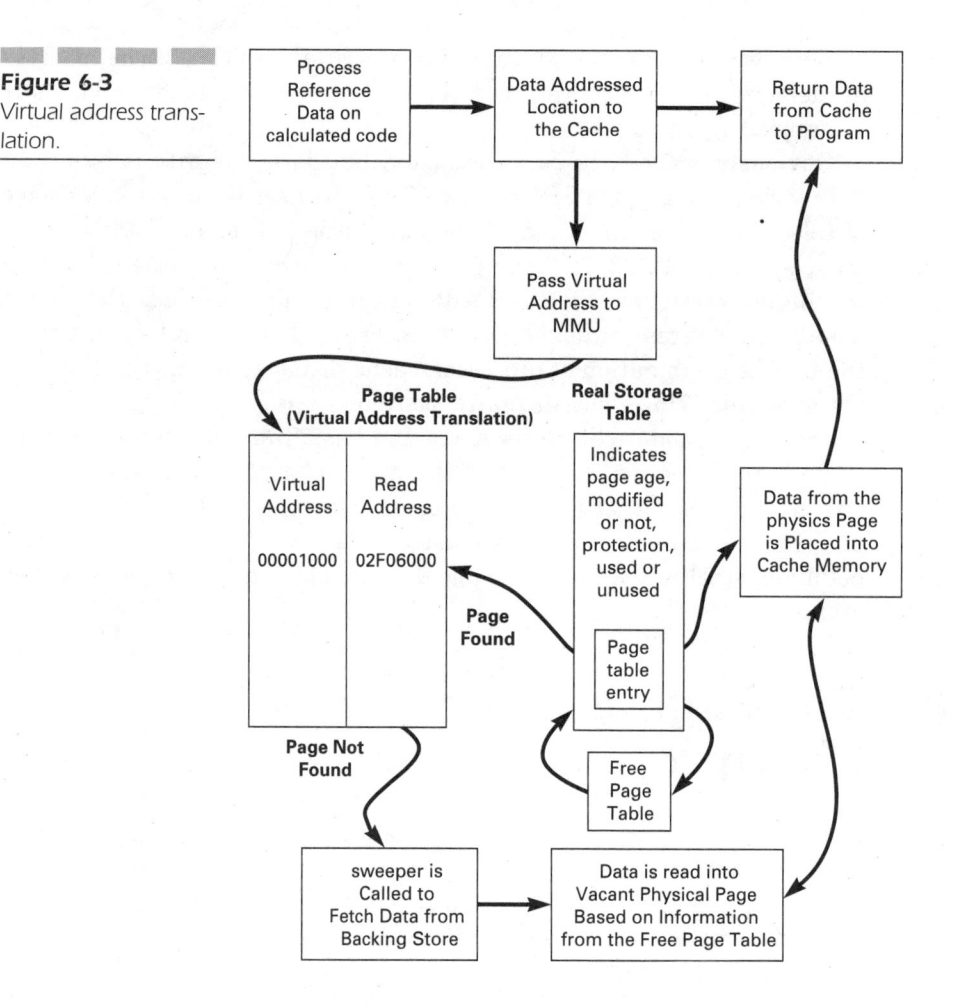

Figure 6-3
Virtual address translation.

brought into memory, the data is placed into the cache and is then passed to the requesting program.

If the request is for a write, the sequence of events is somewhat different. Again, the first thing that occurs is that the program issues an instruction that references the location in virtual memory at which the data is located. And, again, the cache (all levels if there is more than one level) is checked to see if the data has been referenced recently. If it has been, the data is updated; if it has not, the data is placed into the cache.

What happens next depends on the type of cache: *write-through* or *write-back*. With write-through cache, the data is also immediately copied to virtual memory. This implies that the page, just as before when reading the data, must be located in physical storage; if it is not there, it is brought in.

With write-back cache, the data is not written from the cache to virtual memory until the process is swapped out or exited or the address is referenced again.

Obviously, write-back cache is faster, but data integrity is less than with write-through. On SPARC machines, the user is not given a choice of selecting one or the other. Write-back cache is used on the lower-end models (SS1 and SS2, for example), and write-through cache is used on the higher-end ones (SS10, SPARCcenters). For Intel-based systems, usually the system automatically detects which mode is best based on the unique combination of processor, cache memory, and motherboard in the machine. However, in many systems, it is possible to manually select which mode will be used via the basic input/output system, or BIOS setup program. Overall, if there is an "auto-detect" option, it is best to use that. Otherwise, the choice is left to the performance analyst or system administrator, who must decide which factor is more compelling: a small increase in possible data loss or somewhat faster performance.

The Paging Process in Multiprocessor Machines

In a multiprocessor system, as one would expect, cache access is more complex than in a uniprocessor system. This is because each CPU, in addition to its processor, has its own virtual address cache and MMU. When a cache lookup occurs and it is not found in the cache of the CPU doing the lookup, before going to virtual memory, all other processors must be polled to ensure that they are not holding the data. Because of this, the system bus is much busier in a multiprocessor system than in a uniprocessor system, as is the vehicle used by the CPUs to communicate with each other in addition to the other components of the system.

The process of polling the other processors in order to perform the cache lookup is a special technique known as *cache snooping*. There are three possible outcomes of a cache snoop operation:

1. The data is not found in any other cache; therefore the requesting CPU proceeds as it would if it were operating in uniprocessor mode.

2. The request was for a *read* and the data was found in another cache; the data is copied to requesting processor's local cache and used.

3. The request was for a *write* and the data is found in another cache; the data is copied to the local cache and written, and all other copies of the data in other caches must be flushed.

Note that, in a multiprocessor system, every time a write to cache occurs, a synchronization of all of the processor caches must occur to make sure that any old data is flushed.

Components and Structures of Virtual Memory

There are three major components of systemwide virtual memory: the physical memory of the system (RAM), the swap space, and the local and mounted file systems.

Within each process address space, the components of the address space are divided into two major categories, those that are *named* and those that are *unnamed*. Named objects include things that have names such as ordinary files, named pipes, sockets, directories, and physical devices. Unnamed objects include things like private pages, interprocess communication objects, uninitialized data segments, and stack segments.

Regardless of whether the object is named or unnamed, it must ultimately correspond to a physical object—every virtual address must correspond to a physical address, either in physical memory or the backing store (swap space or the file system).

Process Address Space Components

Management of the process address space components starts at the process address space level via the proc* structure. The proc structure consists of an address space, the as structure. The address space consists of segments (a seg structure and a segment structure specific to the object) that in turn map to pages via a vnode structure. These pages contain addressing information specific to the object via the hardware address translation (hat) layer.

---

*Each of these structures is implemented as a header file in the /usr/include/vm directory. For instance, the proc structure is defined in /usr/include/vm/proc.h.

The kernel is unique in that it does not have a `proc` structure associated with it. Instead, the kernel uses a special entry point that is a special address space structure, `kas`.

Management of the Systemwide Components

At the system level, most activity is centered around the management of the physical memory pages. The physical memory pages available for use by user programs, and therefore by the virtual memory manager, all consist of physical memory except the amount of physical memory used by the kernel program and its associated data structures.

The system maintains five major lists related to the management of physical pages: the page structure pool, the freelist, the `vnode` page list, the page `hash` list, and the anonymous memory pool.

The page structure pool is a statically sized structure allocated during the initialization of the system. After the kernel has loaded and allocated all of the data structures it will lock down in memory, an entry is created in the pool for every physical page that has not been locked down by the kernel. Subsequently, the virtual memory manager can use a page in the pool as a `page` structure to be mapped to a process virtual address space.

The freelist is a dynamically sized structure that contains pointers to all of the physical pages on the system that are available. Pages are allocated from the front of the list, and pages that become available are added to the end of the list. Doing so implements a least recently used (LRU) allocation algorithm. For most systems, this is the most efficient way to allocate pages.

The page `hash` table and `vnode` page list are used to make quick lookups of pages that are in use.

The anonymous memory pool contains the pointers to the swap space on the system, either swap partitions or files that have been designated as swap.

Memory Management

When a process starts, a new address space is allocated for the process. The system loads the executable program, sets up the data areas based on information in the executable, and creates the initial user stack in the virtual memory of the process address space. After these actions have been performed, control is transferred to the user program.

As the process address space was loaded with these objects (executable, data, and user stack), the objects were also loaded into physical memory. If there is an abundance of memory in the machine, these objects will remain in the physical memory for an indeterminate length of time. While they remain in the physical memory, no paging of the address space occurs, although the hardware must still translate virtual addresses to physical addresses.

Even though the process sees a large address space, most of that space is unoccupied. The unoccupied space is not allocated virtual memory space until it is used; therefore, the virtual memory does not occupy any physical space until it is used.

It is only when the system finally reaches the point at which the amount of virtual memory in use exceeds the amount of physical memory does paging begin. At this point, requests for objects in memory can result in a page fault.

A page fault is a request by the MMU to bring a page from the backing store into physical memory. All page-in requests occur because a process tries to access a virtual memory address that is not mapped to a physical memory address. Assuming there is ample physical memory, each page fault results in the following actions:

The virtual address cache (VAC) of the processor is checked to see if there is an entry for the requested page.

The MMU is checked to see if the page translation is valid.

If it is valid, the address is resolved and execution continues.

If it is not valid and this is a multiprocessor system, the other MMUs on the other processors are checked to see if they can resolve the address.

If the address was not resolved, the page is not resident; therefore, a physical page is allocated from the freelist, the requested page is read from the backing store, and the physical memory location is mapped to the virtual memory of the process address space.

As can be seen, there are two possible things that can happen. If a physical memory page is free (perhaps another process just finished and released all of its physical memory pages), the requested page can use an available physical memory page. Eventually, though, all of physical memory will become occupied and a physical page will not be free. The system must then decide which physical memory page should be moved to the backing store to make room for the requested page that is *paged in*.

Because this process is so extremely important and common, two processes are dedicated to aspects of this function: the `swapper` process and the `pager` process.*

In order to manage the physical memory, the system must make some determination of what is an acceptable number and the minimum acceptable number of free physical pages. These two values are represented by kernel variables that vary depending on machine architecture:

`minfree` = 25 pages (50 on sun4d machines)

`lotsfree` = 128 pages (256 on sun4d machines)

Solaris uses these values to implement the *two-handed clock algorithm* for managing the removal and replacement policies of the physical memory of the system. A pointer (the fronthand) sweeps through the page structure pool and resets the reference indicator bit for every page. At a later point in time, the second pointer (the backhand) sweeps through the page structure pool again to check the reference indicators. If the bit is still off, the page has not been referenced recently and will be added to the page-out list. If the bit has been set to active, the page is left in physical storage.

Four times per second the amount of free physical memory pages is tested by the kernel. If the amount is less than `lotsfree`, the `pager` daemon is activated. The daemon has two threads, one scans the physical memory and creates a list of pages to page out and the second thread performs the physical I/O of the page-out process. The kernel variable `slowscan` rate is used as an indicator of how often to scan through the page structure pool and the kernel variable `handspreadpages` to determine how far behind the fronthand the backhand should be.

As the amount of available physical memory decreases, the system increases the scan rate up to the amount defined by the kernel variable `fastscan`. The `fastscan` value is used to define the high-end limit for scanning the page structure pool as the system approaches the `minfree` value of physical pages.

---

*The swapper process always runs as process id 0 and the pager process always runs as process id 2.

When the `minfree` value has been reached and the page structure pool has been scanned at the `fastscan` twice and has still not been able to free up any pages, the system becomes desperate and will activate the `swapper`. The `swapper` runs once every second and pages entire threads or processes out at a time. It uses three kernel variables for this process:*

nswapped   The number of threads swapped out

runout   A flag to indicate there is no more work for the swapper

runin   A flag used to indicate there is a need to swap a process in, but there is no room in physical memory to do so

The basic swap-out procedure is

1. For each scheduling class, a swap-out routine is called.
2. Each routine selects a thread (process) to be swapped out.
3. The `swapper` selects the lowest-priority thread from the routines and swaps that thread out to the swap file.
4. The variables `runout` and `nswapped` are incremented by 1.
5. If `runin` is not set on, `runin` is set on.
6. If the amount of available physical memory is still less than `minfree`, go to step 1.

Once the amount of available physical memory is acceptable, the swap-in procedure starts:

1. A swap-in routine specific to each scheduling class is called.
2. Each routine nominates a thread to swap in.
3. The swapper selects the highest-priority thread and swaps the process back in.
4. The variables `nswapped` and `runout` are decremented by 1.
5. If `nswapped` and `runout` both equal zero, `runin` is set to off.
6. If `runin` is off and `nswapped` is equal to zero, the `swapper` goes to sleep.
7. If `runin` is on, but there is not enough physical memory to swap a waiting thread back in, the `swapper` sleeps and the starts swapping things out again.

---

*At one point, there was a parameter that told the kernel at what point desperation swapping should occur. This parameter does not exist in Solaris 2.4 or greater.

Once the swapper has stopped because all of the swapped processes have been brought back into physical memory, the pager resumes regular processing. The scanning thread of the pager process will stop when the entire page structure pool has been scanned twice and no pages are found waiting to be paged out. The I/O thread of the pager process sleeps whenever the list of pages to page out is empty.

Ideally, the swapper will never be invoked. When paging reaches the rate at which the swapper must be invoked, the system is under stress. If this is a temporary and infrequent occurrence, it may be acceptable; however, it is a very pronounced indicator that memory shortage problems are imminent.

Tuning can sometimes help. For example, if the value of lotsfree were made larger, the pager would start sooner. Similarly, if the swap space is distributed over several disk drives, the pager will be able to drive a higher I/O rate, which in turn allows for a higher paging rate without causing the swapper to start.

Summary

Virtual memory is implemented on the physical memory of the machine as a mechanism for extending the capability of the system to support additional processes. This virtual memory is made possible because of the paging subsystem. Therefore, the majority of the discussion in this chapter was related to understanding the concepts of physical and virtual memory and exploring the paging subsystem and the components and structures of the virtual memory and how paging differs in uniprocessor and multiprocessor machines.

Following up on this discussion, process and thread management form the basis of the next chapter.

Process and Thread Management

Every activity on the system is implemented via a process or a thread within a process. Every process on the system competes with all other processes for the resources of the system: execution time, storage, and input/output services.

Solaris divides the time of the system processing units among the executing processes by *time-slicing*. Each process is alloted a maximum amount of time in which it may run. During the period of time the process is running, the process is said to be *in control* of the system. If the maximum time limit is reached, the kernel stops the current process and schedules another process to run. Processes that have been stopped are referred to as *sleeping*.

In many cases, a process never uses its entire allotment of time because the process "voluntarily" gives up control. This occurs most often whenever an input or output operation is performed. Although this surrender is not really voluntary, it is perfectly reasonable. In general, when a process is waiting for an input or output operation to complete, it cannot perform any additional instructions until that I/O is complete. It is not reasonable for the processor to lie idle while a process is waiting for an input or output operation to complete. Therefore, the kernel gives control of the processor to another process as soon as an I/O is initiated.

In addition to voluntarily giving up control, processes may involuntarily give up control of the processor. Every process of the system is scheduled by the kernel based on a priority and the ability of the process to run. When the scheduler selects a process to run, it always selects the highest-priority process on the system that is not waiting for an external event, like I/O. However, unlike most other UNIX-based operating systems, Solaris provides for process preemption; the kernel can preempt most running processes to serve another, higher-priority process. In fact, even many kernel processes are preemptible. Because of this capability, Solaris can provide bounded dispatch behavior (more commonly know as *real-time* execution) that other UNIX variants cannot.

The scheduling of processes is performed by the highest-priority kernel process, `sched`, also known as the `swapper` and as *process 0* because it always runs under process ID zero. Every process on the system is created as a child of process 1, *init,* by means of the `fork` (or `vfork`) system call (Table 7-1).

TABLE 7-1	Allocate a new *proc(ess)* structure
Process Creation Overview	Copy parent *proc* structure to child *proc* structure
	Set up new information (process id, CPU time, etc.)
	Set up file structures (*inodes*) for sharing
	Set up shared memory for child process
	Split into two processes
	Allocate real storage for child process
	Copy *text, data,* and *stack* regions from parent
	Copy *user* structure from parent
	Access new program and read in headers
	Check memory requirements

The `fork` system call tells the kernel to create a child process for the requesting process. The child process is created by duplicating the parent process; the image of the parent process is copied into the new address space. Although the kernel assigns a new process id to the child, the child address space shares many of the parent's facilities; in particular, when the `fork` system call is used, the two address spaces share text areas and file descriptor.* Furthermore, although the data and stack areas are not shared, the `fork` system call does copy the information from the parent's data and stack areas to the child when the child process is created.

The *exec* system call is then used to load the new program into the child process (Fig. 7-1). Without the *exec* system call, the child process would execute the same program as the parent.

There is quite a bit of overhead in performing all of this information copying from the parent to the child. In most cases, this overhead is unjustified because a new program will be loaded into the child process. To circumvent this problem, the `vfork` system call is used. This system call, which is a relatively new addition, only creates a new process address space; it does not copy information from parent to child. It is assumed that a `vfork` call will be followed by an `exec` call to load a program into the address space.

---

*The child process even has the same file location pointers.

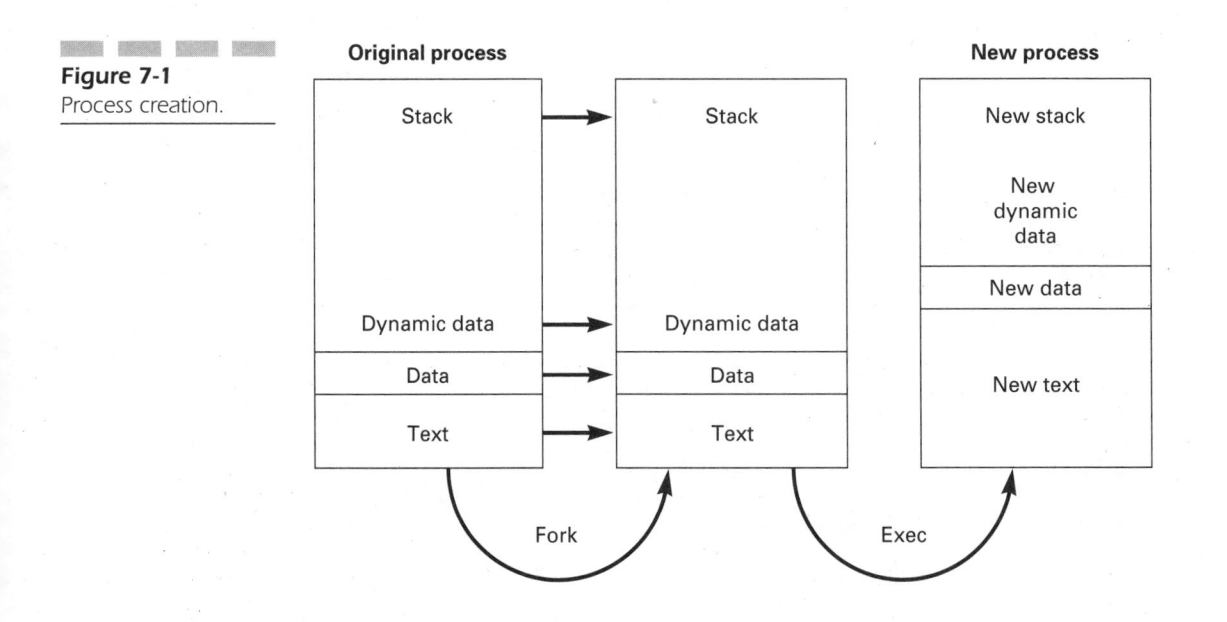

Figure 7-1
Process creation.

A process can either terminate itself normally or be abnormally terminated via the SIGKILL system call (Fig. 7-2). A process cannot terminate until the kernel has "cleaned up" all of the resources the process has used. While the process is waiting for the kernel to clean up, the process is in a *zombie,* or *defunct,* state. In general, processes pass through this state quickly (Table 7-2). However, in unusual circumstances zombie processes can exist for long periods of time. The most common cause of long-running zombie processes is system or application

Figure 7-2
Scheduling priorities.

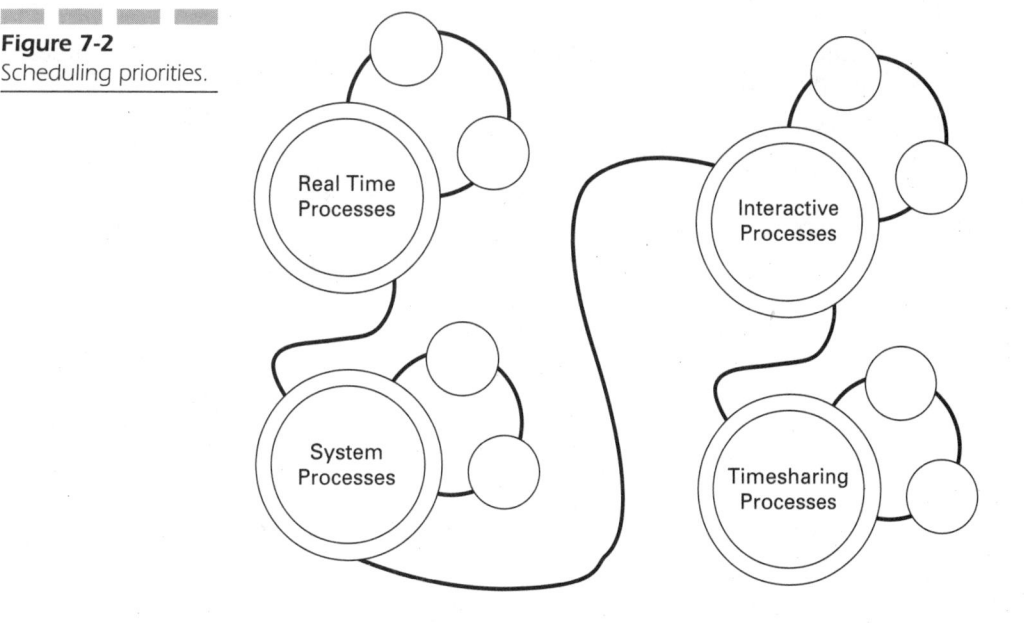

TABLE 7-2

Process Termination Overview

Release all memory used by process except *user* structure

Reduce all files reference counts; close if necessary

Detach from shared memory areas

Change process state to *zombie*

Mark *exit* status in process table entry

Release *user* structure

Signal parent process

Attach remaining child processes to *init* process

Switch control to another process

failure. In these cases, the zombie process usually can only be terminated by shutting down the system.

Threads

Threads are sequences of instructions that are executed within a program. In most programs, there is one thread that starts with the call to `main()` and ends when `exit()` is called. Traditionally, when concurrent paths of execution were needed in a program, separate processes were used. Good examples of this are most Web servers. As each new request for information comes in, the Web server spawns a new process to service the request. These processes are created via the traditional `fork()` system call and communicate with each other (if necessary) via lock files, signals, semaphores, or some other method. This method works well, but it generates a lot of system overhead because the new process creation and all communication between the processes is mediated by the kernel in some way.

In Solaris, programs with concurrent paths of execution may use threads instead of separate processes. Essentially, threads allow for the implementation of concurrent execution paths in one program—what has been traditionally known as private multitasking. This is because the kernel is not involved in the multitasking the process is doing via the threads.

Each thread within a process behaves as if it were an independent program. In fact, threads have all of the properties of a process. Threads have their own identity. That is, each thread has its own stack, program counter, registers, and priority. Every thread within a process is independent of other threads, and as in the case of processes, there is no way to predict the order of execution or completion of threads. Threads are invisible outside the process in which they are running, and the number of threads within a process is not known by the threads within the process.

Because threads execute in a common address space, threads can communicate via library calls rather than system calls. Threads have access to processwide resources; therefore, threads can share data easily through global data in the process address space. However, because every thread is a part of the process, calling `exit()` from a thread will cause all threads in a process to terminate.

Threads are used extensively in Solaris, particularily in the kernel. Normally, when a process (like the kernel) makes a system call, the entire process stops until the request is fulfilled. When threads are used, only the requesting thread is stopped; other threads with work to do may continue to run. In a multiprocessor environment, if threads are used, the threads from a single process can be dispatched on multiple processors. For example, the kernel can process an I/O request via a thread on one processor while dispatching a user process via a separate thread on another processor. A process (such as the kernel) not using threads may only run on one of the CPUs at any given time. In this case, the kernel would have to wait for the I/O request to complete before dispatching the user process.

Lightweight Processes

Ultimately, a process must make its threads known to the kernel. If this were not the case, the thread would not be runable. This is done through the lightweight processes (LWPs). LWPs are threads within the kernel that are used solely for running user threads.

When the program creates a thread, it makes a call to the thread library to set up the thread and all of its associated structures in the process address space. The kernel does not know anything about the thread at this point. Within the thread library is a user-level scheduler that is called by a user process to schedule threads. This user-level scheduler selects a user thread to run and builds an LWP in the kernel based upon the identity of the user thread that is to run. The LWP information is mapped to the kernel thread, and the thread is then dispatched. When the thread completes execution, the LWP is returned to the kernel for use by another thread. The complete LWP birth and death process is outlined in Table 7-3.

An *unbound* LWP can be used and reused by several user threads. An LWP can also be *bound,* which means that it will only be used by a specific thread. An LWP may be bound programmatically to enhance thread performance.

Multiprocessing

When Solaris is running on a processor with more than one CPU, it runs in *tightly coupled* mode. This means that there is only one copy of the

TABLE 7-3 Lightweight Process Life Cycle	After process starts, the thread library creates the number of LWPs necessary to execute all unbound threads.
	The LWP assumes the identity of its parent: registers, program counter, stack, and priority.
	The LWP starts to execute.
	If the thread becomes blocked, the thread library selects another unbound thread not currently assigned to an LWP to run on the now-available LWP.
	If all threads are blocked, the kernel sends a SIGWAITING to the parent process. If the signal handler detects any runable unbound threads, the handler assigns the thread to a newly created LWP.
	When the thread completes, the thread library assigns a runable thread, not currently bound, to the newly available LWP. If there are no runable threads, the LWP becomes idle. If an LWP remains idle for 5 min, it is destroyed by the thread library.

operating system, and all of the processors share the system clock and physical memory. All of the management of resources is centralized in the one copy of the kernel, so much of the work of coordinating the processors is simplified.

However, this does not imply that the kernel is therefore bound to one particular processor. The kernel in Solaris comforms to the *symmetric multiprocessing* (SMP) model. The kernel and its functions are divided into functional pieces via the threads, which operate, for the most part, independently of one another. Any thread can run on any available processor. Therefore, the kernel is not bound to operation on one processor. In fact, kernel functions can be running on all available processors if there is just cause.

The only case of a thread being bound to a processor (having *processor affinity*) is an interrupt thread. Because of the nature of its work, an interrupt thread must complete all of its processing on a single processor.

Preemption, Interrupts, and Real-Time Support

An interrupt occurs when a process is stopped because some type of request must be serviced immediately. The most common types of service requests are from hardware devices, I/O completion, for example, and signals, such as SIGKILL. In most situations, when an interrupt is received, the current process is stopped, the interrupt is serviced, and the original process is restarted. The original process does not lose control of the processor.

Preemption occurs when one process takes over control of a CPU so that it may run. Most commonly, preempts occur when a process with a higher-priority level than the current task becomes runable. The current task is switched out and the higher-level priority process is given control of the CPU. At some later time, the lower-level priority process will be allowed to run again.

By introducing the ability to run real-time applications, a significant change to the traditional UNIX kernel was introduced in Solaris: the preemptability of the kernel. However, because there are certain kernel activities that should never be interrupted because they would make the system unstable (such as interrupting a preemption request), the kernel is not fully preemptable.

Because of these nonpreemptable activities, Solaris cannot really run processes in real-time. A defining point of real-time processing is that the real-time process has instant access to the CPU whenever it is necessary. Therefore, what Solaris really offers is what is called *bounded dispatch latency* processing. This means that a process will be dispatched for execution within a bound period of time. The amount of bounded time varies depending on the processor model and architecture being used. The highest time on SPARC processors is found on a SPARCstation 1, where the maximum time is 4.5 ms.

Scheduling

In Solaris, the basic element of scheduling is the thread. Scheduling of threads is based on priority and scheduling class. This is known as *deterministic scheduling* because the execution characteristics and behavior of a thread are defined and bound.

At any given time, there are a number of threads that are runable. These dispatchable threads are placed in the system dispatch queue* based upon their thread types, scheduling class, and priority. The dispatch queue is a linked list of threads, ordered by priority, where each link points to the runable threads of a particular priority.

---

*On a multiprocessor system, there is a dispatch queue associated with each processor, but the principles are the same.

The system organizes and classifies threads in four priorities based on type or usage. By order of priority these are

Interrupt threads

Kernel threads

User threads

Idle threads*

Scheduling Classes

Within the user threads, Solaris defines three basic scheduling classes: interactive (IA), timesharing (TS), and real-time (RT)† Kernel threads are assigned to the system (SYS) scheduling class.

Within each one of the scheduling classes, a thread is assigned a priority. In most cases, the initial priority of a thread is the same as the priority level of the thread that created it. Priority values are assigned from high to low; therefore, a thread with a priority of 50 will run before a thread with a priority of 25.

The timesharing class is used for most user threads. In this class, threads are scheduled using a timesharing algorithm. Threads only run for a designated period of time and, if not finished, are switched out so that another thread may run. The length of the time-slice changes is based on the priority of the thread within the class. However, the priority of threads within the class is adjusted every time a context switch occurs. This is because the priority of a process is lowered as it uses ever-more CPU cycles. This helps to ensure that one thread does not monopolize the system.

The interactive class is a special case of the timesharing class that is designed to give a performance boost to the current window of users running X-Windows. This is accomplished by putting the window server in the IA scheduling class. By definition, all of its children will also be in this class. Whenever the focus is on one of these windows, the IA scheduling routines raise the priority of the active window by 10.

The system class is used for running system processes. Threads in this class have a fixed priority and are not time-sliced. They run until they are blocked, preempted, or completed. User threads cannot be

---

*These are scheduled when there are no "real" threads ready to run.

†The system administrator can define other classes if so desired.

scheduled or assigned to the SYS class, but the kernel moves user threads to the SYS class for the duration of system calls.

The real-time class is self-explanatory. It is a fixed priority class that does time-slicing. Real-time threads are scheduled for execution based solely on priority.

Interrupt threads and idle threads have separate scheduling classes. All idle threads run with the absolute lowest possible priority, -1. Interrupt threads are always the highest-priority threads in the system and, as discussed earlier, cannot be preempted or interrupted.

The Scheduler

When a processor becomes available, the scheduler scans the dispatch queues and selects the first thread on the first nonempty dispatch queue. Because the dispatch queues are in priority order, this will be the highest-priority task on the system. Threads are dispatched from the front of the list and added to the end of the list when their execution time-slice is over; this is the classic *round-robin* scheduling algorithm.

If all processors are busy, the kernel will check to see if any of the threads in current execution have exceeded their time-slice. If a thread hasn't, it is allowed to continue execution. If it has, the thread is switched out, its priority is recalculated, the thread is placed on the appropriate dispatch queue based on its new priority, and the new thread is dispatched.

A user thread can be preempted by an interrupt thread, a system thread, or a user thread of higher priority. However, instead of placing the preempted task at the end of the dispatch queue, the preempted task is placed at the beginning of its applicable dispatch queue. Because the user thread's time-slice did not expire, the thread receives its entire time-slice before other threads of equal priority. The same is true of a system thread that is preempted; it is always placed at the beginning of the applicable dispatch queue.

Multiprocessor Considerations.   In a uniprocessor environment, there is one set of dispatch queues. In a multiprocessor environment, there is a set of dispatch queues for each CPU. It would be extremely inefficient if all of the dispatch queues on every CPU had to be examined when a process is preempted or is switched out because its time-slice has expired.

To alleviate this, Solaris implements *loose affinity* for timesharing and interactive class threads running in a multiprocessor environment. Basically, once a user thread has started on one processor, it will remain there for the duration of its execution unless something unusual occurs. An example of an unusual situation would be when a kernel thread monopolizes the CPU. In this case, when the maximum execution wait time for the user process is reached, the user process is migrated to another CPU.

Real-time class threads do not have any affinity. The scheduler will also select the dispatch queue associated with the lowest-priority CPU.

Most system threads also do not have any affinity. If these threads are preempted, they are scheduled for execution on the next available processor. Other system threads, however, must complete all of their work on one processor; these are said to have *tightly coupled affinity* to the processor.

Interrupt threads are preemptable only by higher-priority interrupt threads. All interrupt threads are tightly coupled to their processor.

Priority Inheritance

Priority inheritance is a mechanism that is used to avoid a certain type of *deadlock* situation called *priority inversion*. This common type of deadlock occurs when thread A is blocked waiting for a resource owned by thread B, but thread B cannot release the resource because it is running at a lower priority than thread A. In effect, the priorities of the threads are interchanged or inverted.

The solution is to allow thread B to inherit the priority of thread A, at least temporarily, to speed up the release of the locked resource.

The system performs this function, even when complicated chains of dependencies are involved. When the dependencies are resolved, the threads revert to their regular priorities.

Priorities

Priorities on the system are determined by what scheduling classes have been loaded. Some priorities are constant. For instance, the idle threads always run at priority -1. The timesharing and interactive classes run in priorities 0 through 59. Normally, the system class runs in priorities 60 through 99. However, if the system administrator has created a new user class, the system priorities are moved up, relative to the new user class.

Above the system class, the real-time class uses priorities from 100 through 159. If the real-time class is loaded, the interrupt class uses priorities 160 through 169. However, if the real-time class is not loaded, the interrupt classes load at priorities 100 through 109.

The priorities on the system are adjusted as needed when new scheduling classes are loaded. If the real-time class was not loaded at boot-time, the interrupt class uses priorities 100 through 109. If the real-time class were added later, it would not be loaded above the interrupt class. Instead, the interrupt class would be moved, as necessary, to a higher priority than anything in the real-time class. The same shifting-up effect would affect the system, real-time, and interrupt classes if a new user class were loaded.

Summary

This chapter has discussed how Solaris implements processes and uses threads as a means to do so. The three major considerations in relationship to processes are type, underlying implementation, and assignment of priority within the system. Given these considerations, LWPs, multiprocessing, preemption, interrupts, scheduling and scheduling classes, and priorities were assessed.

In the following chapter, we will look at file system implementation.

## CHAPTER 8

File System Fundamentals

Solaris supports a number of different types of file systems. This chapter discusses the various types of file systems found in Solaris and their purpose, implementation, and use. Bear in mind, in the following discussion, the somewhat confusing general interchangability of the term *file system* as it is used when discussing UNIX-based systems. It is used in two different ways:

In a generic way, to indicate a type of file system implementation

In a specific way, to indicated an actual hierarchical implementation of user or system data

Examples of this usage are commonplace: The root file system is implemented as a UNIX file system (UFS) and the /tmp file system is implemented as a TMPFS file system.

Types of File Systems

In Solaris, file systems can be divided into three different types:

1. Physical media based

2. Network based

3. Pseudo file systems

Physical Media-based File Systems

Physical media file systems are stored on either hard disks, CD-ROMs, or disks. All three media types support *the UFS,* which is the most commonly used file system on Solaris systems. It is based upon the BSD Fast Fat file system, not the System V file system. This is because the System V file system imposes limits on a file system that are not acceptable in the Solaris environment.*

On CD-ROM media, Solaris also supports the *High Sierra file system* (HSFS), which was the first CD-ROM file system type, and the ISO 9660 standard, which is the version of High Sierra codified by the International Standards Organization (ISO). Solaris also supports supplements to the ISO 9660 standard, known as the Rock Ridge extensions. The Rock Ridge extensions provide HSFS with all of the functionality of UFS except for writability and hard links.

On disks, Solaris supports DOS-formatted disks via the *PC file system* (PCFS).

Network-based File Systems

Sharing of file systems over a network is accomplished most commonly via the *Network file system* (NFS). Solaris also supports distributed file systems via the *distributed file system* (DFS) type. What is implemented on the remote machine as either an NFS- or DFS-type file system is implemented on the host as a regular UFS-type file system.

NFS and DFS are very similar in function. In both, the file systems are shared across the network and appear to be mounted locally on a

---

*These limits include a maximum of 64K files in a file system, no quota facility, and a maximum of 14 characters in the file name.

given workstation (or server). But, DFS supports *domains* and the sharing of a physical device.

The support of domains in DFS allows a file system to be shared among a select group of users or workstations as opposed to the network as a whole.

Sharing physical devices allows hardware to be used by several machines. A very common application of this is to use DFS to share a common tape drive (for backup) among several workstations.

Pseudo File Systems

The pseudo file systems are used to implement access to the virtual and physical memory of the system. There are several different types of pseudo file systems, but only three are of practical everyday use. The *process file system* (PROCFS) is used to provide an interface to the virtual memory space of processes in the /proc directory (Fig. 8-1). It contains the list of active processes, in process number order. The system tuning and monitoring commmands (such as ps) get their information from the data that is stored in the /proc directory. The /proc directory does not require any system administration. Generally, all operations upon it are handled by the kernel.

The *loopback file system* (LOFS) is used to create virtual file systems, primarily as an alternative means of accessing files. A common use of this to enable read/write access to a portion of a file system that is normally read-only. For example, a loopback mount of /usr/local/bin could be created under another mount point* with read/write access to allow for the installation of a new software package. This would allow update access to /usr/local/bin but leave the rest of /usr/local read-only.

The most significant pseudo file type, from an administration perspective, is the *temporary file system* (TMPFS). By default, the /tmp directory is implemented through TMPFS.

TMPFS uses the virtual memory system to implement a UFS-type file system. Because data is not directly stored on a physical medium, access to files in a TMPFS file system is much faster than to files in a UFS file system. However, as its name suggests, the files in a TMPFS are not permanent. When the file system is unmounted or when the system is shut down (or crashes), all of the files in a TMPFS are lost.

---

*An example is /tmp, the new loopback mount point being /tmp/usr/local/bin.

Figure 8-1
Output of the `ls -l`
`/proc` command.

```
ls -l /proc
total 373672
-rw-------   1 root     root            0 Sep 22 11:21 00000
-rw-------   1 root     root       782336 Sep 22 11:21 00001
-rw-------   1 root     root            0 Sep 22 11:21 00002
-rw-------   1 root     root            0 Sep 22 11:21 00003
-rw-------   1 root     root      1908736 Sep 22 11:22 00110
-rw-------   1 root     root      1372160 Sep 22 11:22 00112
-rw-------   1 root     root      1646592 Sep 22 11:22 00118
-rw-------   1 root     root      2756608 Sep 22 11:22 00120
-rw-------   1 root     root      1511424 Sep 22 11:22 00122
-rw-------   1 root     root      1339392 Sep 22 11:22 00127
-rw-------   1 root     root      1474560 Sep 22 11:22 00134
-rw-------   1 root     root      1798144 Sep 22 11:22 00141
-rw-------   1 root     root      1421312 Sep 22 11:22 00145
-rw-------   1 root     root      1802240 Sep 22 11:22 00147
-rw-------   1 root     root      1318912 Sep 22 11:22 00172
-rw-------   1 root     root      1851392 Sep 22 11:22 00182
-rw-------   1 root     root      2527232 Sep 22 11:22 00197
-rw-------   1 root     root      1331200 Sep 22 11:22 00205
-rw-------   1 root     root      1961984 Sep 22 11:22 00206
-rw-------   1 root     root       704512 Sep 22 11:22 00214
-rw-------   1 root     root      2502656 Sep 22 11:22 00225
-rw-------   1 root     other      737280 Sep 22 11:22 00226
-rw-------   1 root     other      745472 Sep 22 11:22 00229
-rw-------   1 root     root      1789952 Sep 22 11:22 00242
-rw-------   1 root     other      638976 Sep 22 11:22 00265
-rw-------   1 root     other      745472 Sep 22 11:22 00266
-rw-------   1 root     other     1368064 Sep 22 11:22 00267
-rw-------   1 root     other      819200 Sep 22 11:22 00268
-rw-------   1 root     other      700416 Sep 22 11:22 00285
-rw-------   1 root     root      1208320 Sep 22 11:22 00330
-rw-------   1 root     root      1998848 Sep 22 11:22 00332
-rw-------   1 root     root      1359872 Sep 22 11:22 00336
-rw-------   1 root     root      1245184 Sep 22 11:22 00341
-rw-------   1 root     root      1261568 Sep 22 11:22 00342
-rw-------   1 root     root      1728512 Sep 22 11:22 00348
-rw-------   1 root     root      1191936 Sep 22 11:22 00349
-rw-------   1 root     root      1339392 Sep 22 11:22 00350
-rw-------   1 root     root      2359296 Sep 23 14:45 03087
-rw-------   1 root     other     1982464 Sep 30 15:39 14998
-rw-------   1 root     nobody    2490368 Oct  1 00:17 15622
-rw-------   1 nobody   nobody    2707456 Oct  1 15:23 16608
-rw-------   1 nobody   nobody    2707456 Oct  1 16:28 16693
-rw-------   1 mchorazy devlpmnt  1359872 Oct  2 12:03 18104
-rw-------   1 nobody   nobody    2715648 Oct  2 12:13 18112
-rw-------   1 nobody   nobody    2797568 Oct  2 13:02 18170
-rw-------   1 nobody   nobody    2707456 Oct  2 13:31 18252
-rw-------   1 nobody   nobody    2707456 Oct  2 16:49 18586
-rw-------   1 nobody   nobody    2772992 Oct  2 17:04 18647
-rw-------   1 nobody   nobody    2715648 Oct  2 17:35 18726
-rw-------   1 nobody   nobody    2715648 Oct  2 18:04 18910
-rw-------   1 nobody   nobody    2715648 Oct  2 18:44 18932
-rw-------   1 nobody   nobody    2691072 Oct  3 08:26 19645
-rw-------   1 root     other      204800 Oct  3 10:08 19736
-rw-------   1 nobody   nobody    2715648 Oct  3 11:56 19841
-rw-------   1 nobody   nobody    2715648 Oct  3 13:05 19947
-rw-------   1 nobody   nobody    2691072 Oct  3 14:21 20005
-rw-------   1 nobody   nobody    2715648 Oct  3 14:23 20008
-rw-------   1 nobody   nobody    2715648 Oct  3 14:23 20009
-rw-------   1 nobody   nobody    2772992 Oct  3 14:25 20017
```

Figure 8-1
(Continued)

```
-rw-------    1 nobody    nobody     2707456 Oct  3 15:19 20189
-rw-------    1 nobody    nobody     2707456 Oct  3 15:24 20227
-rw-------    1 nobody    nobody     2699264 Oct  3 15:55 20280
-rw-------    1 nobody    nobody     2699264 Oct  3 16:00 20297
-rw-------    1 nobody    nobody     2699264 Oct  3 16:58 20367
-rw-------    1 root      other      1249280 Oct  3 17:35 20410
-rw-------    1 nobody    nobody     2830336 Oct  3 18:00 20455
-rw-------    1 nobody    nobody     2699264 Oct  3 18:01 20459
-rw-------    1 nobody    nobody     2699264 Oct  4 09:44 21101
-rw-------    1 nobody    nobody     2707456 Oct  4 09:48 21102
-rw-------    1 nobody    nobody     2764800 Oct  4 10:59 21136
-rw-------    1 nobody    nobody     2699264 Oct  4 11:31 21174
-rw-------    1 nobody    nobody     2691072 Oct  4 11:45 21178
-rw-------    1 nobody    nobody     2707456 Oct  4 11:46 21187
-rw-------    1 nobody    nobody     2699264 Oct  4 12:27 21245
-rw-------    1 nobody    nobody     2691072 Oct  4 13:32 21319
-rw-------    1 nobody    nobody     2756608 Oct  4 13:59 21341
-rw-------    1 nobody    nobody     2699264 Oct  4 13:59 21342
-rw-------    1 nobody    nobody     2756608 Oct  4 15:05 21434
-rw-------    1 nobody    nobody     2764800 Oct  4 15:19 21446
-rw-------    1 nobody    nobody     2691072 Oct  4 15:36 21456
-rw-------    1 nobody    nobody     2699264 Oct  4 15:44 21467
-rw-------    1 nobody    nobody     2691072 Oct  4 16:58 21525
-rw-------    1 nobody    nobody     2691072 Oct  4 17:57 21565
-rw-------    1 nobody    nobody     2605056 Oct  5 12:02 22282
-rw-------    1 nobody    nobody     2764800 Oct  5 12:06 22290
-rw-------    1 nobody    nobody     2531328 Oct  5 12:34 22318
-rw-------    1 nobody    nobody     2523136 Oct  5 13:02 22367
-rw-------    1 nobody    nobody     2523136 Oct  5 13:03 22368
-rw-------    1 nobody    nobody     2523136 Oct  5 13:03 22369
-rw-------    1 nobody    nobody     2514944 Oct  5 13:03 22370
-rw-------    1 nobody    nobody     2531328 Oct  5 13:06 22372
-rw-------    1 root      root       1433600 Oct  5 13:06 22373
-rw-------    1 fcervone   sys       1359872 Oct  5 13:06 22375
-rw-------    1 fcervone   sys        741376 Oct  5 13:08 22397
```

Because of these characteristics, TMPFS is used most commonly for holding the work files that are used during the course of compilations, database queries, or cgi-scripts running on WWW servers.

Because a TMPFS is subject to the vagaries of virtual storage just as processes in memory are, TMPFS file systems use the swap space on the system as a backing store. Because of this, a TMPFS file system can run out of space if all of the swap space is occupied. Alternatively, processes can abend or be stopped if a TMPFS has expanded to occupy all of the swap space.

The *cache file system* (CacheFS) is used to store frequently used information from either a CD-ROM or a remote file system implemented through NFS or DFS. The data from the original file system is read and stored on a local disk. By doing so, network traffic is reduced, and access time is greatly enhanced. The CacheFS is interesting in that it is not a distinct file system type; it is implemented on the system via UFS file systems.

The other types of pseudo file systems are used for implementation of various Solaris functions. These include

- *FIFOFS (first-in first-out).* Used to implement both named and anonymous pipes
- *FDFS (file descriptors).* Provides explicit names for opening files using file descriptors (i.e., /dev/stdin for /dev/fd/0, /dev/stdout for /dev/fd/1, and /dev/stderr for /dev/fd/2)
- *NAMEFS.* Used by the STREAMS interface for dynamic mounts of file descriptors on top of files, (e.g., for implementing redirection)
- *SPECFS (special).* Used to access character special and block devices
- *SWAPFS.* Is used to implement the swapping subsystem

These file system types are not directly accessible to the user via commands and do not require administration.

UFS

UFS is the default file system for physical media. Most commonly, it is implemented on hard disks, but it can be used on CD-ROMs and diskettes. Depending on the media, UFS supports file systems up to 1 terabyte (1TB) with files as large as 4GB. Spanning of a file system across multiple physical disks is not supported directly by UFS but in conjunction with SunSoft Disksuite.

Before a UFS file system can be created on a hard disk, the disk must be partitioned into *slices,** which are a contiguous range of blocks.† Within each slice, one type of file system may be created, usually UFS but possibly TMPFS or SWAPFS.

In order to provide for better management and extendability within the slice of a UFS file system, the physical space is organized into areas called *cylinder groups.* Each cylinder group is composed of one or more consecutive disk cylinders (Fig. 8-2). Within the individual cylinder

---

*A maximum of eight per disk is supported.

†The smallest physically addressable unit of storage on the device.

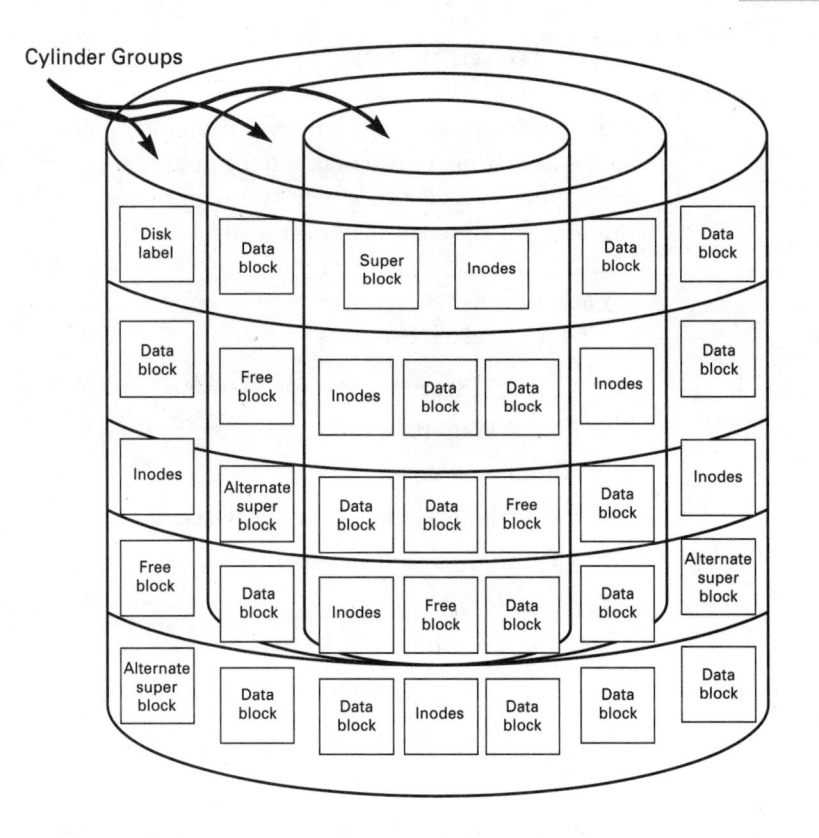

Figure 8-2
Disk layout in Solaris.

Cylinder Groups

groups, further subdivision into blocks is made. These blocks are used to control and organize the structure of the files within the cylinder group.

Within each cylinder group of a UFS file system, there are five types of block:

1. Boot block
2. Superblock
3. Inodes
4. Data blocks
5. Free blocks

The Boot Block

The *boot block* contains the instructions used to boot the system from the disk. This block is blank if the file system is not used for booting the system. The boot block is only contained in the first cylinder group (cylinder group 0) and is limited in size to 8K.

The Superblock

The *superblock* stores the information about the file system. It is located at the beginning of the disk partition and is also replicated in each cylinder group. In order to ensure maximum recoverability, the offset of the replicas within each cylinder group is different. If the file system spans multiple volumes, at least one copy of the superblock is also replicated to each volume.

The superblock contains

- Size and status of the file system
- File system name
- Volume name
- Logical block size of the file system
- Last update timestamp
- Cylinder group size
- Number of data blocks in a cylinder group
- File system state: clean, stable, or active
- Path name of last mount point
- Summary information block

Except for the summary information, all of the above data is in each superblock replica. The summary information block is grouped with the first superblock. The summary information block is used for tracking the changes that occur as the file system is used. In addition, it contains the number of inodes, directories, fragments, and storage blocks within the file system.

Inodes

Inodes (index nodes) are 128-byte data structures that contain basic information about files except for the name of the file. File names are stored in a separate directory and relate to the file via the inode number of the file. Within each inode, the following information is kept:

- Type of file
  - Regular
  - Directory

- Block special
- Character special
- Symbolic link
- Named pipe (FIFO)
- Socket

- Mode (read, write, execute permissions)
- Number of hard links to the file
- User id of the owner
- Group id to which the file belongs
- Size of the file in bytes
- Address array for locating data blocks
- Timestamp of last access
- Timestamp of last modification
- Creation timestamp

The address array is an array of 15 elements that point to the data blocks that store the actual data in the file. The first 12 (addresses 0 through 11) are direct addresses (Fig. 8-3). They point to the first 12 logical storage blocks of the file. If the file is larger than 12 blocks, the thirteenth block points to an *indirect block*. An indirect block is simply another data addressing structure. It is one block in size. Within it is a list of addresses of the additional data blocks of a file. If needed, the fourteenth block is used as a *double indirect block*. The double indirect block points to a one-block data structure that contains the addresses of indirect blocks. If needed, the fifteenth block is used as a *triple indirect block*.

As the size of a file grows, the number of pointers to be traversed to find the actual data of the file increases. However, the use of the indirect addressing structure allows for expedient access to the data of smaller files while, at the same time, balancing the access issues of larger files against the maximization of disk use.

Data Blocks

All of the used space in a file system not occupied by the other three types of blocks is used for *data blocks*. Data blocks are used to store the contents of regular files and the inode number and file names for directories.

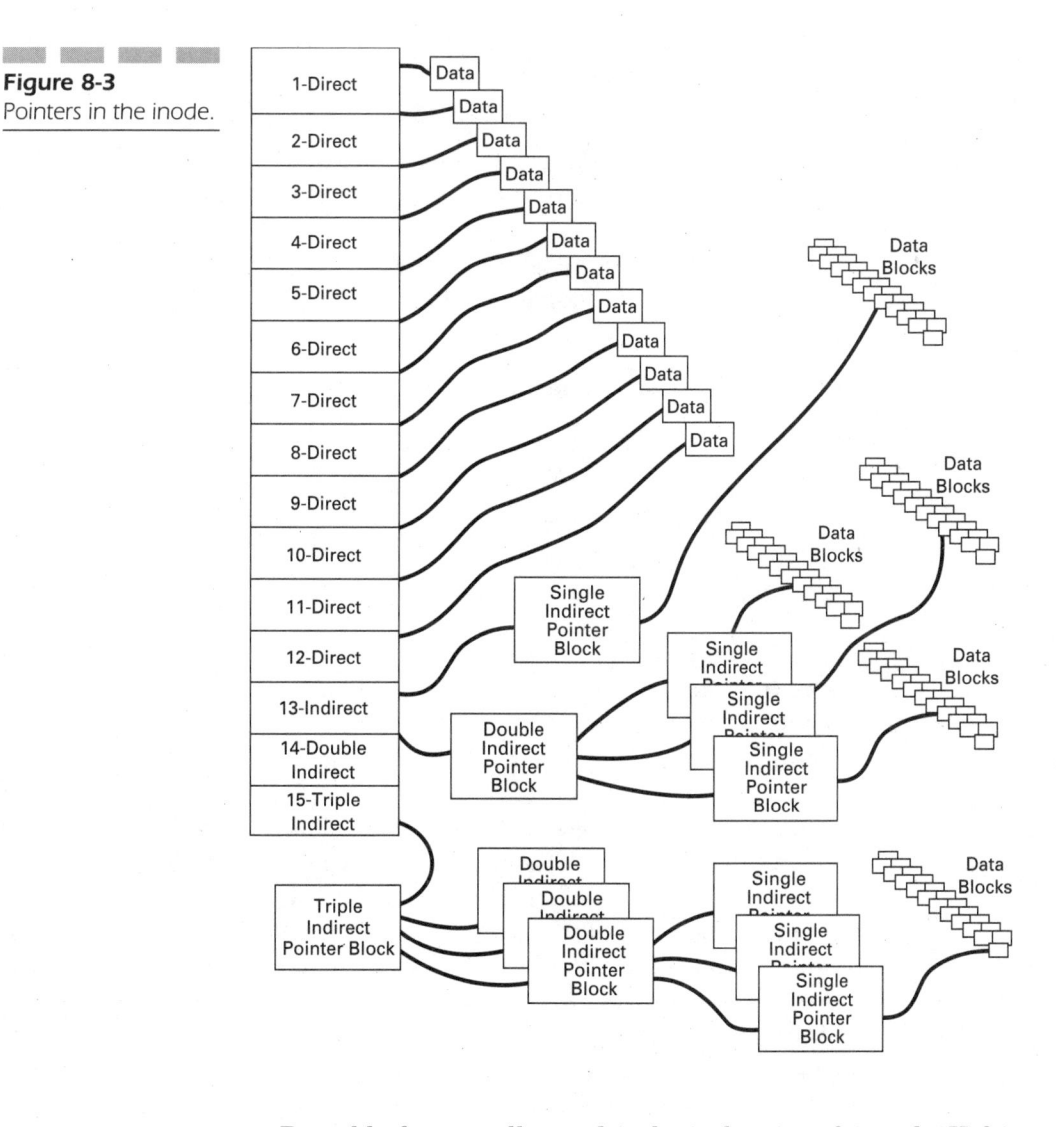

Figure 8-3
Pointers in the inode.

Data blocks are allocated in logical units of 8 and 1K fragments. Unlike other UNIX-based operating systems, Solaris does not require that a file occupy an entire block. Instead, files smaller than 8K occupy *fragments* of a block. This is done to increase the efficiency at which files are stored on the physical media.

The logical block may be (and usually is) different from the physical block size of the storage media. The logical block size, not the physical block size, is the unit that Solaris uses to read and write information on the storage media.

NFS and DFS

NFS and DFS enable users on different machines to share information in a relatively transparent manner. After the initial configuration has been set up, the remote user is not normally aware of any difference between an NFS/DFS file system and a local UFS file system. The NFS/DFS file system appears to the remote user as if it were a local UFS file system.

Sharing through NFS and DFS spans the range from an entire file system down to a single file. When a remote resource is mounted through NFS, the user is not restricted to mounting an entire file system as they are with UFS file systems. Any directory or file in the remote system's file system can be mounted, and access will only be granted to that file or directory and the objects beneath it.

NFS file systems are implemented on the server side through regular UFS file systems. Therefore, the concerns and constraints of UFS file systems affect the implementation of NFS file servers. In addition, the server runs special networking software that implements the protocol used to allow NFS sharing.

On the client end (e.g., remote user), networking software is also used to implement the NFS protocol. In addition, the client may set up a cache file system to help improve the access rate of NFS files.

In both cases, a major factor in performance is the network that connects the two machines. This is the topic of the next chapter.

Summary

Understanding the implementation of file systems on Solaris involves many different topics:

- Types of file systems in general
- Physical media upon which file systems are implemented
- Network-based file systems
- Pseudo file systems

A majority of the chapter was dedicated to discussion of the UFS file system type, which is the most commonly implemented file system used with Solaris. Basic concepts of the UFS file system were explained, including

- Boot block
- Superblock
- Inodes
- Data blocks

The chapter concluded with a discussion of NFS and DFS.

The next chapter further investigates networking and communication.

9

Networking and Communication Fundamentals

In this chapter, the focus is on communication, both locally and over the network. The discussion begins with an overview of input/output in Solaris. After that, network topologies and technologies are discussed. Finally, an overview of connectivity to the outside network services is provided.

Basic Input and Output

UNIX-based operating systems, such as Solaris, handle input and output differently from most other operating systems. Typically, operating systems divide input and output functions into two distinct subsystems: device- and file-level I/O. In UNIX-based operating systems, devices are not viewed by the I/O system as being any different from files; devices are accessed through the same routines that are used for file I/O. Every device on the system is associated with a *special file* that is used to communicate with the device. This I/O implementation allows for the creation of special files that manage system resources other than real I/O devices, such as memory or virtual terminals.

These special files are not actually files on a disk but are paths to a device. Associated with each special file is a *device driver*. Device drivers are programs that serve as the interface between the kernel and a device (Fig. 9-1). The Solaris kernel does not contain built-in code that allows it to control physical devices. All code to control and access devices is loaded from separate modules (in the /dev directory) during boot-time. There, loading instructions for a specific device are routed though the module to the special file and device driver used with the device. It is the responsibility of the device driver to interpret the command sent to the device and translate that into the appropriate commands for the device being controlled. Because of this modular approach, devices can be added to the system while Solaris is running. In many other UNIX-based operating systems, adding new devices requires a regeneration of the kernel.

Devices are categorized as either block or character. Block devices, such as tape or disk drives, generally perform I/O with blocks of data. This allows large quantities of data to be sent at a single time. Almost all other devices are character devices, which perform I/O via a stream of bytes, a byte at a time. Examples of character devices include terminals, printers, and modems. Block devices may often have a character driver, in addition to the block driver, for special-purpose, low-level I/O functions.

Partitions on a disk drive may be used in "raw mode." When used in this way, the partition does not necessarily contain a file system that Solaris is aware of. The application program uses direct commands to read and write from the disk. This technique is primarily used by database management systems to improve performance.

Figure 9-1
Application to device
interface.

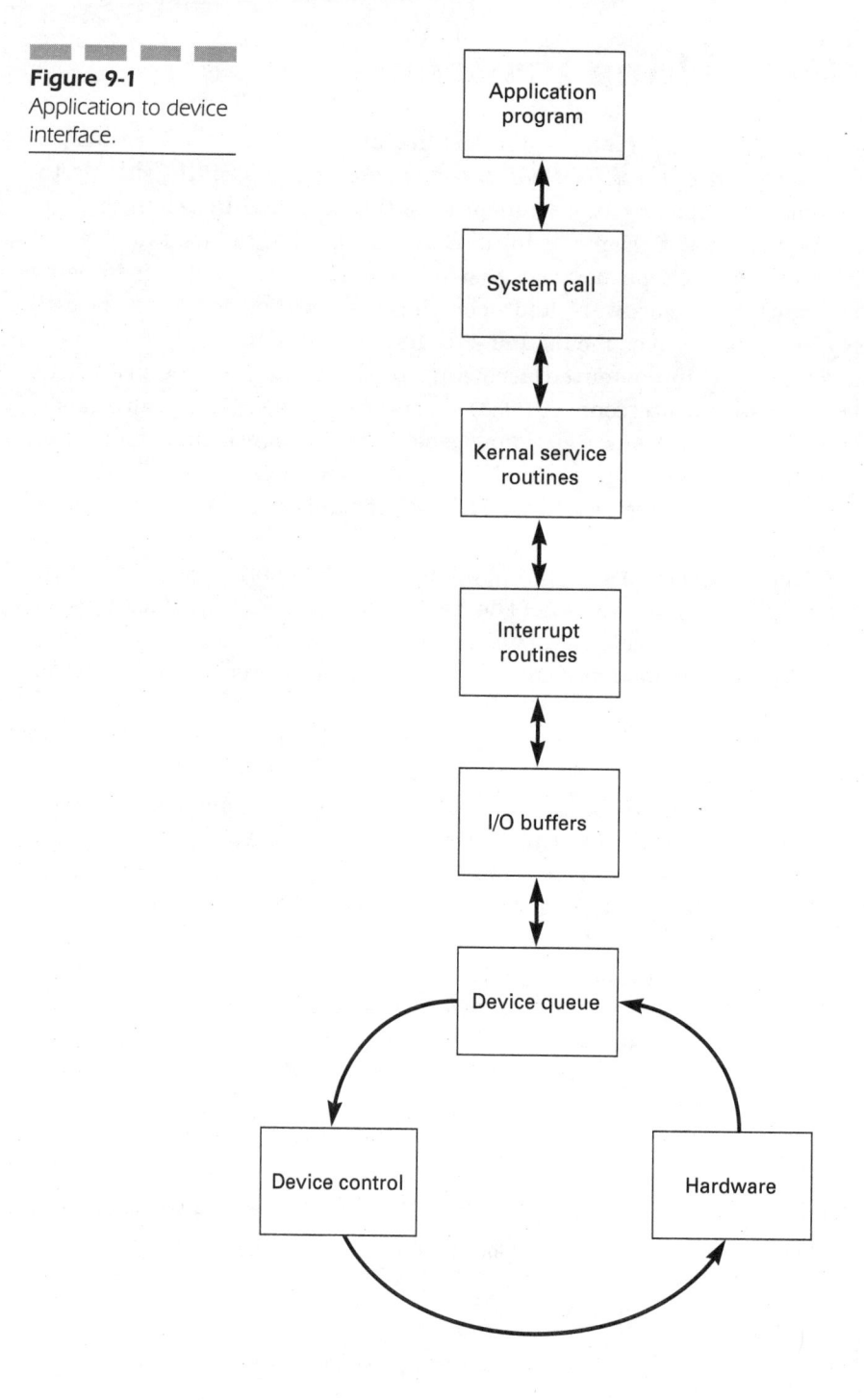

Figure 9-1
Application to device
interface.

Networking Protocols

By far, the most common networking protocol used with Solaris is *Transmission Control Protocol / Internet Protocol,* or TCP/IP. This protocol was developed under the auspices of the Advanced Research Projects Agency of the U.S. Department of Defense (DARPA) to facilitate host-to-host interconnection between dissimilar systems. In addition to being independent of hardware and operating system considerations, TCP/IP is also designed to be media and data link independent.

TCP/IP is implemented according to the basic architecture of the Open Systems Interconnect (OSI) seven-layer model. Briefly, this model separates the various functional aspects of a network implementation into layers that build on and interact with each other (Table 9-1). Because of these design points, TCP/IP is flexible and can be implemented easily.

TCP/IP supports two types of application communication: *connection-oriented* and *connectionless*. The TCP part of TCP/IP provides for connection oriented, reliable, peer-to-peer communications. Examples of this type of application communication are file transfers and terminal sessions.

Connectionless communication is used for data transfers that do not require the reliability and continuity provided for by TCP. An example of this type of communication is where a client application sends an asynchronous request for data to a server application. At some later point, the server replies to the client application. This communication protocol, called User Datagram Protocol, or UDP, is very fast compared to TCP, but it is less reliable. It does not provide for error notification or message sequencing; that is, the entire communication from one application to another must fit in a single transmission unit.

TCP/IP also includes several basic network support functions: file transfer (via the File Transfer Protocol, or FTP), terminal access (via

TABLE 9-1	**ISO Layer**	**Network Function**
TCP/IP Network Functions and Their Relationship to ISO Layers	Application	FTP, TELNET, rlogin, NFS, applications using sockets
	Presentation	Library routines, stream modules
	Session	Sockets, remote procedure calls
	Transport	TCP
	Network	IP
	Data Link & Physical	Ethernet, Token-Ring, x.25

TELNET), and electronic mail (via the Simple Mail Transfer Protocol, or SMTP). In addition to these basic applications, the Network File System (NFS) is implemented via TCP/IP.

The Internet Protocol (IP) part of TCP/IP provides the addressing, data segmentation, and numbering functions for messages to be routed through the network.

Figure 9-2 demonstrates the relationship between the various components of TCP/IP.

Solaris also provides support for a basic intermachine communication mechanism called *uucp* in deference to the most famous command in the protocol. Although used quite extensively in the past for UNIX-to-UNIX connectivity and communications, this networking facility has been superceded, for the most part, by the superior facilities of TCP/IP. It will not be discussed any further in this book.

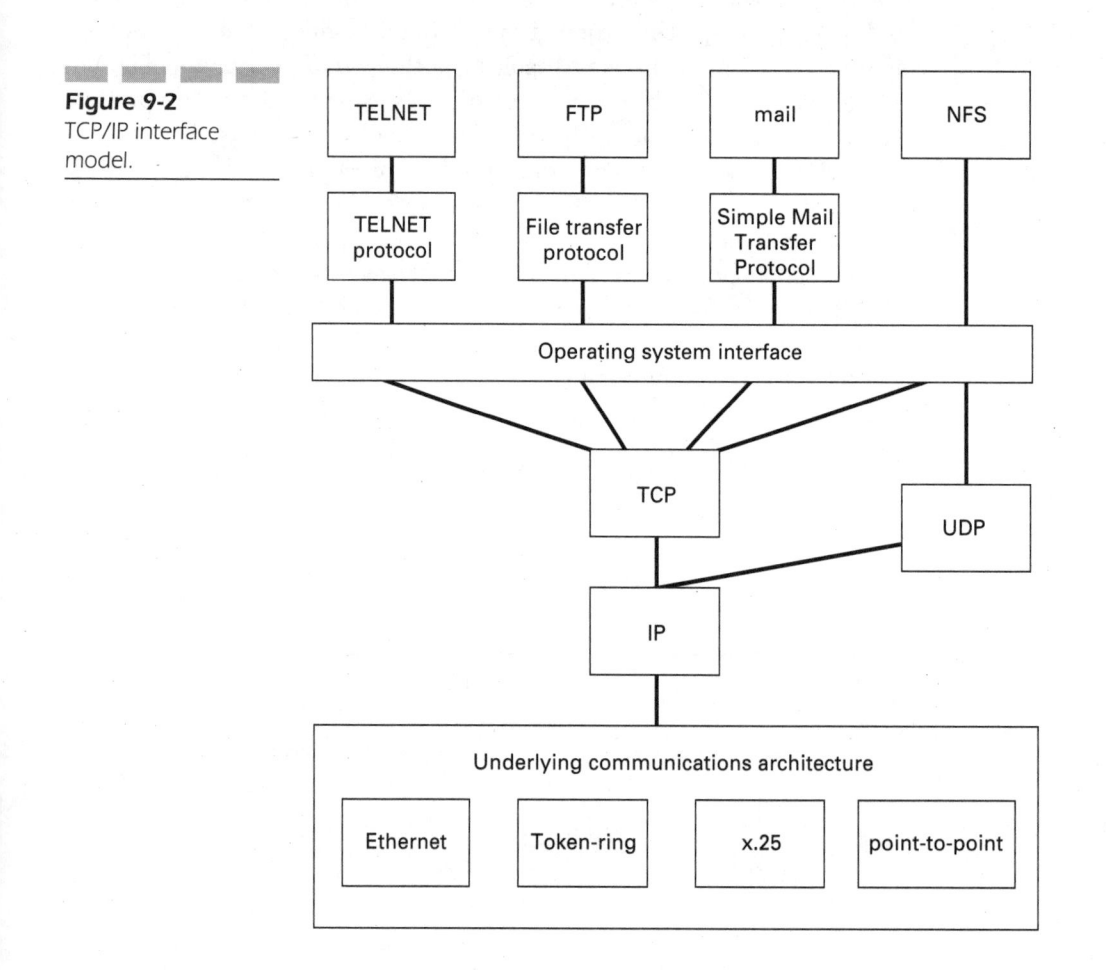

Figure 9-2
TCP/IP interface model.

Network Topologies

Discussions of network topology are usually broken into two phases: local area networks (LANs) and wide area networks (WANs). Although most networks are built in a LAN-centric manner, any discussion of networking needs to include both LANs and WANs. It is rare today to find a system that is not connected to some kind of WAN such as a closed, corporate facility, the Internet, or both.

Networks come in three major topologies.* The simplest is a *daisy chain* or *bus* topology (Fig. 9-3) where every machine is connected to a single stretch of cable. In a star topology (Fig. 9-4), machines are connected serially to a central device that provides interconnection services for the machines. These can be connected hierarchically to extend the size of the network. The third type of topology is a ring (Fig. 9-5). In this layout, every machine is connected in a manner similar to that of the bus topology except that there is no defined beginning or end. A very common variation of the ring topology is the *collapsed star* topology. In this version, the machines are not directly connected to the ring but instead are connected serially to a device called a multistation access unit (MSAU), which performs the functions of the ring. This implementation also lends itself to a hierarchical organization that extends the size of the network.

These topologies are used to implement several types of networking technologies. For local area networks, the two most common networking technologies are Ethernet, which uses a bus or star topology, and Token-Ring, which uses a ring topology. For wide area networks, the two most common networking technologies are asynchronous transfer mode

---

*There are other topologies, but these are infrequently used.

Figure 9-3
Bus topology.

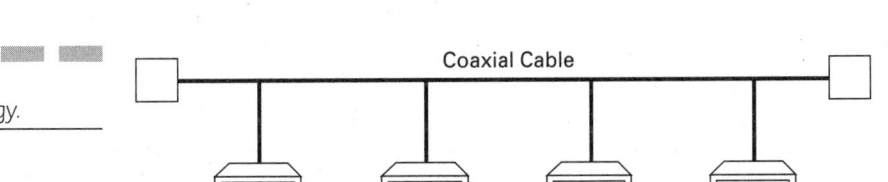

Coaxial Cable

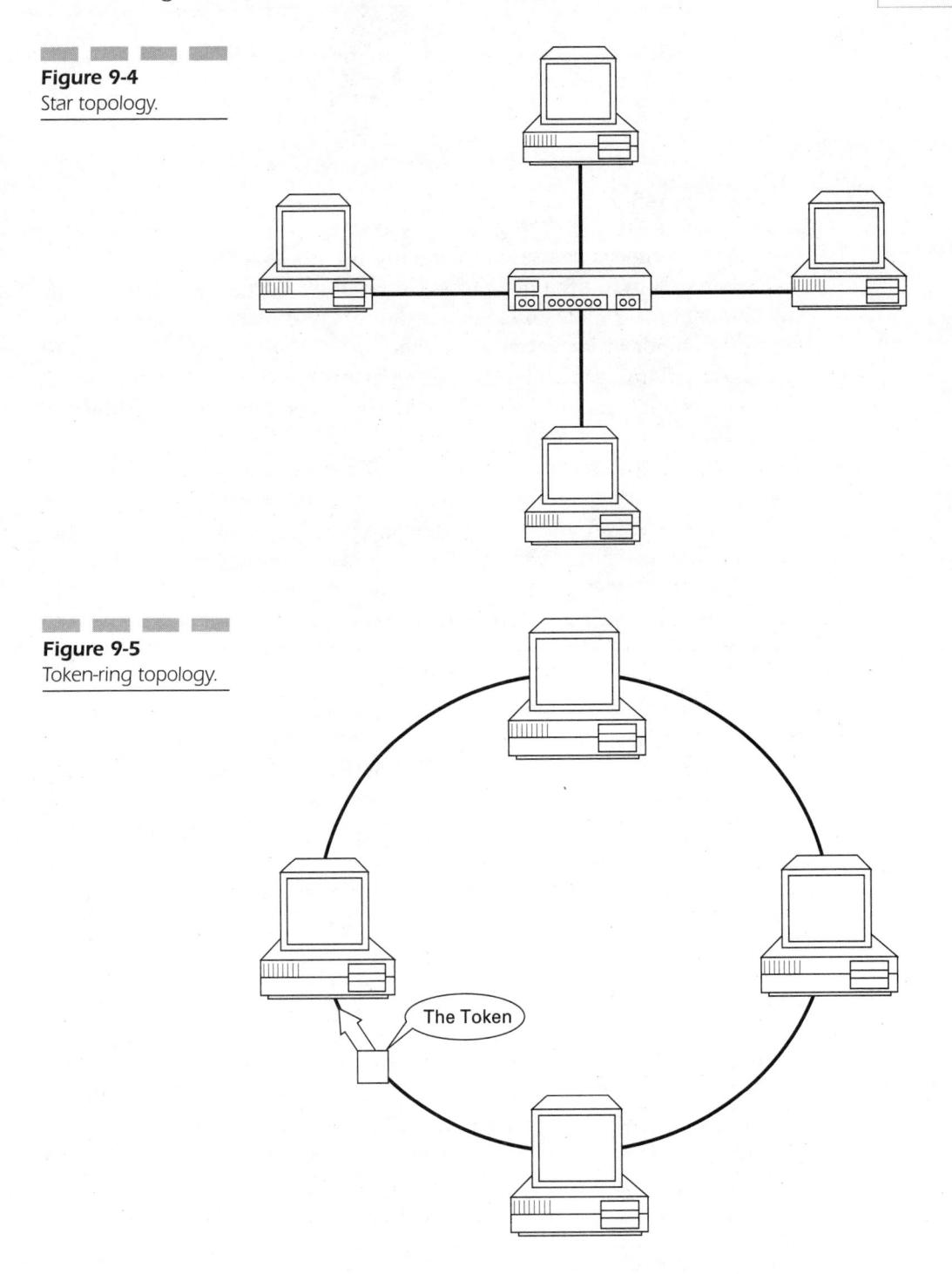

Figure 9-4
Star topology.

Figure 9-5
Token-ring topology.

The Token

(ATM), which uses a star technology, and fiber distributed data interface (FDDI), which uses a ring topology.

Ethernet

By far, Ethernet is the most commonly used networking technology on Solaris-based local area networks. Ethernet was developed in the 1970s by Xerox at the Palo Alto Research Center (PARC) as a simple, nonproprietary standard for networking. The underlying architecture is based on Carrier Sense Multiple Access/Collision Detection (CSMA/CD). Simply put, whenever a machine needs to send something to the network, it first senses to see if another transmission is in progress. If it does not sense anything, it starts sending data. If during the course of the transmission, data from another machine arrives on the network, both stations sense the *collision* and stop sending. After a random amount of time on both machines' part, each tries to resend.

Ethernet networks are shared networks. Every machine sees all of the network traffic regardless of its final destination, and each machine must wait for the network to become idle before it can successfully begin a transmission. In this regard, Ethernet networks are similar to the telephone party lines of long ago.

Because of this, the number of machines that can be connected to an Ethernet network at any one time is limited. To deal with this problem, Ethernet networks are divided into *segments,* which are parts of the overall network. The segments of the network are tied together by additional network devices—most commonly by routers and bridges. Both of these devices isolate the internal traffic on one segment from the internal traffic on another. This helps reduce the overall load on the LAN.

Media

Ethernet networks can be implemented with various types of wiring media. Although the basic operation of an Ethernet network is the same, regardless of media, there are some differences that should be noted.

The original Ethernet wiring media was coaxial cable.* This was the same type of cable used at the time for cable TV. The cable itself consists

---

*This is known as 10Base5 wiring.

Figure 9-6
Collapsed star topolo-
gy.

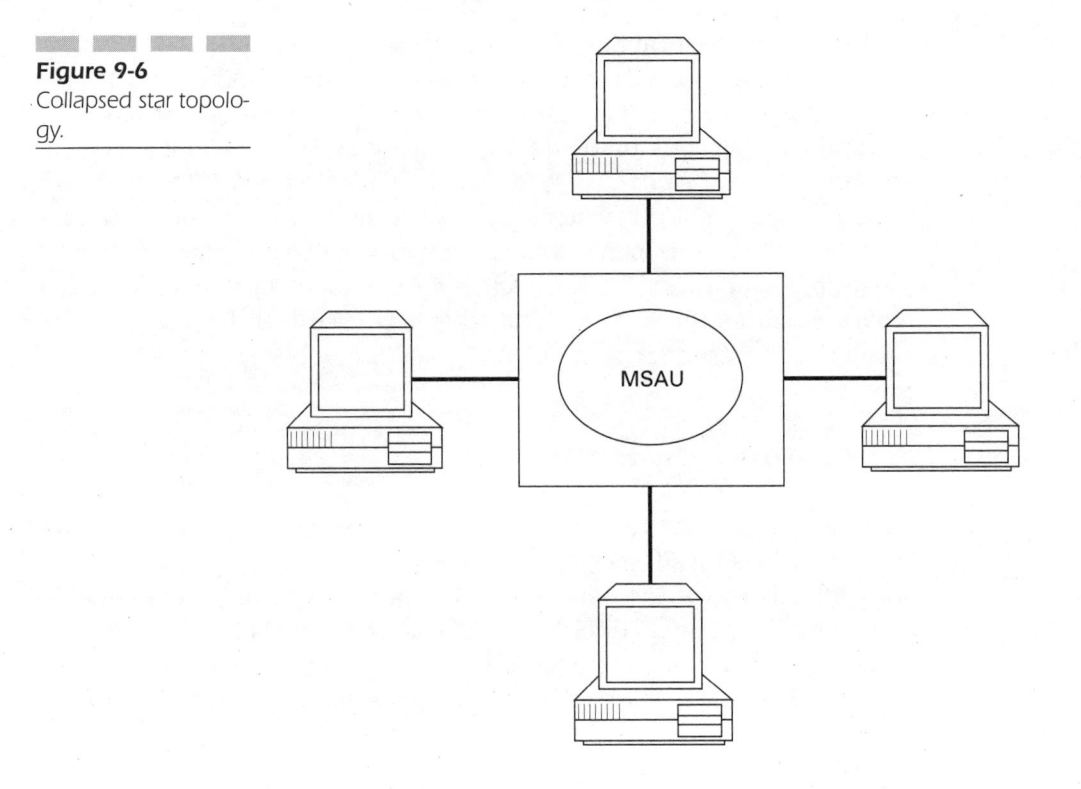

Figure 9-6
Collapsed star topology.

of two parts, the center conductor and the shield conductor, which is used to ground the cable. When this type of cable is used, each machine on a segment "taps" into a single run of the cable via a device called a *media access unit,* or MAU (Fig. 9-6). These devices pierce into the cable to make contact with the center conductor and the shield conductor. In addition, at the very end of the cable, a terminator must be installed. The terminator absorbs the signal that reaches the end of the cable, preventing feedback onto the cable.

Even though thinner coaxial cable* can now be used for Ethernet networks, the major problems with this type of cabling remain. Because all of the machines are essentially joined together in one long string, a break anywhere along the line brings the entire segment down. Furthermore, bad connections to the line from MAUs (or T-connectors on Thin Ethernet) can cause "noise" or random transmissions on the line, which, in turn, increases the rate at which data must be retransmitted.

---

*This is referred to as either Thin Ethernet or 10Base2.

In most modern cabling systems, twisted-pair (or 10BaseT) wiring is used. This wire is similar to regular telephone wire. Unlike coaxial cable Ethernet wiring schemes, 10BaseT networks are not run on a single strand of cable but instead use separate wire connections to each machine from a central device called a *hub* (Fig. 9-7). The hub is a repeater that send every signal it receives on to each of the ports connected to it. In this manner, a hierarchical network structure can be developed that allows for many more devices than is possible on coaxial cable-based networks. When this scheme is used with fiber optic cable, instead of twisted-pair, it is called 10BaseFL.*

Transmission Rates

The maximum data throughput rate of the original Ethernet network implementation is 10 megabits per second (Mbps). In practice, the data throughput rate of the network will never achieve this speed. Ignoring the overhead of the protocol itself, such as message headers, trailers, and other control information, the fundamental principle of CSMA/CD prevents an Ethernet network from reaching maximum theoretical speed. In

---

*The FL stands for fiber link.

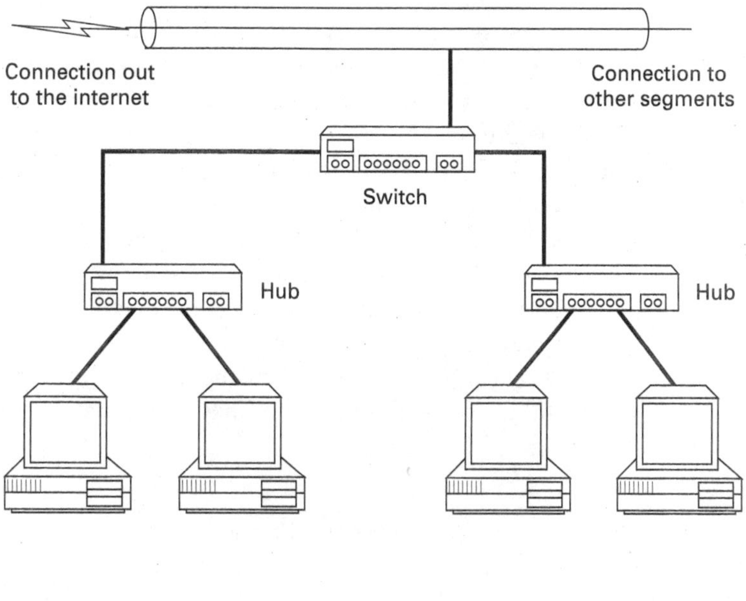

Figure 9-7
A typical Ethernet 10Base-T network diagram.

the best of circumstances, the maximum data throughput rate of an Ethernet network is only about 70 percent of the theoretical maximum.

However, the amount of interference caused by the CSMA/CD mechanism is highly dependent on the network configuration. As the number of machines on the network increases, the number of collisions increase. In turn, the amount of time a machine must wait to transmit or retransmit increases. All of this makes it possible for an Ethernet network with many active nodes to become *saturated,* that is, running at its maximum capacity, when throughput is only 30 percent of its theoretical maximum.

Fast Ethernet

To address this problem, faster versions of Ethernet have been developed. The first of these is *Fast Ethernet,* or 100BaseT, which is 10BaseT running at 100 Mbps instead of 10. Because the protocol and operation is exactly the same as 10BaseT or "standard" Ethernet,* implementing 100BaseT is relatively simple. Fast Ethernet offers a migration option to higher bandwidth simply and cost effectively because most Fast Ethernet products support 10- and 100-Mbps Ethernet connections and allow for speed autonegotiation.

In modern wiring plants that have Category 5 cable, implementation only involves changing the network interface card to support the higher speed of transmission.

Switched Ethernet

Along with 100BaseT, *Switched Ethernet* is becoming more commonly used. In a Switched Ethernet system, the hub is replaced by a switching device. The switching device essentially isolates every port from the others, which in effect creates independent segments for each port. It does not broadcast all data on the network to every port but only broadcasts data to the port that is actually to receive the data. Switched Ethernet is particularly useful for isolating server traffic to and from the WAN from server traffic that remains within the LAN.

---

*The only difference is that Fast Ethernet can use full-duplex, whereas standard Ethernet only uses half-duplex.

Gigabit Ethernet

Still in the beginning stages of deployment is *Gigabit Ethernet* (1000BaseT), which has a theoretical data throughput rate of 1 gigabit per second (gbps). Switching is an integral component of 1GB Ethernet implementations.

Gigabit Ethernet helps to alleviate the data transfer limits some networks are facing now that 100BaseT is being deployed on end-user workstations. Gigabit Ethernet is expected to be used primarily to interconnect 10/100BaseT switches and as a connection to high-performance servers.

Gigabit Ethernet supports a new full-duplex transmission mode for switch-to-switch and switch-to-end station connections. For shared connections using repeaters and the CSMA/CD access method, Gigabit Ethernet supports half-duplex operating mode.

Currently, Gigabit Ethernet only operates over fiberoptic cabling. But, over time, it is expected that Gigabit Ethernet will also support operation over Category 5 unshielded twisted-pair (UTP) wiring.

Asynchronous Transfer Mode

ATM was originally designed to simplify and standardize telecommunications over wide area networks. ATM networks are based on a cell-switching technology that uses small fixed-sized packets, or cells, that can concurrently travel over multiple paths to the destination. This architecture was designed to be very efficient over the regular telephone network. However, the complexity of the equipment that is used to transform the network traffic to fixed-size packets and multiplex the transmission has kept the cost of ATM high and has limited the widespread adoption of ATM for local area networks. Because ATM is *deterministic,* that is, it allows for the specification of explicit routes for data transmission, it is not necessarily the best technology for regular TCP/IP traffic, which is nondeterministic.

Fiber Distributed Data Interface

FDDI is a full-featured, ANSI standard technology for 100-Mbps local area networks. Originally implemented over fiber media, the technology is now also available over copper wire, referred to as CDDI. The topology of FDDI is different from the Ethernet family and ATM in that it is a double ring-based topology.

Data is passed through the network via tokens. A frame of data, known as the token, is passed from one machine to another around the first network ring. The token contains control information such as who is transmitting to whom and the message length. When a machine wants to send data, it must wait to receive the token. When it receives the token, it modifies it to indicate that data is being sent and sends the token and the data out onto the network. Both the token and data are then passed along the ring until they reach the destination. When the data is successfully received, the sending machine modifies the token again to indicate that another machine may now send. The token continues to be passed around the ring until a machine wishes to transmit and the process is repeated.

The second network ring is used for error recovery should the token in the first ring become lost. This can happen due to programming or hardware errors.

Because only one system can be transmitting at a time, no collisions are possible, such as those found in Ethernet technologies. However, the performance of the system does not remain constant under increasing utilization. As the demand for use of the token increases, the time it takes to acquire the token increases as well. However, given that token passing is a deterministic process, the performance of an FDDI network is more predictable than an Ethernet network.

FDDI is most often used to interconnnect lower-speed LANs.

Token-Ring

Token-Ring networks are, in many ways, the local area equivalent of FDDI. The primary differences between Token-Ring networks and FDDI are

Token-Ring is limited to 16 Mbps.

There is only one ring, which is used for all traffic.

Token-Ring is implemented primarily on copper cable.

Originally, Token-Ring was developed by IBM to allow internetworking between mainframes and smaller machines, and it is still used today primarily in areas where IBM mainframe connectivity is important. It is rarely found in other environments.

Outside Connectivity

Connecting the internal network to the outside world is performed through some type of connection to the national telecommunications network—the phone system. This network was originally designed for voice communications. As such, telecommunications services are offered in capacities that relate to the base unit of transmission in the phone system—the amount of data required for the transmission of a digitized phone conversation.

Analog Modems

Analog modems are used to transfer information over standard phone lines. Although the basic infrastructure of the phone system is primarily digital, connections between telephone company offices and users are primarily analog. Therefore, analog connections are prevalent and readily available.

The maximum amount of data a standard telephone line can carry is 64 kilobits per second (kbps). However, this data throughput rate cannot be achieved using analog modem technology. Because of the technical characteristics of the analog phone system, the fastest speed achievable with completely analog modems is 33.6 kbps.

Because of this slow throughput rate, analog modems are generally only used to allow dial-in access to a server. Except for connection to infrequently used services, analog modems are not appropriate for use in server-to-server or server-to-WAN applications.

Integrated Services Digital Network

Integrated Services Digital Network (ISDN) is primarily used when noncontinuous, high-throughput connectivity from a server to the phone network is needed. Because the service is entirely digital, much greater throughput rates are possible than would be via an analog connection. For example, an analog phone connection typically takes 10 s for connection, whereas dialing a phone number and making a connection on an ISDN line is almost instantaneous.

There are two types of ISDN service. The most common type is Basic Rate Interface (BRI). BRI ISDN uses two 64-kbps lines for data (called B, or bearer, channels) and one D, or, *delta,* channel for controlling the connection. The second type is Primary Rate Interface (PRI). In the United States, a PRI ISDN connection uses twenty-three 64-kbps B channels and one D channel. In Europe, PRI ISDN uses thirty 64-kbps B channels and one D channel.

Leased Lines

Leased lines are used where continuous high-throughput connectivity from a server to the phone network is needed. Although leased lines can be used for analog connections, leased lines are primarily digital connections.

A basic digital line operates at the standard telephone line speed of either 56 or 64 kpbs.* As such, it is suitable for light data transmission loads.

Digital Service One (DS1) lines are the continuous connection equivalent of a PRI ISDN connection. In the United States, DS1 lines are referred to as T1 lines and in Europe they are known as E1 lines. In the United States, a full T1 line consists of twenty-three 64-kbps data channels and one control channel, which yields a data capacity of 1.544 Mbps. In Europe, full E1 lines correspond to the European version of PRI ISDN: thirty 64-kbps data channels and one control channel for a data capacity of 2.048 Mbps. Because the full throughput rate may not be needed for all applications, it is possible to split up a DS1 line, which results in a fractional DS1 line. Fractional DS1 lines run from 64 kbps up to the maximum speed of a full DS1.

DS3 (or T3) is the next step up from DS1. Connections on DS3 lines in the United States operate at 44.736 Mbps. The majority of the backbone of the Internet runs on DS3 lines.

At the upper end of speed is SONET OC-12, which runs at 622 Mbps. This service is used primarily for running ATM backbones.

Finally, Frame Relay is a service that provides for "shared" leased lines. To access a Frame Relay network, the server connects to an endpoint connection of the relay network. The end point, in turn, connects to at least one leased line that terminates at another end point. Information that is to be exchanged over the network is formatted into small, variable-length frames that are routed through the network via a per-

---

*The speed depends on whether a portion of the bandwidth is used for controlling the connection or not.

manent virtual circuit (PVC). A PVC is simply a predetermined path that defines how information from one machine is routed to another over the interconnected leased lines. A new addition to frame relay is switched virtual circuits (SVC), which allows for dynamic connections to be made between systems.

Summary

Networking and intersystem communication are fundamental to the implementation of Solaris systems. This chapter focused on the physical implementation of networks, both in the local enterprise and in the larger global scheme. Beginning with a discussion of basic input and output and network protcols, the topics were expanded to include various network toplogies such as Ethernet, Switched Enternet, ATM, FDDI, and Token-Ring. Based upon this fundamental information, the latter part of the chapter focused on external connectivity through analog modems, ISDN, and leased lines.

The next section is about System Performance Tuning. As such, it will discuss

- Monitoring activity and workloads
- Memory management
- I/O performance management
- Network hardware and services performance management
- Kernel tuning

System
Performance
Tuning

This section discusses the activities involved in performance tuning and capacity planning in a Solaris environment. The chapters of this section cover the management of

- Processes
- Memory
- I/O
- The network

Throughout the section, reporting and monitoring techniques are discussed in relationship to the issue at hand.

Perhaps the most important thing about solving performance problems is to keep an open mind about what the problem may be. A cursory examination of the system is not sufficient for proper diagnosis. All systems are different. Their workloads differ as do their interaction with other machines, if they are on a network. No single cookbook approach will work in all cases. Knowledge of the system and intelligent judgment of the performance data are the most important tools a performance analyst can have.

10

Monitoring Activity and Workloads

This chapter is concerned with processes on the system—what they are doing and how they are affecting each other. It will discuss some of the commands used to monitor process activity and how workload behavior can be influenced using commands available in Solaris.

The performance of a computer system depends on two things: how the system allocates its resources and how the system uses the allocated resources. If a computer is connected to a network, the performance of the computer is also affected by the interactions among the systems on the network.

Locating the source of a performance problem requires careful detective work because the source of a problem is not always obvious. Unless the performance of the system is monitored on a regular basis, it is difficult, if not impossible, to know what "normal" or expected performance should be. Without regular monitoring, performance degradation may not be noticed until it reaches a critical stage, at which point solving the problem will be much more difficult than had it been discovered earlier.

What Is the System Doing?

Generally, the first question asked when a performance problem arises is What is the system doing? There are three ways of looking at the issue. One is from a global scale by finding out what the *system load average* is (e.g., what the average process activity on the system is). The second is to look at what individual users are up to. And the third is to study the detailed statistics of all the currently executing processes via the ps command.

Uptime—The System Load Average

The uptime command is used to display the system load average. The load average is defined as the average number of processes in the run queue during a particular interval. Generally, a process is in the run queue if

- It is not waiting for terminal I/O.
- It is not in a voluntary wait (it hasn't called wait).
- It is not stopped (e.g., waiting to terminate).

The uptime command display one line of output that contains

- The current time
- The length of time the system has been up
- The average number of jobs in the run queue in the last 1, 5, and 15 min

For example,

```
$ uptime
10:47am up 55 day(s), 20:42, 14 users, load average: 0.79, 0.62,
0.59
```

This example was performed at 10:47 in the morning. The system has been up for 55 days, 22 h, and 42 min. On average, there are 14 users. In the last minute, the number of active processes was 0.79, in the last 5 min, 0.62, and in the last 15, 0.59.

Based on this information, the system load average is going up. If the system is performing slowly, the administrator will want to periodically observe this statistic to monitor the situation.

uptime does have some limitations. The load average used by uptime does not account for the scheduling priority; that is, it does not differentiate between jobs running at high priority (and consuming a lot of CPU cycles) and jobs running at low priority (and consuming few, if any, CPU cycles). Furthermore, the system load average includes processes that are waiting for disk I/O, including NFS requests. If a remote NFS server fails, a process can wait indefinitely for the server, which increases the reported load average even though no work is actually being done by these waiting processes.

An acceptable load average varies depending on the implementing system, but one basic formula can be used. In general, performance of a system is OK as long as the number of active processes per CPU is three or less. If the number of active processes is greater than five per CPU, the system will experience severe performance degradation.

In the example above, the current load average is 0.79 on a machine with four processors. By dividing the load average by the number of processes, the calculation is

$$\frac{0.79}{4} = 0.1975$$

which is clearly OK. If the load average had been 28.89, then the result

$$\frac{28.89}{4} = 7.225$$

would indicate a significant problem.

w—Who Is logged In and What Are They Doing?

The w command (Table 10-1) is used to provide a quick snapshot of all of the logged in users and what their current foreground process is. The first line of a w display is the same as that displayed by the uptime com-

TABLE 10-1

w—Who Is Logged
In and What They
Are Doing

```
w [ -hlsuw ][ user ]
```

Options	Purpose
-h	Suppresses the heading line.
-l	Produces a long form of output (the default).
-s	Produces a short form of output; the tty is abbreviated and the login time and CPU times are left off, as are the arguments to commands.
-u	Produces the heading line, which shows the current time, the length of time the system has been up, the number of users logged into the system, and the average number of jobs in the run queue over the last 1, 5, and 15 min.
-w	Produces a long form of output, identical to the −l option.

Figure 10-1

w command
example.

```
w
 12:54pm  up 12 day(s), 19:16,  14 users,  load average: 0.17, 0.11,
0.10
User       tty           login@  idle  JCPU  PCPU  what
sskevoul  pts/0       12:09pm    15     2           telnet ted.cs
lsadler   pts/3       12:38pm           2     2     vi /tmp/snd.27540
kgiglio   pts/4       12:48pm     3                 pine
bhavel    pts/6       12:54pm                       pine -i
gandrus   pts/5       26Sep97 9days     2           -csh
mdeter    pts/7       10:17am    14    21           elm
scho      pts/8       12:42pm    12                 pine
jbergen   pts/9       12:44pm           1     1     lynx
wdalton   pts/10      12:46pm                       pine
fcervone  pts/12      12:53pm                       w
prahman1  pts/1       Fri12am 3days                 /bin/tcsh
ggordon   pts/23      23Sep97 2days   1:13    55    telnet hawk
slytinen  pts/31      Mon 1pm 4days   1:20    46    /usr/bin/csh -i
wkrueger  pts/32      25Sep9710days     1           pg Assignment1.html
wkrueger  pts/34      25Sep97 9days     5           vi index.html
```

mand. Following that, the command displays a line for each user with the following information (Fig. 10-1):

- User's login name
- Name of the tty the user is on
- Time of day the user logged on
- Idle time*
- CPU time used by all processes and their children on that terminal
- CPU time used by the currently active processes

---

*The number of minutes since the user last typed something.

■ Name and arguments of the current process

A user name can be included in the command, for example,

```
w fcervone
```

in which case, the output information is restricted to information about that user.

The information about the current process is determined by finding either the highest-numbered process on the terminal that is not ignoring interrupts or the highest-numbered process on the terminal. This could lead to misleading results when the user is in critical sections of programs like the shell and `vi` or when erroneous programs in the background fork and fail to ignore interrupts.

CPU time, as reported by the command, is only an estimate. For example, if a user leaves a background process running after logging out, the time that process uses could be assigned to the next person using the terminal. In addition, background processes are not shown at all, even though they can account for much of the activity of a user.

whodo—Who Is Doing What?

In many respects, the `whodo` command (Table 10-2) is similar to the `w` command, except that `whodo` displays more detailed information that also likely to be more accurate. This is because it derives and compiles its statistics from several sources of process information: the `/var/adm/utmp`, `/tmp/ps_data`, and `/proc/pid` files.

Figure 10-2 shows that the output of the command begins with a line detailing the date, time, and machine name. For each user on the system, the device name, user id, and login time of the user is shown. This is followed by separate lines for each of the active processes associated

TABLE 10-2

whodo—Who Is
Doing What

`/usr/sbin/whodo [ -h ] [ -l ] [ user ]`

Option	Purpose
-h	Suppresses the heading line.
-l	Produces a long form of output. The fields displayed include the user's login name, the name of the tty the user is on, the time of day the user logged in, the idle time, the CPU time used by all processes and their children, the CPU time used by the currently active processes, and the name and arguments of the current process.

```
whodo                                       pts/32          12599    0:00 tcsh
Sun Oct  5 12:54:41 CDT 1997                pts/32          17879    0:00 pg
condor
                                    pts/34          wkrueger 11:34
pts/0           sskevoul 12:09              pts/34          12633    0:00 tcsh
    pts/0           26833    0:00 tcsh      pts/34          17663    0:00 vi
    pts/0           27561    0:00 telnet

pts/3           lsadler 12:38
    pts/3           27518    0:00 tcsh
    pts/3           27540    0:02 elm
    pts/3           27879    0:00 sh
    pts/3           27880    0:00 vi

pts/4           kgiglio  12:48
    pts/4           27790    0:00 tcsh
    pts/4           27810    0:00 pine

pts/6           bhavel  12:54
    pts/6           27972    0:00 tcsh
    pts/6           27991    0:00 pine

pts/5           gandrus  15:30
    pts/5            4505    0:00 csh

pts/7           mdeter   10:17
    pts/7           24353    0:00 tcsh
    pts/7           25917    0:00 elm

pts/8           scho     12:42
    pts/8           27623    0:00 tcsh
    pts/8           27641    0:00 pine

pts/9           jbergen  12:44
    pts/9           27672    0:00 tcsh
    pts/9           27695    0:01 lynx

pts/10          wdalton  12:46
    pts/10          27722    0:00 tcsh
    pts/10          27744    0:00 pine

pts/12          fcervone 12:53
    pts/12          27931    0:00 tcsh
    pts/12          28015    0:00 whodo

pts/1           prahman1  0:20
    ?               11065    0:00 cmdtool
    pts/1           11104    0:00 tcsh

pts/23          ggordon   9:50
    pts/23           5705    0:00 tcsh
    pts/23          11384    0:55 telnet

pts/31          slytinen 13:20
    pts/31           7632    0:00 tcsh
    pts/31           7667    0:31 emacs
    pts/35           7753    0:00 csh
    pts/35           7046    0:00 lisp
    pts/35           7047    0:15 cl

pts/32          wkrueger 11:34
```

Figure 10-2

whodo command example.

with the user id. These process lines include the device name, process id, CPU minutes and seconds used, and process name.

As with `w`, output can be restricted to a single user by specifying a user on the command line, that is,

```
whodo fcervone
```

This would limit the output to the information for `fcervone`.

ps—Process Status

The `ps` command is one of the most useful commands when a quick diagnosis of a performance problem is needed. It enables the administrator to monitor the execution status of the processes on the system. It can uncover memory, CPU hogging, and I/O problems by user and process.

The basic function of the `ps` command is to print information about active processes. With no options, `ps` displays information about the processes associated with the invoking terminal. This output is limited in its usefulness because it contains only the process id, terminal identifier, and cumulative execution time.

The real functionality of the `ps` command comes from the many options of the command (Table 10-3). In this section, the focus will be on the two most useful formats, `ps -ecf` and `ps -el`. These two options are most useful because they display comprehensive information on a systemwide basis.

The first example, `ps -ecf` (Fig. 10-3), focuses on the priority and scheduling classes of the processes. The report contains a line for each process on the system. The information reported on the processes includes

UID—the user id of the process's owner

PID—the process id

PPID—the parent process id

CLS—the scheduling class of the process, either

> TS for timesharing
>
> SYS for system
>
> IA for interactive (the active window on an X-Windows display station)
>
> REL for real time

TABLE 10-3

ps Command
Options

Option	Purpose
-a	Prints information about all processes most frequently requested except process group leaders and processes not associated with a terminal.
-c	Prints information in a format that reflects scheduler properties as described in priocntl(1). The -c option affects the output of the -f and -l options.
-d	Prints information about all processes except session leaders.
-e	Prints information about every process running.
-f	Generates a full listing. (See below for significance of columns in a full listing.)
-j	Prints session id and process group id.
-l	Generates a long listing. (See below.)
-g grplis	Lists only process data whose group leader's id number(s) appears in grplist.
-p proclist	Lists only process data whose process id numbers are given in proclist.
-s sidlist	Lists information on all session leaders whose id's appear in sidlist.
-t term	Lists only process data associated with terminal term.
-u uidlist	Lists only process data whose user id number or login name is given in uidlist. In the listing, the numerical user id will be printed unless the -f option is used.

Display formats

With the -f option, ps tries to determine the command name and arguments given when the process was created by examining the user block. If this is not possible, the command name is printed as it would have appeared without the -f option.

The column headings and the meaning of the columns in a ps listing are listed below. The letters f and l indicate the option (full or long) that causes the corresponding heading to appear; all means that the heading always appears.

Format	Option	Meaning
F	(1)	Flags (hexadecimal and additive) associated with the process. These flags are available for historical purposes; currently, no particular meaning is ascribed to the various combinations.
S	(1)	The state of the process.

TABLE 10-3
(Continued)

ps Command
Options

Format	Option	Meaning
UID	(f,1)	The user ID number of the process owner. The login name is printed when the -f option is used.
PID	(all)	The process id of the process.
PPID	(f,1)	The process id of the parent process.
C	(f,1)	Processor utilization for scheduling. Not printed when the -c option is used.
CLS	(f,1)	Scheduling class. Printed only when the -c option is used.
PRI	(1)	The priority of the process. Without the -c option, higher numbers mean lower priority. With the -c option, higher numbers mean higher priority.
NI	(1)	Nice value, used in priority computation. Not printed when the -c value is used. Only processes in the timesharing class have a nice value.
ADDR	(1)	The memory address of the process.
SZ	(1)	The size of the swappable processes' image in main memory.
WCHAN	(1)	The address of an event for which the process is sleeping. If blank, the process is running.
STIME	(f)	The starting time of the process, given in hours, minutes, and seconds. (A process started more than 24 h before the inquiry is executed is given in months and days.)
TTY	(all)	The cumulative execution time for the process.
COMMAND	(all)	The command name (the full command name and its arguments are printed with the -f option). A process that has exited but still is attached to a parent is marked <defunct>

PRI—the process's scheduling priority*

STIME—the time the process started

TTY—the terminal associated with the process

TIME—the total amount of CPU time used by the process since it was
started

COMD—the command used to start the process

As can be seen in Fig. 10-4, the information reported with the second
option (ps -el) is significantly different from the prior example. In the
second example the report focuses more closely on the state of the
process. For each process, the following information is reported:

---

*The higher the number, the lower the priority.

```
ps -ecf
      UID    PID  PPID  CLS PRI    STIME TTY        TIME COMD
     root      0     0  SYS  96  Sep 22 ?         0:01 sched
     root      1     0  TS   58  Sep 22 ?         6:31 /etc/init -
     root      2     0  SYS  98  Sep 22 ?         0:07 pageout
     root      3     0  SYS  60  Sep 22 ?       395:49 fsflush
     root    664     1  TS   58  Sep 22 ?         0:01
/usr/openwin/bin/xdm -nodaemon
     root    323     1  TS   58  Sep 22 ?         6:33 /usr/sbin/rpcbind
   sryner    893   868  TS   58  14:16:53 pts/0   0:01 elm
     root      8     1  TS   58  Sep 22 ?         0:38 vxconfigd -m boot
     root    331     1  TS    2  Sep 22 ?         0:00 /usr/sbin/kerbd
     root    340     1  TS   58  Sep 22 ?         7:35 /usr/sbin/inetd -s
     root    315     1  TS   58  Sep 22 ?        15:50 /usr/sbin/in.routed
-q
     root    343     1  TS   58  Sep 22 ?         0:00 /usr/lib/nfs/statd
     root    325     1  TS   58  Sep 22 ?         0:00 /usr/sbin/keyserv
     root    345     1  TS   58  Sep 22 ?         0:01 /usr/lib/nfs/lockd
     root    365     1  TS    0  Sep 22 ?         0:00
/usr/lib/autofs/automountd
     root    369     1  TS   58  Sep 22 ?        10:36 /usr/sbin/syslogd
     root    379     1  TS   53  Sep 22 ?         4:41 /usr/sbin/cron
     root    666     1  TS   58  Sep 22 ?         0:02
/usr/local/etc/httpd/htbin/httpd
     root    612     1  TS   59  Sep 22 ?         0:00
/usr/local/bin/xntpd
     root    654     1  TS   58  Sep 22 ?         0:00
/usr/software/SPSS/bin/lmgrd -c /usr/software/SPSS/licenses/license.dat
   nobody   1099   666  TS   60  14:23:44 ?       0:00
/usr/local/etc/httpd/htbin/httpd
 prahman1  11065 10912  TS   58  Oct 03 ?         0:01
/usr/openwin/bin/cmdtool
     root    567     1  TS   33  Sep 22 ?         0:00 /usr/sbin/nsrexecd
     root    844   340  TS   58  Sep 22 ?         0:01 rpc.ttdbserverd
     root    549     1  TS   58  Sep 22 ?         1:53 /usr/lib/utmpd
   mdeter  25917 24353  TS   48  11:27:54 pts/7   0:03 elm
     oipr   6079 11795  TS   60  Oct 03 ?         0:00
/condor/oiprstaf/oipr/httpd/apache -d /condor/oiprstaf/oipr/httpd
     root    660   654  TS   58  Sep 22 ?         0:06 HLM_SPSS -T condor
3 -c /usr/software/SPSS/licenses/license.dat
     root  12596   340  TS   18  Sep 25 ?         0:00 in.telnetd
     root    672   663  TS   58  Sep 22 ?         0:00 /usr/lib/saf/listen
tcp
     root   7625   340  TS   18  Sep 29 ?         0:00 in.telnetd
   sryner    868   866  TS   30  14:16:47 pts/0   0:01 -tcsh
     root  18289     1  TS   58  Oct 03 ?         0:02 nmbd -D
   nobody   1093   666  TS   60  14:23:39 ?       0:00
/usr/local/etc/httpd/htbin/httpd
   oracle    681     1  TS   58  Sep 22 ?         0:00 ora_pmon_cnd1
     root    579   578  TS   53  Sep 22 ?         0:00 vxnotify -f -w 15
   oracle    778     1  TS   58  Sep 22 ?         0:01 ora_reco_cnd1
   nobody    931   666  TS   60  14:18:50 ?       0:01
/usr/local/etc/httpd/htbin/httpd
   oracle    772     1  TS   58  Sep 22 ?         0:36 ora_smon_cnd1
  slytinen   7047  7046  TS   51  Oct 01 pts/35   0:16 cl
   bhavel  27972 27970  TS   55  12:54:03 pts/6   0:00 -tcsh
     root   1114   340  TS   42  14:24:38 ?       0:00 in.telnetd
     root    652     1  TS   51  Sep 22 ?         0:00 /usr/lib/nfs/mountd
     root    650     1  TS   12  Sep 22 ?         0:00 /usr/lib/nfs/nfsd -
a 16
   oracle    730     1  TS   58  Sep 22 ?         0:00 ora_lgwr_cnd1
```

Figure 10-3

ps -ef command output example.

```
    root 18355 18297   TS  58   Oct 03 ?          0:01 smbd -D
wkrueger 12633 12631   TS  58   Sep 25 pts/34     0:01 -tcsh
  nobody  1142   666   TS  58 14:25:01 ?          0:00
/usr/local/etc/httpd/htbin/httpd
  nobody  1064   666   TS  54 14:22:35 ?          0:00
/usr/local/etc/httpd/htbin/httpd
  oracle   781     1   TS  59   Sep 22 ?          0:00 ora_s000_cnd1
    scho 27641 27623   TS  58 12:42:04 pts/8      0:01 pine
    root   573     1   TS  30   Sep 22 ?          0:00 /sbin/sh -
/usr/lib/vxvm/bin/vxsparecheck root
    root   673   663   TS  58   Sep 22 ?          0:00 /usr/lib/saf/ttymon
    root   559     1   TS  58   Sep 22 ?          0:08 /usr/sbin/vold
    root   578   573   TS  55   Sep 22 ?          0:00 /sbin/sh -
/usr/lib/vxvm/bin/vxsparecheck root
prahman1 11104 11065   TS  58   Oct 03 pts/1      0:00 /bin/tcsh
  nobody  1140   666   TS  48 14:25:00 ?          0:00
/usr/local/etc/httpd/htbin/httpd
  mdeter 24353 24351   TS  58 10:17:03 pts/7      0:01 -tcsh
    root 19896     1   IA  42   Oct 03 ?          0:00 xconsole -geometry
590x77+316-762 -daemon -notify -verbose -fn fixed -exitOnFai
  oracle   699     1   TS  58   Sep 22 ?          0:00 ora_dbwr_cnd1
    root  1040 22725   TS  58 14:22:16 ?          0:00 /usr/lib/sendmail -
bd -q10m
 nmurphy  1035  1033   TS  20 14:22:03 pts/3      0:01 -tcsh
    yliu 12464     1   TS  36   Oct 03 ?          0:00 httpd
prahman1 10902     1   TS  58   Oct 03 ?          0:00 vkbd -nopopup
    root   663     1   TS  58   Sep 22 ?          0:00 /usr/lib/saf/sac -t
300
    root   688   664   IA  59   Sep 22 ?          0:50 /usr/openwin/bin/X
:0 -auth /var/tmp/A:0-a000AO
    root   469     1   TS  58   Sep 22 ?          0:02 /usr/lib/lpsched
    root   483   479   TS  58   Sep 22 ?          0:02 suntechd -T condor
3 -c /etc/opt/licenses/licenses_combined
    root   479     1   TS  58   Sep 22 ?          0:01
/etc/opt/licenses/lmgrd.ste -c /etc/opt/licenses/licenses_combined
    root   478   469   TS  58   Sep 22 ?          0:00 lpNet
    root   484   478   TS  58   Sep 22 ?          0:02 lpNet
  oracle   790     1   TS  50   Sep 22 ?          0:00 ora_d000_cnd1
  nobody  1113   666   TS  58 14:24:29 ?          0:00
/usr/local/etc/httpd/htbin/httpd
 nmurphy  1057  1035   TS  58 14:22:18 pts/3      0:01 pine
    root 13910     1   TS   0   Sep 22 ?         58:34 /usr/bin/perl
name_server
  nobody  1089   666   TS  60 14:23:34 ?          0:00
/usr/local/etc/httpd/htbin/httpd
    oipr 15940 11795   TS  58   Oct 02 ?          0:01
/condor/oiprstaf/oipr/httpd/apache -d /condor/oiprstaf/oipr/httpd
    root   866   340   TS  55 14:16:46 ?          0:00 in.telnetd
    root 27970   340   TS  18 12:54:03 ?          0:00 in.telnetd
    root  1033   340   TS  51 14:22:03 ?          0:00 in.telnetd
  nobody  1145   666   TS  58 14:25:05 ?          0:00
/usr/local/etc/httpd/htbin/httpd
  nobody  1092   666   TS  60 14:23:38 ?          0:00
/usr/local/etc/httpd/htbin/httpd
  nobody  1144   666   TS  58 14:25:04 ?          0:00
/usr/local/etc/httpd/htbin/httpd
prahman1 10965 10912   TS  58   Oct 03 ?          0:00 olwmslave
prahman1 11063 10912        0                     0:02 <defunct>
wkrueger 12599 12596   TS  58   Sep 25 pts/32     0:01 -tcsh
    oipr 11795     1   TS  58   Sep 22 ?          0:00
/condor/oiprstaf/oipr/httpd/apache -d /condor/oiprstaf/oipr/httpd
```

Figure 10-3

(Continued) `ps -ef` command output example.

```
     root 12631    340    TS  18    Sep 25 ?         0:00 in.telnetd
  ggordon  5705   5703    TS  58    Sep 23 pts/23    0:01 -tcsh
   sryner   916    893    TS  38 14:18:05 pts/0      0:00 sh -c emacs
/tmp/snd.893
     oipr 20266  11795    TS  60    Oct 02 ?         0:01
/condor/oiprstaf/oipr/httpd/apache -d /condor/oiprstaf/oipr/httpd
     root  5703    340    TS  18    Sep 23 ?         0:00 in.telnetd
     root  1111    340    TS  58 14:24:27 ?          0:00 in.comsat
prahman1 10909      1    TS  50    Oct 03 ?          0:00 ttsession -s
slytinen  7046   7753    TS   8    Oct 01 pts/35     0:00 /bin/csh
/usr/local/bin/lisp
slytinen  7632   7625    TS  58    Sep 29 pts/31     0:01 -tcsh
     root  4503    340    TS  18    Sep 26 ?         0:00 in.telnetd
fcervone  1146   1116    TS  20 14:25:10 pts/9       0:02 ps -ecf
     root 27677    478    TS  58    Sep 24 ?         0:00 lpNet
wkrueger 17663  12633    TS  58    Sep 25 pts/34     0:00 vi index.html
wkrueger 17879  12599    TS  52    Sep 25 pts/32     0:00 pg Assignment1.html
     root   420  27932    TS  58 14:02:54 ?          0:03 /usr/lib/sendmail -
bd -q10m
slytinen  7667   7632    TS  58    Sep 29 pts/31     0:32 emacs grammar-
handout.tex
prahman1 10912      1    TS  58    Oct 03 ?          0:01 olwm
  nobody  1100    666    TS  28 14:23:45 ?           0:00
/usr/local/etc/httpd/htbin/httpd
     root 27621    340    TS  55 12:41:57 ?          0:00 in.telnetd
     root 27932  22725    TS  45 12:52:59 ?          0:00 /usr/lib/sendmail -
bd -q10m
  nobody  1070    666    TS  58 14:22:44 ?           0:00
/usr/local/etc/httpd/htbin/httpd
  nobody  1106    666    TS  58 14:23:50 ?           0:00
/usr/local/etc/httpd/htbin/httpd
slytinen  7753   7667    TS  58    Sep 29 pts/35     0:00 /usr/bin/csh -i
  ggordon 11384   5705    TS  58    Sep 24 pts/23    0:56 telnet hawk
     oipr 25099  11795    TS  58 10:49:55 ?          0:00
/condor/oiprstaf/oipr/httpd/apache -d /condor/oiprstaf/oipr/httpd
   bhavel 27991  27972    TS  58 12:54:10 pts/6      0:00 pine -i
     root 19881    664    IA  41    Oct 03 ?         0:00
/usr/openwin/bin/xdm -nodaemon
   sryner   917    916    TS  58 14:18:05 pts/0      0:01 emacs /tmp/snd.893
     root 18297      1    TS  48    Oct 03 ?         0:00 smbd -D
  gandrus  4505   4503    TS  58    Sep 26 pts/5     0:01 -csh
     root    69    340    TS  42 13:52:24 ?          0:00 in.telnetd
    csheu    71     69    TS  58 13:52:24 pts/4      0:01 -tcsh
     scho 27623  27621    TS  53 12:41:58 pts/8      0:00 -tcsh
fcervone  1116   1114    TS  58 14:24:39 pts/9       0:01 -tcsh
     oipr 20121  11795    TS  60    Oct 03 ?         0:01
/condor/oiprstaf/oipr/httpd/apache -d /condor/oiprstaf/oipr/httpd
     root 24351    340    TS  55 10:17:03 ?          0:00 in.telnetd
     root 22725      1    TS  58    Oct 02 ?         1:28 /usr/lib/sendmail -
bd -q10m
     oipr 25618  11795    TS  58    Oct 04 ?         0:00
/condor/oiprstaf/oipr/httpd/apache -d /condor/oiprstaf/oipr/httpd
```

Figure 10-3

(Continued) `ps -ef` command output example.

```
ps -el
 F S   UID   PID  PPID  C PRI NI    ADDR     SZ   WCHAN TTY      TIME
COMD
19 T     0     0     0 74   0 SY e01d6a18     0           ?        0:01
sched
 8 S     0     1     0 80  41 20 f7345cd8   211 f7345ea8 ?        6:31
init
19 S     0     2     0 80   0 SY f7345678     0 e01c4078 ?        0:07
pageout
19 S     0     3     0 80   0 SY f7345018     0 e01d7104 ?      395:49
fsflush
 8 S     0   664     1 80  41 20 f7346998   616 f7e663ee ?        0:01
xdm
 8 S     0   323     1 80  41 20 f7b5a660   414 f7a0ed6e ?        6:33
rpcbind
 8 S 17488   893   868 80  41 20 f89b8998   279 f89b8a02 pts/0    0:01
elm
 8 S     0     8     1 80  41 20 f755fce0   481 f7a0e18e ?        0:38
vxconfig
 8 S     0   331     1 10  97 20 f7b5b320   369 f7a0eb66 ?        0:00
kerbd
 8 S     0   340     1 80  51 20 f7b5acc0   375 f7a0e3be ?        7:35
inetd
 8 S     0   315     1 80  41 20 f7560340   300 f7a0eb16 ?       15:50
in.route
 8 S     0   343     1 20  41 20 f7b5b980   417 f7a0ee0e ?        0:00
statd
 8 S     0   325     1 11  41 20 f7b5a000   333 f7a0e756 ?        0:00
keyserv
 8 S     0   345     1 74  41 20 f7db0988   517 f7a0ecf6 ?        0:01
lockd
 8 S     0   365     1 12  99 20 f7dafcc8   358 f7a0e706 ?        0:00
automoun
 8 S     0   369     1 80  41 20 f7daf008   356 f7a0e6b6 ?       10:36
syslogd
 8 S     0   379     1 80  46 20 f7ddc990   439 f7dc4aee ?        4:41
cron
 8 S     0   666     1 80  41 20 f7e5d000   391 f7e5d1d0 ?        0:02
httpd
 8 S     0   612     1 14  40  8 f75609a0   368 f7560b70 ?        0:00
xntpd
 8 S     0   654     1 50  41 20 f7daf668   329 f7e668c6 ?        0:00
lmgrd
 8 S 60001  1099   666 18  39 20 f8327cc8   397 f7d97e38 ?        0:00
httpd
 8 S     0  1147   340  9  41 20 f7c32340   296 f79aea36 ?        0:00
rquotad
 8 S 22900 11065 10912 80  41 20 f809a670   856 f82230d6 ?        0:01
cmdtool
 8 S     0   567     1  4  66 20 f7e67668   302 f7a0ee86 ?        0:00
nsrexecd
 8 S     0   844   340 60  41 20 f7e559a0   576 f7e66696 ?        0:01
rpc.ttdb
 8 S     0   549     1 80  41 20 f7e68328   172 f7a0eeae ?        1:53
utmpd
 8 S 10439 25917 24353 80  51 20 f7e5dcc0   301 f7efc63e pts/7    0:03
elm
 8 S 30082  6079 11795 50  39 20 f8149338   402 f7d960b0 ?        0:00
apache
 8 S     0   660   654 80  41 20 f7e54020   341 f7e6675e ?        0:06
HLM_SPSS
```

Figure 10-4

ps -el command output example.

```
   8 S     0 12596   340 17  81 20 f7b60000    350 f7f496c6 ?           0:00
in.telne
   8 S     0   672   663 20  41 20 f7e2acc8    291 f7e6607e ?           0:00
listen
   8 S     0  7625   340 18  81 20 f7c329a0    350 f79ae7de ?           0:00
in.telne
   8 S 17488   868   866 51  69 20 f89b7cd8    306 f89b7ea8 pts/0       0:01
tcsh
   8 S     0 18289     1 80  41 20 f849d340    374 f79ae64e ?           0:02
nmbd
   8 S 60001  1093   666 24  39 20 f8492338    397 f86bce90 ?           0:00
httpd
   8 S   106   681     1 24  41 20 f7ea0988   6328 f7f3802c ?           0:00
oracle
   8 S     0   579   578  5  46 20 f7e67008    155 f7a0eac6 ?           0:00
vxnotify
   8 S   106   778     1 80  41 20 f7e9f008   6336 f7f3806c ?           0:01
oracle
   8 S 60001   931   666 73  41 20 f7f18020    402 f79ae716 ?           0:01
httpd
   8 S   106   772     1 80  41 20 f7eb0cd0   6350 f7f3805c ?           0:36
oracle
   8 S  2722  7047  7046 80  48 20 f7b61320   5163 f79aeb26 pts/35      0:16
cl
   8 S  1031 27972 27970 44  44 20 f7c35010    306 f7c351e0 pts/6       0:00
tcsh
   8 S     0  1114   340 16  57 20 f7e47018    350 f79ae73e ?           0:00
in.telne
   8 S     0   652     1 27  48 20 f7ddc330    409 f7e66d4e ?           0:00
mountd
   8 S     0   650     1  6  87 20 f7ddb670    295 f7e667fe ?           0:00
nfsd
   8 S   106   730     1 39  41 20 f7e47678   6346 f7f3804c ?           0:00
oracle
   8 S     0 18355 18297 80  41 20 f7ef3990    479 f79ae69e ?           0:01
smbd
   8 S  1420 12633 12631 63  41 20 f8184cc8    307 f8184e98 pts/34      0:01
tcsh
   8 S 60001  1142   666  9  39 20 f8281000    397 f86bcfb0 ?           0:00
httpd
   8 S 60001  1064   666 31  39 20 f849cce0    399 f86bc230 ?           0:00
httpd
   8 S   106   781     1 13  40 20 f7f18ce0   6330 f7f3807c ?           0:00
oracle
   8 S  1667 27641 27623 80  41 20 f8185328    958 f79ae14e pts/8       0:01
pine
   8 S     0   573     1 15  69 20 f7eb1330     76 f7eb139a ?           0:00
vxsparec
   8 S     0   673   663 37  41 20 f7e2b328    327 f7e2b4f8 ?           0:00
ttymon
   8 S     0   559     1 80  41 20 f7eb0010    438 f7e663c6 ?           0:08
vold
   8 S     0   578   573  6  44 20 f7e67cc8     76 f7e5a156 ?           0:00
vxsparec
   8 S 22900 11104 11065 21  41 20 f7b61980    303 f7d60b26 pts/1       0:00
tcsh
   8 S 60001  1140   666  5  51 20 f8282980    397 f7b2a07e ?           0:00
httpd
   8 S 10439 24353 24351 80  41 20 f7ddbcd0    311 f7ddbea0 pts/7       0:01
tcsh
```

Figure 10-4

(Continued) `ps -el` command output example.

```
8 S     0 19896     1 14  57 20 f7c31020   579 f7a0e026 ?        0:00
xconsole
8 S   106   699     1 28  41 20 f7e48338  6347 f7f3803c ?        0:00
oracle
8 S     0  1040 22725 42  39 20 f7e48998   503 f830f7e8 ?        0:00
sendmail
8 S 21125  1035  1033 68  79 20 f7f18680   310 f7f18850 pts/3    0:01
tcsh
8 S 35086 12464     1 50  63 24 f8148018   312 f7d8f55e ?        0:00
httpd
8 S 22900 10902     1 36  41 20 f7b60660   832 f822378e ?        0:00
vkbd
8 S     0   663     1 20  41 20 f7eb0670   308 f7e7e82e ?        0:00
sac
8 S     0   688   664 80  40 20 f7e2a008  2205 f7e6684e ?        0:50
Xsun
8 S     0   469     1 80  41 20 f7ec7018   620 f7e6698e ?        0:02
lpsched
8 S     0   483   479 80  41 20 f7ec7cd8   354 f7e669b6 ?        0:02
suntechd
8 S     0   479     1 80  41 20 f755f020   331 f7e66a06 ?        0:01
lmgrd.st
8 S     0   478   469 17  41 20 f7ec8338   325 f7e66a56 ?        0:00
lpNet
8 S     0   484   478 80  41 20 f7ec7678   379 f7e6693e ?        0:02
lpNet
8 S   106   790     1 20  49 20 f7e17678  6348 f7f3808c ?        0:00
oracle
8 S 60001  1113   666 14  41 20 f8282320   397 f851567e ?        0:00
httpd
8 S 21125  1057  1035 80  41 20 f7eb1990   798 f79ae0d6 pts/3    0:01
pine
8 S     0 13910     1 80  99 20 f7e7fcc8  2524 f825463e ?       58:34
name_ser
8 S 60001  1089   666 40  39 20 f7e2a668   399 f817f890 ?        0:00
httpd
8 S 30082 15940 11795 80  41 20 f7e47cd8   404 f7e66916 ?        0:01
apache
8 S     0   866   340 14  44 20 f7c31680   350 f7e6689e ?        0:00
in.telne
8 S     0 27970   340 16  81 20 f8328988   350 f7a0e076 ?        0:00
in.telne
8 S     0  1033   340 15  48 20 f7f19340   350 f7e6652e ?        0:00
in.telne
8 S 60001  1145   666  6  61 20 f8281cc0   397 f81670a6 ?        0:00
httpd
8 S 60001  1092   666 25  51 20 f7c35cd0   399 f79ae356 ?        0:00
httpd
8 S 60001  1144   666  5  39 20 f7e68988   399 f817f590 ?        0:00
httpd
8 S 22900 10965 10912 28  41 20 f809a010   817 f8223fae ?        0:00
olwmslav
8 Z 22900 11063 10912 80   0                                     0:02
<defunct>
8 S  1420 12599 12596 80  41 20 f7ddb010   317 f7ddb1e0 pts/32   0:01
tcsh
8 S 30082 11795     1 49  41 20 f7e80328   373 f7e804f8 ?        0:00
apache
8 S     0 12631   340 16  81 20 f8491018   350 f7e6611e ?        0:00
in.telne
```

Figure 10-4

(Continued) `ps -el` command output example.

8	S	1403	5705	5703	80	41	20	f84b7008	321	f84b71d8	pts/23	0:01
tcsh												
8	S	17488	916	893	4	61	20	f89b7018	181	f89b7082	pts/0	0:00
sh												
8	S	30082	20266	11795	80	39	20	f7e17018	402	f7d97a18	?	0:01
apache												
8	S	0	5703	340	18	81	20	f84b8988	350	f7f49e6e	?	0:00
in.telne												
8	S	0	1111	340	8	41	20	f7e54680	287	f7d9eaf6	?	0:00
in.comsa												
8	S	22900	10909	1	34	49	20	f7e5d660	735	f82237de	?	0:00
ttsessio												
8	S	2722	7046	7753	11	91	20	f7b60cc0	218	f7b60e90	pts/35	0:00
lisp												
8	S	2722	7632	7625	80	41	20	f89b7678	313	f89b7848	pts/31	0:01
tcsh												
8	S	0	4503	340	15	81	20	f84af338	350	f79ae32e	?	0:00
in.telne												
8	O	1440	1148	1116	80	99	20	f89b8338	181		pts/9	0:01
ps												
8	S	0	27677	478	24	41	20	f809b990	385	f7f49176	?	0:00
lpNet												
8	S	1420	17663	12633	30	41	20	f8184008	268	f873ca0e	pts/34	0:00
vi												
8	S	1420	17879	12599	7	47	20	f8328328	177	f8800cfe	pts/32	0:00
pg												
8	S	0	420	27932	80	41	20	f7e54ce0	522	f808904e	?	0:03
sendmail												
8	S	2722	7667	7632	80	41	20	f7c33cc0	998	f7e664de	pts/31	0:32
emacs												
8	S	22900	10912	1	80	41	20	f7e2b988	518	f822341e	?	0:01
olwm												
8	S	60001	1100	666	21	39	20	f7e18998	399	f7f04430	?	0:00
httpd												
8	S	0	27621	340	15	44	20	f7e5e320	350	f7e66f06	?	0:00
in.telne												
8	S	0	27932	22725	8	54	20	f8491678	514	f84916e2	?	0:00
sendmail												
8	S	60001	1070	666	40	41	20	f7ef2cd0	397	f851514e	?	0:00
httpd												
8	S	60001	1106	666	25	39	20	f80eb328	399	f86bcef0	?	0:00
httpd												
8	S	2722	7753	7667	42	41	20	f84aecd8	229	f84aeea8	pts/35	0:00
csh												
8	S	1403	11384	5705	80	41	20	f80eb988	325	f7f493f6	pts/23	0:56
telnet												
8	S	30082	25099	11795	3	41	20	f7e18338	373	f8750068	?	0:00
apache												
8	S	1031	27991	27972	50	41	20	f7c36990	738	f7e66cfe	pts/6	0:00
pine												
8	S	0	19881	664	14	58	20	f7ec8998	626	f7a0eb3e	?	0:00
xdm												
8	S	17488	917	916	55	41	20	f849c020	891	f79ae176	pts/0	0:01
emacs												
8	S	0	18297	1	3	51	20	f849c680	395	f80ede16	?	0:00
smbd												
8	S	1401	4505	4503	64	41	20	f84ae018	236	f7afa366	pts/5	0:01
csh												
8	S	0	69	340	16	57	20	f7f199a0	350	f79ae0ae	?	0:00
in.telne												

Figure 10-4

(Continued) ps -el command output example.

```
 8 S   1355     71     69 80   41 20 f7e7f668    308 f834432e pts/4     0:01
tcsh
 8 S   1667 27623 27621 44   46 20 f7e55340    306 f7e55510 pts/8     0:00
tcsh
 8 S   1440  1116  1114 57   41 20 f7db0328    306 f7db04f8 pts/9     0:01
tcsh
 8 S  30082 20121 11795 66   39 20 f7c31ce0    404 f74a62f8 ?         0:01
apache
 8 S      0 24351   340 15   44 20 f809b330    350 f79ae87e ?         0:00
in.telne
 8 S      0 22725     1 80   41 20 f7c35670    495 f842180e ?         1:28
sendmail
 8 S  30082 25618 11795 17   41 20 f7c33660    402 f74a6598 ?         0:00
apache
```

Figure 10-4

(Continued) ps -el command output example.

TABLE 10-4	State	Meaning
Process States	S	Sleeping: Process is waiting for an event to complete.
	R	Runable: Process is on run queue.
	I	Idle: Process is being created.
	Z	Zombie state: Process is terminated and parent is not waiting.
	T	Traced: Process is stopped by a signal because parent is tracing it.
	X	SXBRK state: Process is waiting for more primary memory.

- F—the state of the process. (Table 10-4)
- S—the dispatch state of the process.
- UID—the user id of the owner of the process.
- PID—the process id.
- PPID—the parent process id.
- C—processor utilization used for scheduling.
- PRI—the processes' scheduling priority.*
- NI—the nice number of the process (used as a factor in computing priority; lowering the nice number lowers the priority).
- ADDR—memory address of the process control block.
- SZ—amount of virtual memory used by the process.

---

*See prior footnote.

- WCHAN—address of the event the process is waiting for; if blank, the process is running.
- TTY—terminal associated with the process.
- TIME—the total amount of CPU time used by the process since it began.
- COMD—the command used to start the process.

It is important to remember that the ps command provides a snapshot of the system. Things change while ps is running. The snapshot it provides is only accurate for the split second of time the ps command was gathering data.

It is also important to note that ps checks stdin, stdout, and stderr (in that order) to determine the controlling terminal for purposes of reporting. If stdin, stdout, and stderr are all redirected, ps will not be able to find a controlling terminal, so there will be no report for the process.

mpstat—Multiprocessor Status

On machines with more than one processor, the mpstat command can be used to determine how the load is being balanced across processors.

When run with no options, each line of the output represents the activity of a processor since the time the system was started. For each processor, the following information is displayed:

- CPU—processor id
- minf—minor faults
- mjf—major faults
- xcal—interprocessor cross-calls
- intr—interrupts
- ithr—interrupts as threads, not counting clock interrupts
- csw—context switches
- icsw—involuntary context switches
- migr—thread migrations to another processor
- smtx—spins on mutexes (lock not acquired on first try)
- srw—spins on readers/writer locks (lock not acquired on first try)
- syscl—system calls

- usr—percentage of user time

- sys—percentage of system time

- wt—percentage of wait time

- idl—percentage of idle time

The `mpstat` command can also be run in continuous mode by specifying an interval and count, where the interval is expressed as a number of seconds (Fig. 10-5).

For example, to run the `mpstat` command every hour for the next 12 h, the performance analyst would use the command

```
mpstat 3600 12
```

Managing the Workload

Solaris provides commands that allow the user, in some cases, and the system administrator to influence the execution of processes on the system.

The priority of a process is determined by its scheduling class and its *nice number.* Confusing the situation somewhat is that processes in Solaris have two priority numbers: an execution priority number and a nice number.

The nice number is used to rank a process relative to other active processes. By default, a process always starts with the same nice number as its parent. A user can "be nice" and lower the priority of a process by starting it with the `nice` command. Or, after the process begins, the user can lower the priority with the `renice` command. However, a user cannot raise the priority of a process. This ability is reserved for the system administrator (and root).

```
mpstat
CPU minf mjf xcal  intr ithr  csw icsw migr smtx  srw syscl  usr sys  wt
idl
  0   19   0    0   109    9   37    1   10    3    0   122    2    3    9
86
  1   18   0    0    92   92   35    0   10    3    0   117    2    4    9
85
  2   18   0    0     1    0   38    1   10    3    0   123    2    3   10
86
  3   18   0    0     1    0   37    1   10    3    0   123    2    3   10
86
```

Figure 10-5
`mpstat` command output example.

nice—Change the Starting nice Value of a Process

The `nice` command uses the following syntax:

```
nice -value command_name
```

where *value* is the amount to lower the nice value by, and *command_name* is the command to be executed. Nice numbers range from −20 to 20, but a user can only set values in the range of 1 through 19. Also worth noting is that because they indicate the amount by which to lower priority, setting a nice value to −19 actually *raises* the priority of a process. For example, the following command

```
nice -19 ps -ecl
```

will run the command with a nice number that is 19 less than the nice value of the parent process (which is probably the user's shell). However, the command

```
nice −19 ps -ecl
```

will run the command with a nice number that is 19 greater than that of the parent process. Again, though, only the system administrator and root can raise the priority of a process.

renice—Change the nice Value of a Running Process

But what about a process that is already running? The `renice` command alters the scheduling priority of one or more running processes. By default, the processes to be affected must be specified by their process id's. Other than root and the system administrator, users may only alter the priority of processes they own, incrementing the nice value one step at a time within the range 0 to 20. This means that a user who wants to raise the priority of a process (let's say process id 134) to a nice number of 15 will have to issue the command `renice 0 -p 134` followed by `renice 1 -p 134`, repeating the process until 15 is reached. This peculiar restriction is in place to prevent users from abusing the facility. Note that if this procedure is not followed, the system will not issue an error message; it simply ignores the command. The privileged users (root and the system administrators) may alter the priority of any process and set the priority to any value in the range −20 to 20.

For both `nice` and `renice` the following statements about nice values are true:

With a nice value of 19, the affected process will run only when nothing else in the system wants to.

The nice value of 0 is the base scheduling priority.

Any negative value will make things run faster.

If a process id is not specified in the `renice` command, that is, with only the priority is specified, the current process is used.

The `renice` command allows for all of the processes of a user to be modified with the `-u user1 user2`...option. To change the nice values of all of the processes of a process group,* use the option `-g PPid1 PPid2`...

It should be noted that if the nice number of a process is set to a very negative number, it is possible that the process will not be interruptable. To regain control, the priority must be elevated to greater than zero.

priocntl—Display or Set Scheduling Parameters of Specified Process(es)

The `nice` and `renice` commands are standard UNIX-based operating system commands. Solaris provides a command, `priocntl`, that supersedes both of these commands. The `priocntl` command combines and extends the functions of the `nice` and `renice` commands. In addition, `priocntl` is used to display the configuration information of the process scheduler.

In Solaris, processes fall into distinct classes, each with a separate scheduling policy. These include the real-time class, the timesharing class, the interactive class, and any user-defined classes that may exist. Each class has its own characteristics. In the default configuration, a runable real-time process will run before any other process. Therefore, real-time processes have the highest user priority on the system, and inappropriate use of or behavior in this class can have a devastating impact on performance. Next in priority are the system class, the inter-

---

*A process group is a parent process and all of its children.

active class, and the time-sharing class, which is at the bottom of the hierarchy.

Because the use of the `priocntl` command differs for the different scheduling classes, a quick overview of the aspects is in order.

Characteristics of the Real-Time Class.   The real-time class provides a fixed-priority preemptive scheduling policy for processes that require fast and (relatively) deterministic response. When the real class is defined, it has control of the highest scheduling priorities. Because of this, a runable real-time process is given CPU time before any process belonging to any other class. The real-time class has a range of priority values that may be assigned to processes within the class. Real-time priorities range from 0 to x, where x is the highest value that has been configured. The value of x can be displayed with the command

```
priocntl -l
```

The real-time scheduling policy is a fixed-priority one. The priority of a real-time process never changes unless the user or application makes an explicit request to do so. Within the real-time class, the nice value, or *rtpri* (real time priority value), is equivalent to the scheduling priority of the process. Numerically higher rtpri values represent higher priorities.

In addition to providing control over priority, `priocntl` also provides for control of time quantums allocated in the real-time class. The value so specified determines the maximum amount of time a process may run. This assumes three things:

The process does not finish before the time quantum is over.

The process does not go into a wait state during the time quantum.

Another process, at a higher priority, does not become runable.

Only root and system administrators can change a process to the real-time class. A user can change the rtpri or time quantum value of processes they own, but the user must be running a real-time shell in order to do so.

Characteristics of the Timesharing Class.   The timesharing scheduling policy tries to balance the needs of all processes so that there is a fair and optimal allocation of processor resources. Because of the varying CPU consumption characteristics of processes in this class, the primary objective in this class is to provide good response time to interactive processes and good throughput to CPU-bound jobs.

The timesharing class has a range of priority values that may be assigned to processes. Priorities are configurable and range from $-x$ to $+x$. The value of $+x$ is 1 less than the lowest value in the system class. Priority is used in this class to provide some degree of user/application control over the scheduling of processes. Raising or lowering the nice or *tsupri* value in this class raises or lowers the scheduling priority of the process. But this does not guarantee that a timesharing process with a higher tsupri value will run before one with a lower value. This is primarily because it is only one factor used in determining scheduling priority in this class. The system also factors the amount of CPU usage and I/O in scheduling priority for processes in the timesharing class. By definition, then, the system dynamically changes the value of the scheduling priority of timesharing processes.

In addition to global system limits, there is a per-process user priority limit (the *tsuprilim* value) that specifies the maximum tsupri value a given process can take. Any timesharing process may lower its tsuprilim value, but only root or system administrator processes can raise a tsuprilim value.

Characteristics of the Interactive Class.   The interactive class is very similar to the timesharing class. The primary use of the interactive class is to give a priority boost to the active window of X-Window users. Only root and the system administrator have explicit access to the interactive class. The user has no direct control over scheduling policies in the interactive class.

Using the priocntl Command.   The options of the `priocntl` command are outlined in Table 10-5. The follow examples demonstrate its use in various situations.

For real-time processes, the `priocntl` command needs to know, in addition to the priority, the time quantum associated with the command. For example, the command

```
priocntl -s -c RT -t 2 -i pid 3220
```

sets the class of the non-real-time process 3220 to real-time with a default priority of 0, and a time quantum of 2 ms.

To invoke a command in real time, the `priocntl` command is used as follows:

```
priocntl -e -c RT -p 5 -t 10 ps -ecf
```

	Options	Meaning
TABLE 10-5 `priocntl` options	-l	Display a list of the classes currently configured in the system along with class-specific information about each class.
	-d	Display the scheduling parameters associated with a set of processes.
	-s	Set the scheduling parameters associated with a set of processes.
	-e	Execute a specified command with the class and scheduling parameters associated with a set of processes.
	-i idtype	This option, together with any `idtype` arguments, specifies one or more processes to which the command is to apply. The interpretation of `idlist` depends on the value of `idtype`. The valid `idtype` arguments and corresponding interpretations of `idlist` are as follows:

-i pid—`idlist` is a list of process id's. The command applies to the specified processes.

-i ppid—`idlist` is a list of parent process id's. The command applies to all processes whose parent process id is in the list.

-i pgid—`idlist` is a list of process group id's. The command applies to all processes in the specified process groups.

-i sid—`idlist` is a list of session id's. The command applies to all processes in the specified sessions.

-i class—`idlist` consists of a single class name: RT for real time, TS for timesharing, or IA for interactive. The command applies to all processes in the specified class.

-i uid—`idlist` is a list of user id's. The command applies to all processes with an effective user id equal to an id from the list.

-i gid—`idlist` is a list of group id's. The command applies to all processes with an effective group id equal to an id from the list.

-i all—The command applies to all existing processes. No `idlist` should be specified. If one is, it is ignored.

Permission restrictions described

-c class specifies the class to be set. The valid arguments are RT for real time, TS for timesharing, or IA for interactive. If the specified class is not already configured, it will automatically be configured.

Valid class-specific options for setting real-time parameters

-p rtpri—Set the real-time priority of the specified processes to rtpri.

-t tqntm [-r res]—Set the time quantum of the specified processes to tqntm. You may optionally specify a resolution as explained below.

TABLE 10-5

(Continued)
priocntl options

Valid class-specific options for setting time-sharing parameters
-m tsuprilim—Set the user priority limit of the specified processes to tsuprilim.
-p tsupri—Set the user priority of the specified processes to tsupri.

Valid class-specific options for setting interactive parameters
- m iamode—Mark the specified processes as currently interactive or not.

This example executes ps -ecl in the real-time class with a real-time priority of 5 and a time quantum of 10 ms.

Setting the process to the timesharing class is performed with a command similar to this:

```
priocntl -s -c TS -i uid fcervone
```

In this example, all of the nontimesharing processes of user fcervone are selected and moved to the timesharing class with a default user priority limit and user priority of 0.

The following example is equivalent to the prior nice command example:

```
nice —19 ps -ecl
```

With the command

```
priocntl -e -c TS -m 0 -p -19 ps -ecl
```

the program ps -ecl is executed with a priority of −19 and a user priority limit of 0.

The priocntl command can also be used on processes that are already in the timesharing class to change their priority. The priocntl equivalent of the

```
renice 0 -p 134
renice 1 -p 134
  .
  .
  .
```

sequence above would be

```
priocntl -s -c TS -p 15 -i pid 134
```

It is not possible to change the class of any process to SYS. This special scheduling class exists for the purpose of scheduling the execution of certain system processes (such as the swapper) only. In addition, any processes that are in the system scheduling class that are included in a set of processes specified by *idtype* and *idlist* are ignored. However, the init process (process id 1) is a special case. The priocntl command can be used to change the class and other scheduling parameters of this process. To do so, the system administrator must use the *idtype/idlist* form -i pid 1. Nothing else may be included. Theoretically, the init can be assigned to any configured class, but the timesharing class is usually where it is run from; other choices may be highly undesirable and cause system failure.

pbind—Control and Query Bindings of Processes to Processors

In multiprocessor systems, it may be advantageous to bind processes to certain processors. In those cases, the pbind command is used to do so.

pbind performs three functions: It binds all the lightweight processes (LWPs) of a process to a processor, it removes such bindings, or it displays the current bindings.

The -b option binds all of the LWPs of the indicated processes to the specified processor. The processor must be present and on-line. This can be determined by using the psrinfo command. For example, the command

```
pbind -b 3 10966
```

will bind process id 10966 to processor 3.

Once an LWP is bound to a processor, it will only execute on that processor except when it requires a resource that is only available on another processor. Any binding that is made is not exclusive; the processor can run other processes as well. Bindings are inherited, so new LWPs and processes created by a bound LWP will have the same binding as their parent. For example, binding a user's shell will bind all commands executed by the shell as well.

The system administrator or root may bind or unbind any process. Users can use pbind to bind or unbind any process that belongs to the user.

The -q option displays the bindings of the specified processes. If a process is composed of multiple LWPs, each with different bindings, the bindings of only one LWP will be shown. For example, in the following command, the query is made against a bound and unbound process:

```
pbind -q 10966 12394
```

This command would display the following report:

```
process id 10966: 3
process id 12394: not bound
```

This is what would be expected because process 10966 is currently bound to processor 3 and process 12394 is not bound to any processor.

The -u option removes the bindings from all the LWPs of the specified processes. They may then execute on any available processor. To unbind the processes bound in the previous example, the command would be

```
pbind -u 10966
```

dispadmin—Process Scheduler Administration

Root and the system administrator can modify the process scheduler on the fly while the system is in use. The dispadmin command implements this ability. This command builds the new scheduling values for the table supplied as input. It does a limited amount of checking on the values supplied in the table, mainly to verify that the values are within required bounds. The checking does not, in any way, attempt to analyze the effect the new values will have on performance. As one would guess, inappropriate values can really mess things up.

Typically, the command is used twice. First, it is used to dump the current options to a file. The file is modified and then the command is used again to read the table and update the values.

The first step is accomplished with a command similar to the following:

```
dispadmin -c TS -g -r 100 >/usr/local/mods/TS_scheduler
```

This command retrieves the current scheduler parameters for the time-sharing class from the kernel memory and writes them to standard output, which is redirected to the file /usr/local/mods/TS_scheduler.

At this point, modifications are made to the table in the /usr/local/mods/TS_scheduler file (Fig. 10-6). The table consists of a line for each priority level that details six data items:

PRIORITY LEVEL—the dispatch priority.

ts_quantum—the number of CPU ticks (at a rate of 100 ticks per second) the process is allowed to run before being switched out.

ts_tqexp—the new priority of the process the next time it runs if it uses all of the ts_quantum time.

ts_slpret—the priority of the process when it becomes runable after sleeping.

ts_maxwait—the maximum number of seconds a process will wait before getting its full time quantum. A value of zero indicates no wait.

ts_lwait—new priority of a process that has waited maxwait and has not used all of its ts_quantum.

Once the modifications to the file are complete, the following command can be used to overwrite the current scheduler values with the values in the /usr/local/mods/TS_scheduler file:

```
dispadmin -c TS -s /usr/local/mods/TS_scheduler
```

The new values will take effect immediately. However, they will not remain in effect over a system reboot.

Some Common Problems and Suggestions for Improvement

There is a class of problems regarding system activity and workload management that are very common. The following areas are some items to look out for:

- *Identical jobs owned by the same user.*   In almost all cases this is some type of error, either by the user or the program.

- *Processes with large amounts of CPU time.*   This is a classic symptom of a program in an infinite loop.

- *Processes consuming large amounts of memory.*   This is another classic symptom of a program problem.

```
dispadmin -c TS -g
# Time Sharing Dispatcher Configuration
RES=1000
```

# ts_quantum	ts_tqexp	ts_slpret	ts_maxwait	ts_lwait	PRIORITY	LEVEL
200	0	50	0	50	#	0
200	0	50	0	50	#	1
200	0	50	0	50	#	2
200	0	50	0	50	#	3
200	0	50	0	50	#	4
200	0	50	0	50	#	5
200	0	50	0	50	#	6
200	0	50	0	50	#	7
200	0	50	0	50	#	8
200	0	50	0	50	#	9
160	0	51	0	51	#	10
160	1	51	0	51	#	11
160	2	51	0	51	#	12
160	3	51	0	51	#	13
160	4	51	0	51	#	14
160	5	51	0	51	#	15
160	6	51	0	51	#	16
160	7	51	0	51	#	17
160	8	51	0	51	#	18
160	9	51	0	51	#	19
120	10	52	0	52	#	20
120	11	52	0	52	#	21
120	12	52	0	52	#	22
120	13	52	0	52	#	23
120	14	52	0	52	#	24
120	15	52	0	52	#	25
120	16	52	0	52	#	26
120	17	52	0	52	#	27
120	18	52	0	52	#	28
120	19	52	0	52	#	29
80	20	53	0	53	#	30
80	21	53	0	53	#	31
80	22	53	0	53	#	32
80	23	53	0	53	#	33
80	24	53	0	53	#	34
80	25	54	0	54	#	35
80	26	54	0	54	#	36
80	27	54	0	54	#	37
80	28	54	0	54	#	38
80	29	54	0	54	#	39
40	30	55	0	55	#	40
40	31	55	0	55	#	41
40	32	55	0	55	#	42
40	33	55	0	55	#	43
40	34	55	0	55	#	44
40	35	56	0	56	#	45
40	36	57	0	57	#	46
40	37	58	0	58	#	47
40	38	58	0	58	#	48
40	39	58	0	59	#	49
40	40	58	0	59	#	50
40	41	58	0	59	#	51
40	42	58	0	59	#	52
40	43	58	0	59	#	53
40	44	58	0	59	#	54
40	45	58	0	59	#	55
40	46	58	0	59	#	56
40	47	58	0	59	#	57
40	48	58	0	59	#	58
20	49	59	32000	59	#	59

Figure 10-6

dispadmin command output example.

■ *Processes running with too high of a priority.*   A process that is running as a real-time process will block the execution of all timesharing process. Verify that processes are running with correct priority by using the `ps -ecf` command.

■ *Too many long running jobs are active.*   Traditional "batch" jobs should be run during nonpeak times, if at all possible. Either lower the priority of the job, if it must run during peak time, or use the `at` command or `cron` table (Chap. 11) to schedule the job at a more convenient time.

■ *Don't run daemons that aren't necessary.*   For example, if the system does *not* use NFS, don't run the NFS daemons *automountd, mountd,* and *nfsd*. This seems simple, but many systems run daemons that are never really used. Stop *lp* and *lpsched* if the system does not support printing and disable *routed* unless the machine is really acting as a router. Don't run *nisd, cachemgr,* and *rpc.nisd_resolv* if the system does not use NIS+.

■ *Have users minimize directory search paths.*   As much as possible, limit the number of directories that are in the search path. Place large directories and directories that are used frequently at the beginning of the search path. These actions will minimize the start-up time for a command.

Other Useful Commands

The following commands are not strictly related to performance measurement or management. However, they can be useful in diagnosing some types of problems that may manifest themselves as performance problems.

prtconf—Print the System Configuration Data

The `prtconf` command is used to print system configuration information. The output (Fig. 10-7) details the total amount of memory and the configuration of system peripherals formatted as a device tree.

```
prtconf
System Configuration:  Sun Microsystems   sun4d
Memory size: 256 Megabytes
System Peripherals (Software Nodes):

SUNW,SPARCserver-1000
    packages (driver not attached)
        disk-label (driver not attached)
        deblocker (driver not attached)
        obp-tftp (driver not attached)
    options, instance #0
    aliases (driver not attached)
    memory (driver not attached)
    virtual-memory (driver not attached)
    openprom (driver not attached)
    boards (driver not attached)
        bif (driver not attached)
        bif (driver not attached)
    cpu-unit, instance #0
        TI,TMS390Z55, instance #0
        bootbus, instance #0
            zs, instance #0
            zs, instance #1
            eeprom (driver not attached)
            sram (driver not attached)
            leds (driver not attached)
    cpu-unit, instance #1
        TI,TMS390Z55, instance #1
    cpu-unit, instance #2
        TI,TMS390Z55, instance #2
        bootbus, instance #1
            zs, instance #2
            zs, instance #3
            eeprom (driver not attached)
            sram (driver not attached)
            leds (driver not attached)
    cpu-unit, instance #3
        TI,TMS390Z55, instance #3
    mem-unit, instance #4
    mem-unit, instance #5
    io-unit, instance #6
        sbi, instance #0
            dma, instance #0
                esp, instance #0
                    sd (driver not attached)
                    st (driver not attached)
                    sd, instance #0
                    sd, instance #1
                    sd, instance #2 (driver not attached)
                    sd, instance #3 (driver not attached)
                    sd, instance #4 (driver not attached)
                    sd, instance #5 (driver not attached)
                    sd, instance #6
                    st, instance #0 (driver not attached)
                    st, instance #1 (driver not attached)
                    st, instance #2 (driver not attached)
                    st, instance #3 (driver not attached)
                    st, instance #4
                    st, instance #5
                    st, instance #6 (driver not attached)
                lebuffer, instance #0
```

Figure 10-7

prtconf example output.

```
           le, instance #0
       cgsix, instance #0
       SUNW,soc, instance #0
           SUNW,pln (driver not attached)
               SUNW,ssd (driver not attached)
           SUNW,pln (driver not attached)
               SUNW,ssd (driver not attached)
           SUNW,pln, instance #0
               ssd, instance #0
               ssd, instance #1
               ssd, instance #2
               ssd, instance #3 (driver not attached)
               ssd, instance #4 (driver not attached)
               ssd, instance #5
               ssd, instance #6
               ssd, instance #7
               ssd, instance #8 (driver not attached)
               ssd, instance #9 (driver not attached)
               ssd, instance #10
               ssd, instance #11
               ssd, instance #12
               ssd, instance #13 (driver not attached)
               ssd, instance #14 (driver not attached)
               ssd, instance #15
               ssd, instance #16
               ssd, instance #17
               ssd, instance #18 (driver not attached)
               ssd, instance #19 (driver not attached)
               ssd, instance #20
               ssd, instance #21
               ssd, instance #22
               ssd, instance #23 (driver not attached)
               ssd, instance #24 (driver not attached)
               ssd, instance #25
               ssd, instance #26
               ssd, instance #27
               ssd, instance #28 (driver not attached)
               ssd, instance #29 (driver not attached)
io-unit, instance #7
    sbi, instance #1
        dma, instance #1
            esp, instance #1
                sd (driver not attached)
                st (driver not attached)
                sd, instance #15 (driver not attached)
                sd, instance #16 (driver not attached)
                sd, instance #17 (driver not attached)
                sd, instance #18 (driver not attached)
                sd, instance #19 (driver not attached)
                sd, instance #20 (driver not attached)
                sd, instance #21 (driver not attached)
                st, instance #7 (driver not attached)
                st, instance #8 (driver not attached)
                st, instance #9 (driver not attached)
                st, instance #10 (driver not attached)
                st, instance #11 (driver not attached)
                st, instance #12 (driver not attached)
                st, instance #13 (driver not attached)
        lebuffer, instance #1
            le, instance #1
pseudo, instance #0
```

Figure 10-7

(Continued) `prtconf` example output.

Four options are available:

-P Includes information about pseudo devices

-v Specifies verbose mode

-F Returns the device pathname of the console frame buffer, if one exists (SPARC only)

-p Displays information derived from the device tree provided by the firmware (SPARC only)

prtdiag—Print System Diagnostic Information

prtdiag displays system configuration and diagnostic information. The diagnostic information lists any failed Field Replaceable Units (FRUs) in the system. prtdiag is supported only on sun4d or later machines. When used with the -v option, the command also displays the time of the most recent ac power failure and the most recent system watchdog information.

psrinfo—Prints Information about Configured Processors

psrinfo shows information on configured processors (Fig. 10-8). Without arguments, it prints a line for each processor, indicating whether it is on-line or off-line and when the status last changed. When used with the -v option, the command also shows information about the processor type and clock speed.

```
$ psrinfo
0       on-line     since 09/22/97 17:38:18
1       on-line     since 09/22/97 17:38:18
2       on-line     since 09/22/97 17:38:18
3       on-line     since 09/22/97 17:38:18
```

Figure 10-8
psrinfo example output.

psradm—Set Processors On-line or Off-line

psradm takes a processor off-line or brings it on-line. An off-line processor does little or no work. The actual effect of being off-line may vary from machine to machine.

The options used by the command are:

-f procid... Take the specified processor procid off-line.

-n Bring the specified processors on-line.

-a Perform the action on all processors or on as many as possible.

-v Output a message giving the results of each attempted operation.

This command may only be executed by root or the system administrator. A processor may not be taken off-line if there are LWPs that are bound to the processor. On some architectures, it might not be possible to take certain processors off-line if the system depends on some resource provided by the processor.

At least one processor must always be on-line.

sundiag—Hardware Diagnostic Program

sundiag is a diagnostic utility that runs stress tests on hardware devices. Only the system administrator or root can use the command.

The sundiag program consists of the sundiag window-based user interface, along with modules and executable files that perform the actual tests. A command-based interface is also available.

For further information on sundiag, consult the *SunDiag User's Guide*.

Summary

In this chapter, the basic procedures and commands for monitoring activity and workloads were investigated. These commands can be divided into three categories:

- **System monitoring** (uptime, w, whodo, ps, mpstat)
- **Process management** (nice, renice, priocntl, pbind, dispadmin)

■ System configuration and maintenance (`prtconf`, `prtdiag`, `psrinfo`, `psradm`, `sundiag`)

In the next chapter, we will look at the commands that are used for managing and monitoring memory on the system.

Memory Management

Memory can become a constraining factor in system performance when the running processes require more physical memory than is present on the machine. In Chap. 6, the concept of virtual memory was introduced. In that discussion, it was stated that the complete address space of the process does not have to reside in physical memory at all times. Those parts of the process that are not currently being used may be *paged out,* that is, copied to a backing store for retrieval at a later point. Once the page is copied out to the backing store, the system can reuse the physical page for another process.

When a process is paged out, its overall performance decreases. Even with the fastest processor and I/O system, some degradation will occur. When several processes are being paged, overall system performance will suffer.

In some respects, memory problems are very simple: Either there is enough or there isn't. However, the answers to memory problems are not simple. In most cases, there is no cost justification to having extended amounts of memory available just to prevent paging. Of course, there are some exceptions to this, but in the majority of cases, some paging is normal and even expected.

The purpose of this chapter is to outline the methods used to determine whether and how much paging is occurring. After having identified the problem, some methods of alleviating performance problems due to paging will be discussed.

Paging versus Swapping

In Solaris, as with all UNIX-based operating systems, a differentiation is made between *paging* and *swapping*. Paging moves individual pages of a process to and from the *swap space* on disk. Swapping moves the entire address space of the process to and from the swap space in one fell swoop. Clearly, swapping is a more drastic action than paging.

There are two circumstances under which swapping can occur. The first is somewhat benign and is more related to housekeeping than any actual problem. Solaris will set a process *eligible* for swap if the process goes into a sleep state for more than 20 s.* Note that this does not mean the process will be swapped; it only indicates the process is eligible for swapping. This is a perfectly reasonable thing to do. If the process is not doing anything, there is no reason for it to be occupying physical memory that could be better used for other processes.

The second circumstance that leads to swapping is not good and indicates a serious performance problem. In the second case, the number of free memory pages falls below the minimum amount specified by the *minfree* or *desfree* parameters in the /etc/system table.† Because the paging mechanism is not able to handle the requests for physical memory pages, the swap mechanism is invoked to free up more pages quickly. Unfortunately, this is a relatively slow process that involves a lot of I/O. Although the swap mechanism tries to avoid swapping active processes, interactive process performance will degrade quickly and significantly whenever there is paging.

---

*This value can be changed with the maxslp parameter in the /etc/system file.

†In Solaris 2.4, these values are automatically set by the kernel and are not easily modified by the system administrator.

The reason for this seeming anomaly is simple: Interactive processes tend to be inactive most of the time. Editors, shells, and data entry applications spend most of their time waiting for user input. During this time, they are inactive and are prime candidates for swap out when the system is overburdened.

Demand Paging

The basic underlying principle of *demand paging* is that the operating system does not bring a page for process into physical storage until the page is actually needed. This makes for very efficient use of system resources, but it can also skew paging and swapping statistics.

When a new process starts, Solaris uses the demand paging mechanism to load the new process. Instead of copying the entire program into memory, Solaris only sets up the memory maps for the address space. Once set up, a jump is performed to the beginning address of the program. This, in turn, causes a page fault, which results in the first page of the program being read into physical memory. As the program executes, additional pages are read into physical memory as needed.

As a result of this, page-in (for the program) and swap-in (for the address space as a whole) activity may happen with great frequency. It is completely normal and expected and does not indicate a type of memory shortage problem. Neither of these variables are useful in locating performance problems.

Paging Problem Indicators

The important statistics to monitor for indications of paging problems are the number of page outs and swap outs. As discussed above page ins and swap ins are not necessarily indicative of excessive or abnormal system load. Page outs and swap outs do point to a lack of adequate physical storage given the current workload.

Paging and swapping are designed to help alleviate problems. This implies that their application by the system indicates a problem. This may or may not be true. If a system is continually paging out, it is time to consider a memory upgrade. If a system swaps out often (e.g., several times a day), a memory upgrade is required. However, if a system swaps out only on occasion, due to unusual circumstances, it is probably nothing to worry about. Furthermore, if a system consistently has a low page-out rate that does not seem to significantly affect performance, that is probably acceptable as well. But, the situation needs to be monitored carefully to ensure that the paging rate does not slowly creep up and develop into a major problem.

Monitoring Paging and Swapping

There are two primary tools for monitoring paging and swapping. The sar command generates detailed long-term reports and is discussed in Chap. 12. The most commonly used command for "snapshot" reporting is vmstat.

vmstat

The vmstat command reports on virtual memory statistics and CPU load: paging, swapping, context switches, CPU utilization by state. The syntax of the command is

```
vmstat [-cisS] [d1 d2 d3 d4] [interval [count]]
```

When used without options, vmstat displays a one-line summary of activity since the system was booted. If *interval* is specified, the following lines summarize activity during the last *interval* seconds, repeating until the command is interrupted via user intervention. When a *count* is also supplied, the statistics are displayed for the *count* number of times.

If a disk name (e.g., d1, d2, etc.), is specified, these disks are given display priority. Normally, the first four disk devices on the system are displayed. Because only four devices can be displayed on a line, this option allows the performance analyst to override the default display option.*

As seen in Fig. 11-1, the vmstat command displays several fields of information:

procs   Reports on the number of processes in the three states:

      r—in run queue waiting to run

      b—blocked for resources (I/O, paging, etc.)

---

*Disk names generally follow the naming convention of id, sd, xd, or xy (depending on type and I/O interface), followed by a number (e.g., id0, sd2, xd1, etc.).

procs			memory		page							disk				faults			cpu		
r	b	w	swap	free	re	mf	pi	po	fr	de	sr	s0	s1	sd	sd	in	sy	cs	us	sy	id
0	0	0	15332	3064	0	75	20	9	18	0	3	3	3	0	0	104	488	148	2	3	95
0	0	0	797596	53392	0	6	0	0	0	0	0	2	0	0	0	45	138	81	0	2	98
0	0	0	798080	53632	0	3	0	0	0	0	0	0	0	0	0	41	92	91	0	1	99
0	0	0	798724	53948	0	0	0	0	0	0	0	0	0	0	0	26	47	53	0	0	100
0	0	0	798724	53932	0	0	6	0	0	0	0	0	0	0	0	55	319	97	1	2	97
0	0	0	798724	53920	0	1	0	0	0	0	0	0	0	0	0	66	196	122	0	1	99
0	0	0	798724	53900	0	0	6	0	0	0	0	1	0	0	0	84	400	125	0	2	98
0	0	0	798432	53868	0	41	0	0	0	0	0	0	0	0	0	126	467	164	0	4	96
0	0	0	797968	53688	0	89	0	0	0	0	0	0	0	0	0	65	336	103	1	1	98
0	0	0	797356	53504	0	38	0	0	0	0	0	0	0	0	0	45	140	84	0	2	98

Figure 11-1
vmstat command output.

w—runable but swapped out

memory   Reports on virtual and real memory:

swap—amount of swap space currently available in kilobytes

free—size of the free list in kilobytes

page   Reports information about paging activity in numbers per second:

re—page reclaims from the free list

mf—minor faults; address space or hardware address translation faults

pi—kilobytes paged in

po—kilobytes paged out

fr—kilobytes freed

de—anticipated short-term memory shortfall in kilobytes

sr—pages scanned by clock algorithm

disk   Reports the number of disk I/Os per second for up to four disks faults   Reports the system trap and interrupt rates per second:

    in—device interrupts, not including system clock interrupts

    sy—system calls

    cs—CPU context switches

cpu—A breakdown of percentage of CPU time. On multiprocessor systems, this is an average across all processors:

    us—user time

    sy—system time

    id—idle time

Four optional flags may be used with the vmstat command. The -c flag (Fig. 11-2) changes the output to report cache flushing statistics, if the machine has a virtual address cache. The report includes the total number of each kind of cache flushed since the system was booted. The six cache types are user, context, region, segment, page, and partial-page.

The -i flag (Fig. 11-3) changes the output to report the number of interrupts. Per-device statistics are given if a device name is supplied, as in d1, d2, etc., and monitoring is being performed at the device level.*

The -s flag (Fig. 11-4) displays a summary report of system events from the time the system was booted.

The -S flag (Fig. 11-5) modifies the "generic" report to give information on swapping rather than paging activity. This option changes two fields in the display: instead of the re and mf fields, si (swap ins) and so (swap outs) are used instead.

---

*See Chap. 12 for information on turning device-level monitoring on.

Figure 11-2
vmstat -c command output.

```
$ vmstat -c
flush statistics: (totals)
     usr       ctx       rgn       seg       pag       par
       0         0         0         0         0         0
```

Figure 11-3
vmstat -i command output.

```
vmstat -i
interrupt              total      rate
-------------------------------------
clock            110649076       100
-------------------------------------
Total            110649076       100
```

Figure 11-4
vmstat -s com-
mand output.

```
vmstat -s
        0 swap ins
        0 swap outs
        0 pages swapped in
        0 pages swapped out
 83375114 total address trans. faults taken
  1863365 page ins
   607581 page outs
  5702283 pages paged in
  2511209 pages paged out
   958355 total reclaims
   936793 reclaims from free list
        0 micro (hat) faults
 83375114 minor (as) faults
  1099996 major faults
 23921604 copy-on-write faults
 14518470 zero fill page faults
  3860092 pages examined by the clock daemon
       60 revolutions of the clock hand
  5015417 pages freed by the clock daemon
   631523 forks
   114631 vforks
   571709 execs
164166764 cpu context switches
226657284 device interrupts
118985597 traps
540600976 system calls
191707572 total name lookups (cache hits 4294967295%)
   238332 toolong
  8826063 user    cpu
 14447036 system cpu
377801586 idle    cpu
 41524705 wait    cpu
```

Worth noting is that the *interval* and *count* options are not valid with either the -i or -s options.

swap

The other useful command for monitoring paging and swapping is the swap command. The swap command is the general interface to adding, deleting, and monitoring the system swap areas.

The swap -s command is used to print summary information about swap space usage and availability. For each space, the columns in the report (Fig. 11-6) include

```
Symbol 0    Courier New $ vmstat 1 5 -S procs          memory                              page
          disk           faults        cpu r b w   swap   free   re   mf  pi po fr de sr
 s1 s2 s3 s5   in    sy   cs us sy id 0 0 0    4996   1544    0    3   0  0  0  0  0
  0  0  0  0  201   47   18  1  3 97 0 0 0   80812   1936    0   12   0  0  0  0  0
  0  0  0  0  0  176   15   15  0  4 96 0 0 0   80812   1936    0    0   0  0  0  0  0
  0  0  0  0  0  189   11   17  0  0 100 0 0 0   80812   1936    0    0   0  0  0  0  0
  0  0  0  0  0  178   11   12  0  0 100 0 0 0   80812   1936    0    0   0  0  0  0
  0  0  0  0  0  0  184   11   14  0  1 99
```

Microsoft Word 6.0 Document   MSWordDoc   Word.Document.6

Figure 11-5

vmstat -S command output.

```
swap -s
total: 37004k bytes allocated + 52640k reserved = 89644k used, 82212k
available
```

Figure 11-6
swap -s command output.

allocated	Total amount of swap space (in 1K blocks) currently allocated
reserved	Total amount of swap space (in 1K blocks) not allocated but claimed for future use
used	Total of the allocated and reserved areas
available	Total swap space (in 1K blocks) that is not current allocated or reserved

These numbers include swap space from all configured areas as well swap space in the form of physical memory.

The swap -l command is used to list the status of each individual swap area. The report produced (Fig. 11-7) has five columns:

path	Path name for the swap area
dev	Major/minor device number in decimal if it is a block special device; zeros otherwise
swaplo	*Swaplow* value for the area in 512-byte blocks
blocks	*Swaplen* value for the area in 512-byte blocks
free	Number of 512-byte blocks in the area that are not currently allocated

The value *INDEL* appears in a sixth column if the area is in the process of being deleted.

The syntax for the swap command when adding a swap space is

```
swap -a swapname [swaplow [swaplen]]
```

This form of the command can only be used by root or the system administrator. The person using this command must be very careful because no checking is done to ensure that the swap area does not overlap an existing file system.

Figure 11-7
swap -l command output.

```
swap -l
swapfile            dev  swaplo blocks   free
/dev/dsk/c0t3d0s1   32,25      8 132040 119944
/dev/dsk/c0t1d0s1   32,9       8 132040 120176
```

In the command syntax, *swapname* denotes the name of the swap file, either a slice (or partition) of a disk, such as /dev/dsk/c0t0d3s1, or a regular file.

Optionally, *swaplow* and *swaplen* may be specified. *swaplow* is used to indicate where the swap area is to begin. It is an offset (in 512-byte blocks) from the first block of the file or slice. If *swaplow* is not specified, the swap area begins at the second block of the file or slice.* *swaplen* denotes the length of the swap area in 512-byte blocks. If no *swaplen* is specified, the space from *swaplow* to the end of the file or slice will be allocated as swap space. If the value is specified, it cannot be less than 16. When both are specified, *swaplow+swaplen* must be less than or equal to the size of the swap file.

Once defined with the swap command, swap areas are added to the system automatically during system start-up via the /sbin/swapadd script, which adds all swap areas that are defined in the /etc/vfstab file.

Swap space may be deleted with the command

```
swap -d swapname
```

Once the last process using the space has exited, the swap space will be removed from the system.

Paging Performance Tips

In general, the following guidelines can be used to determine whether a problem exists.

Swap space should never go below 32MB.   When swap space goes below this point, the system can quickly run out of virtual memory. At this point, process should be stopped or swap space should be added. When swap space goes below 4MB, the system will soon run out of swap space. Some applications should be terminated immediately. If swap space goes below 1MB, programs will fail and the kernel may panic. If it is still possible, applications should be terminated until the swap amount returns to a level above 32MB.

---

*The first block of any swap area is used for storing control information about the swap area.

The freepage scan rate should not go over 192 pages per second. Scan rates greater than this indicate a serious physical memory shortage is developing. If the scan rate rises above 320 pages, active as well as inactive pages will be stolen from processes. This can easily lead to a *thrashing* situation where the kernel is simply paging *processes* in and out and not doing any real work.

Resolving and Avoiding Memory Problems

In all cases, adding memory to a system will help alleviate problems associated with physical memory. But there are also many other actions that can be taken to forestall or mitigate physical memory shortfalls.

Program Development Issues

Performance tuning starts during the application development phase. The following items should be considered during programming:

- *Ensure that all programs use shared libraries.* Shared libraries allow multiple programs to share common code in library routines. Although shared libraries is the default in all of the SUN compilers, an individual can override this. Contrary to what some may believe, there is no performance penalty for using shared libraries.

- *Perform quality control.* Make sure programs maximize *locality of reference** and allocate and deallocate memory appropriately. Holding onto memory blocks when they are not needed is not good for the system overall; however, allocating and reallocating the same memory over and over is not effective either.

- *Use the* mmap *system call for file access.* This function maps files into the process address space, bypassing the overhead of copying to and from a user buffer. Because files may be shared

---

*Locality of reference refers to the concept of concentrating references to specific areas of memory rather than scattered access to various parts of memory. This is especially an issue regarding access to data items in arrays.

with this call, more efficient memory use will result if a file is used by more than one process at a time.

■ *Always use the highest level of compiler optimization possible.* For most compilers, this is level -O3 or, if available, -O4. For device drivers, the *volatile* keyword must be specified if a level higher than -O2 is to be used.

■ *If the process uses multiple threads use the parallelizing optimizer.* This will enable the process to use multiple processors on machines that have them.

End-user Application Execution Issues

Although the user environment can be customized to constrain a program that is using too many system resources, this is easily overridden by the user. Therefore, it is limited in its usefulness as a serious system performance tuning tool. More information on these limits can be found in Chap. 15.

System Configuration Issues

Unlike many other UNIX-based operating systems, the Solaris kernel does not, in general, need buffer tuning. Solaris is designed to expand and contract these pools as needed, so the traditional advice in regard to these items is inappropriate for Solaris.

There are, however, three tunable parameters that can significantly affect the memory subsystem. The first is the distribution and size of the swap areas. In general, swap space should be distributed across as many different disk drives as possible. The exception to this is when there are disk drives that are significantly slower or more heavily used than others. For example, consider a machine running on an Intel architecture with both SCSI and IDE drives. In this case, the system administrator would want to keep the swap space off the IDE drives because they are inherently less efficient than a SCSI drive.* Furthermore, on a SPARC-based machine, the swap areas would probably not be placed on the same drives as those used for a major transaction processing database. The contention would most likely be too great.

---

*This is discussed more completely in Chap. 12.

The second parameter is the value of the *maxslp* variable in the /etc/system file. As stated previously, any process that has been asleep for more than 20 s is eligible to be swapped. Because several system tasks (disk synchronization and system clock, to name two) sleep for periods longer than this, they become eligible for swapping with great frequency. The system will only keep track of process sleep time for a maximum of 127 s because the process sleep time value is stored in a single byte. By setting the value of *maxslp* to 128, it is possible to suppress this check for process sleep time entirely.

The final set of parameters that can be explored is to modify the paging mechanism so scanning for free pages starts sooner and occurs more quickly if paging is not happening fast enough. Alternatively, these can also be used to slow paging down if too many pages are going onto the free list unnecessarily. This is done by modifying the values of *fastscan, slowscan,* and *handspreadpages* in the /etc/system file. In general, modifying these parameters is not recommended. Versions of Solaris after 2.3 are quite adept at adapting to the changing workload of a system. It is unlikely that manual modification of these parameters will have a positive effect on system performance.

Summary

Memory management primarily involves the control and administration of the paging and swapping activity of the system. The vmstat and swap commands are the major ones used to monitor this activity. In addition, this chapter examined the major indications of memory problem and how to resolve and avoid them. The concluding part of the chapter discussed the memory issues related to program development, end-user application execution, and system configuration.

The next chapter discusses the issues involved in managing and tuning the I/O subsystem.

CHAPTER **12**

I/O Performance Management

Issues in I/O performance management divide very neatly between hardware and software. Both factors must be considered when evaluating performance problems. The most efficiently constructed file system will not perform well if it is implemented on slow hardware, regardless of the tuning effort expended. In this chapter, the physical and logical implementations of file systems will be investigated, along with some common problems and solutions.

Disk Performance Tuning Basics

In most, but not all, systems, disk performance is the most critical aspect of performance tuning. Considering that disk performance affects data caching, swapping, and print spooling, this is not surprising.

In general, tuning disk performance revolves around two basic optimizations:

1. Overall system disk I/O throughput

2. Disk storage efficiency

These are often incompatible goals.

Overall system disk throughput optimization starts at the process level. If a system can deliver outstanding per-process throughput rates, most likely the overall system throughput rate will also be outstanding. But this is not guaranteed. Processes can and do compete for the same resources. One example would be the case where one process is reading a file sequentially and another process is reading the same file randomly. The conflicting usage pattern between the two will slow down access for both processes. The same is true for two processes that are reading separate files where one file is at the outside edge of the disk and the second file is at the inside edge of the disk.

Optimizing storage efficiency often has a negative impact on access efficiency. The classic example of this is increasing the block size of a file system to enhance throughput. Larger block sizes waste more space on disk than small block sizes, although Solaris has provided block fragmenting (discussed below) to help alleviate this problem.

Hardware Considerations

The three factors affecting the physical performance of a disk are *seek latency, rotational latency,* and *data transfer rate.*

As discussed in Chap. 2, *seek latency* (Fig. 12-1) is the time that is required to position the disk head over the desired cylinder. Once the head has been positioned, *rotational latency* (Fig. 12-2) is the amount of time it takes for the required block to spin under the head. Once the data has been read, the *data transfer rate* determines how quickly the data reaches the system unit. Each factor contributes to the overall speed of data transfer.

Figure 12-1
Seek latency.

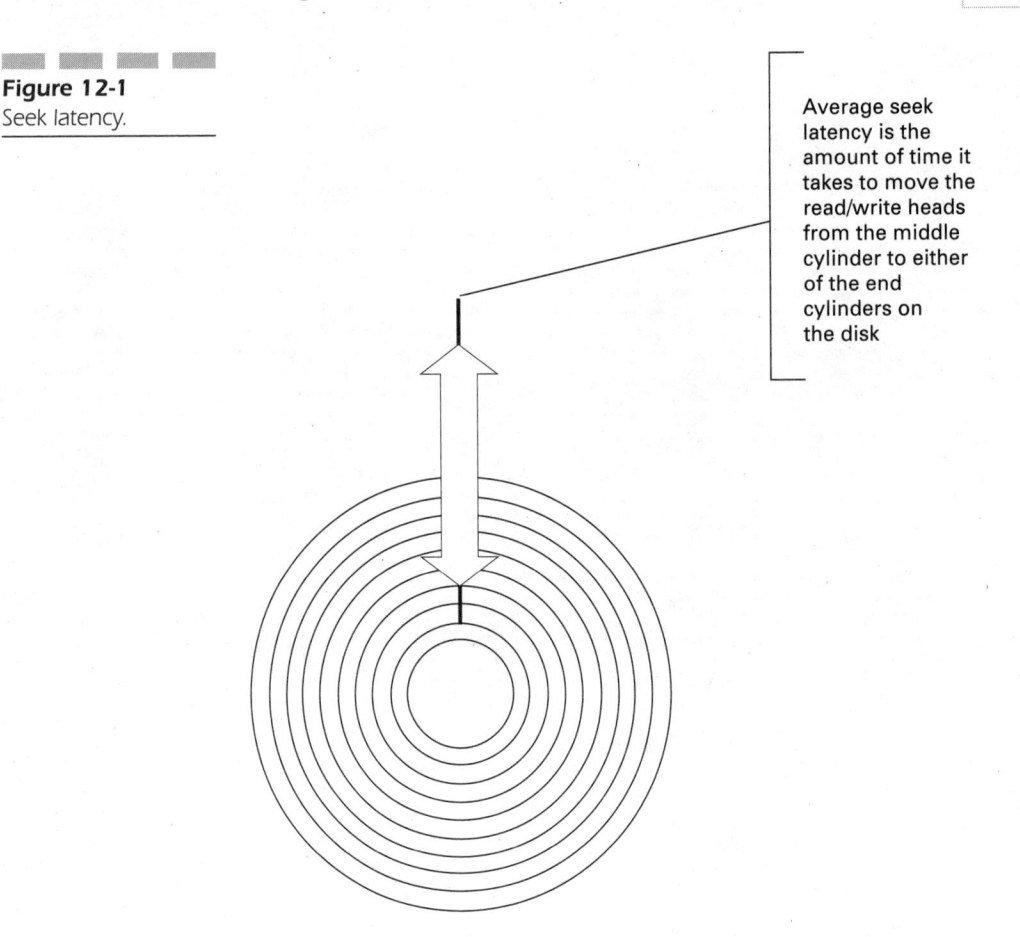

Average seek latency is the amount of time it takes to move the read/write heads from the middle cylinder to either of the end cylinders on the disk

In the best of circumstances, there will be no seek or rotational latency. This, of course, is a very rare occurrence. In most cases, the read/write head will have to be positioned and wait for the data to rotate underneath it. The average amount of time it takes for this to happen is expressed as the *access time* of the device.

In general, the formula for determining the access time is

Access time = average seek latency time + average rotational latency
              time

The problem is that there is no standard definition of either average seek latency or average rotational latency.

The *full-travel* time of a disk is the amount of time it takes to position the head from the innermost track to the outermost track. The *track-to-*

Figure 12-2
Rotational latency.

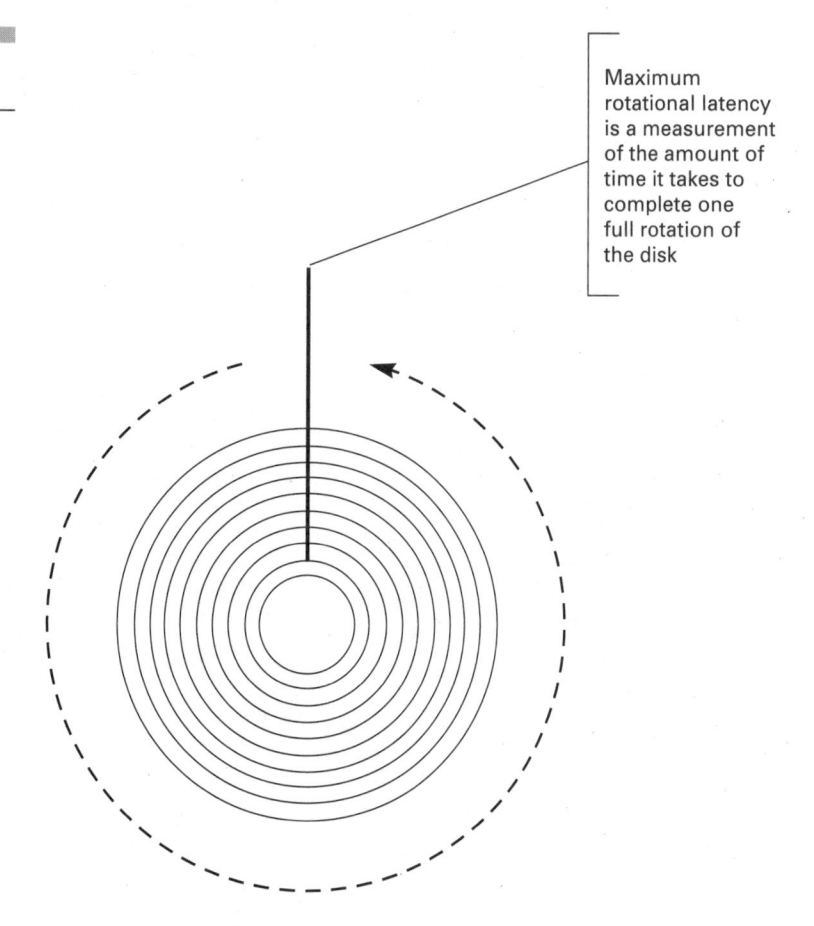

Maximum
rotational latency
is a measurement
of the amount of
time it takes to
complete one
full rotation of
the disk

track time is the time it takes to move the head one track. Some manufacturers compute the average time as

$$\text{Average seek latency} = \frac{\text{full-travel time} + \text{track-to-track time}}{2}$$

Others compute it as the amount of time it takes to move from either of
the edge tracks to the middle track of the disk. Still others use the
amount of time it takes to move from the edge to one-third of the way
into the disk. This is justified by studies that show that "average" seeks
do not move all the way, or even half the way, across a disk but instead
move about a third of the way through. The important issue is that if
the performance analysts do not do their own measurements, they must
be careful to ensure that comparisons among average times are based on
average times that are based on the same criteria.

Rotational latency is less obscure. In the worst case, the read/write head will be positioned to the proper cylinder just as the desired block has just started to pass underneath. This will lead to a *maximum rotational latency* time, which is the amount of time it takes for the disk to complete one full revolution. As one could guess, rotational latency is dependent on rotational speed of the disk platters. The faster the rotation, the lower the rotational latency. The average rotational latency speed is the maximum speed divided by 2.

Computing Maximum Throughput Rate

In addition to the above ratings, disk drives are usually rated in relationship to size. Size is determined by the number of platters and, by extension, the number of heads available to read data and the number of tracks per platter. The size is influenced by how the disk is formatted, which determines the number of sectors* per track and their size.

Knowing these factors and the rotational speed of the disk, it is relatively simple to compute the peak sustained data rate of the device:†

$$\text{Peak sustained data rate per second} = \frac{(\text{number of sectors} * \text{sector size in bytes} * \text{rotational speed})}{60}$$

Now having said this, this still is only an approximate guess. The above calculation assumes that all tracks store an equivalent amount of data and rotate at the same speed. By definition, the geometry of disk devices makes the outside tracks larger and rotate faster. As the heads move from the outside to the inside track, the performance decreases and the data density lowers.

In older disk drives, the drive was calibrated to the speed and density of the innermost tracks. Therefore, a lot of space was wasted on the outermost tracks. In order to make better use of the outermost tracks, all modern disk drives use a technique called *zoned encoding* (or *zoned bit rate*), which allows for more data to be stored on the outer tracks of the disk than on the inner tracks. This means that the number of sectors per track is not constant. A side effect of this is that access to data on

---

*In most cases, sectors are interchangeable with blocks.

†For reference, the formatted size of a device (that is, the size usable after formatting) is computed by the formula. Size in kilobytes = (number of sectors * sector size in bytes * number of heads * number of tracks)/1024.

the outermost tracks will be faster. Therefore, slice 0 (outermost) will be faster than slice 7 (innermost) on any given disk drive.

Disk Controllers and Interfaces

On Intel-based machines, there are two types of disk interfaces: AT Attachment/Integrated Drive Electronics (ATA/IDE) and Small Computer System Interface (SCSI). Each of these types has several subtypes that reflect the ongoing developments in technology. On SPARC-based machines, only SCSI types of interfaces are supported.

The combinations of SCSI types can be very confusing. The first implementation of SCSI, known as SCSI-1, used an 8-bit data bus at 5 MHz that yields a maximum throughput rate of about 5 Mbps. A single interface card supported concurrent operations on up to seven devices. SCSI-2, or *fast SCSI,* added a number of additional commands to enhance performance in addition to increasing the data rate to 10 Mbps. Soon after the release of fast SCSI, a *wide* option was made available that used 16-bit data paths and expanded the number of devices on a single interface to 15. *UltraSCSI* increases the data rate to 20 MB on an 8-bit data path. A wide UltraSCSI connection has a transfer rate of 40 Mbps. However, with UltraWide UltraSCSI has a transfer rate of 80 Mbps because the data path is 32 bits.

The SCSI-3 is a newly emerging standard that provides the basis for connections via high-speed interfaces such as fiber channel. The fiber channel interface is used by the SPARCstorage Disk Array. The interface has two 25-Mbps data channels that support bidirectional data transfer, unlike SCSI-1 and SCSI-2, which are unidirectional.

ATA/IDE interfaces are only used in Intel-based machines. A legacy of the original IBM PC implementation, the ATA/IDE interface is not as flexible or extendible as SCSI. However, given its widespread availability, ATA/IDE disk drives tend to be less expensive than SCSI drives.

The ATA/IDE interface uses a 16-bit wide interface and supports up to two drives with a maximum transfer rate of 3.33 Mbps. The ATA/IDE interface does not support concurrent operations, however, so only one device may be active on an interface at a time.

Enhancements to the ATA/IDE standard (known variously as ATA-2, FastATA, or EIDE) provide higher data transfer rates of up to 16.7 Mbps. This, of course, assumes the disk drives support that data transfer rate.

Obviously, the best performance will be gained by using the fastest interface possible. But it is important that the devices connected to the interface also run at a comparable speed. For example, very often, disk drives are shipped from the factory set to use the SCSI-1 interface, because it is the lowest common denominator. The performance analyst should check all disk drives attached to the system to make sure the jumper settings are correct given the SCSI interface card that is being used.

RAID

Redundant Arrays of Inexpensive Disk (RAID) is used for both performance and data integrity reasons. RAID systems can be implemented in software, such as Solstice DiskSuite, or used with hardware controllers to combine two or more disks in such a way that they function as if they were a single "unit" to Solaris. This allows for data to be distributed across multiple disks, which can increase fault tolerance and/or improve performance.

There are several levels of RAID implementations. The basic ones, RAID levels 0 through 5, are fairly standard across manufacturers. Some manufacturers supplement these with proprietary implementations with names such as RAID 30, RAID 50, etc.

RAID 0 is technically not RAID at all. When it is used, it is not implemented to increase fault tolerance but is used solely to increase performance. A RAID 0 array consists of two or more disk drives that are used in sequence to *stripe* the data (Fig. 12-3). Striping data simply means that the disk controller splits the data and places it on multiple drives. When the data is read, the controller pulls the information from all of the disks and reassembles it. Because the I/O load is distributed among the various disk drives, RAID 0 enhances overall I/O performance significantly for both read and write operations. However, because there is no redundancy, the failure of a single drive can cause data problems for all files stored on the array.

RAID 1 (Fig. 12-4) is also known as *mirroring*. In RAID 1, every device in the array contains the exact same data. RAID 1 provides a high level of fault tolerance and very good performance on read operations. However, write operations can result in very poor performance because the information must be updated on every drive in the array. RAID 1 is usually used only for applications where the majority of I/O

Figure 12-3
RAID 0.

Data blocks are evenly distributed over all disk devices, no redundancy

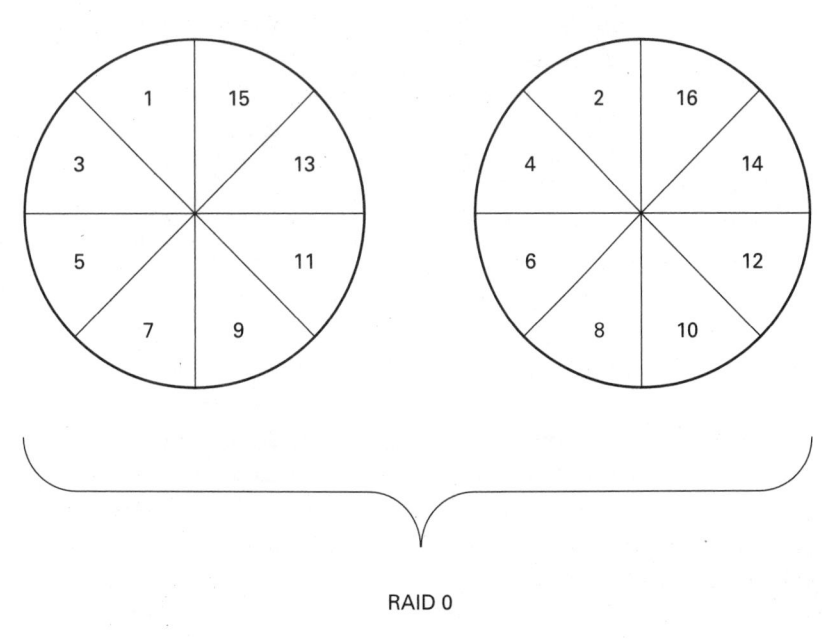

RAID 0

Figure 12-4
RAID 1.

Data blocks are duplicated over all disk devices; complete redundancy

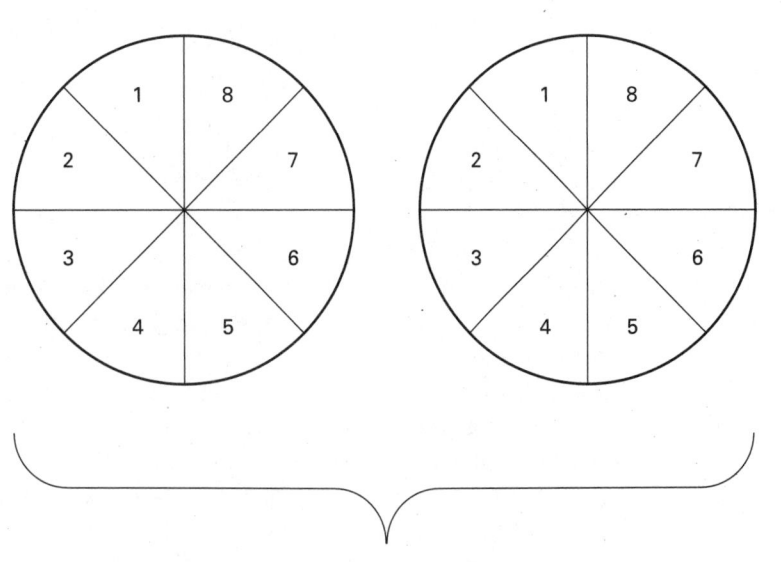

RAID 1

activity consists of reads, not writes. It would be an extremely poor choice for storing a database of a transaction processing system.

In RAID 2 systems, the data is organized in some word-size manner using either 8, 16, or 32 bits. Each bit of the word is sent to a different disk, and Hamming code error correction is applied to eliminate errors (Fig. 12-5). Because of the large investment in disk drives and the undue complexity given most applications, RAID 2 is rarely used.

RAID 3 (Fig. 12-6) uses all of the disks in the array except one for striping data in byte-sized units. The other disk is used to store parity information about the data on the other disks. RAID 3 provides good performance, almost as good as RAID 0, except that it includes fault tolerance. The parity disk allows errors to be detected and fixed. An important consideration with level 3 RAID is that if the parity disk goes bad, there is no fault tolerance.

RAID 4 is essentially the same as RAID 3 except that it uses block-sized units for striping and the parity disk instead of byte-sized units.

RAID 5 (Fig. 12-7) uses the concept of blocking from RAID 4 but intermingles the parity information across all drives. By using this mechanism, it provides for a high level of fault tolerance and good per-

Figure 12-5
RAID 2.

Data is divided into words and distributed over all disk devices; error correction code is used to eliminate errors; no data redundancy

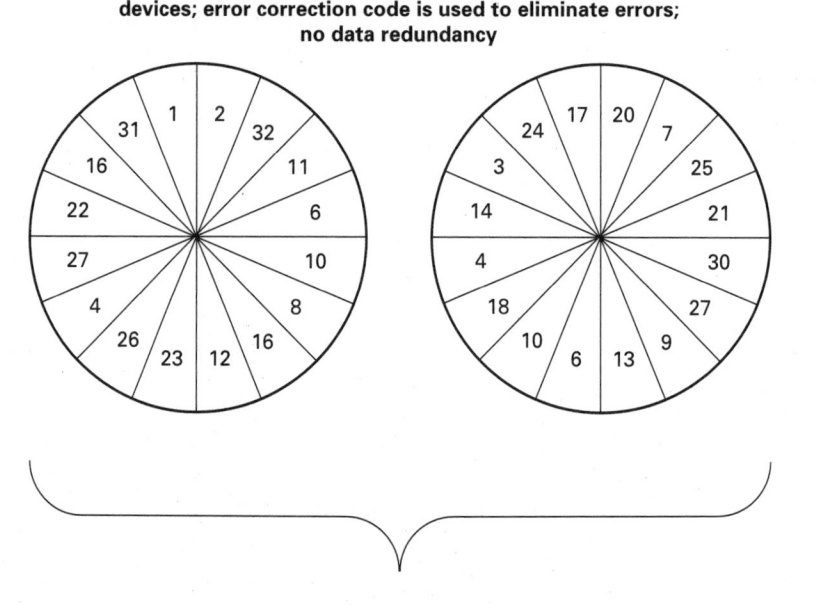

RAID 2

Figure 12-6
RAID 3.

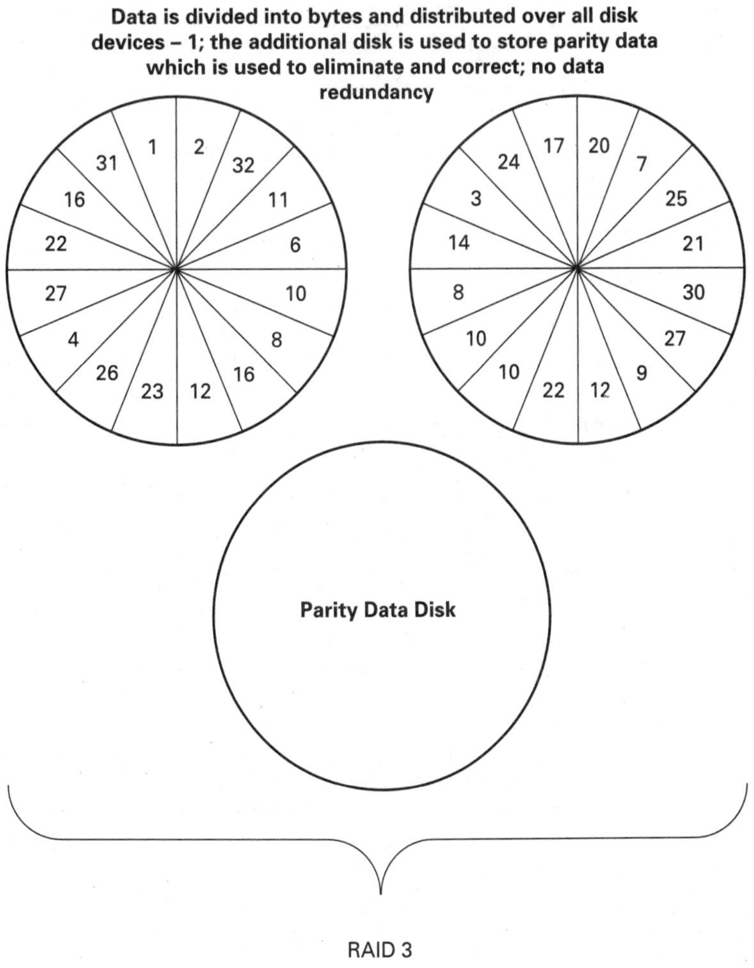
Data is divided into bytes and distributed over all disk devices – 1; the additional disk is used to store parity data which is used to eliminate and correct; no data redundancy
1
2
32
11
6
10
8
16
12
23
26
4
27
22
16
31
17
20
7
25
21
30
27
9
12
22
10
10
8
14
3
24
Parity Data Disk
RAID 3

formance. By intermingling the parity information across all drives, a RAID 5 array can lose a disk drive and still recover (actually, recreate) all of the lost data. This allows the array to be *hot swappable*; that is, a new drive can be insert while the system is running and the lost data can be rebuilt on the new drive based on the parity information from the existing drives. Finally, because RAID 5 uses blocking, the performance level is usually slightly better than RAID level 3 but not as good as level 0.

Figure 12-7
RAID 5.

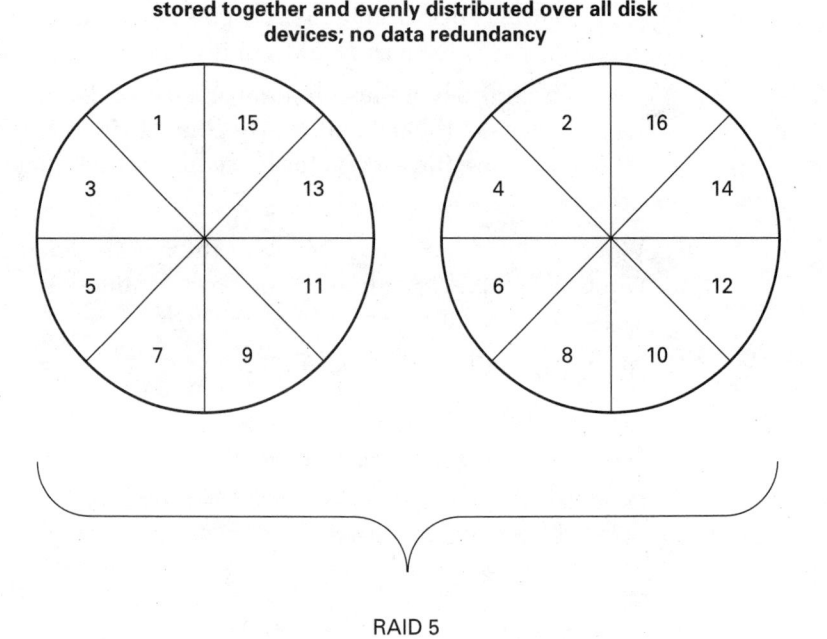

Data blocks and their associated parity information are
stored together and evenly distributed over all disk
devices; no data redundancy

RAID 5

File System Implementation Considerations

The parameters that affect file system performance are set when the file system is initially defined. Before delving into the specifics of what can be tweaked when creating a new file system, some general considerations about file systems should be outlined.

When considering the layout of a system, several factors should influence the design:

- I/O workload should be distributed as evenly as possible across the disk drives on the system; use Solstice DiskSuite to help automate this for most file systems.*

- Manually distribute swap areas across as many devices as possible; never create swap areas as files in existing file systems— always use a unique slice for the swap space, preferably slice 0.

---

*Bear in mind that Solstice DiskSuite cannot be used for the / (root) and /usr file systems.

■ Keep the number of file systems on any one disk to a minimum. Solaris is better able to manage fragmentation of a file system in a larger slice (partition) than it is in a small, crowded one.

■ If a large set of files (in number, size, or both) has characteristics that make them significantly different from "typical" files, create a separate file system for these files that is tuned to their requirements.

When a file system is created with the `newfs` command, a set of default values is applied to define the file system unless specifically overridden. These default values are

Block size of 8K.

Fragment size of 1K.

Minimum free space is 10 percent.

One inode for each 2K of space in the file system, and optimization is for space rather than speed.

Although it is possible to use the `tunefs` command to modify some of the parameters after definition, not all parameters can be changed after the file system is created, so it is simpler to use the `newfs` command* and define the file system as desired right from the beginning.†

Creating Optimized File Systems

`newfs` is a front end to the `mkfs` program and its subprograms. It is used to create file systems on disk partitions.

The `newfs` command is usually run without specifying the optional parameters that affect performance. To a great degree this is because the default parameters are OK in most cases. `newfs` calculates the appropriate parameters to use based on the information it can ascertain about the drive and calls the `mkfs` command, which actually creates the file system.‡ However, the performance analyst can optimize a file system for specific purposes by using the optional parameters wisely.

---

*The newfs command does not directly create a file system. The newfs command calls a lower-level command, mkfs, to perform the actual file system creation. There is no advantage to calling the command directly.

†On the other hand, some parameters of `tunefs` are not available in the `newfs` command.

‡Actually `mkfs`, in turn, calls other lower-level programs, such as `mkfs_ufs`, to create specific file system types.

The `newfs` command has two sets of option flags. The first set consists of only two flags, `-N` and `-v`. When the `-N` flag is used, the command does not create a file system, but only displays the system information about the file system, if it were to be created. This is demonstrated in Fig. 12-8. If this flag is used on an existing file system, this command *does not* display the current information from the file system; it displays what would happen if the file system were recreated. The other flag in this group, `-v`, displays the flags of the second group of options, also known as the `mkfs` options. The `-v` flag, if used by itself, will create a new file system. To see the flags that would be used if a new file system were created, make sure the `-N` option is also specified.

The `mkfs` options are used to control various aspects of the physical structure of the file system. These options include

-a abc. The number of alternate blocks per cylinder (SCSI devices only) to reserve for bad block replacement. The default value is 0.

-b bsize. The logical block size of the file system in bytes. The default is 8192, but this can be reduced to 4096.

-c cgize. The number of cylinders in a cylinder group. Valid values are 1 through 32. The default is 16.

-d gap. The expected minimum time, in milliseconds, to complete a data transfer and initiate a new request on the same cylinder. It is used to decide how much rotational spacing to place between adjacent blocks in a file. The default is disk-type dependent. For devices with track buffering, this value should be set to 0.

-f fragsize. The smallest amount of disk space in bytes to allocate to a file. The value must be a power of 2 greater than 512 but less than or equal to the logical block size. Legal values are 512, 1024, 2048, 4096, and 8192 if the logical block size 8192. The default is 1024.

-i nbpi. The number of bytes per inode. This number is used to calculate the fixed number of inodes in the file system. It should reflect the

```
newfs -n /dev/dsk/c0t1d0s1
/dev/rdsk/c0t1d0s1:      132048 sectors in 131 cylinders of 14 tracks, 72
sectors
      64.5MB in 9 cyl groups (16 c/g, 7.88MB/g, 3776 i/g)
super-block backups (for fsck -F ufs -o b=#) at:
 32, 16240, 32448, 48656, 64864, 81072, 97280, 113488, 129696,
```

Figure 12-8
newf -n command output.

expected average size of files in the file system. Large numbers of small files drive this number up, and small numbers of extremely large files drive this number down. The default is 2048.

-m free. The minimum percentage of free space to maintain in the file system. This space is off limits to normal users. Once the file system is filled to this threshold, only the superuser can continue writing to the file system. The default is 10 percent.

-n nrpos. The number of different rotational positions in which to divide a cylinder group. The default is 8.

-o opt. Takes one of the two values, space or time. Time instructs the file system to try to minimize the time spent allocating blocks, and space indicates that the file system should try to minimize the space fragmentation on the disk. If the minimum free space threshold is less than 10 percent, space optimization will be used.

-r rpm. The speed of the disk in revolutions per minute. The default is 3600.

-s size. The size of the file system in sectors. The default is to use the entire slice (partition).

-t tracks. The number of tracks per cylinder. The default is taken from the disk label.

-C maxcontig. The maximum number of blocks, belonging to one file, that will be allocated contiguously before inserting a rotational delay. For a file system with a logical block size of 4K, the default is 14; for an 8K file system, the default is 7. If the file system is on a disk array, the *maxcontig* value should be multiplied by the number of disks in the array. For example, a file system on an array with six disks using 8K blocks should define the value of *maxcontig* to be 42 (7 blocks * 6 disks). This parameter also controls clustering. Regardless of the value of -d gap, clustering is enabled only when *maxcontig* is greater than 1.

Of these flags, the most important from a performance perspective are -f, -o, and -r. Unless the performance analyst knows a great deal about both the architecture of the hardware and the fine details of the file system to be implemented, the -d and -n flags should be avoided.

Where previously a performance analyst might worry about physical block size, the -f flag allows for the implementation of partial block use by small files. If a file system has a great number of files less than 512 bytes long, the -f 512 option should be used. On the other hand, if most of the files in a file system will be larger than 8K, fragmentation should be turned off by specifying -f 8192 because allowing fragmentation does involve a small bit of overhead.

The use of -o is obvious and is the decision of the performance analyst. If the default, as described above, is not acceptable, this parameter should be specified.

The -r rpm parameter is perhaps the most important option flag. Many new drives operate at speeds much faster than 3600 rpm. However, the newfs command cannot automatically adjust this parameter based on information from the disk drive. Therefore, a significant source of performance degradation can be traced to an incorrect specification here. This is because the speed of the drive is a factor in calculating many other aspects of the physical structure of the disk.

The maximum number of blocks that will be allocated contiguously before inserting a rotational delay (-C maxcontig) is an example of a factor that depends on an accurate reporting of revolutions per minute. On drives that have no internal buffer, the default value is 1; that is, no contiguous blocks will be allocated. On drives that do have an internal buffer, the value is calculated such that a maximum value less than 64K is used. If the revolutions per minute value is incorrect, performance could actually decrease by using contiguously allocated blocks.

Monitoring File System Performance

The primary tool for monitoring I/O workload is the iostat command. iostat reports on terminal and disk I/O activity, as well as CPU utilization. As with the vmstat command, the first line of output reports statistics since the system was booted. Each subsequent line reports information for the requested interval.

The information used to compute the statistics is maintained via a number of counters in the kernel. For each disk, the kernel counts the number of reads and writes along with the number of bytes transferred during each operation. Residence time is also tracked via time stamps taken at device queue entry and exit points. This allows for the reporting of cumulative residence-length products for each queue.

These values enable iostat to produce very accurate measures of throughput, utilization, queue lengths, transaction rates, and device service times.

For terminals, the kernel simply counts the number of input and output characters collectively.

In Solaris, this command has three major formats. The default format uses no option flags and is similar in syntax and format to the vmstat command.

Looking at Fig. 12-9, it can be seen that the default format

```
iostat [count [interval]]
```

produces 18 columns of information.

The first set of columns is related to terminal I/O activity. The columns are

tin   Number of characters input per second

tout   Number of characters output per second

Kps   Number of kilobytes transferred per second

tps   Transfer operations per second

```
iostat 2 10
        tty          sd0          sd1          ssd0         ssd1
cpu
  tin tout Kps tps serv  Kps tps serv  Kps tps serv  Kps tps serv  us sy
wt id
    6  293  17   3  64   46   3  61    2   0  15    1   0  13    2  3
9 85
    3  932  17   3  13    2   1  12    0   0   0    0   0   0    1  1
5 92
    6    8  41   8  11    0   0   0    0   0   0    0   0   0    1  3
12 85
    2   55   0   0   0    0   0   0    0   0   0    0   0   0    0  1
0 99
    4  330   0   0   0    0   0   0    0   0   0    0   0   0    0  0
0 100
    8   22  42   5 277   30   6  57    0   0   0    0   0   0    0  6
10 85
    8 1881 148  23  60    2   1  16    1   1  15    0   0   0    6  7
30 56
    8   24  25   5  12    0   0   0    0   0   0    0   0   0    1  2
6 91
    4   10   2   1  13    0   0   0    0   0   0    0   0   0    0  1
0 99
    2    2   0   0   0    0   0   0    0   0   0    0   0   0    0  0
0 100
```

Figure 12-9
iostat command output.

The next four groups of columns report information on the first four disk devices (including floppy disks and CD-ROMs) on the system. For each device, these columns detail

Kps Number of kilobytes transferred per second

tps Transfer operations per second

serv Average service time in milliseconds

The final group of columns reports on CPU utilization:

us Percentage of time in the user state

sy Percentage of time in the system state

wt Percentage of time in the wait state

id Percentage of time idle.

The second format of the `iostat` command uses the `-D` option flag. In this format (Fig. 12-10), the output format is different and focuses on device transfer rate and utilization. In the report, the first two columns display information about terminal devices in a manner similar to that used in the default format. The next four column groups report information on the first four disk devices (excluding floppy disks and CD-ROMs). For each device, these columns detail

rps Read operations per second

wps Write operations per second

util Average device utilization

The final group of columns gives statistics about CPU utilization:

us Percentage of time in the user state

ni Percentage of time running processes that have been `niced` or `reniced`

sy Percentage of time in the system state

id Percentage of time idle

The third format of the `iostat` command uses the `-x` option flag to display detailed information about the first four disk devices. In this format (Fig. 12-11), a separate line is displayed for each disk device; it identifies the following performance indicators:

Figure 12-10
`iostat -D` command output.

```
iostat -D
           sd0              sd1              ssd0             ssd1
    rps wps util    rps wps util    rps wps util    rps wps util
      0   2  3.5      1   2  4.4      0   0  0.2      0   0  0.1
```

```
iostat -x
```

					extended	disk	statistics		
disk	r/s	w/s	Kr/s	Kw/s	wait	actv	svc_t	%w	%b
sd0	0.3	2.5	1.3	15.9	0.0	0.2	64.2	0	3
sd1	0.8	2.5	13.2	33.0	0.0	0.2	61.1	0	4
ssd0	0.2	0.0	1.4	0.2	0.0	0.0	14.7	0	0
ssd1	0.2	0.0	1.3	0.1	0.0	0.0	12.8	0	0
ssd10	0.4	0.2	2.5	1.2	0.0	0.0	36.2	0	1
ssd11	0.4	0.2	2.5	1.1	0.0	0.0	37.1	0	1
ssd12	0.4	0.1	2.5	0.9	0.0	0.0	36.5	0	1
ssd15	0.4	0.2	2.5	1.3	0.0	0.0	36.8	0	1
ssd16	0.2	0.1	2.7	0.8	0.0	0.0	19.4	0	0
ssd17	0.3	0.1	2.4	0.8	0.0	0.0	29.9	0	0
ssd2	0.2	0.0	1.7	0.2	0.0	0.0	18.2	0	0
ssd20	0.3	0.2	2.6	1.3	0.0	0.1	192.9	0	1
ssd21	0.1	0.1	1.3	0.8	0.0	0.1	583.7	0	0
ssd22	0.0	0.0	0.4	0.1	0.0	0.0	26.4	0	0
ssd25	0.0	0.0	0.1	0.0	0.0	0.0	73.7	0	0
ssd26	0.0	0.3	0.3	3.2	0.0	0.0	24.8	0	1
ssd27	0.1	0.0	0.9	0.1	0.0	0.0	11.6	0	0
ssd5	0.2	0.6	1.2	4.7	0.0	0.0	51.3	0	1
ssd6	0.4	0.2	2.5	1.3	0.0	0.0	37.0	0	1
ssd7	0.4	0.2	2.5	1.1	0.0	0.0	37.8	0	1

Figure 12-11
iostat -x command output.

disk	The device the information applies to
r/s	Read transfer operations per second
w/s	Write transfer operations per second
Kr/s	Number of kilobytes read per second
Kw/s	Number of kilobytes written per second
wait	Average number of commands waiting in the device queue
actv	Average number of command in process*
svc_t	Service time†
%w	Percentage of time waiting in queue
%b	Percentage of time the device is busy

*This will only be greater than 1 for SCSI devices that are using tag queuing.

†The service time is the average time taken to service a command. This includes time spent waiting for prior commands in the queue to be processed.

On the line detailing the first disk drive, the terminal statistics (as discussed above) are reported, in addition to CPU statistics in the same format as the default report.

fusage—Disk Access Statistics

The `fusage` command (Fig. 12-12) reports on the block I/O transfers on all locally mounted file systems. The count data is cumulative from the time the file system was mounted.

The report includes a section for each local and remote file system. The sections are ordered by device name; advertised resources that are not complete file systems will follow the sections of the file system in which they are located.

Identifying Performance Problems

At the device level, performance problem identification is best done by monitoring service and device busy times.

In general, disks that have sustained service times of greater than 50 ms or are busy more than 30 percent of the time are, or will shortly become, performance bottlenecks. In general, these indicate device performance problems. This can be checked by using the utilization and forced flow laws discussed in Chap. 4 to determine what the maximum throughput can be. It is possible that these formulas will show that the device is not overloaded. In that case, the service and busy times could be a symptom of another problem, excessive wait time.

When wait time becomes excessive, the problem is not the individual disk drive but the I/O controller the disk is attached to. In this case, performance can only be improved by reducing the number of devices on the controller.

In general, a SCSI controller operating at a speed of 5MB cannot effectively support more than two frequently accessed disks. This recommendation scales to a maximum of four busy disks on a 10MB controller and eight on a 20MB controller.

The `df` command is used to display the number of free disk blocks and files in a file system. It is of interest in performance tuning because the command

```
df -ka
```

Figure 12-12
fusage command
output.

```
FILE USAGE REPORT FOR condor

/dev/dsk/c0t0d0s0        /dev/dsk/c0t0d0s0
                         /
                         condor          0 KB
/dev/dsk/c0t0d0s6        /dev/dsk/c0t0d0s6
                         /usr
                         condor          0 KB
/proc                    /proc
                         /proc
fd                       fd
                         /dev/fd
                         condor     278524 KB
/dev/vx/dsk/tmp/vol01    /dev/vx/dsk/tmp/vol01
                         /tmp
                         condor          0 KB
/dev/vx/dsk/opt/vol01    /dev/vx/dsk/opt/vol01
                         /opt
                         condor          0 KB
/dev/vx/dsk/condor/vol01      /dev/vx/dsk/condor/vol01
                         /condor
                         condor          0 KB
/dev/vx/dsk/datasets/vol01      /dev/vx/dsk/datasets/vol01
                         /datasets
                         condor          0 KB
/dev/vx/dsk/rootdg/vol01      /dev/vx/dsk/rootdg/vol01
                         /var/mail
                         condor          0 KB
/dev/vx/dsk/software/vol01      /dev/vx/dsk/software/vol01
                         /usr/software
                         condor          0 KB
/dev/vx/dsk/software/vol02      /dev/vx/dsk/software/vol02
                         /usr/local
                         condor          0 KB
/dev/vx/dsk/software/vol03      /dev/vx/dsk/software/vol03
                         /var/aux

                         condor          0 KB
-hosts                   -hosts
                         /net
                         condor          0 KB
condor:vold(pid559)      condor:vold(pid559)
                         /vol
                         condor     150188 KB
```

```
df -ka
Filesystem                kbytes      used    avail capacity  Mounted on
/dev/dsk/c0t0d0s0          88879     53869    26130    67%     /
/dev/dsk/c0t0d0s6         217671    188266     7645    96%     /usr
/proc                          0         0        0     0%     /proc
fd                             0         0        0     0%     /dev/fd
/dev/vx/dsk/tmp/vol01     963631     94898   772373    11%      /tmp
/dev/vx/dsk/opt/vol01     960860    476860   387920    55%      /opt
/dev/vx/dsk/condor/vol01 5766264   4820693   368951        93%      /condor
/dev/vx/dsk/datasets/vol01 5766264 2964428  2225216       57%      /datasets
/dev/vx/dsk/rootdg/vol01  654749    500676    88603      85%      /var/mail
/dev/vx/dsk/software/vol01 2883124 2280159   314655      88%
/usr/software
/dev/vx/dsk/software/vol02 480311   342315    89966       79%     /usr/local
/dev/vx/dsk/software/vol03 481299    78112   355067       18%     /var/aux
-hosts                         0         0        0     0%     /net
condor:vold(pid559)            0         0        0     0%     /vol
```

Figure 12-13
df -ka command output.

(Fig. 12-13) displays the amount of free space in each file system. Performance of a file system degrades significantly when free space falls below 90 percent; therefore, this command is useful in locating file systems that need to be cleaned up.

Tuning File System Performance

The tunefs command is used to change the dynamic parameters of a file system. All of the dynamic parameters are related to the way data is laid out physically on disk.

Although the tunefs command can be used on a system in multiuser mode, it cannot be used on a mounted file system. Therefore, before the tunefs command is used on a file system, the file system must be unmounted.

It is generally recommended that file systems should be optimized for time unless the file system is over 90 percent full, in which case it should be optimized for space.

The parameters that can be changed are outlined below. As can be seen, this is a much smaller set of options than are available when the file system is initially created. The changeable options are

-a maxcontig.   The maximum number of blocks, belonging to one file, that will be allocated contiguously before inserting a rotational delay. For disk drives that do not support buffering, this value should be 1. For disk drives that do support buffering, this should be the largest value that will result in a data transfer size less than or equal to 64K. If the file system is on a disk array, the *maxcontig* value should be multiplied by the number disks in the array. Regardless of the value of -d gap, clustering is enabled only when *maxcontig* is greater than 1.

-d gap.   The expected minimum time, in milliseconds, to complete a data transfer and initiate a new request on the same cylinder. It is used to decide how much rotational spacing to place between adjacent blocks in a file. The default is disk-type dependent. For devices with track buffering, this value should be set to 0.

-e maxbpg.   Indicates the maximum number of blocks a single file can allocate from a cylinder group before it is forced to allocate blocks from another cylinder group. Usually, this is set to one-quarter of the total blocks in a cylinder group. This prevents any single file from using all the blocks in a cylinder group and degrading access times for files subsequently allocated in the cylinder group. Because this causes large files to be subject to more frequent long seeks, file systems with a great number of large files should have this parameter set higher.

-m free.   The minimum percentage of free space to maintain in the file system. This space is off-limits to normal users. Once the file system is filled to this threshold, only the superuser can continue writing to the file system. The default is 10 percent. This can be set to 0 percent, but a significant performance degradation may result. If the value is raised above the current usage level, users will be unable to allocate files until the specified amount of free space required becomes available.

-o [space | time].   Changes the optimization strategy. *Space* conserves space, and *time* attempts to organize file layout to minimize access time.

Tuning Solstice DiskSuite

In general, the use of RAID techniques, either in hardware or software, is not a performance enhancement technique. It is an availability enhancement technique. For this reason, the implementation of the array subsystem can be a major factor affecting system performance.

Depending on the level of RAID selected, writes may be propagated to two or more devices. When defining the concatenation set, ensure that writes are issued simultaneously on all devices and not sequentially. Simultaneous writes allow the write to be performed on all devices at the same time; the write is considered complete when the last drive to finish reports success. Sequential writes will have a significant negative impact on overall performance because each write is performed in sequence on each drive of the concatenation set. A new write can only be issued after the prior drive completes the write request. And the write request as a whole is only considered complete after the last drive is successful.

Read strategy on a RAID system is more complex. Four strategies are possible, but the last two are only applicable to mirrored partitions. The simultaneous read strategy requests the data from each device. This may provide fast response on a lightly loaded system but quickly bogs down a heavily loaded system.

The alternate read strategy provides a semblance of load balancing, but it does not allow the system to take advantage of prefetching that may be done at the hardware level.

The fixed singular read strategy is only useful for two heavily used mirrored partitions. In this case, the reads for one of the partitions are always (except in the case of failure) performed on one disk, and the reads for the other partition are always performed from the other disk.

The fourth option is for a single mirrored partition. In this case, the partition is divided into two parts where the primary drive is used to read the first part of the partition and the secondary drive is used to read the last part of the partition. This option cuts the seek time in half because only half of the partition is being serviced by either disk. This is a particularly useful option when the workload consists primarily of random reads.

The following are some additional performance considerations when setting up a concatenation set:

- Partitions on the same drive should not be concatenated together. Doing so can create seek performance problems.
- Mirrors should always be set up on separate drives. Not doing so effectively doubles the I/O rate of the device and failure of the drive means the loss of all the data, which defeats the purpose of mirroring.

- UFS file systems that are logged should put the log on a device that is separate from the devices on which the data is located. Failing to do so creates seek performance problems on the device with the log.

- As much as possible, devices in a concatenation group should be on separate I/O controllers. This mitigates the interference multiple I/O commands may have in relationship to each other.

- Do not mix disks or controllers of differing performance characteristics in a concatenation set. Doing so can degrade performance significantly, especially if some disks or controllers are significantly slower than others.

Imposing Limits on Disk Usage

Imposing limits on the usage of disk space is intimately related to the capacity planning function. Disk space can be controlled in Solaris through the disk quota system. Disk quotas set up maximum limits for each user: the maximum number of files that can be created and the maximum amount of disk space than can be used.

Each quota has two values: the hard limit and the soft limit. The soft limit serves as a warning level. When this value is exceeded, the user receives warning messages for a specified period of time, but the additional allocation is granted. When the time limit expires, the soft limit is treated as if it were a hard limit. When the hard limit level is reached, the system stops allocating resources.* Further resources are not allocated until the usage level has been reduced to a level below the soft limit.

Using disk quotas involves some system overhead—each request for new space has to be checked against the defined quotas. This checking process is detailed in Fig. 12-14. Because of this overhead, disk quotas are generally used only when disk space is tight or an additional level of security is needed.

---

*Hard limits do not apply to root.

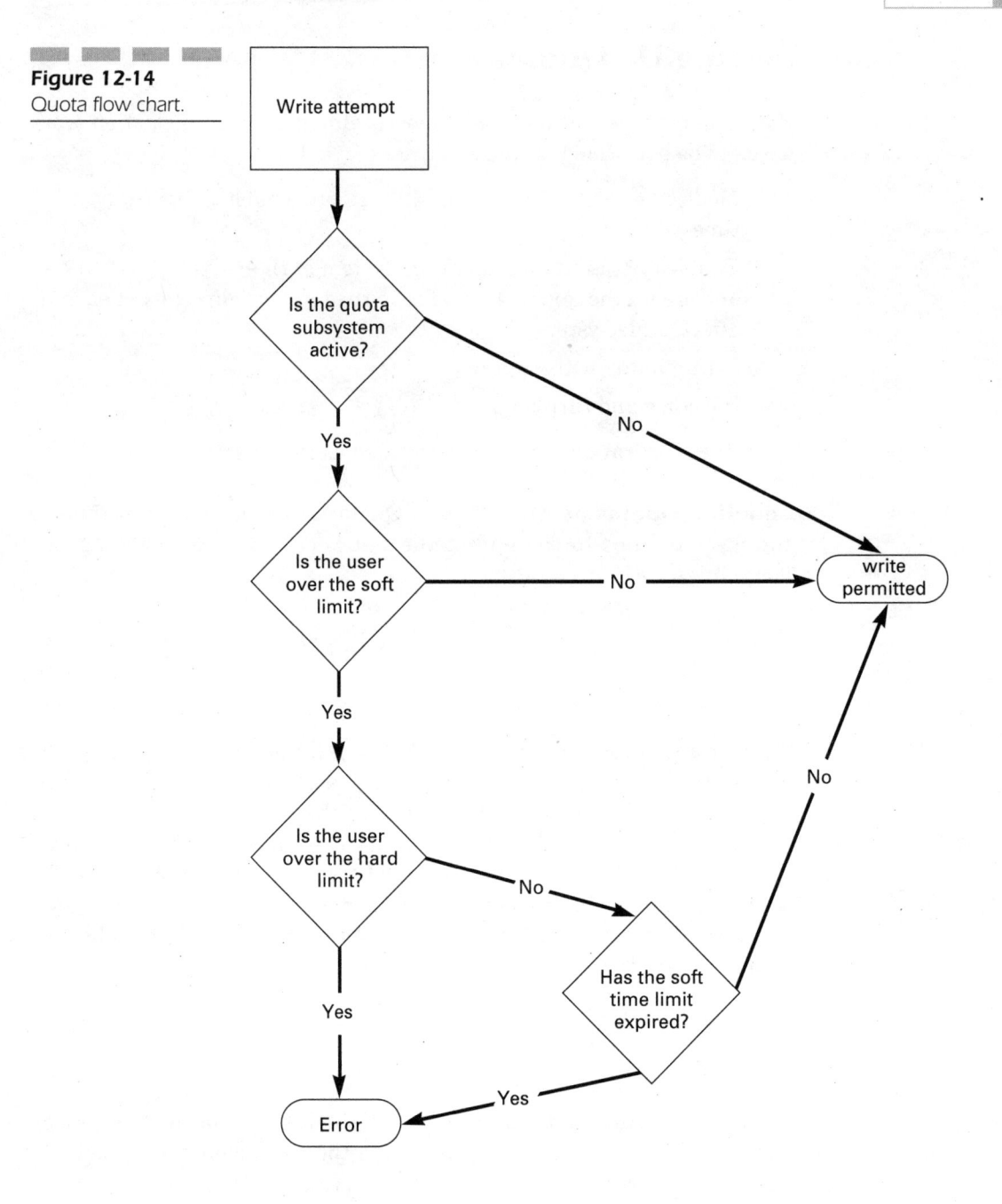

Figure 12-14
Quota flow chart.

Setting Up Quotas

Before quotas can be imposed, some preliminary administration work needs to be performed. These steps are

- Modify `/etc/rc2.d/S01MOUNTFSYS` and enable quotas at boot time
- Enable quotas on individual file system in the `/etc/vfstab` file and create the `quota` limits file in the top-level directory of each affected file system
- Set up limits with `edquota`
- Initialize and turn on limits

All of these operations must be performed as the root user.

Enabling Quotas at Boot Time. Quotas are enabled at boot time by adding four lines to the end of the `/etc/rc2.d/S01MOUTFSYS` file. These lines are

```
echo -n 'Checking quotas:' > /dev/console
/usr/sbin/quotacheck -a > /dev/console 2>&1
echo 'Enabling quota limits' > /dev/console
/usr/sbin/quotaon -a > /dev/console 2>&1
```

Enabling Quotas on Individual File Systems. For each file system that is to be protected by disk quotas, two operations must be performed. The first is to add an option to the file system entry in the `/etc/vfstab` file. The change adds the value `rq` to the `mount options` field for the file system. The second operation, after the `/etc/vfstab` has been modified, is to add a `quotas` file to the top-level directory of the affected file system(s). For each directory, the following commands are issued:

```
cd /file_system
touch quotas
chmod 600 quotas
```

The first command changes to the top-level directory of the file system. The second creates the `quotas` file, and the third changes the permissions to read/write for root only.

Set Up Limits with edquota. Setting up quotas involves editing a file that defines the `quotas` for a user. In most cases, a prototype file is created that is then used as the basis for real users on the system.

In any case, the edquota command is used to edit the appropriate user profile. For example,

```
edquota fcervone
```

enables viewing and editing of the quota information for user fcer-vone.

The information that is displayed consists of a line for each file system that has quotas enabled. An example is

```
fs /home blocks (soft = 0, hard = 0) inodes (soft = 0, hard = 0)
```

In this case, for this user the limits in the /home file system are 0 in all cases. The use of zero indicates that there are no limits associated with the user in this file system. To change this, simply change the limit for blocks and inodes, both soft and hard as appropriate, and save the file.

To use a profile as a prototype, edit the prototype profile and then issue the edquota command with the -p option:

```
edquota -p proto_user user1 user2 user3 user4…
```

This command will copy the quota profile of the *proto_user* to *user1, user2,* etc.

Initialize and Turn On Quotas.   In this step, the commands added to the /etc/rc2.d/S01MOUNTFSYS file are performed manually to enable quota checking. The commands issued are

```
/usr/sbin/quotacheck -a
```

to initialize the disk quota system and

```
/usr/sbin/quotaon -a
```

to enable quota monitoring.*

Monitoring Quotas.   Monitoring quotas can be performed manually or as part of a regularly scheduled script. The quota command displays

---

*Quotas may be turned off completely with the quotaoff -a command.

a user's disk quota and usage information. When used without any options, the quota command displays warnings about mounted file systems (local and remote) where usage is over quota. The -v option is used to display the current user's quota on all mounted file systems where quotas exist. The -v username option allows the root user or system administrator to display the user quota of a specific user.

The repquota command is used to generate a summary quota report for a UFS file system. The current number of files and amount of space (in kilobytes) are printed for each user along with any quotas.

The -a option is used to report on all mounted UFS file systems. The -v option is used to report quotas for all users, even those who are not using any resources.

Summary

I/O performance management is one of the most complex areas in performance tuning. Starting with a discussion of disk performance tuning basics, the focus of the first part of the chapter was related to hardware considerations: computing maximum throughput, disk controllers and interfaces, RAID configurations, file system implementation, and optimization.

In addition to performance considerations, the latter part of the chapter focused on creating disk space limits and monitoring disk space utilization.

In the following chapter, the focus will turn to managing the physical hardware of the network.

13

Network Performance Management

Network performance management is the most difficult aspect of performance tuning and capacity planning. This is because the performance of the network does not hinge on the performance of one machine, but instead performance is dependent on all machines on the network—clients, servers, routers, hubs, and gateways.

A common misconception is that it is easy to identify whether problems are caused by the network or by the server. Common wisdom has it that a network problem exists when operations that involve the network seem slow but other operations proceed at a "normal" rate. This can be used as a very general rule in some cases, but in a complex environment this advice means little. Particularly when both NFS and NIS + are used, it often takes quite a bit of investigative work to determine where the real bottleneck lies when performance is suffering.

Network services on Solaris machines run on TCP/IP. Application services rely primarily on two of the protocols in the suite: Transmission Control Protocol (TCP) and Unreliable Datagram Protocol (UDP). Both protocols are used to send information from one system to another over arbitrary network topologies and configurations,* but how they do this is substantially different.

TCP is used to provide reliable delivery of transmission packets. It is connection-oriented and stateful. Because of this, all parties know to whom they are communicating and the status of the communication. The protocol handles transmission error recovery, and all parties to the communication can signal a request for error recovery if something goes awry.

In order to provide reliability, TCP uses *positive acknowledgment*. When a packet is sent to a remote machine, the sender sets a timer and waits for an acknowledgment of receipt from the remote machine. If the acknowledgment (ACK) does not arrive within the designated amount of time, the packet is retransmitted. However, to increase network throughput, TCP uses *adaptive retransmission*. The retransmission rate is constantly adjusted to account for the amount of time it is actually taking for packets to be sent and acknowledged.

Another performance enhancement technique groups packets together for transmission. It is inefficient to send one packet and wait for an acknowledgment for the one packet. When the connection is negotiated between the communicating machines, each advertises the maximum number of bytes it can accept at one time. The lowest common denominator among the systems is set as the *window size* for the transmission. The default value is typically 6 times the size of a packet. On an Ethernet network, packets are usually 1500 bytes long.

UDP, on the other hand, is a much simpler protocol. It is connectionless and nonstateful. Because of this, it is primarily used for sending a single transmission packet from one machine to another. The sending machine does not know when, or even if, the receiver gets the message. If an application uses the UDP protocol, it is the application's responsibility to perform error recovery in the event of lost transmissions, duplicated transmission, or corrupted data packets. The protocol itself provides no mechanisms for addressing these issues.

As mentioned previously, network services are implemented using both TCP and UDP, depending on the level of reliability and (to some

---

*This is one of the defining characteristics of TCP/IP.

degree) security needed. This is why the trivial file transfer protocol (tftp) uses UDP, but the regular file transfer protocol (ftp) uses TCP. However, sometimes the choice of protocol seems to defy logic. For example, the network file system (NFS) is implemented over UDP instead of TCP. And, the same port offers different services on a port depending on what protocol is used: port 514 is the *shell* service if TCP is the protocol and the *syslog* service if UDP is used.

Latency, Bandwidth, and Utilization

These three items, latency, bandwidth, and utilization, are the primary factors in network performance.

Latency is the amount of time it takes for a single data packet to travel from one system to another. It is, therefore, a measure of the total amount of time it takes to pass through the communications network. Latency is not inherently related to the amount of data sent or its transmission rate, but it can be affected by both to varying degrees. Latency is a simple measure of a propagation rate of a signal from one system to another.

Latency is inherent in the transmission of electronic signals. It is also introduced into the network by the intermediate equipment between two systems: Routers, bridges, and hubs are the most common examples. Each of these must perform some type of processing on the signal, processing that slows transmission to some degree. Finally, the methods used by the media access control (CSMA/CD in Ethernet, for example) and congestion avoidance also introduce delays that contribute to the overall amount of latency time.

As the distance between machines increases, so does the latency (Fig. 13-1); this is a fundamental principle of physics. Because of this, latency can become especially evident when Internet connections are involved, given the greater number of intermediate devices and physical connections between the communicating machines.

Latency manifests itself in several ways:

New connections for network services take longer to establish.

Ongoing conversations occur more slowly due to the propagation delay.

Server processes tend to increase because requests cannot be satisfied quickly.

Figure 13-1 Latency
affects all networks
small or large.

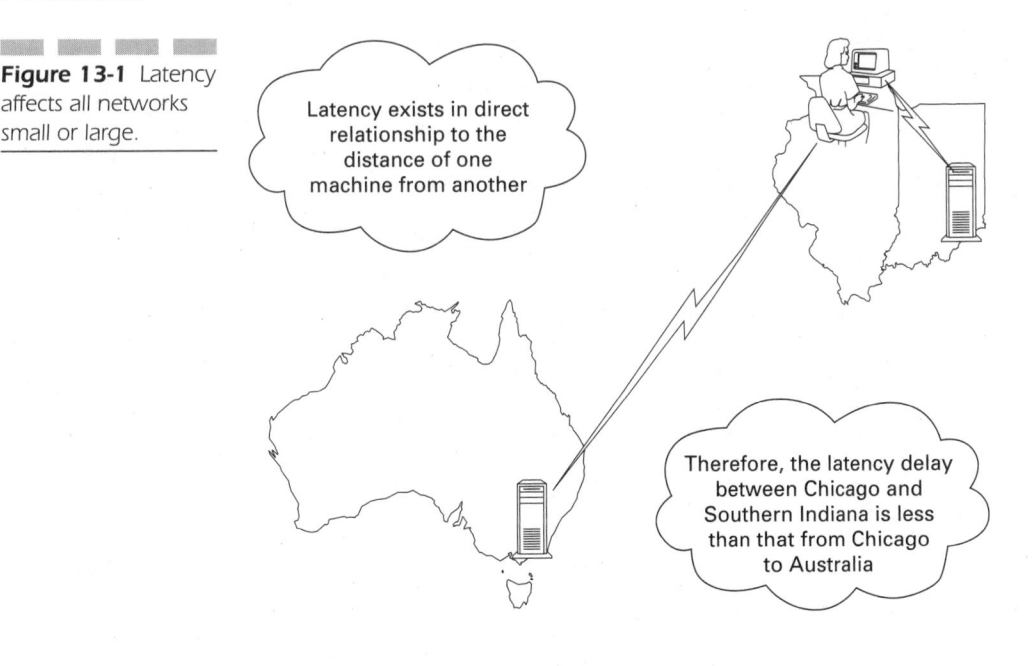

The most effective way to reduce latency is to locate the communicating machines as close as possible to each other. Locally, this would mean placing machines that communicate frequently on the same network segment (Fig. 13-2). In highly distributed environments, this could involve the creation of *mirror sites,* servers that duplicate the content of another server at a remote location (Fig. 13-3).

Bandwidth is the limiting factor in network performance. Bandwidth is the measure of the maximum amount of data traffic that can be sent across the network in a given time period. For example, on a 10Base-T Ethernet, the theoretical maximum speed is 10 Mbps, which is equivalent to 1250 kbps. The problem is that this maximum speed can never be attained. Protocol overhead, media access control, and congestion avoidance will introduce delays that decrease the overall effective bandwidth rate. These issues are true, to differing degrees, with all network topologies and architectures.

Utilization is the measure of the amount of network bandwidth that is used. As the number of data transfers over the network increases, so does utilization of the network. The increase in utilization decreases network availability, because the network is busy. In turn, the lack of availability slows the overall throughput rate of the network. Utilization problems can be solved in two ways: increase bandwidth and/or redistribute the workload over the network.

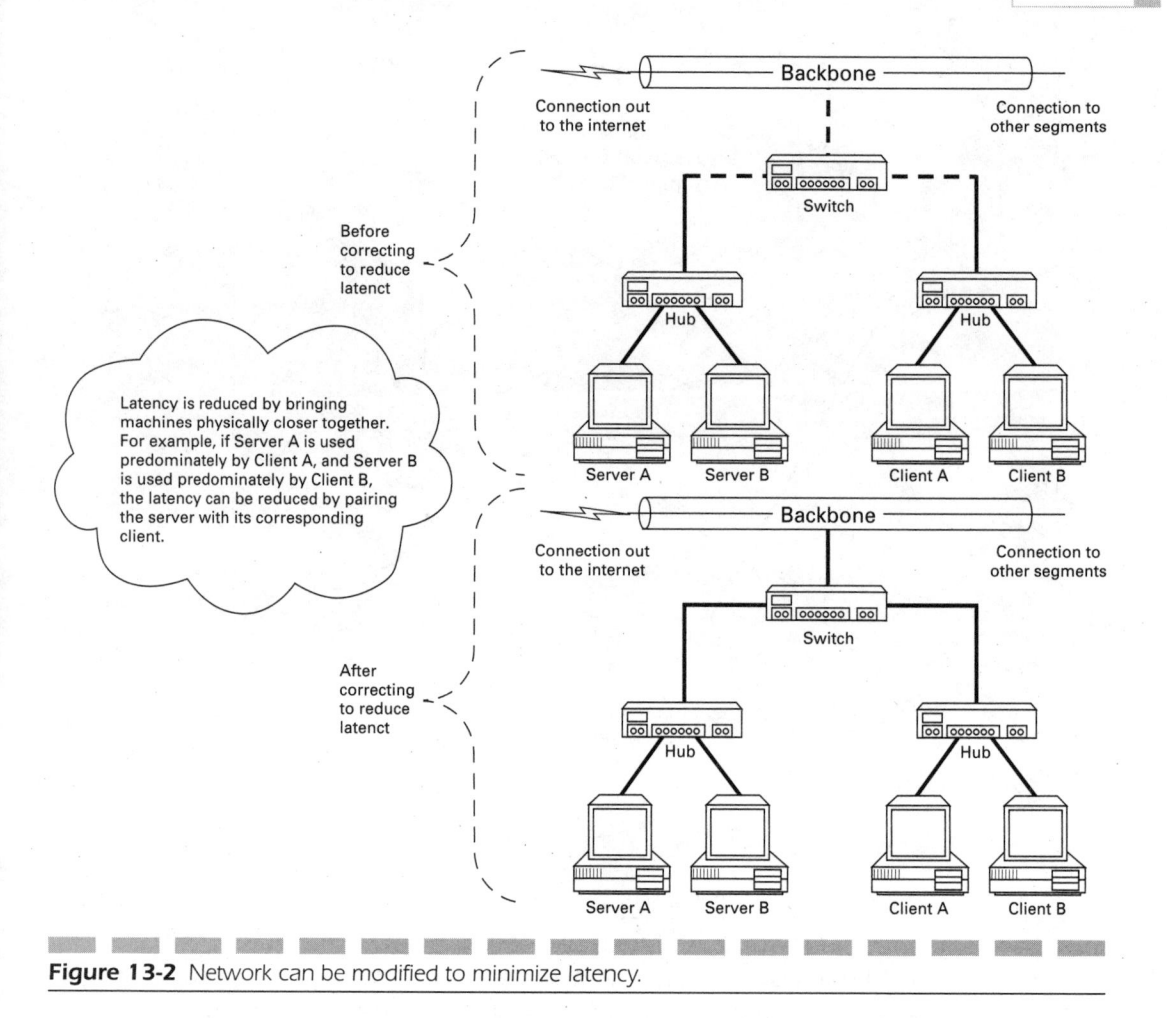

Figure 13-2 Network can be modified to minimize latency.

Identifying Performance Problems

There are two primary tools in Solaris for identifying latency and utilization problems. For latency problems, the ping command is the most commonly used tool.

ping

The ping command measures latency on a network. It does this by using the Internet Control Message Protocol (ICMP) to send

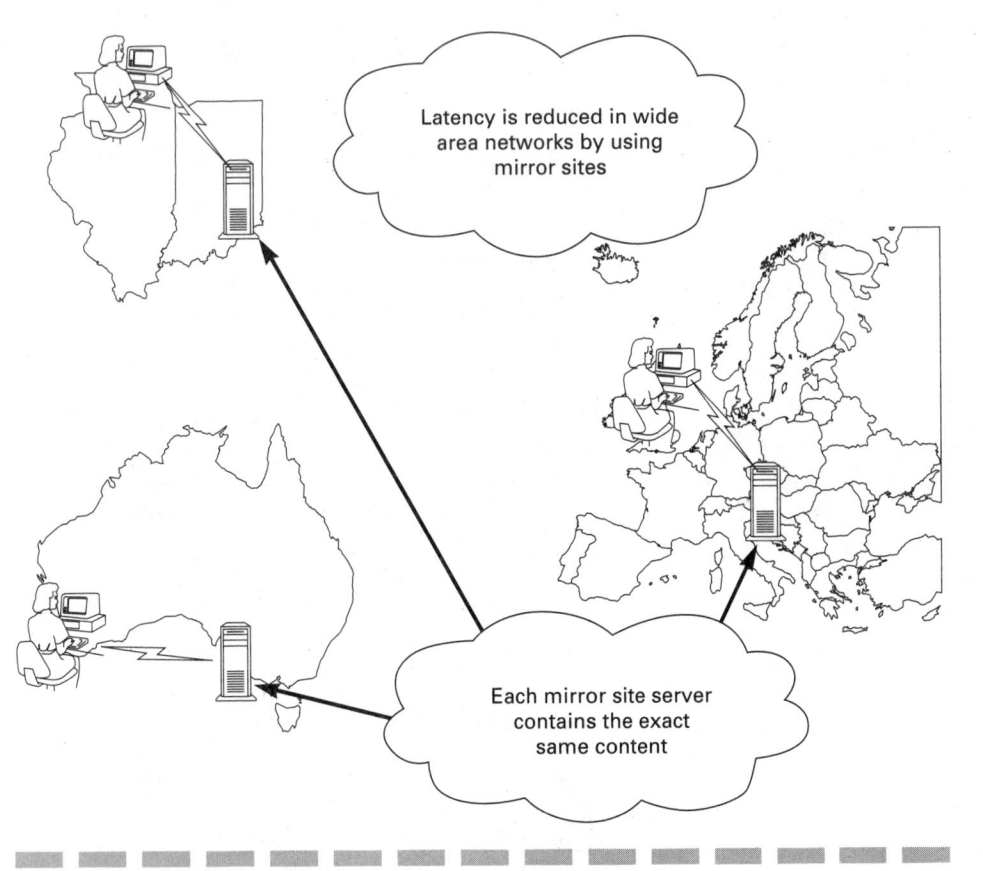

Figure 13-3 Latency can be reduced with mirror sites.

echo_request messages to a remote host. When the host receives the request, it sends a packet back to the sender. `ping` determines network latency time by measuring the amount of time it takes for the remote host's *echo_response* packet to be returned.

The basic form of the command is used just to tell if a machine is up. The syntax for this form of the command is

```
ping host [ timeout]
```

If the *host** responds within the *timeout* number of seconds, `ping` directs a message

```
host is alive
```

---

*This may be specified as an IP address or as a DNS name.

(where *host* is replaced by the actual machine name) to standard output and exits. The default value of *timeout* is 20 s. If the remote host does not respond within the *timeout* number of seconds, ping directs the message

```
no answer from host
```

to standard output and exits.

Of more interest for performance analysis is the second form of the ping command:

```
ping [ -s ] [ -dlLnrRv ] [ -i interface ]
[-I interval ][ -t ttl ] host [ packetsize ]
[ count ]
```

With this form of the command, ping -s, one *echo_request* datagram is sent each second (unless overridden by the -I flag). For each *echo_response* received, one line of output is displayed; no output line is displayed if there is no response to the *echo_request*. The command produces a summary report when the command is terminated (with Ctrl-C) or after the requested number of datagrams (as specified by *count*) have been sent. This report details minimum, average, and maximum response times along with packet loss statistics (Fig. 13-4).

The default datagram packet size is 64 bytes. For many terminal-based interactions this may be an appropriate value to use for testing. However, to test differing workloads and traffic patterns, this value can

```
ping -s www.sun.com
64 bytes from www.Sun.COM (192.9.9.100): icmp_seq=0. time=148. ms
64 bytes from www.Sun.COM (192.9.9.100): icmp_seq=1. time=150. ms
64 bytes from www.Sun.COM (192.9.9.100): icmp_seq=2. time=67. ms
64 bytes from www.Sun.COM (192.9.9.100): icmp_seq=3. time=68. ms
64 bytes from www.Sun.COM (192.9.9.100): icmp_seq=4. time=147. ms
64 bytes from www.Sun.COM (192.9.9.100): icmp_seq=5. time=74. ms
64 bytes from www.Sun.COM (192.9.9.100): icmp_seq=6. time=70. ms
64 bytes from www.Sun.COM (192.9.9.100): icmp_seq=7. time=65. ms
64 bytes from www.Sun.COM (192.9.9.100): icmp_seq=8. time=67. ms
64 bytes from www.Sun.COM (192.9.9.100): icmp_seq=9. time=84. ms

----www.sun.com PING Statistics----
10 packets transmitted, 10 packets received, 0% packet loss
round-trip (ms)  min/avg/max = 65/94/150
```

Figure 13-4 ping -s command output.

be modified by specifying a *packetsize* (Fig. 13-5). Note in comparing Figs. 13-4 and 13-5 how the overall latency time can increase as the amount of data transferred increases.

Some of the optional flags are useful in determining the route packets take, which allows for more detailed analysis of actual network routing patterns. The combination `ping -sv1R` prints a report (Fig. 13-6) that displays the route a packet takes to get to its destination. The flags used are:

-1 Loose source routing. Does not require that all datagrams use the same path to get to the destination.

-R Record route. This stores the route of the packet within the IP header.

-v Verbose output. Required to display the -R information.

The other flags may be useful in diagnosing other types of performance problems:

-L Turn off loopback of multicast packets. Normally, a copy of the multicast packets will be delivered to the local machine.

-n Show network addresses as numbers. Suppresses DNS resolution of IP addresses to names.

```
ping -s www.Sun.Com 4096
4104 bytes from www.Sun.COM (192.9.9.100): icmp_seq=0. time=156. ms
4104 bytes from www.Sun.COM (192.9.9.100): icmp_seq=1. time=148. ms
4104 bytes from www.Sun.COM (192.9.9.100): icmp_seq=2. time=154. ms
4104 bytes from www.Sun.COM (192.9.9.100): icmp_seq=3. time=148. ms
4104 bytes from www.Sun.COM (192.9.9.100): icmp_seq=4. time=174. ms
4104 bytes from www.Sun.COM (192.9.9.100): icmp_seq=5. time=197. ms
4104 bytes from www.Sun.COM (192.9.9.100): icmp_seq=6. time=159. ms
4104 bytes from www.Sun.COM (192.9.9.100): icmp_seq=7. time=155. ms
4104 bytes from www.Sun.COM (192.9.9.100): icmp_seq=8. time=147. ms
4104 bytes from www.Sun.COM (192.9.9.100): icmp_seq=9. time=175. ms
4104 bytes from www.Sun.COM (192.9.9.100): icmp_seq=10. time=145. ms
4104 bytes from www.Sun.COM (192.9.9.100): icmp_seq=11. time=148. ms
4104 bytes from www.Sun.COM (192.9.9.100): icmp_seq=12. time=175. ms
4104 bytes from www.Sun.COM (192.9.9.100): icmp_seq=13. time=176. ms

----www.sun.com PING Statistics----
14 packets transmitted, 14 packets received, 0% packet loss
round-trip (ms)  min/avg/max = 145/161/197
```

Figure 13-5 Ping command output using a larger packet size.

```
ping -svlR www.sun.com
64 bytes from condor.depaul.edu (140.192.1.6): icmp_seq=0. time=47. ms
   IP options:  <loose source route> dep-dgc.chicago.cic.net
(131.103.14.34) <record route> dep-dgc.chicago.cic.net (131.103.14.34),
dgc-dep.chicago.cic.net (131.103.14.33), cicrtr.depaul.edu
(140.192.1.11), condor.depaul.edu (140.192.1.6),  (End of record)
64 bytes from condor.depaul.edu (140.192.1.6): icmp_seq=1. time=54. ms
   IP options:  <loose source route> dep-dgc.chicago.cic.net
(131.103.14.34) <record route> dep-dgc.chicago.cic.net (131.103.14.34),
dgc-dep.chicago.cic.net (131.103.14.33), cicrtr.depaul.edu
(140.192.1.11), condor.depaul.edu (140.192.1.6),  (End of record)
64 bytes from condor.depaul.edu (140.192.1.6): icmp_seq=2. time=43. ms
   IP options:  <loose source route> dep-dgc.chicago.cic.net
(131.103.14.34) <record route> dep-dgc.chicago.cic.net (131.103.14.34),
dgc-dep.chicago.cic.net (131.103.14.33), cicrtr.depaul.edu
(140.192.1.11), condor.depaul.edu (140.192.1.6),  (End of record)
64 bytes from condor.depaul.edu (140.192.1.6): icmp_seq=3. time=80. ms
   IP options:  <loose source route> dep-dgc.chicago.cic.net
(131.103.14.34) <record route> dep-dgc.chicago.cic.net (131.103.14.34),
dgc-dep.chicago.cic.net (131.103.14.33), cicrtr.depaul.edu
(140.192.1.11), condor.depaul.edu (140.192.1.6),  (End of record)
ICMP Host redirect from gateway cicrtr.depaul.edu (140.192.1.11)
 to 140.192.1.120 for cls171.sac232.depaul.edu (140.192.9.171)
ICMP Host redirect from gateway cicrtr.depaul.edu (140.192.1.11)
 to 140.192.1.120 for shanghai.upit-sac.depaul.edu (140.192.8.250)
64 bytes from condor.depaul.edu (140.192.1.6): icmp_seq=4. time=114. ms
   IP options:  <loose source route> dep-dgc.chicago.cic.net
(131.103.14.34) <record route> dep-dgc.chicago.cic.net (131.103.14.34),
dgc-dep.chicago.cic.net (131.103.14.33), cicrtr.depaul.edu
(140.192.1.11), condor.depaul.edu (140.192.1.6),  (End of record)
64 bytes from condor.depaul.edu (140.192.1.6): icmp_seq=5. time=96. ms
   IP options:  <loose source route> dep-dgc.chicago.cic.net
(131.103.14.34) <record route> dep-dgc.chicago.cic.net (131.103.14.34),
dgc-dep.chicago.cic.net (131.103.14.33), cicrtr.depaul.edu
(140.192.1.11), condor.depaul.edu (140.192.1.6),  (End of record)
64 bytes from condor.depaul.edu (140.192.1.6): icmp_seq=6. time=15. ms
   IP options:  <loose source route> dep-dgc.chicago.cic.net
(131.103.14.34) <record route> dep-dgc.chicago.cic.net (131.103.14.34),
dgc-dep.chicago.cic.net (131.103.14.33), cicrtr.depaul.edu
(140.192.1.11), condor.depaul.edu (140.192.1.6),  (End of record)
64 bytes from condor.depaul.edu (140.192.1.6): icmp_seq=7. time=72. ms
   IP options:  <loose source route> dep-dgc.chicago.cic.net
(131.103.14.34) <record route> dep-dgc.chicago.cic.net (131.103.14.34),
dgc-dep.chicago.cic.net (131.103.14.33), cicrtr.depaul.edu
(140.192.1.11), condor.depaul.edu (140.192.1.6),  (End of record)
64 bytes from condor.depaul.edu (140.192.1.6): icmp_seq=8. time=102. ms
   IP options:  <loose source route> dep-dgc.chicago.cic.net
(131.103.14.34) <record route> dep-dgc.chicago.cic.net (131.103.14.34),
dgc-dep.chicago.cic.net (131.103.14.33), cicrtr.depaul.edu
(140.192.1.11), condor.depaul.edu (140.192.1.6),  (End of record)
64 bytes from condor.depaul.edu (140.192.1.6): icmp_seq=9. time=28. ms
   IP options:  <loose source route> dep-dgc.chicago.cic.net
(131.103.14.34) <record route> dep-dgc.chicago.cic.net (131.103.14.34),
dgc-dep.chicago.cic.net (131.103.14.33), cicrtr.depaul.edu
(140.192.1.11), condor.depaul.edu (140.192.1.6),  (End of record)
64 bytes from condor.depaul.edu (140.192.1.6): icmp_seq=10. time=27. ms
   IP options:  <loose source route> dep-dgc.chicago.cic.net
(131.103.14.34) <record route> dep-dgc.chicago.cic.net (131.103.14.34),
dgc-dep.chicago.cic.net (131.103.14.33), cicrtr.depaul.edu
(140.192.1.11), condor.depaul.edu (140.192.1.6),  (End of record)
64 bytes from condor.depaul.edu (140.192.1.6): icmp_seq=11. time=77. ms
```

Figure 13-6 ping -sv1R output tracks the route of the data packets.

```
   IP options:  <loose source route> dep-dgc.chicago.cic.net
(131.103.14.34) <record route> dep-dgc.chicago.cic.net (131.103.14.34),
dgc-dep.chicago.cic.net (131.103.14.33), cicrtr.depaul.edu
(140.192.1.11), condor.depaul.edu (140.192.1.6),  (End of record)
64 bytes from condor.depaul.edu (140.192.1.6): icmp_seq=12. time=9. ms
   IP options:  <loose source route> dep-dgc.chicago.cic.net
(131.103.14.34) <record route> dep-dgc.chicago.cic.net (131.103.14.34),
dgc-dep.chicago.cic.net (131.103.14.33), cicrtr.depaul.edu
(140.192.1.11), condor.depaul.edu (140.192.1.6),  (End of record)

----www.sun.com PING Statistics----
13 packets transmitted, 13 packets received, 0% packet loss
round-trip (ms)  min/avg/max = 9/58/114
```

Figure 13-6 (Continued) `ping  -sv1R` output tracks the route of the data packets.

-r Bypasses the normal routing tables and sends the request directly to a host on an attached network. If the recipient is not on a directly attached network, an error is returned.

-i interface   Specifies the interface to use for multicast packets. Normally, the default interface, as determined by the routing tables, is used.

-I interval   Overrides the default interval of one second.

-t ttl   Overrides the default IP time to live for unicast and multicast packets. The default time to live for unicast packets is set with ndd via the *icmp_def_ttl* variable. The default time to live for multicast is one hop.

netstat

netstat is a generalized tool for monitoring network activity. The first form of the command

```
netstat [ -anv ]
```

displays a list of active sockets for each protocol. This is useful for determining the amount of network activity.

The second form

```
netstat [ -g | -m | -p | -s | -f address_family ]
[-n ] [ -P protocol ]
```

is used to display information from among various network data structures.

The third form

```
netstat {[ -i ] [ -I Interface ]} [ interval ]
```

shows the state of the interfaces. This form is useful for gathering general statistics about each network interface card.

The fourth form

```
netstat -r [ -anv ]
```

displays the routing table, and the fifth form

```
netstat -M [ -ns ]
```

displays the multicast routing table.

For performance analysis, the -i and -s flags are most often used.

netstat -i. As seen in Fig. 13-7, the output of a netstat -i count command details the current status of all network interfaces. The first output group displays information since the system was booted, and each subsequent group displays information specific to that interval.

For each interface, the following information is displayed:

mtu   Maximum transmission unit—the maximum datagram size*

net/dest Name and type of interface

address   Device name

ipkts   Number of input packets

ierrs   Number of input packet errors

opkts   Number of output packets

---

*Typical values for this setting differ according to network typology: For Ethernet the value is 1500, for Token-Ring it is 4089, and for dial-up modems it is 576.

```
netstat -i
Name  Mtu  Net/Dest      Address          Ipkts    Ierrs Opkts    Oerrs Collis
Queue
lo0   8232 loopback      localhost        256375 0    256375 0     0
0
le0   1500 140.192.1.0   condor.depaul.edu 33784091 0    25132192 0
387443 0
```

Figure 13-7 netstat -i command output.

oerrs   Number of output packet errors

collis   Number of collisions

The number of input and output packets is useful in determining the overall activity rate of an interface. However, because peak transmission rate, packet length, or packet type information is not kept, it is only a general guide.

The input error column represents a number of different problems: packet length errors, consistency errors, shortage of network buffers, bad interface on network, or a loose cable. The number of input errors should be small, less than 1 percent of all incoming packets. If it is not, it could indicate that packet corruption is occurring somewhere in the network or that the number of network buffers is inadequate. It should be investigated immediately.

The output error column represents the number of times a packet could not be transmitted. This is most usually due to loss of carrier, the maximum collision retry count has been exceeded, or there is a lack of buffers in the transmit queue. If this value is over 1 percent of all outgoing packets, a serious problem exists.

The collisions column represents the number of collisions detected by the interface adapter. When this value is 5 percent of all outgoing packets or greater, the performance of the network is significantly affected.

netstat -s. The netstat -s command (Fig. 13-8) displays detailed information, per protocol, about the operation of the overall operation of the network interfaces. Some of the fields indicate set limits, and others are event counters.

The report is divided into five sections, one for each of the following protocols (in report order): UDP, TCP, IP, ICMP, and IGMP.

The UDP report only details three statistics:

Number of input packets

Number of output packets

Number of input packet errors

Ideally, the input packet error level will be zero. A level greater than 5 percent merits investigation.

The TCP report details a number of statistics. Considerations for this protocol are the following ratios:

Outgoing data segments (tcpOutDataSegs) to retransmitted segments (tcpRetransSegs); a high ratio indicates network transmission problems.

■ ■ ■ ■
Figure 13-8
netstat -s com-
mand output gives
detailed statistics
on network
performance.

```
netstat -s

UDP
      udpInDatagrams      =6868241  udpInErrors          =       0
      udpOutDatagrams     =5463967

TCP   tcpRtoAlgorithm     =       4  tcpRtoMin            =     200
      tcpRtoMax           =   60000  tcpMaxConn           =      -1
      tcpActiveOpens      =  116862  tcpPassiveOpens      =1144396
      tcpAttemptFails     =   38988  tcpEstabResets       =117333
      tcpCurrEstab        =      33  tcpOutSegs           =17114469
      tcpOutDataSegs      =14329097  tcpOutDataBytes      =-1610793485
      tcpRetransSegs      =  668254  tcpRetransBytes      =385361515
      tcpOutAck           =2707090   tcpOutAckDelayed     =1170874
      tcpOutUrg           =     217  tcpOutWinUpdate      =  14178
      tcpOutWinProbe      =   15725  tcpOutControl        =2675988
      tcpOutRsts          =  136253  tcpOutFastRetrans    =  32851
      tcpInSegs           =25518280
      tcpInAckSegs        =11958764  tcpInAckBytes        =-1719667085
      tcpInDupAck         =1157913   tcpInAckUnsent       =       0
      tcpInInorderSegs    =9088773   tcpInInorderBytes    =1827049075
      tcpInUnorderSegs    =   85312  tcpInUnorderBytes    =42201105
      tcpInDupSegs        =   15112  tcpInDupBytes        =2845714
      tcpInPartDupSegs    =    1625  tcpInPartDupBytes    =1059490
      tcpInPastWinSegs    =     377  tcpInPastWinBytes    =-848182812
      tcpInWinProbe       =     150  tcpInWinUpdate       =    7816
      tcpInClosed         =   90372  tcpRttNoUpdate       =253527
      tcpRttUpdate        =2351614   tcpTimRetrans        =1099716
      tcpTimRetransDrop   =    3273  tcpTimKeepalive      =    2583
      tcpTimKeepaliveProbe=     702  tcpTimKeepaliveDrop  =      10

IP    ipForwarding        =       2  ipDefaultTTL         =     255
      ipInReceives        =30215200  ipInHdrErrors        =       6
      ipInAddrErrors      =       0  ipInCksumErrs        =       0
      ipForwDatagrams     =       0  ipForwProhibits      =       0
      ipInUnknownProtos   =       0  ipInDiscards         =      26
      ipInDelivers        =30226003  ipOutRequests        =25101908
      ipOutDiscards       =       0  ipOutNoRoutes        =       0
      ipReasmTimeout      =      60  ipReasmReqds         =    1394
      ipReasmOKs          =    1392  ipReasmFails         =       2
      ipReasmDuplicates   =       0  ipReasmPartDups      =       0
      ipFragOKs           =    5166  ipFragFails          =       0
      ipFragCreates       =   28094  ipRoutingDiscards    =       0
      tcpInErrs           =    7671  udpNoPorts           =   37931
      udpInCksumErrs      =       0  udpInOverflows       =    2408
      rawipInOverflows    =       3

ICMP  icmpInMsgs          =224206   icmpInErrors         =       0
      icmpInCksumErrs     =       3  icmpInUnknowns       =       0
      icmpInDestUnreachs  =    6916  icmpInTimeExcds      =    3229
      icmpInParmProbs     =       0  icmpInSrcQuenchs     =     875
      icmpInRedirects     =181729   icmpInBadRedirects   =142211
      icmpInEchos         =    9338  icmpInEchoReps       =  22115
      icmpInTimestamps    =       0  icmpInTimestampReps  =       0
      icmpInAddrMasks     =       1  icmpInAddrMaskReps   =       0
      icmpInFragNeeded    =     444  icmpOutMsgs          =  42311
      icmpOutDrops        =       2  icmpOutErrors        =       0
      icmpOutDestUnreachs =   32972  icmpOutTimeExcds     =       0
      icmpOutParmProbs    =       0  icmpOutSrcQuenchs    =       0
      icmpOutRedirects    =       0  icmpOutEchos         =       0
      icmpOutEchoReps     =    9338  icmpOutTimestamps    =       0
```

Figure 13-8 (Continued) netstat -s command output gives detailed statistics on network performance.

```
                   icmpOutTimestampReps=    0    icmpOutAddrMasks   =      0
                   icmpOutAddrMaskReps =    1    icmpOutFragNeeded  =      0
                   icmpInOverflows     =    0
           IGMP:
                       1 message received
                       0 messages received with too few bytes
                       0 messages received with bad checksum
                       0 membership queries received
                       0 membership queries received with invalid field(s)
                       0 membership reports received
                       0 membership reports received with invalid field(s)
                       0 membership reports received for groups to which we belong
                       0 membership reports sent
```

Incoming data segments (tcpInSegs) to input acknowledgment messages (tcpInAckSegs); indicates poor use of service windows if acknowledgments are high.

Input acknowledgment messages (tcpInAckSegs) to the number of duplicate acknowledgment messages (tcpInDupAck); a high ratio indicates severe transmission delays.

Segments received in order (tcpInInorderSegs) to those received out of order (tcpInUnorderSegs); a low ratio indicates little network congestion and good routing.

Total segments received (tcpInInorderSegs)+(tcpInUnorderSegs) to the number of duplicated segments (tcpInDupSegs)+(tcpInPartDupSegs); a high ratio of duplicated segments indicates network congestion and possible routing problems.

The IP protocol report gives a high- (or lower, depending on your view) level report on the performance of the network.

All of the following fields should be monitored to ensure that the counters are ideally at zero or at the very least remain very low in comparison to the total number of input packets (i.e., less than 1 percent of all input packets):

ipInHdrErrors   Input header errors; should be low.

ipInAddrErrors   Input addressing errors; should be low.

ipInCksumErrs   Input checksum errors; should be low.

ipInDiscards   Input discards because the network buffers were full.

ipOutDiscards   Output discards because transmission could not be completed.

ipOutNoRoutes   No routes available.

ipReasmReqds   Packet reassemblies required.

ipReasmOKs	Successful packet reassemblies; should be high in relationship to ipReasmReqds.
ipReasmFails	Failed packet reassemblies.
ipReasmDuplicates	Duplicate reassemblies.
ipReasmPartDups	Partial duplicate reassemblies.
ipFragFails	Should be low in relationship to ipFragOKs.
udpNoPorts	High values indicate not enough server processes to satisfy requests.
rawipInOverflows	Should be low; indicates shortage of network buffers.

The detailed statistics that are produced for ICMP and IGMP, although interesting in some circumstances, are not generally of much use when diagnosing the problems a server may be having in relationship to the network.

syncstat

The syncstat command is used to report driver statistics from a synchronous serial link. The syntax of the command is

```
syncstat [-c] devname [count]
```

The -c option flag is used to clear the counters.

The report is either a snapshot of the accumulated totals or a *count,* a series of samples showing incremental changes in the last interval, is specified. The event statistics are maintained by the driver for each physical channel that it supports.

syncstat output contains the following information:

speed	The line speed of the device
ipkts	The total number of input packets
opkts	The total number of output packets
undrun	The number of transmitter underrun errors
ovrrun	The number of receiver overrun errors
abort	The number of aborted received frames
crc	The number of received frames with cyclical redundancy check (CRC) errors
isize	The average size (in bytes) of input packets

osize   The average size (in bytes) of output packets

The fields *underrun, overrun, frame-abort,* and *CRC errors* have a number of possible causes. Typically, the communication protocol handles these errors and initiates recovery of the transmission. Small numbers of such errors are not usually a big problem. However, the overhead involved in recovering from a link error can be much greater than that of normal operation, so high error rates will greatly degrade overall link throughput. As is true with most network equipment, high error rates are often caused by problems in the link hardware, such as cables, connectors, interface electronics, or telephone lines.

The percentages for input and output line utilization may occasionally be greater than 100 percent because of inexact sampling times and differences in the accuracy between the system and the modem clocks. If the percentage of use greatly exceeds 100 percent, or never exceeds 50 percent, the baud rate set for the device probably does not accurately reflect the speed of the modem.

spray

spray is used to generate network traffic. It is most useful for determining maximum network load to a specific host. This is not necessarily the maximum network bandwidth though. spray sends a one-way stream of packets to the designated host using remote procedure calls (RPC) and reports on how many of the packets were received and the overall transfer rate. The results of this operation do not necessarily indicate network bandwidth because spray can report a large number of packets that were dropped because spray was sending packets faster than they could be buffered by the sending machine.

The format of the command is:

```
spray [ -c count ] [ -d delay ] [ -l length ]
[-t nettype ] host
```

where

-c count.   Specifies how many packets to send. The default value is the number of packets that would be required to generate a stream of 100,000 bytes.

-d delay.   Specifies the number of microseconds to wait before sending another packet. The default is zero.

-l length.   The number of bytes in the packet that contains the RPC call message. When greater than 1514, the RPC call cannot be encapsulated in one Ethernet packet; therefore the *length* field no longer corresponds to the packet size. The default length is 86 bytes (the size of the RPC and UDP headers).

-t nettype.   Specifies the class of transport. The default is netpath. See rpc(3N) for more information.

host.   Either a name or an IP address.

snoop

snoop is used to capture and inspect network packets. Using both the network packet filter and streams buffer modules, captured packets can be displayed as they are received or saved for later analysis. This is an extremely useful tool in tracking what network activity is being generated by client machines.

Packets can be displayed in a single-line summary form or in verbose multiline form. In the summary form, only the data pertaining to the highest-level protocol is displayed unless the verbose options are used, in which case all underlying frame information is also displayed.

The syntax and options of snoop are outlined in Table 13-1.

Diagnosis using snoop can be very laborious, especially if many machines are being traced at once. And processing overhead is much higher when real-time packet interpretation is used. Because of this, the packet drop count may be significantly higher than when using log files. It follows then that more reliable captures are possible when the packet capture data is output to a file (using the -o option) and the packets are analyzed off-line.

Also, snoop is likely to generate extra packets as an effect of its use. It may use a network name service (NIS or NIS+) to convert IP addresses to host names, for example. Obviously, capturing into an NFS-mounted file will also generate extra packets.

Tuning Network Parameters

ndd is a generalized kernel driver configuration tool. However, it is used exclusively for network tuning because only TCP/IP protocol drivers are supported by the tool at the present time.

TABLE 13-1

snoop—Capture and Inspect Network Packets

```
snoop [ -aPDSvVNC ] [ -d device] [ -s snaplen] [ -c maxcount] [ -i
filename] [ -o filename] [- n filename] [ -t [ r | a | d ] ] [ -p
first [,last] ] [ -x offset[,length] ] [ expression ]
```

Options	Meaning
-a	Listen to packets on /dev/audio.
-P	Capture packets in nonpromiscuous mode. Only broadcast, multicast, or packets addressed to the host machine will be seen.
-d device	Receive packets from the network using the interface specified by device. Normally snoop will automatically choose the first nonloopback interface it finds.
-s snaplen	Truncate each packet after snaplen bytes. Usually the whole packet is captured. This option is useful if only certain packet header information is required. The packet truncation is done within the kernel, giving better utilization of the streams packet buffer. This means less chance of dropped packets due to buffer overflow during periods of high traffic. To capture only headers, use a snaplen of 34 for IP. For UDP use 42, for TCP use 54, for RPC headers use 80, and for NFS use 120 bytes.
-c maxcount	Quit after capturing maxcount packets. Otherwise keep apturing until there is no disk left or until interrupted with CTRL-C.
-i filename	Display packets previously captured in filename. If a filename.names file is present, it is automatically loaded as an address-to-name mapping table.
o-filename	Save captured packets in filename as they are captured. During packet capture, a count of the number of packets saved in the file is displayed.
-n filename	Use filename as an IP address-to-name mapping table. This file must have the same format as the /etc/hosts file.
-S	Display size of the entire Ethernet frame in bytes on the summary line.
-t [r	a	d]	Timestamp presentation. Timestamps are accurate to within 4 ms. The default is for times to be presented in d (delta) format—the time since receiving the previous packet. Option a (absolute) gives wall-clock time. Option r (relative) gives time relative to the first packet displayed. This can be used with the -p option to display time relative to any selected packet.
-v	Verbose mode. Print packet headers with extensive detail.
-V	Verbose summary mode. Instead of displaying just the summary line for the highest-level protocol in a packet, it displays a summary line for each protocol layer in the packet.

TABLE 13-1

(Continued)
snoop—Capture
and Inspect Net-
work Packets

Options	Meaning
-p first[,last]	Select one or more packets to be displayed from a capture file. The first packet in the file is packet #1.
-x offset[,length]	Display packet data in hexadecimal and ASCII format. The offset and length values select a portion of the packet to be displayed. To display the whole packet, use an offset of 0.
-N	Create an IP address-to-name file from a capture file. This must be set together with the -i option that names a capture file. The address-to-name file has the same name as the capture file with .names appended. Packets are not displayed when this flag is used.
-C	List the code generated from the filter expression for either the kernel packet filter or snoop's own filter.
expression	Select packets either from the network or from a capture file. Only packets for which the expression is true will be selected. If no expression is provided, it is assumed to be true. A filter expression consists of a series of one or more boolean primitives that may be combined with boolean operators (AND, OR, and NOT). Normal precedence rules for boolean operators apply. Order of evaluation of these operators may be controlled with parentheses. Because parentheses and other filter expression characters are known to the shell, it is often necessary to enclose the filter expression in quotes. The primitives are:
	host hostname—True if the source or destination address is that of hostname.
	ipaddr or etheraddr—Literal addresses; both IP dotted and ethernet color are recognized.
	from or src—A qualifier that modifies the following host, net, ipaddr, etheraddr, port, or rpc primitive to match just the source address, port, or RPC reply.
	to or dst—A qualifier that modifies the following host, net, ipaddr, etheraddr, port, or rpc primitive to match just the source address, port, or RPC reply.
	ether—A qualifier that modifies the following host primitive to resolve a name to an Ethernet address. Normally, IP address matching is performed.
	ethertype number—True if the Ethernet-type field has a value number.
	ip, arp, rarp—True if the packet is of the appropriate ethertype.
	broadcast—True if the packet is a broadcast packet.
	multicast—True if the packet is a multicast packet.
	apple—True if the packet is an Apple Ethertalk packet.

TABLE 13-1

(Continued)
snoop—Capture
and Inspect Net-
work Packets

Options	Meaning
	decnet—True if the packet is a DECNET packet.
	greater length—True if the packet is longer than length.
	less length—True if the packet is shorter than length.
	udp, tcp, icmp—True if the IP protocol is of the appropriate type.
	net net—True if either the IP source or destination address has a network number of net.
	port—True if either the source or destination port is port.
	rpc prog[,vers[,proc]]—True if the packet is an RPC call or reply packet for the protocol identified by prog. The prog may be either the name of an RPC protocol from /etc/rpc or a program number. The vers and proc may be used to further qualify the program version and procedure number.
	gateway host—True if the packet used host as a gateway.
	nofrag—True if the packet is unfragmented or is the first in a series of IP fragments.
	expr op expr—True if the relation holds, where op is one of $>$, $<$, $> =$, $< =$, $=$, $! =$, and expr is an arithmetic expression composed of numbers, packet field selectors, the length primitive, and arithmetic operators $+$, $-$, $*$, $\&$, $|$, $\wedge$, and $\%$. The arithmetic operators within expr are evaluated before the relational operator, and normal precedence rules apply between the arithmetic operators, such as multiplication before addition. Parentheses may be used to control the order of evaluation.

Each driver chooses which variables to make visible via the ndd interface; some are modifiable and some parameters may be read-only. These parameters are tightly coupled to the implementation of the driver, and they may change from release to release.

ndd operates in two modes: set and display. When the -set flag is not used, ndd queries the named driver (such as /dev/tcp, /dev/ip, or /dev/udp) and prints the current value of the associated parameter. As an example, the following command would display the current IP forwarding table:

```
ndd /dev/ip ip_ire_status
```

When the -set flag is used, ndd passes the specified value to the driver, which then assigns it to the parameter. So, to disable IP forwarding, the following command would be issued to set that value of the *ip_forwarding* parameter to false:

```
ndd -set /dev/ip ip_forwarding 0
```

A complete list of all parameters supported by a driver can be displayed by using an escaped question mark (\?) as the parameter to display. For example, the command

```
ndd /dev/tcp \?
```

will display the information in Fig. 13-9—all of the configuration parameters for TCP. Figures 13-10 and 13-11 display the configuration parameters for IP and UDP, respectively.

Tuning TCP Parameters

The TCP parameters that are most often tuned are*

`tcp_conn_req_max` (the listen backlog queue)

`tcp_xmit_hiwat` (transmit buffer size)

`tcp_recv_hiwat` (receive window sizes)

`tcp_rexmit_interval_min` (the minimum time to wait before retransmission)

The listen backlog queue needs to be adjusted on all versions of Solaris because the default value (32 in Solaris 2.5 and above) is simply not enough. This parameter is used to control the maximum number of connections in process that TCP will queue for a specific socket. This is especially critical if the machine is hosting a busy `http` (Web) server. All Netscape `http` servers and many others assume that the size of the listen backlog queue is 128. The maximum value of the listen queue in Solaris 2.5, and above that is 1024. For most sites a value of 128 or 256 will provide much better performance than the default value. Increasing the listen queue to the maximum value is *not* recommended, because this could cause the other parts of the system to become overloaded—memory, processor, etc.

Also related to `http` servers, the `tcp_keepalive_interval` can have a significant performance impact. In HTTP v1.0, each element on a Web page is separately requested. This means that the client connects and disconnects from the server multiple times during the course of a

---

*Consult Paging Parameters (Chap. 15) for information on making permanent changes to these parameters.

Figure 13-9 nnd is
used to display the
configurable parame-
ters for tcp.

```
ndd /dev/tcp
tcp_close_wait_interval       (read and write)
tcp_conn_req_max              (read and write)
tcp_conn_grace_period         (read and write)
tcp_cwnd_max                  (read and write)
tcp_debug                     (read and write)
tcp_smallest_nonpriv_port     (read and write)
tcp_ip_abort_cinterval        (read and write)
tcp_ip_abort_interval         (read and write)
tcp_ip_notify_cinterval       (read and write)
tcp_ip_notify_interval        (read and write)
tcp_ip_ttl                    (read and write)
tcp_keepalive_interval        (read and write)
tcp_maxpsz_multiplier         (read and write)
tcp_mss_def                   (read and write)
tcp_mss_max                   (read and write)
tcp_mss_min                   (read and write)
tcp_naglim_def                (read and write)
tcp_old_urp_interpretation    (read and write)
tcp_rexmit_interval_initial   (read and write)
tcp_rexmit_interval_max       (read and write)
tcp_rexmit_interval_min       (read and write)
tcp_wroff_xtra                (read and write)
tcp_deferred_ack_interval     (read and write)
tcp_snd_lowat_fraction        (read and write)
tcp_sth_rcv_hiwat             (read and write)
tcp_sth_rcv_lowat             (read and write)
tcp_dupack_fast_retransmit    (read and write)
tcp_ignore_path_mtu           (read and write)
tcp_rwin_credit_pct           (read and write)
tcp_rcv_push_wait             (read and write)
tcp_smallest_anon_port        (read and write)
tcp_largest_anon_port         (read and write)
tcp_xmit_hiwat                (read and write)
tcp_xmit_lowat                (read and write)
tcp_recv_hiwat                (read and write)
tcp_fin_wait_2_flush_interval (read and write)
tcp_co_min                    (read and write)
tcp_rtt_updates               (read and write)
tcp_status                    (read only)
tcp_bind_hash                 (read only)
tcp_listen_hash               (read only)
tcp_conn_hash                 (read only)
tcp_queue_hash                (read only)
name to get/set ?
```

transmission. TCP connections can be reused, but the default limit on
the keep-alive time is too low for this to have much practical effect for
`http` connections. By increasing the `tcp_keepalive_interval` to 240,
the chances of reusing an existing TCP connection are greatly increased.
This is not as large of an issue with HTTP v1.1 because it bunches
requests together on a single connection. This is much more efficient
and faster.

Excessive TCP retransmission can indicate a network hardware problem. But in many cases, a high retransmission rate simply indicates
that the machine is not waiting long enough for acknowledgments. If,
indeed, there are no hardware problems, the retransmission rate is set

Figure 13-10 nnd
can also be used for
ip parameters.

```
ndd /dev/ip
ip_ill_status                      (read only)
ip_ipif_status                     (read only)
ip_ire_status                      (read only)
ip_rput_pullups                    (read and write)
ip_forwarding                      (read and write)
ip_respond_to_address_mask_broadcast(read and write)
ip_respond_to_echo_broadcast       (read and write)
ip_respond_to_timestamp            (read and write)
ip_respond_to_timestamp_broadcast(read and write)
ip_send_redirects                  (read and write)
ip_forward_directed_broadcasts(read and write)
ip_debug                           (read and write)
ip_mrtdebug                        (read and write)
ip_ire_cleanup_interval            (read and write)
ip_ire_flush_interval              (read and write)
ip_ire_redirect_interval           (read and write)
ip_def_ttl                         (read and write)
ip_forward_src_routed              (read and write)
ip_wroff_extra                     (read and write)
ip_ire_pathmtu_interval            (read and write)
ip_icmp_return_data_bytes          (read and write)
ip_send_source_quench              (read and write)
ip_path_mtu_discovery              (read and write)
ip_ignore_delete_time              (read and write)
ip_ignore_redirect                 (read and write)
ip_output_queue                    (read and write)
ip_broadcast_ttl                   (read and write)
ip_icmp_err_interval               (read and write)
ip_reass_queue_bytes               (read and write)
ip_strict_dst_multihoming          (read and write)
name to get/set ?
```

Figure 13-11

nnd/dev/udp
command output.

```
ndd /dev/udp
udp_wroff_extra                    (read and write)
udp_def_ttl                        (read and write)
udp_smallest_nonpriv_port          (read and write)
udp_trust_optlen                   (read and write)
udp_do_checksum                    (read and write)
udp_smallest_anon_port             (read and write)
udp_largest_anon_port              (read and write)
udp_xmit_hiwat                     (read and write)
udp_xmit_lowat                     (read and write)
udp_recv_hiwat                     (read and write)
udp_status                         (read only)
```

too low and must be adjusted for the network; retransmissions on a slow network will make it even slower. If the number of retransmissions, as determined by the ratio of `tcpOutDataSegs` to `tcpRetransSegs` from the `netstat -s` command, is greater than 30 percent, the retransmission delay rate should be increased (starting from 1200) until the proportion of retransmits drops below 15 percent.

As a general rule of thumb, both `tcp_xmit_hiwat` and `tcp_recv_hiwat` should be set to the maximum value possible, 65,535. This allows negotiation on windows size to occur without setting artificial limits on the maximum size. These two parameters are important in environments that use NFS V3.0, which uses TCP, instead of UDP, to send large blocks of data. The settings of these two variables define the maximum block size that the `nfsd` daemon can negotiate.

Tuning UDP Parameters

The UDP parameters that are most often tuned are

`udp_xmit_hiwat` (transmit buffer size)

`udp_recv_hiwat` (receive window size)

As with TCP, both `tcp_xmit_hiwat` and `tcp_recv_hiwat` should be set to the maximum value possible, 65,535. This allows negotiation on windows size to occur without setting artificial limits on the maximum size. This is especially important in environments that use NFS V2.0. The settings of these two variables define the maximum block size that the `nfsd` daemon can negotiate.

Summary

Understanding latency, bandwidth, and utilization is critical to network performance management. Identification of performance problems on the network is done with commands such as `ping`, `netstat`, `syncstat`, `spray`, and `snoop`. Once an understanding of the utilization characteristics of the network has been arrived at, it is possible to tune the network.

The next chapter discusses the issues involved in optimizing the applications and services that run on the network.

14

Network Services
Performance
Management

Tuning the performance of the network is generally not enough. Many of the problems that exist in networked systems may not be related to the network per se but to the services that implement the network. These would include the network file system (NFS), the network information system (NIS and NIS+), the domain name server (DNS), and various other applications. Understanding, monitoring, and tuning these services can result in significant improvements in overall system and network performance.

Network File System

NFS is one of the most popular network services because it allows multiple clients to share files mounted on a server. This allows users on any host in the network to access their home directory. NFS permits the concept of diskless workstations by having the files that normally would be on a local disk be resident on a server on the network.

There are two versions of NFS that are currently being used: Version 2 and Version 3. All versions of Solaris support Version 2 of NFS, which is integrated into the kernel; it is an inherent part of the operating system. As part of the operating system, much of the code has been optimized for performance. Solaris 2.5 and subsequent versions support the latest version of NFS, Version 3. This version adds extended functionality to NFS and even greater efficiency. By default, Solaris 2.5 and above will use NFS Version 3 if the client will support it.

Because NFS is a relatively simple protocol, tuning NFS involves balancing system resources rather than tweaking daemons. The following are important considerations for file systems served by NFS to the network:

- The file systems being served by NFS should be balanced, as much as possible, over the entire disk subsystem.

- Unless absolutely required, file systems should always be mounted *read-only*; this will make more effective use of NFS caching techniques.

- The default mount retry value is much too high (10,000); it should be lowered to a value that is appropriate for the given environment.

- The default time-out value (1.1 s) may be too low for many environments and should be raised until all valid requests are satisfied within the limit.

- The `nointr` mount option should never be used; doing so can result in client workstations that lock up due to interrupted NFS requests.*

NFS is served by the `nfsd` daemon; it is the process that handles client file system requests. Normally, `nfsd` is automatically invoked during system start-up, in run level 3 with the `-a` option. By default, the

---

*This is not so much a performance concern as it is an availability concern.

script starts the daemon to support an unlimited number of connections that are supported by 16 threads. In most cases, it is appropriate to modify the start-up procedure* so that the maximum number of connections (and threads to serve them) may be set. In general, it is not a bad idea to have an equal number of threads to connections. The nfsd threads generate very little system overhead when there is no processing to do, and so the benefits of satisfying requests as soon as possible outweigh any performance overhead concerns. To modify the number of connections and processes, find the line in the script that starts nfsd and modify it with the new options. For example, to change the maximum number of connections to 64, the following line would be appropriate:

```
/usr/lib/nfs/nfsd -a -c 64 64
```

The -c 64 flag sets the number of connections to 64 and the second 64 sets the number of threads to 64. This second value sets the maximum number of concurrent NFS requests the server can handle. This concurrency is achieved by running, in the kernel, a number of threads as needed up to the number specified.

Unlike other implementations of NFS, in Solaris it is not necessary to worry about the block size of the NFS file system transfers. The nfsd daemon negotiates with the client to send the maximum-size block whenever possible. If the client does not support negotiation, a standard size block of 8K is used. See Sec. 13.3 for information on the TCP parameters that affect this negotiation process.

Two other daemons are associated directly with NFS: the lockd (lock manager) and statd (status manager) daemons. Neither daemon has options that affect performance, so they will not be discussed further.

nfsstat

The nfsstat command displays information about the NFS and Remote Procedure Call (RPC) interfaces to the kernel. It is also used to reinitialize these counters.

When no specific option flags are used, the default generates a report as if the

```
nfsstat -cnrs
```

---

*This can be found in the /etc/rc3.d directory as S15nfs.server.

```
nfsstat

Server rpc:
calls       badcalls    nullrecv    badlen      xdrcall     dupchecks
dupreqs
2607359     0           0           0           0           3376        0

Server nfs:
calls       badcalls
2607357     0
Version 2: (2607355 calls)
null        getattr     setattr     root        lookup      readlink    read
0 0%        58962 2%    951 0%      0 0%        2420123 92% 71 0%       102186
3%
wrcache     write       create      remove      rename      link
symlink
0 0%        1954 0%     178 0%      223 0%      42 0%       3 0%        7 0%
mkdir       rmdir       readdir     statfs
9 0%        9 0%        22561 0%    76 0%

Client rpc:
calls       badcalls    retrans     badxids     timeouts    waits
newcreds
4364        0           12          0           12          0           0
badverfs    timers      toobig      nomem       cantsend    bufulocks
0           63          0           0           0           0

Client nfs:
calls       badcalls    clgets      cltoomany
4364        0           4364        0
Version 2: (4364 calls)
null        getattr     setattr     root        lookup      readlink    read
0 0%        4359 99%    0 0%        0 0%        0 0%        0 0%        0 0%
wrcache     write       create      remove      rename      link
symlink
0 0%        0 0%        0 0%        0 0%        0 0%        0 0%        0 0%
mkdir       rmdir       readdir     statfs
0 0%        0 0%        0 0%        5 0%
```

Figure 14-1

nfsstat command output.

had been entered. This command will display all counters (Fig. 14-1) and not perform any reinitialization.* The command options used represent the following:

-c Display client information

-n Display NFS information

-r Display RPC information

-s Display server information

---

*Counters are reinitialized by entering nfsstat -z.

In the report, each NFS call type is displayed along with statistics on how many times it was used. These are broken down into requests as a client and services provided as a server.

For servers, the following additional NFS fields are reported:

- calls—the total number of NFS calls received
- Badcalls—the total number of calls rejected by the NFS

and the following fields related to RPC are shown:

- calls—the total number of RPC calls received
- Badcalls—the total number of calls rejected by the RPC layer (the sum of badlen and xdrcall)
- nullrecv—the number of times an RPC call was not available when it was thought to be received
- Badlen—the number of RPC calls with a length shorter than a minimum-sized RPC call
- Xdrcall—the number of RPC calls whose header could not be decoded by XDR

On clients, the following additional NFS fields are displayed:

- calls—the total number of NFS calls received
- Badcalls—the total number of calls rejected by NFS
- nclget—the number of times a CLIENT handle was received
- cltoomany—the number of times a call had to sleep while awaiting a handle

and the following RPC fields are shown:

- calls—the total number of RPC calls made
- Badcalls—the total number of calls rejected by the RPC layer
- Retrans—the number of times a call had to be retransmitted due to a time-out waiting for a reply from the server
- Badxid—the number of times a reply from a server was received that did not correspond to any outstanding call
- Timeout—the number of times a call timed out for a reply from the server
- Wait—the number of times a call had to wait because no client handle was available
- Newcred—the number of times authentication information had to be refreshed

- Timers—the number of times the calculated time-out value was greater than or equal to the minimum specified time-out value for a call

The other major display format of the nfsstat command is invoked by the -m flag (Fig. 14-2). This format displays statistics for each NFS mounted file system including

Server name and address

Mount flags

Current read and write sizes

Retransmission count

Timers used for dynamic retransmission

The *srtt* value contains the smoothed (average) round-trip time for requests, the *dev* value indicates the estimated deviation of *srtt,* and the *cur* value is the current time-out value for retransmission.

automountd—The Automounter

The automountd daemon is used to NFS mount and unmount file systems as necessary. Unlike mountd, which is used to NFS mount file systems for, theoretically, the duration of the system run, automountd is used to NFS mount file systems that are required only for a specific period of time. When the required period is over, the NFS mount is released.

```
/home/fcervone from fullerton:/usr/home/fcervone
 Flags:
vers=2,proto=udp,auth=unix,hard,intr,dynamic,rsize=8192,wsize=8192,retrans=5
 Lookups: srtt=11 (27ms), dev=8 (40ms), cur=5 (100ms)
 Reads:   srtt=4 (10ms), dev=4 (20ms), cur=2 (40ms)
 Writes:  srtt=8 (20ms), dev=7 (35ms), cur=4 (80ms)
 All:     srtt=14 (35ms), dev=9 (45ms), cur=6 (120ms)

/opt/scripts from fullerton:/opt/scripts
 Flags:
vers=2,proto=udp,auth=unix,hard,intr,dynamic,rsize=8192,wsize=8192,retrans=5
 Lookups: srtt=7 (17ms), dev=7 (35ms), cur=4 (80ms)
 Reads:   srtt=15 (37ms), dev=7 (35ms), cur=5 (100ms)
 All:     srtt=8 (20ms), dev=6 (30ms), cur=4 (80ms)
```

Figure 14-2

nfsstat -m command output.

The most commonly `automounted` files are home directories of users. When used in this manner, after users sign onto a participating system, their home directory is automatically mounted via NFS. When they sign off, the NFS mapping is automatically deleted.

Neither `mountd` nor `automountd` have any special flags that control or optimize performance. And neither is generally a performance problem, especially in Solaris 2.5 and later. In these versions, the `automountd` daemon was modified to be mutithreaded, which allows multiple mounts or demounts to occur simultaneously. However, the performance analyst should bear in mind that file systems that are frequently mounted and unmounted on a particular system are good candidates for permanent mounting via `mountd` rather than automounting.

NFS and the Cache File Systems

Other than a fast network connection, the most significant performance enhancement that can be made on the client side when using NFS is to implement a *cache file system* for any NFS mounted directories. A cache file system on the client allows a local disk to be used to store information from the remote NFS file system. The cache file system can also be used on an NFS server to cache data from CD-ROMs. The cache file system is unobtrusive; the user accessing a file is never aware that the data is coming from the cache and not the original (i.e., backing) file system.

Cache file systems are created within other UFS file systems; these UFS file systems are referred to as *front-file systems*. Although a separate disk slice or partition can be set aside for a cache file system, a regular UFS file system must be created in the slice (partition) before the cache file system can be allocated.

Cache file systems are administered and monitored with the `cfsadmin` command. The command is used to

Create a cache

Delete a cache

List the contents of a cache and statistics

Adjust parameters of the cache*

When the cache file system is created, it is defined via a group of six parameters. Each of these parameters may be also adjusted after the file

---

*The file system must be unmounted first.

system has been created. These parameters, in and of themselves, do not have much affect on performance, but they do affect the amount of space the cache may occupy in the front file system. These parameters are

- Maxblocks, the maximum amount of storage space that can be used for the cache file system; expressed as a percentage of the total number of blocks in the front file system. The default is 90.

- Minblocks, the minimum amount of storage space that can be used for the cache file system; expressed as a percentage of the total number of blocks in the front file system. The default is 0.

- Threshblocks, the front file system allocation level where further cache file system allocation stops. Once the front file system reaches the *threshblocks* number of allocated blocks, the cache file system will no longer expand, as long as the percentage of allocation in *minblocks* has been reached. The default value is 85.

- Maxfiles, the maximum number of files that can be allocated in the cache file system; expressed as a percentage of the total number of inodes in the front file system. The default is 90.

- Minfiles, the minimum number of files that the cache file system can allocate. The default is 0.

- Threshfiles, the front file system allocation level where further cache file system allocation stops. Once the front file system reaches the *threshfiles* number of allocated inodes, the cache file system will no longer expand, as long as the percentage of allocation in *minfiles* has been reached. The default value is 85.

- Maxfilesize, the largest file size, expressed in megabytes, that the cache file system can allocate. The default is 3. Note: The block or inode allotment for a cache cannot be decreased. To decrease the size of a cache, it must be removed and created.

The `cfsadmin -l` command (Fig. 14-3) is used to display information about the file systems in a cache including statistics on resource utilization and cache resource parameters.

When mounting a file system to be cached by the cache file system, two mount options are important in performance:

1. If the back file system (the file system to be cached) is not a secure NFS file system,* the `local-access` mount option should be

---

*See Solaris 2.x Administering NFS for more information on secure NFS.

Figure 14-3
cfsadmin -1 com-
mand output.

```
cfsadmin: list cache FS information
    maxblocks     90%
    minblocks      0%
    threshblocks  85%
    maxfiles      90%
    minfiles       0%
    threshfiles   85%
    maxfilesize    3MB
```

used. This allows the mode bits on the files in the cache to be checked rather than having to go to the back file system to check the mode bits.

2. If the back file system is read-only, mount the cache file system as read-only and use the noconst mount option. This disables consistency checking between the back file system and the cache; because both are read-only, this is perfectly acceptable and greatly increases performance.

Network Information Service Plus

NIS + is a service that stores information about users, workstations, applications, services, and file systems networkwide in a common database that is shared by all machines on the network. Because of this centralization of information, each workstation and server does not need to store this aforementioned information individually, which, in turn, alleviates the system administration burden.

NIS + is an authorization and authentication system. NIS + can be used to handle all login processing on the network, confirmation of group membership for individual users, verification of authority to use RPC services, and authorization to mount NFS files.

When NIS + is used extensively, the impact on client workstations on the system can be very large. This is primarily because every time a request for a service protected via NIS + is made, the request has to be passed to a NIS + server for validation. Perhaps the greatest amount of overhead is generated when RPC services are protected via NIS +.

The problem with NIS + overhead is that it is very difficult to track unless a tool such as snoop is used. After the NIS + request is passed from the client to the server, the client goes into a wait state until the server responds. If a large number of requests are being sent to the NIS + server, the client can become very slow. This slowness is not related to any activity on the client machine; it is simply spending a lot of time waiting for events on another machine to complete.

The best approach for increasing the performance of NIS + is to alleviate network congestion and interference between the client and server as much as possible. In addition, services that do not need to be provided via NIS + should be provided through other means, local customization files if possible.

The NIS + service is implemented with the rpc.nisd daemon, which is an RPC service that runs on all machines that serve a portion of the NIS + namespace.

rpc.nisd is usually started during system start-up. A complementary service, rpc.nisd_resolv, is invoked when the rpc.nisd daemon is started with the -YB option. These two options start the NIS + server in NIS compatibility mode. In addition, the aforementioned additional daemon provides NIS- (ypserv) compatible DNS forwarding services for NIS host requests.

The only tunable parameter for the rpc.nisd daemon is the -L number option flag. This allows a performance analyst to specify the maximum number of processes the server may spawn to handle NIS + requests. This value must be at least 1 for NIS + to function. The default value is 128, which may not be adequate for a very large root server.

Another ancillary NIS + process that runs on every NIS + participant is the nis_cachemgr daemon. Somewhat deceptively named, this daemon does not cache actual NIS + information, such as authentication credentials, but instead the daemon maintains a cache of the NIS + directory objects, which in turn contain location information necessary to contact the NIS + servers that serve the various directories in the name space. This information includes transport addresses, information needed to authenticate to the server, and a *time to live* field that indicates how long the directory object can be cached.

The cache helps improve the performance of the NIS + clients as they traverse the NIS + name space. The nis_cachemgr daemon is not required to run NIS +, but it is strongly recommended that it be used to improve performance. There is one exception to this, however. If the principal (server) does not have the proper security credentials in the cred.org_dir table for its domain, running the nis_cachemgr daemon without insecure mode turned on (-n) may actually greatly degrade the performance of client processes issuing NIS + requests.

Domain Name Service

DNS is used to provide information about hosts on a network. It is used extensively to translate host names into IP addresses. It is essential for networking on the Internet.

Unlike most other network services on the client side, there is neither a daemon nor particular program that runs to request DNS services. The required routines are compiled into programs via libraries. Programs make resolution calls via the *resolver,* which is a routine that reads a file* that contains a list of possible DNS servers that inquiries can be directed to.

On the server side, the `in.named` daemon provides resolution of host names to IP addresses. When the daemon starts, it reads the configuration files to determine where the starting points are in the network area for locating information to resolve names. As the daemon executes, it caches the information it retrieves, thereby making subsequent lookups faster. Because of this caching mechanism, `in.named` should always be run as a stand-alone process and not from `inetd`. When run from `inetd`, the caching mechanism is rendered useless because the `in.named` daemon is continually started and stopped. Other than this, there are no performance or capacity management options for the `in.named` daemon.

nscd

New in Solaris 2.5 is `nscd`, the name service cache daemon. It is used to improve the performance of name service lookup from NIS, NIS+, DNS, and local files. The `nscd` daemon caches information in the user, password, and group files. The items to cache and amount of time items should be kept in the cache are defined in the `/etc/nscd.conf file`. An example of this file is shown in Fig. 14-4.

inetd

`inetd` is the server process for the standard Internet services, such as `telnet`, `talk`, `finger`, and `bootp`. It is usually started at system

---

*The /etc/resolv.conf file.

```
#
# Copyright (c) 1994 by Sun Microsystems, Inc.
# All rights reserved.
#
#ident       "@(#)nscd.conf    1.2    94/12/09 SMI"
#


#
#      Currently supported cache names: passwd, group, hosts
#

#      logfile                    /var/tmp/nscd.log
#      enable-cache               hosts        no

       debug-level       0

       positive-time-to-live   passwd           600
       negative-time-to-live   passwd           5
       suggested-size          passwd           211
       keep-hot-count          passwd           20
       old-data-ok      passwd          no
       check-files      passwd          yes

       positive-time-to-live   group            3600
       negative-time-to-live   group            5
       suggested-size          group            211
       keep-hot-count          group            20
       old-data-ok      group           no
       check-files      group           yes

       positive-time-to-live   hosts            3600
       negative-time-to-live   hosts            5
       suggested-size          hosts            211
       keep-hot-count          hosts            20
       old-data-ok      hosts           no
       check-files      hosts           yes
```

boot time. The configuration file, /etc/inetd.conf, lists the services that inetd may provide.

Once started, inetd listens for service requests on the TCP or UDP ports associated with each of the services outlined in the configuration file. When a request arrives, inetd starts the server program associated with the service. These services can be configured to be *single-threaded*; that is, inetd waits for the service's server process to finish before a starting a second process for the same service.

inetd itself provides many of the rudimentary Internet services, such as echo, discard, chargen (character generator), daytime (human-readable time), and time (machine-readable time).

Many of the services provided via inetd are superfluous or extremely insecure. These can be turned off by placing a pound sign (#) before the applicable line in the /etc/inetd.conf file. Although most of these services use little processing power, and therefore have little impact on performance overall, it is never a good idea to have services that are not needed.

sendmail

The sendmail daemon and its associated service is the most complex, as far as configuration goes, of all of the services. sendmail is used to send messages, routing the message over whatever networks as necessary. It performs internetwork forwarding as needed to deliver the message to the correct place.

The flag options of sendmail that are related to performance are

- -qtime. Directs sendmail to batch message processing at the specified interval. The *time* interval may be specified as seconds (s), minutes (m), hours (h), days (d), or weeks (w). For example, the command

```
sendmail -bd -q120m
```

causes sendmail to queue outgoing mail for processing every 2 h.

- -oCckpt_value instructs sendmail to checkpoint the queue every *ckpt_value* (default 10) addresses sent. If large mailing lists are commonly used, the default value of 10 is too low and is causing unnecessary overhead.

- -ohhop_count specifies the maximum hop count a message can make. It is assumed that messages over the *value* amount are in a loop and should be discarded. The default value of 25 is too high for systems directly connected to the Internet.

- -ok open_conn defines the maximum number of open connections that will be cached. The default is 1. This delays closing the current connection until either this invocation of sendmail needs to connect to another host or it terminates. Setting this value to zero causes connections to close immediately. Unless persistent mail connections are used, this should be set to zero.

- -oKtimeout sets the maximum amount of time a cached connection can remain idle. When the *timeout* value is exceeded, the connection is immediately closed. This value should be less than 10 min. The default is 5 min.

- -oOListen = queue_size sets the size of the input listen queue; the default value is 10. On very active servers, the amount may need to be increased.

- -oxload_average defines the system load average limit at which sendmail stops sending outgoing mail. All outgoing mail is queued until the system load average falls below this value. The default is 8, which is too high for most small and medium-size systems. This value should not be greater than 2 times the number of processors on the system.

- -oXload_average defines the system load average limit at which sendmail stops accepting incoming mail; that is, all incoming SMTP connections are refused. The default is 12, which is much too high for small and medium-size systems. This value should not be greater than 3 times the number of processors on the system.

- -oY instructs sendmail to deliver each job that is run from the queue in a separate process. This option tends to conserve memory and should be used in memory-constrained environments.

comsat

comsat, also known as the *biff server*, is the inetd process associated with sendmail. comsat listens for incoming mail and notifies users when new mail has arrived. It is invoked as needed and times out if inactive for a few minutes.

Because this service is notoriously buggy and can use quite a bit of CPU time on a very active mail server, it is often turned off. If the new mail notification facility is not absolutely required, comsat should be disabled.

WWW Servers

Tuning for Web server performance is a relatively new area for performance management. In most cases, network speed is the biggest factor that affects http server performance. In Chap. 13, tuning suggestions were given for the two most important TCP parameters from the perspective of an `http` server: `tcp_conn_req_max` and `tcp_rexmit_interval_min`.

In the `http` server itself, several options influence the performance of the server. Although these may have different names depending on the server, the function is the same in the various servers.

In order to provide complete log information, reverse DNS lookups can be performed by the server to translate IP addresses into host names. Generally, this is an unnecessary waste of resources. If possible, the DNS lookup option should be set to a level that only performs the DNS lookup when it is needed to resolve access permissions. When this option is set, the reverse DNS resolution is deferred and must be performed by the access log processing tool.

If the server supports it, keep alive should always be set on. When keep alive is set on, the keep-alive time-out value should be set to a value that will enable slow connections to take advantage of it. A good starting point is 120 s. If the server imposes a restriction on the number of keep-alive processes, the option should be set to its maximum possible value. Keep-alive processing is the single most important performance enhancement that can be used in an `http` server.

Depending on the server, a combination of processes *and* threads (such as on the Netscape server) may be used to implement `http` services. If processes, instead of threads, are used by the server, the performance analyst should ensure that the maximum number of processes is set lower than the systemwide maximum number of processes. Furthermore, if the `http` server sets a limit on the maximum number of connections that can be serviced from a single process before the process is terminated, this value should be set to its maximum value. Finally, if the server supports it, the minimum number of idle threads (or processes) should be set to the average number of concurrent request of the server. The maximum number of idle processes should not be set high; a good guideline would be to set this value to the maximum number of concurrent requests made of the server.

Summary

Network services performance management focuses heavily on tuning the major network services: NFS, NIS+, and DNS. These services can be monitored with commands, such as `nfsstat`, and most network services can be tuned either through configuration files or command options. Finally, at the end of the chapter, tips and hints for optimizing the performance of WWW servers were discussed.

Our next chapter will focus on the issues involved in tuning the kernel.

15

Kernel Tuning

Kernel tuning on Solaris is far simpler than it is on other UNIX-based operating systems. This is due to two things:

Solaris has fewer parameters than do other UNIX-based operating systems.

Solaris, for the most part, automatically adjusts to changing situations as needed, alleviating the need for manual intervention.

Introduction to Kernel Tuning on Solaris

Because of the considerations listed above, it is best to only tune the kernel when a default-value kernel value is seriously out of line with the typical load and, therefore, greatly affecting the performance of a given system. Furthermore, only the standard, well-documented variables should be tweaked. Tweaking obscure or incompletely documented variables can result in extremely poor performance or complete system failure.

Additionally, kernel tuning is complicated by changes between releases of Solaris, where parameters are added or removed, and by differences in platform, where parameters may have different effects depending on platform.

Having said that, a complete list of the tunable kernel parameters can be derived by issuing the following command for Solaris 2.4:

```
/usr/ccs/bin/nm /kernel/unix
```

For Solaris 2.5 and above, it is*

```
/usr/ccs/bin/nm /kernel/genunix /platform/'uname m'/kernel/unix
```

The output of the command is voluminous (Fig. 15-1). There are six columns for each entry:

[Index] Internal identifying index number

Value   Current value of the parameter

Size   Amount of bytes reserved for the parameter

Type   Type of parameter:

      SECT—code section

      OBJT—system object

      FUNC—system function

      FILE—file

      NOTY—the parameter has not been specified

      Bind—either local (LOCL) or global (GLOB)

      Other—not used at the present time

---

*Substitute the actual platform name as reported by the uname -m command for the `uname -m' portion of the directory name.

Figure 15-1
An example
etc/system file.

```
*ident   "@(#)system    1.15    92/11/14 SMI" /* SVR4 1.5 */
*
* SYSTEM SPECIFICATION FILE
*

* moddir:
*
*        Set the search path for modules.  This has a format similar to the
*        csh path variable. If the module isn't found in the first directory
*        it tries the second and so on. The default is /kernel /usr/kernel
*
*        Example:
*                moddir: /kernel /usr/kernel /other/modules


* root device and root filesystem configuration:
*
*        The following may be used to override the defaults provided by
*        the boot program:
*
*        rootfs:          Set the filesystem type of the root.
*
*        rootdev:         Set the root device.  This should be a fully
*                         expanded physical pathname.  The default is the
*                         physical pathname of the device where the boot
*                         program resides.  The physical pathname is
*                         highly platform and configuration dependent.
*
*        Example:
*             rootfs:ufs
*             rootdev:/sbus@1,f8000000/esp@0,800000/sd@3,0:a
*
*        (Swap device configuration should be specified in /etc/vfstab.)


* exclude:
*
*        Modules appearing in the moddir path which are NOT to be loaded,
*        even if referenced. Note that `exclude' accepts either a module name,
*        or a filename which includes the directory.
*
*        Examples:
*                exclude: win
*                exclude: sys/shmsys


* forceload:
*
*        Cause these modules to be loaded at boot time, (just before mounting
*        the root filesystem) rather than at first reference. Note that
```

```
*       forceload expects a filename which includes the directory. Also
*       note that loading a module does not necessarily imply that it will
*       be installed.
*
*       Example:
*               forceload: drv/foo


* set:
*
*       Set an integer variable in the kernel or a module to a new value.
*       This facility should be used with caution.  See system(4).
*
*       Examples:
*
*       To set variables in 'unix':
*
*               set nautopush=32
*               set maxusers=40
*
*       To set a variable named 'debug' in the module named 'test_module'
*
*               set test_module:debug = 0x13


* Begin MDD database info (do not edit)
set md:mddb_bootlist1="sd:17:16 sd:22:16 sd:41:16 sd:46:16"
* End MDD database info (do not edit)
```

Figure 15-1

(Continued) An example etc/system file.

Shndx   Name shared memory index number

Name   parameter name

Again, most of these will never need to be changed.

The performance analyst is much better off using the list of standard kernel variables that are displayed by entering the command

```
sysdef -i
```

At the end of the report (Fig. 15-2), the standard tunable parameters and their current values are listed.

Figure 15-2
Example sysdef -i
command output.

```
sysdef -i
*
* Hostid
*
   807101c4
*
* sun4d Configuration
*
*
* Devices
*
packages (driver not attached)
      disk-label (driver not attached)
      deblocker (driver not attached)
      obp-tftp (driver not attached)
options, instance #0
aliases (driver not attached)
memory (driver not attached)
virtual-memory (driver not attached)
openprom (driver not attached)
boards (driver not attached)
      bif (driver not attached)
      bif (driver not attached)
cpu-unit, instance #0
      TI,TMS390Z55, instance #0
      bootbus, instance #0
            zs, instance #0
            zs, instance #1
            eeprom (driver not attached)
            sram (driver not attached)
            leds (driver not attached)
cpu-unit, instance #1
      TI,TMS390Z55, instance #1
cpu-unit, instance #2
      TI,TMS390Z55, instance #2
      bootbus, instance #1
            zs, instance #2
            zs, instance #3
            eeprom (driver not attached)
            sram (driver not attached)
            leds (driver not attached)
cpu-unit, instance #3
      TI,TMS390Z55, instance #3
mem-unit, instance #4
mem-unit, instance #5
io-unit, instance #6
      sbi, instance #0
            dma, instance #0
                  esp, instance #0
                        sd (driver not attached)
                        st (driver not attached)
                        sd, instance #0
                        sd, instance #1
                        sd, instance #2 (driver not attached)
                        sd, instance #3 (driver not attached)
                        sd, instance #4 (driver not attached)
                        sd, instance #5 (driver not attached)
                        sd, instance #6
                        st, instance #0 (driver not attached)
                        st, instance #1 (driver not attached)
                        st, instance #2 (driver not attached)
```

Figure 15-2

(Continued) Example
sysdef -i com-
mand output.

```
                                          st, instance #3 (driver not attached)
                                          st, instance #4
                                          st, instance #5
                                          st, instance #6 (driver not attached)
                            lebuffer, instance #0
                                  le, instance #0
                      cgsix, instance #0
                      SUNW,soc, instance #0
                            SUNW,pln (driver not attached)
                                  SUNW,ssd (driver not attached)
                            SUNW,pln (driver not attached)
                                  SUNW,ssd (driver not attached)
                            SUNW,pln, instance #0
                                  ssd, instance #0
                                  ssd, instance #1
                                  ssd, instance #2
                                  ssd, instance #3 (driver not attached)
                                  ssd, instance #4 (driver not attached)
                                  ssd, instance #5
                                  ssd, instance #6
                                  ssd, instance #7
                                  ssd, instance #8 (driver not attached)
                                  ssd, instance #9 (driver not attached)
                                  ssd, instance #10
                                  ssd, instance #11
                                  ssd, instance #12
                                  ssd, instance #13 (driver not attached)
                                  ssd, instance #14 (driver not attached)
                                  ssd, instance #15
                                  ssd, instance #16
                                  ssd, instance #17
                                  ssd, instance #18 (driver not attached)
                                  ssd, instance #19 (driver not attached)
                                  ssd, instance #20
                                  ssd, instance #21
                                  ssd, instance #22
                                  ssd, instance #23 (driver not attached)
                                  ssd, instance #24 (driver not attached)
                                  ssd, instance #25
                                  ssd, instance #26
                                  ssd, instance #27
                                  ssd, instance #28 (driver not attached)
                                  ssd, instance #29 (driver not attached)
            io-unit, instance #7
                  sbi, instance #1
                        dma, instance #1
                              esp, instance #1
                                  sd (driver not attached)
                                  st (driver not attached)
                                  sd, instance #15 (driver not attached)
                                  sd, instance #16 (driver not attached)
                                  sd, instance #17 (driver not attached)
                                  sd, instance #18 (driver not attached)
                                  sd, instance #19 (driver not attached)
                                  sd, instance #20 (driver not attached)
                                  sd, instance #21 (driver not attached)
                                  st, instance #7 (driver not attached)
                                  st, instance #8 (driver not attached)
                                  st, instance #9 (driver not attached)
                                  st, instance #10 (driver not attached)
                                  st, instance #11 (driver not attached)
```

Figure 15-2

(Continued) Example
sysdef -i com-
mand output.

```
                                         st, instance #12 (driver not attached)
                                         st, instance #13 (driver not attached)
                             lebuffer, instance #1
                                   le, instance #1
        pseudo, instance #0
              clone, instance #0
              ip, instance #0
              tcp, instance #0
              udp, instance #0
              icmp, instance #0
              arp, instance #0
              sad, instance #0
              consms, instance #0
              conskbd, instance #0
              wc, instance #0
              iwscn, instance #0
              mm, instance #0
              cn, instance #0
              vxio, instance #0
              vxspec, instance #0
              vxspec, instance #1
              vxspec, instance #2
              vxspec, instance #3
              openeepr, instance #0
              log, instance #0
              kstat, instance #0
              ksyms, instance #0
              tl, instance #0
              ptm, instance #0
              pts, instance #0
              logindmux, instance #0
              sy, instance #0
              vol, instance #0
        *
        * Loadable Objects
        *
        misc/dlma
        unix
        drv/arp
        drv/cn
        drv/ip
        drv/logindmux
        drv/logindmux
        misc/strplumb
        drv/arp
        drv/tcp
        drv/leo
        misc/tlimod
        drv/rtvc
        drv/be
        drv/soc
        drv/ssd
        drv/clone
        drv/clone
        misc/swapgeneric
        drv/cn
        exec/elfexec
        exec/intpexec
        exec/aoutexec
        sched/TS_DPTBL
        sched/TS
```

Figure 15-2

(Continued) Example `sysdef -i` command output.

```
drv/conskbd
drv/conskbd
drv/consms
drv/consms
strmod/bufmod
strmod/connld
strmod/dedump
strmod/ldterm
strmod/ms
strmod/sockmod
strmod/timod
strmod/telmod
strmod/rpcmod
strmod/pckt
strmod/rlmod
strmod/pfmod
strmod/pipemod
strmod/ptem
strmod/redirmod
strmod/tirdwr
strmod/ttcompat
strmod/arp
strmod/kb
strmod/hwc
strmod/bd
drv/esp
drv/sd
drv/ssd
drv/pln
drv/vxio
drv/vxspec
drv/icmp
drv/vxspec
misc/consconfig
drv/udp
misc/des
drv/ip
misc/ipc
misc/nfs_dlboot
misc/scsi
drv/pln
drv/isp
misc/klmmod
misc/seg_drv
misc/seg_mapdev
drv/iwscn
drv/iwscn
drv/le
drv/llc1
drv/llc1
drv/options
sys/kaio
sys/c2audit
sys/inst_sync
sys/msgsys
sys/semsys
sys/shmsys
sys/nfs
drv/options
drv/pseudo
drv/pseudo
```

Figure 15-2
(Continued) Example
sysdef -i com-
mand output.

```
drv/qe
drv/sad
drv/sad
fs/lofs
fs/autofs
fs/cachefs
fs/nfs
        hard link:  sys/nfs
fs/procfs
fs/tmpfs
fs/ufs
fs/fifofs
fs/hsfs
fs/specfs
drv/tl
drv/sp
drv/sp
drv/st
drv/st
drv/sy
drv/sy
drv/tcp
drv/tl
drv/udp
drv/xbox
drv/bootbus
drv/bpp
drv/cpu
drv/dma
drv/lebuffer
drv/log
drv/log
drv/mm
drv/mm
drv/openeepr
drv/openeepr
drv/profile
drv/profile
drv/rootnex
drv/vxio
drv/icmp
drv/sbusmem
drv/sbusmem
drv/sd
drv/stc
drv/stc
drv/wc
drv/wc
drv/zs
drv/zsh
drv/zsh
drv/cgsix
drv/cgthree
drv/qec
drv/sbi
*
* System Configuration
*
  swap files
swapfile              dev  swaplo blocks    free
/dev/dsk/c0t0d0s1     32,1      8 1397080 1324952
```

Figure 15-2

(Continued) Example
sysdef -i com-
mand output.

```
*
* Tunable Parameters
*
 5312512     maximum memory allowed in buffer cache (bufhwm)
    3210     maximum number of processes (v.v_proc)
      99     maximum global priority in sys class (MAXCLSYSPRI)
    3205     maximum processes per user id (v.v_maxup)
      30     auto update time limit in seconds (NAUTOUP)
      25     page stealing low water mark (GPGSLO)
       5     fsflush run rate (FSFLUSHR)
      25     minimum resident memory for avoiding deadlock (MINARMEM)
      25     minimum swapable memory for avoiding deadlock (MINASMEM)
*
* Utsname Tunables
*
     5.4   release (REL)
   condor  node name (NODE)
    SunOS  system name (SYS)
Generic_101945-43  version (VER)
*
* Process Resource Limit Tunables (Current:Maximum)
*
Infinity:Infinity cpu time
Infinity:Infinity file size
7ffff000:7ffff000 heap size
  800000:7ffff000 stack size
Infinity:Infinity core file size
      40:     400 file descriptors
Infinity:Infinity mapped memory
*
* Streams Tunables
*
       9        maximum number of pushes allowed (NSTRPUSH)
   65536        maximum stream message size (STRMSGSZ)
    1024        max size of ctl part of message (STRCTLSZ)
*
* IPC Messages
*
       0        entries in msg map (MSGMAP)
       0        max message size (MSGMAX)
       0        max bytes on queue (MSGMNB)
       0        message queue identifiers (MSGMNI)
       0        message segment size (MSGSSZ)
       0        system message headers (MSGTQL)
       0        message segments (MSGSEG)
*
* IPC Semaphores
*
      10        entries in semaphore map (SEMMAP)
      70        semaphore identifiers (SEMMNI)
     200        semaphores in system (SEMMNS)
      30        undo structures in system (SEMMNU)
      25        max semaphores per id (SEMMSL)
      10        max operations per semop call (SEMOPM)
      10        max undo entries per process (SEMUME)
   32767        semaphore maximum value (SEMVMX)
   16384        adjust on exit max value (SEMAEM)
*
* IPC Shared Memory
*
 8388608        max shared memory segment size (SHMMAX)
```

Figure 15-2
(Continued) Example
sysdef -i com-
mand output.

```
        1       min shared memory segment size (SHMMIN)
      100       shared memory identifiers (SHMMNI)
       10       max attached shm segments per process (SHMSEG)
*
* Time Sharing Scheduler Tunables
*
  60    maximum time sharing user priority (TSMAXUPRI)
  SYS   system class name (SYS_NAME)
```

Modifications to kernel variables are made by placing entries in the /etc/system file. All entries in this file should be carefully evaluated and checked. The kernel reads this file during system start-up and applies all of the changes found in the file to the kernel directly. The modifications are neither verified nor validated for accuracy or applicability.

In the event an entry in the /etc/system file causes system failure, the system operator recovers from the situation by rebooting the system using the boot -a option. When prompted for the name of the configuration file, either a backup copy of /etc/system or of /dev/null, which would bypass all kernel customization, can be used.

The format of entries in the /etc/system file for entries that are used to modify kernel variables follows the syntax of

```
set variable = new_value
```

Note that these entries follow the other types of entries in the /etc/system file (Fig. 15-3), such as those that force modules to load, exclude modules from loading, or set paths for locating kernel modules. This is a convention, not a requirement.

```
/kernel/genunix:

[Index]    Value      Size    Type  Bind  Other Shndx   Name

[11]  |         0 |      0 | SECT | LOCL | 0    | 10     |
[2]   |         0 |      0 | SECT | LOCL | 0    | 1      |
[3]   |         0 |      0 | SECT | LOCL | 0    | 2      |
[4]   |         0 |      0 | SECT | LOCL | 0    | 3      |
[5]   |         0 |      0 | SECT | LOCL | 0    | 4      |
[6]   |         0 |      0 | SECT | LOCL | 0    | 5      |
[7]   |         0 |      0 | SECT | LOCL | 0    | 6      |
[8]   |         0 |      0 | SECT | LOCL | 0    | 7      |
[9]   |         0 |      0 | SECT | LOCL | 0    | 8      |
[10]  |         0 |      0 | SECT | LOCL | 0    | 9      |
[14]  |         0 |      0 | SECT | LOCL | 0    | 13     |
[12]  |         0 |      0 | SECT | LOCL | 0    | 11     |
```

Figure 15-3
Abbreviated example nm command output.

```
[13]   |        0|       0|SECT |LOCL |0    |12      |
[2263] |        4|      64|OBJT |GLOB |0    |COMMON  |EIO_vfs
[2895] |    28416|      32|OBJT |GLOB |0    |5       |EIO_vfsops
[2714] |    37628|      28|FUNC |GLOB |0    |2       |OTHERQ
[2881] |   266416|      16|FUNC |GLOB |0    |2       |QLOCK
[1829] |    37656|      20|FUNC |GLOB |0    |2       |RD
[1149] |        4|       4|OBJT |GLOB |0    |COMMON  |SAD_MAJOR
[1158] |    37676|      24|FUNC |GLOB |0    |2       |SAMESTR
[2191] |        0|       0|NOTY |GLOB |0    |UNDEF   |Sysbase
[1054] |        0|       0|NOTY |GLOB |0    |UNDEF   |Syslimit
[2062] |    37712|      19|FUNC |GLOB |0    |2       |WR
[3315] |        0|       0|NOTY |GLOB |0    |UNDEF   |__div64
[1949] |        0|       0|NOTY |GLOB |0    |UNDEF   |__divrem64
[1764] |      772|       8|FUNC |GLOB |0    |2       |__ipltospl
[2651] |        0|       0|NOTY |GLOB |0    |UNDEF   |__mul64
[2060] |        0|       0|NOTY |WEAK |0    |UNDEF   |__tnf_probe_version_1
[2206] |        0|       0|NOTY |WEAK |0    |UNDEF   |__tnf_tag_version_1
[2115] |        0|       0|NOTY |GLOB |0    |UNDEF   |__udivrem64
[1862] |        0|       0|NOTY |GLOB |0    |UNDEF   |_argsbase
[2446] |        0|       0|NOTY |GLOB |0    |UNDEF   |_defaultstksz
[2825] |        0|       0|NOTY |GLOB |0    |UNDEF   |_diskrpm
[46]   |    11200|     436|FUNC |LOCL |0    |2       |_doprint
[1640] |        0|       0|NOTY |GLOB |0    |UNDEF   |_dsize_limit
[2842] |        0|       0|NOTY |GLOB |0    |UNDEF   |_kernelbase
[996]  |        0|       0|NOTY |GLOB |0    |UNDEF   |_maxhandspreadpages
[1439] |        0|       0|NOTY |GLOB |0    |UNDEF   |_maxslp
[3404] |        0|       0|NOTY |GLOB |0    |UNDEF   |_mmu_pagemask
[2265] |        0|       0|NOTY |GLOB |0    |UNDEF   |_mmu_pageoffset
[1606] |        0|       0|NOTY |GLOB |0    |UNDEF   |_mmu_pageshift
[1315] |        0|       0|NOTY |GLOB |0    |UNDEF   |_mmu_pagesize
[1296] |        0|       0|NOTY |GLOB |0    |UNDEF   |_msg_bsize
[2613] |        0|       0|NOTY |GLOB |0    |UNDEF   |_nbpg
[1887] |        0|       0|NOTY |GLOB |0    |UNDEF   |_pagemask
[1487] |        0|       0|NOTY |GLOB |0    |UNDEF   |_pageoffset
[1559] |        0|       0|NOTY |GLOB |0    |UNDEF   |_pageshift
[1253] |        0|       0|NOTY |GLOB |0    |UNDEF   |_pagesize
[1120] |        0|       0|NOTY |GLOB |0    |UNDEF   |_pgthresh
[44]   |    11008|      20|FUNC |LOCL |0    |2       |_pput
[47]   |    11636|     113|FUNC |LOCL |0    |2       |_printn
[45]   |    11028|      20|FUNC |LOCL |0    |2       |_sput
[964]  |        0|       0|NOTY |GLOB |0    |UNDEF   |_ssize_limit
[1988] |        0|       0|NOTY |GLOB |0    |UNDEF   |_userlimit
[1605] |    12512|     256|FUNC |GLOB |0    |2       |access
[53]   |        0|       0|FILE |LOCL |0    |ABS     |access.c
[2344] |        0|       0|NOTY |GLOB |0    |UNDEF   |acct
[2390] |        4|      40|OBJT |GLOB |0    |COMMON  |acctbuf
[1261] |        4|       4|OBJT |GLOB |0    |COMMON  |acctvp
[1631] |    12768|      84|FUNC |GLOB |0    |2       |acl
[54]   |        0|       0|FILE |LOCL |0    |ABS     |acl.c
[1161] |        4|       8|OBJT |GLOB |0    |COMMON  |aclock
[1792] |   376096|     148|FUNC |GLOB |0    |2       |add_class
[2646] |    57596|      20|FUNC |GLOB |0    |2       |add_ns
[2544] |   187576|      37|FUNC |GLOB |0    |2       |add_one_utstop
[866]  |   363640|     216|FUNC |LOCL |0    |2       |add_spec
[911]  |   372636|     112|FUNC |LOCL |0    |2       |add_val
```

Figure 15-3

Abbreviated example nm command output.

```
[2213]   |      2360|     96|FUNC |GLOB |0     |2       |address_in_memlist
[1616]   |         0|    132|FUNC |GLOB |0     |2       |addupc
[1973]   |    253020|    141|FUNC |GLOB |0     |2       |adjfmtp
[2580]   |    206528|    188|FUNC |GLOB |0     |2       |adjmsg
[1249]   |     14416|    328|FUNC |GLOB |0     |2       |adjtime
[56]  |        0|      0|FILE |LOCL |0     |ABS    |adjtime.c
[2655]   |      2952|      4|OBJT |GLOB |0     |5       |aignore
[1066]   |     16188|    312|FUNC |GLOB |0     |2       |aio_cleanup
[1664]   |     16500|    228|FUNC |GLOB |0     |2       |aio_cleanup_exit
[2393]   |     16728|     76|FUNC |GLOB |0     |2       |aio_copyout_result
[61]  |    15668|    332|FUNC |LOCL |0     |2       |aio_done
[60]  |        0|      0|FILE |LOCL |0     |ABS    |aio_subr.c
[1525]   |     14992|    196|FUNC |GLOB |0     |2       |alarm
[57]  |        0|      0|FILE |LOCL |0     |ABS    |alarm.c
[966] |        0|      0|NOTY |GLOB |0     |UNDEF  |alloc_cid
[23]  |      3968|    430|FUNC |LOCL |0     |2       |alloc_hunk
[1931]   |     52992|    152|FUNC |GLOB |0     |2       |allocate_execsw
[1076]   |    256176|    205|FUNC |GLOB |0     |2       |allocate_fmodsw
[854] |   358096|     64|FUNC |LOCL |0     |2       |allocate_modp
[2820]   |    321972|     88|FUNC |GLOB |0     |2       |allocate_vfssw
[2521]   |    204476|    120|FUNC |GLOB |0     |2       |allocb
[554] |   204596|     60|FUNC |LOCL |0     |2       |allocb_tryhard
[2950]   |         4|      4|OBJT |GLOB |0     |COMMON |allocb_tryhard_fails
[1101]   |    254188|    188|FUNC |GLOB |0     |2       |allocb_wait
[1885]   |    254116|     48|FUNC |GLOB |0     |2       |allocband
[2768]   |    248396|    112|FUNC |GLOB |0     |2       |alloclink
[2564]   |    253744|    164|FUNC |GLOB |0     |2       |allocq
[1153]   |    181292|    148|FUNC |GLOB |0     |2       |alloctty
[710] |    26412|      4|OBJT |LOCL |0     |5       |allthreads
[1711]   |         4|     96|OBJT |GLOB |0     |COMMON |ani_free_pool
[1110]   |     15656|     10|FUNC |GLOB |0     |2       |anocancel
[750] |   323276|     60|FUNC |LOCL |0     |2       |anon_addhash
[1007]   |    324168|    244|FUNC |GLOB |0     |2       |anon_alloc
[746] |    25468|      4|OBJT |LOCL |0     |6       |anon_cache
[1532]   |         4|      4|OBJT |GLOB |0     |COMMON |anon_debug
[1094]   |    324412|    336|FUNC |GLOB |0     |2       |anon_decref
[2535]   |    324748|    136|FUNC |GLOB |0     |2       |anon_dup
[3294]   |    324884|     72|FUNC |GLOB |0     |2       |anon_free
[1784]   |    324956|    288|FUNC |GLOB |0     |2       |anon_getpage
[2791]   |         4|      4|OBJT |GLOB |0     |COMMON |anon_hash
[2049]   |         4|      4|OBJT |GLOB |0     |COMMON |anon_hash_size
```

Figure 15-3

(Continued) Abbreviated example nm command output.

maxusers

The maxusers parameter is used to provide a baseline upon which other parameters are sized. Originally, this parameter was specified to size system tables in relationship to the anticipated number of users. Today, though, it neither limits the number of users on the system nor does it reflect the actual number of users that may be using a system at any given point in time.

In Solaris, `maxusers` is automatically configured by the kernel based on the amount of physical memory on the machine (Table 15-1). The maximum value is 2048.

As previously stated, the value of `maxusers` affects the default settings for several other kernel table parameters. The calculations that are used are outlined in Table 15-2.

Other Kernel Variables

Although many of the important kernel variables are tuned via the `maxusers` variable, hundreds of others are not. And, for some variables that are constrained by `maxusers`, the default calculations may not be sufficient. Because of this, several kernel parameters are possible targets for consideration depending on the workload of the system.

TABLE 15-1

Solaris 2.X
maxusers Default
Values

Memory Size (MB)	maxusers value
32	8
40	32
64	40
128	64
>128	128

TABLE 15-2

Kernel Parameters
Affected by
maxusers

Kernel table	Kernel variable	Variable value
Callout	ncallout	16 + max_nprocs
Inode	ufs_ninode	max_nprocs + 16 + maxusers + 64
Name cache lookup	ncsize	max_nprocs + 16 + maxusers + 64
Process	max_nprocs	10 + 16*maxusers
Disk quota structure	ndquot	(maxusers*NMOUNT)/4 + max_nprocs
User processes	maxuprc	max_nprocs-5

The `pt_cnt` variable sets the limit on the number of remote logins. The default value is 48. On a very active system, this limit may need to be increased. On a very overworked system, this value may be decreased to avoid further overburdening the system. The maximum value of this variable is 3000.

The default value of the `ncsize` parameter is controlled by `maxusers`, but the calculation is invalid if the machine is used as an NFS server. This parameter defines the size of the file directory name lookup cache. The default calculation is

$$ncsize = 17 * \text{maxusers} + 90.$$

On systems with 256MB or less RAM, it is suggested that the value be set to 2048 or greater, depending on the NFS load on the system.

On a related vein, the `ufs_ninode` parameter is calculated using the same formula as `ncsize` ($17 * \text{maxusers} + 90$). As could be guessed, this is inadequate as well. This parameter defines the maximum number of inodes that will be cached. It should be set to double the value of `ncsize`.

`maxuprc` limits the number of processes a user may start. The default setting is

$$maxuprc = 16 * \text{maxusers} + 5.$$

This value may be much too high depending on the workload and user mix on the system and should be lowered. However, if not all users can be constrained via a global system limit, consider limiting the maximum number of processes on a per-user basis via individual shell profiles.

The buffer cache is used to cache inode, indirect block, and cylinder group information. The default value allows up to 2 percent of physical memory to be allocated for this purpose. In almost all cases, this is far too much. This table should be limited by specifying a value for `bufhwm`. The `sar -b` report (Chap. 16) details information on buffer usage. Use that report as a base for making changes.

Fixed Parameters

Several parameters that may have been previously specified in the `/etc/system` file to influence the paging subsystem are no longer necessary because Solaris now provides fixed values for these variables or simply no longer uses them.*

In Solaris 2.4 and greater, the value of `minfree` is set to a constant value of 50 pages for sun4d processors and 25 pages for all other processor types. This value is used as a limit to determine when swapping should begin. If the amount of free memory falls below this value for more than 5 s, Solaris will start swapping processes out. Solaris also uses this value as an upper limit for loading programs. If a program is smaller than the value of `minfree`, it will be loaded all at one time rather than being paged in in the normal fashion.

Along the same lines, `desfree` is set to a constant value of 100 pages for sun4d processors and 50 pages for all other processor types in Solaris 2.4 and later. When the free memory in the system falls below the `desfree` value for more than 30 s, Solaris will start swapping processes out. Furthermore, when Solaris starts taking pages from the free list, the amount of free memory is compared to the `desfree` value. If the amount of free memory is less, an immediate wake-up call is sent to the `pageout` daemon.

The `lotsfree` parameter is set to a constant value of 256 pages for sun4d processors and 128 pages for all other processor types starting with Solaris 2.4. `lotsfree` is used as a baseline for the page scan rate. When the amount of free memory is equal to or greater than `lotsfree`, the scan rate is set to the `slowscan` rate.† If the amount of free memory ever drops below the `lotsfree` value, a wake-up call is immediately sent to the `pageout` daemon.

The `tune_t_gpgslo` is no longer used, its function being folded into the `minfree` and `desfree` values.

The `handspreadpages` parameter is set by the kernel to coincide with the value of `fastscan` Paging Parameters.

---

*Technically, these values could be changed by using adb to patch the kernel. This is not advised. Entries in the /etc/system file for these parameters are ignored by Version 2.4 of Solaris and greater. The only exception to this is for the lotsfree parameter. On multiprocessor systems, the default value should be multiplied by the number of processors. On uniprocessor systems, the kernel will automatically override any specification with the default value.

†The `slowscan` rate was fixed at 100 pages per second in Solaris 2.4 and versions thereafter.

Paging Parameters

Although many of the parameters previously used to influence paging have been made fixed values or completely dropped, there are still a number of parameters that can be modified to influence the performance of the system.

The fast page scan rate, fastscan, is used as the upper limit in the page scan mechanism. When memory is freely available, page scanning occurs at the slowscan rate, which is fixed at 100 pages a second. As the number of free pages in the system decreases, the speed of the page scanning process increases up to the limit defined by fastscan. The default value is the number of physical memory pages (or the value specified by physmem*) divided by 4. The maximum rate, regardless of amount of physical memory is 16,384 pages per second.

The maxpgio parameter defines the maximum number of page-out operations per second the system will schedule. The default value is 40 except on sun4d processors, where the value is 60. This value should *always* be tuned to coincide with the I/O load the disk subsystem can support. The I/O load is easily calculated by summing the throughput rates of all disk drives† that are used for swapping.

The autofs parameter defines the maximum age in seconds of a modified file system page in physical memory. Along with the tune_f_fsflushr parameter,‡ these two parameters control the behavior of the fsflush daemon. The fsflush daemon flushes modified (i.e., "dirty") file system pages from physical memory onto the backing store. If a machine has a large amount of physical memory with lots of modified file system pages, the overhead of the fsflush daemon can become excessive. On stable systems, the overhead of the fsflush daemon can be reduced by increasing the amount of time a modified file system page remains in memory. Obviously, the longer a modified page remains in memory and not written to the physical disk, the greater the risk of data loss should the system crash. The costs of overhead versus the risk of data loss must be carefully weighed by the performance analyst.

---

*physmem is used to artificially reduce the amount of physical memory available to the system. Unless special testing is being done, this parameter should not be specified.

†See the *forced flow law* in Chap. 4 for more information on maximum throughput rates.

‡The tune_t_fsflushr parameter defines how often the fsflush daemon will wake up.

In general, the overhead of the `fsflush` daemon should not account for more than 5 percent of the processor usage on a busy system. The amount of CPU time `fsflush` consumes is determined by comparing the amount of CPU time `fsflush` has used to the total amount of elapsed time the system has been up. For example,

```
$ ps -p 3
  PID TTY    TIME CMD
   3 ?       56:00 fsflush
$ uptime
 3:42pm up 12 day(s), 3:31, 1 user, load average: 0.00, 0.00, 0.01
$
```

The calculation =
fsflush time total system uptime =
56 min * 60 (12 days * 86400) + (3 h *
3600) + (31 min * 60) =
3360 1049460 = 0.3 percent of CPU time

This is clearly very acceptable.
This is a second example:

```
% ps -p 3
  PID TTY    TIME COMD
   3 ?     10380:23 fsflush
% uptime
 3:31pm up 77 day(s), 1:27, 9 users, load average:
0.08, 0.09, 0.08
%
```

(10380 min * 60) + 23 (77 days * 86400) + (1
h * 3600) + (27 min * 60) =
622823 6658020 = 9.35 percent of CPU time

In this case, `fsflush` is using too much of the processor, and the amount of overhead is not acceptable.

The `max_page_get` parameter limits the number of pages that can be allocated in one operation. The default is set to one-half the amount of physical memory on the machine. There may be unusual circumstances that require increasing this value, but it should never be increased to more than 90 percent of the physical memory on the machine. Doing so could result in a system deadlock.

Finally, the `use_mxcc_prefetch` parameter is used to control whether or not the next cache subblock is prefetched, that is, retrieved before it is actually needed. This is very useful on systems that are used primarily for running applications that perform intensive floating-point operations in a linear manner. If the workload is not primarily of this type, prefetch is likely to have little beneficial effect and may, in fact, degrade the performance of the system. On large machine architectures, like the SPARCserver 1000 (sun4d), this is set off by default. However, on smaller machines, such as the SPARCstation 20, this value is set on by default. If the machine, regardless of size, is used primarily as a multiuser, multiworkload server, it is probably best to turn this parameter off by specifying

```
set use_mxcc_prefetch = 0
```

Setting Other Parameters

Kernel parameters for specific subsystems can be set in the /etc/system file as well. In these cases, the syntax of the set command in /etc/system is slightly different: The parameter name must be prefixed with its subsystem identifier:

```
set subsystem_id:variable = new_value
```

For instance, the parameters of the shared memory subsystem are often modified in /etc/system based on the specific requirements of application programs.

The TCP, IP, and UDP parameters discussed in Chap. 13 under the ndd command may be specified in /etc/system as well. For example, to set the TCP listen backlog queue to 128 entries, the following line could be added to /etc/system:

```
set tpc:tcp_conn_req_max = 128
```

The advantage of using this method, as opposed to creating new startup scripts or modifying existing ones, is that it reduces script maintenance by concentrating changes in a central location.

Summary

Kernel tuning primarily revolves around the changes made to system parameters in the /etc/system file. These parameters can be groups into four groups: `maxusers`, fixed parameters, paging parameters, and miscellaneous parameters.

With this chapter, the section on performance tuning concludes. The next section focuses on the capacity planning function.

Capacity
Planning

T his final section discusses some of the aspects of long-term capacity planning and monitoring.

The first part of the section is devoted to a discussion of the Solaris tools and methods that enable long-term reporting and monitoring of the system. After that, the elements involved in developing a proactive strategy and reporting structure are discussed.

16

System Activity

Solaris uses two major tools for long-term reporting and logging of system data. The focus of this chapter is the System Activity Data Collector (sadc). The function of the sadc is to gather statistics on a systemwide basis. The next chapter discusses system accounting and focuses on statistics at the user level. This chapter is not concerned with using the results as reporting mechanisms for others within the organization; that is the focus of a latter chapter.

System Activity Data Collector

sadc is a program that collects system activity data on a regular basis. The data that is gathered by sadc is collected from the counters in the Solaris kernel. These counters include information about CPU utilization, buffer usage, I/O activity, terminal device activity, mode switching, system call activity, file access, queue activity, interprocess communications (IPC) calls, and paging. Once collected, the data is analyzed with the System Activity Reporter (sar) program.

Setting Up System Data Collection

In most circumstances, sadc is not invoked directly. In order to collect data on a regular basis, the system activity data collector is normally run via a crontab entry for the script /usr/lib/sa/sa1. This shell script is used to collect and store data in the binary file /var/adm/sa/sadd where dd is the current day. A typical example would be the following entries in the sys crontab. The first entry collects sadc data every 30 min during the hours of 9 P.M. to 5 A.M., Monday through Friday. The second entry collects data every 10 min from 6:00 A.M. to 8:00 P.M., Monday through Friday. The third entry collects data every hour on the weekends:

```
0,30 21-5 * * 1-5 /usr/lib/sa/sa1
0,10,20,30,40,50 6-20 * * 1-5 /usr/lib/sa/sa1
0* * * 6-7 /usr/lib/sa/sa1
```

The only time the data collector is directly invoked is at system boot time, when booting to multiuser mode. The entry made marks the time at which the counters are reset to zero. When system accounting is enabled, boot-up script /etc/rc2.d/S21perf is run during the startup. In this script, the sadc is invoked directly to write the restart mark to the daily data file with the command:

```
su sys -c "/usr/lib/sa/sadc /var/adm/sa/sa`date +%d`"
```

sar—The System Activity Reporter

sar has two modes of operation. The most common mode extracts data from a sadc collection file. sar extracts data from the system activity daily data file `/var/adm/sa/sadd` (where *dd* represents the current day) by default. However, data from an previous data collection file can be used if the `-f filename` option is used. In both cases, though, the start and end times of the report may be bound using the `-e` (for end) and `-s` (for stop) arguments with the time specified in *hh:mm:ss* form. The data intervals in the file are used for reporting purposes unless overridden by the `-i seconds` option, in which case the specified interval is used.

The second mode of operation monitors the system in real-time. `sar` samples the cumulative activity counters in the kernel for a specified intervals every specified number of seconds. For example,

```
/usr/lib/sa/sar -a 20 30
```

would run the option `a` report (discussed below) every 20 times at 30-s intervals. When used in real-time, the interval specified should always be 5 s or greater. If an interval of less than 5 s is used, the results of the monitoring are significantly affected by the overhead of `sar` itself. The `-o filename` option may be used to save the samples collected in a data collection format file.

A `sar` shell script is provided (`/usr/lib/sa/sa2`) to allow for the automatic daily reporting. The output is sent to a file named `/var/adm/sa/sardd`, where *dd* represents the current date. As with the data collector, an entry must be made in the sys `crontab` entry `/var/spool/cron/crontabs/sys` to run the reporting script. The following entry would run at 6:00 P.M. every day and report important activities on an hourly basis from 8:00 A.M. to 6:00 P.M.:

```
5 18 * * 1-5 /usr/lib/sa/sa2 -s 8:00 -e 18:01 -i 1200 -A
```

The System Activity Reports

The various reports are selected by the System Activity Reporter via option flags. The report option flags are specified after any other flags, such as start and end times. The `-A` report option reports on all data. It is equivalent to specifying `/usr/lib/sa/sar -abcdgkmpqruvwy`.

File System and I/O Device Reports

The `-a` option is used to report information collected by the file access system routines (Fig. 16-1). The report contains three fields:

Figure 16-1

sar -a command
output.

```
sar -a
SunOS fullerton 5.4 Generic_101945-46 sun4m     09/23/97

00:00:01   iget/s namei/s dirbk/s
01:00:01        0        0        0
02:00:02       28       48       34
03:00:03        0        1        0
04:00:01        1        1        1
05:00:01        0        0        0
06:00:01        0        0        0
07:00:01        0        0        0
08:00:01        0        1        1
09:00:00        0        2        2
10:00:01        0        2        2
11:00:03        0        5        4
12:00:01        0        5        5
13:00:01        0        7        6
14:00:01        0        5        4
15:00:02        0        6        6
16:00:02        0        9        5
17:00:01        0       12        7
18:00:01        0        6        6
19:00:01        0        3        3
20:00:00        0        3        4
21:00:01        0        6        5
22:00:01        0        3        2
23:00:01        0        1        1

Average          1        5        4
```

- iget/s—the number of inode gets per second
- namei/s—the number of file name gets per second
- dirblk/s—the number of directory blocks read per second

As the kernel spends more time accessing files, the values in these fields will increase. This report is useful for establishing a baseline for "average" system usage. There are no inherently good or bad values.

The -d option (Fig. 16-2) is used to report activity for block device (e.g., disk or tape drives) with the exception of XDC disks and tape drives. For each device, the activity data reported is

- %busy—busy time, the portion of time the device was busy servicing a request
- avque—the average number of requests outstanding during that time
- r + w/s—number of read/write transfers to or from a device per second

```
sar -d
SunOS fullerton 5.4 Generic_101945-46 sun4m      09/23/97

00:00:01  device    %busy   avque  r+w/s  blks/s  avwait  avserv

01:00:01  sd1         0      0.0     0      0       0.0     0.0
          sd2         0      0.0     0      0       0.0     19.0
          sd3         0      0.0     0      1       0.0     58.2
          sd5         0      0.0     0      0       0.0     18.9

02:00:02  sd1         0      0.0     0      0       0.0     0.0
          sd2         1      0.0     1      9       0.0     22.6
          sd3         4      0.2     2      23      0.0     94.1
          sd5         1      0.0     1      8       0.0     24.2

03:00:03  sd1         0      0.0     0      0       0.0     0.0
          sd2         0      0.0     0      0       0.0     17.8
          sd3         0      0.0     0      2       0.0     59.4
          sd5         0      0.0     0      0       0.0     14.8

04:00:01  sd1         0      0.0     0      0       0.0     0.0
          sd2         0      0.0     0      0       0.0     52.0
          sd3         0      0.0     0      2       0.0     78.6
          sd5         0      0.0     0      0       0.0     51.9

05:00:01  sd1         0      0.0     0      0       0.0     0.0
          sd2         0      0.0     0      0       0.0     16.8
          sd3         0      0.0     0      1       0.0     62.6
          sd5         0      0.0     0      0       0.0     0.0

06:00:01  sd1         0      0.0     0      0       0.0     0.0
          sd2         0      0.0     0      0       0.0     17.0
          sd3         0      0.0     0      1       0.0     50.6
          sd5         0      0.0     0      0       0.0     15.4

07:00:01  sd1         0      0.0     0      0       0.0     0.0
          sd2         0      0.0     0      0       0.0     19.6
          sd3         0      0.0     0      1       0.0     50.7
          sd5         0      0.0     0      1       0.0     19.9

08:00:01  sd1         0      0.0     0      0       0.0     0.0
          sd2         0      0.0     0      0       0.0     21.9
          sd3         0      0.0     0      1       0.0     57.9
          sd5         0      0.0     0      0       0.0     18.2

09:00:00  sd1         0      0.0     0      0       0.0     0.0
          sd2         0      0.0     0      0       0.0     21.4
          sd3         0      0.0     0      3       0.0     62.0
          sd5         0      0.0     0      0       0.0     18.0

10:00:01  sd1         0      0.0     0      0       0.0     0.0
          sd2         0      0.0     0      1       0.0     25.0
          sd3         0      0.0     0      4       0.0     60.6
          sd5         0      0.0     0      1       0.0     18.9

11:00:03  sd1         0      0.0     0      0       0.0     0.0
          sd2         0      0.0     0      1       0.0     32.4
          sd3         1      0.0     0      5       0.0     91.0
          sd5         0      0.0     0      1       0.0     21.4

12:00:01  sd1         0      0.0     0      0       0.0     0.0
```

Figure 16-2

sar -d command output.

	sd2	0	0.0	0	2	0.0	35.4
	sd3	1	0.0	0	6	0.0	87.1
	sd5	0	0.0	0	1	0.0	21.6
13:00:01	sd1	0	0.0	0	1	0.0	47.2
	sd2	0	0.0	0	1	0.0	41.9
	sd3	1	0.0	0	6	0.0	88.9
	sd5	0	0.0	0	1	0.0	27.9
14:00:01	sd1	0	0.0	0	0	0.0	0.0
	sd2	0	0.0	0	1	0.0	35.7
	sd3	1	0.0	0	5	0.0	87.7
	sd5	0	0.0	0	0	0.0	22.8
15:00:02	sd1	0	0.0	0	3	0.0	16.7
	sd2	0	0.0	0	1	0.0	40.4
	sd3	1	0.1	1	15	0.0	62.5
	sd5	0	0.0	0	1	0.0	29.8
16:00:02	sd1	0	0.0	0	1	0.0	14.8
	sd2	0	0.0	0	2	0.0	36.8
	sd3	1	0.1	1	9	0.0	111.7
	sd5	0	0.0	0	1	0.0	21.8
17:00:01	sd1	0	0.0	0	0	0.0	14.0
	sd2	0	0.0	0	2	0.0	42.2
	sd3	1	0.1	1	9	0.0	117.9
	sd5	0	0.0	0	1	0.0	23.7
18:00:01	sd1	0	0.0	0	0	0.0	20.9
	sd2	0	0.0	0	2	0.0	40.6
	sd3	1	0.0	0	6	0.0	93.9
	sd5	0	0.0	0	1	0.0	25.3
19:00:01	sd1	0	0.0	0	0	0.0	10.4
	sd2	0	0.0	0	1	0.0	28.0
	sd3	0	0.0	0	3	0.0	62.0
	sd5	0	0.0	0	0	0.0	23.3
20:00:00	sd1	0	0.0	0	0	0.0	0.0
	sd2	0	0.0	0	1	0.0	29.9
	sd3	0	0.0	0	3	0.0	57.7
	sd5	0	0.0	0	0	0.0	21.7
21:00:01	sd1	0	0.0	0	1	0.0	27.7
	sd2	0	0.0	0	1	0.0	36.3
	sd3	1	0.0	0	6	0.0	77.0
	sd5	0	0.0	0	1	0.0	27.7
22:00:01	sd1	0	0.0	0	0	0.0	15.4
	sd2	0	0.0	0	1	0.0	30.5
	sd3	0	0.0	0	3	0.0	67.7
	sd5	0	0.0	0	0	0.0	22.9
23:00:01	sd1	0	0.0	0	0	0.0	10.8
	sd2	0	0.0	0	0	0.0	25.8
	sd3	0	0.0	0	2	0.0	67.2
	sd5	0	0.0	0	0	0.0	19.0
Average	sd1	0	0.0	0	0	0.0	17.2
	sd2	0	0.0	0	1	0.0	30.3
	sd3	1	0.0	0	5	0.0	84.2
	sd5	0	0.0	0	1	0.0	24.1

Figure 16-2 (Continued) `sar  -d` command output.

■ blks/s—the number of bytes transferred, in 512-byte units per second

■ avseek—average service time, number of milliseconds per average seek

In general, average wait time, queue length, and busy time will increase in a linear relationship with each other as access to user files increases. It is possible to have average wait time and queue length increase but also have busy time remain small. This seeming anomaly is the result of "normal" flushing activity—the kernel is ensuring that all altered file blocks are written to disk; it is generally not a cause for concern.

The report generated with option -b (Fig. 16-3) is related to buffer activity:

■ bread/s—buffer reads per second

■ lread/s—read accesses satisfied from buffers

■ %rcache—read cache hit ratios (bread/lread) as a percentage

■ bwrit/s—buffer writes per second

```
sar -b
SunOS fullerton 5.4 Generic_101945-46 sun4m     09/23/97

00:00:01 bread/s lread/s %rcache bwrit/s lwrit/s %wcache pread/s pwrit/s
01:00:01       0       0      98       0       0      52       0       0
02:00:02       2      25      94       1       2      60       0       0
03:00:03       0       0      98       0       0      62       0       0
04:00:01       0       1      95       0       0      58       0       0
05:00:01       0       0      96       0       0      54       0       0
06:00:01       0       0      97       0       0      47       0       0
07:00:01       0       0      96       0       0      52       0       0
08:00:01       0       0      98       0       0      56       0       0
09:00:00       0       1     100       0       0      56       0       0
10:00:01       0       1      99       0       1      58       0       0
11:00:03       0       3     100       0       1      61       0       0
12:00:01       0       3     100       0       1      61       0       0
13:00:01       0       3     100       0       1      63       0       0
14:00:01       0       2     100       0       1      61       0       0
15:00:02       0       3      99       0       1      63       0       0
16:00:02       0       3      99       1       2      63       0       0
17:00:01       0       4     100       1       2      62       0       0
18:00:01       0       3     100       0       1      61       0       0
19:00:01       0       2     100       0       1      58       0       0
20:00:00       0       2     100       0       1      60       0       0
21:00:01       0       3     100       0       1      61       0       0
22:00:01       0       1     100       0       1      58       0       0
23:00:01       0       1     100       0       0      58       0       0

Average        0       3      97       0       1      61       0       0
```

Figure 16-3
sar -b command output.

- lwrit/s—write accesses satisfied via buffers
- %wcache—write cache hit ratios (bwrit/lwrit) as a percentage
- pread/s—read transfers using raw device mechanism
- pwrit/s—write transfers using raw device mechanism

On the cache report, the most important indicators are the cache hit ratios. In general, the read hit ratio should be high; 90 percent or better is ideal. The write cache hit ratio is not as important. In general, the write cache hit ratio will only be high if a small group of records are repeatedly updated, which is not typical behavior in most systems. If the hit ratios are low, it may help to increase the bufshwm kernel parameter, but carefully monitor the results of such activity. Increasing the size of the file buffer could decrease overall performance due to an increase in page stealing or thrashing in the cache because the cache is too big.

Terminal Activity

The -y option reports on terminal (TTY) device activity (Fig. 16-4). For each terminal, the following statistics are provided:

- rawch/s—raw input character rate

Figure 16-4

sar -y command output.

```
sar -y
SunOS fullerton 5.4 Generic_101945-46 sun4m    09/23/97

00:00:01 rawch/s canch/s outch/s rcvin/s xmtin/s mdmin/s
01:00:01       0       0       0       0       0       0
02:00:02       0       0       0       0       0       0
03:00:03       0       0       0       0       0       0
04:00:01       0       0       0       0       0       0
05:00:01       0       0       0       0       0       0
06:00:01       0       0       0       0       0       0
07:00:01       0       0       0       0       0       0
08:00:01       0       0       0       0       0       0
09:00:00       0       0       0       0       0       0
10:00:01       0       0       0       0       0       0
11:00:03       0       0       0       0       0       0
12:00:01       0       0       0       0       0       0
13:00:01       0       0       0       0       0       0
14:00:01       0       0       0       0       0       0
15:00:02       0       0       3       0       0       0
16:00:02       0       0      12       0       0       0
17:00:01       0       0       3       0       0       0
18:00:01       0       0       0       0       0       0
19:00:01       0       0       0       0       0       0
20:00:00       0       0       0       0       0       0
21:00:01       0       0       0       0       0       0
22:00:01       0       0       0       0       0       0
23:00:01       0       0       0       0       0       0

Average        0       0       1       0       0       0
```

■ canch/s—canonical* input character rate

■ outch/s—output character rate

■ rcvin/s—characters received

■ xmtin/s—characters transmitted

■ mdmin/s—modem interrupt rate

Each statistic is reported on a transfer per second rate. If the number of modem interrupts is greater than the characters received and characters transmitted, there is a strong likelihood there is some type of problem with the communications equipment that is causing a performance problem.

System Calls, Message, and Semaphore Activity

Systems calls are reported on when the -c option (Fig. 16-5) is used. The information displayed includes

*Loosely interpreted, this is the number of displayable characters.

Figure 16-5

sar -c command output.

```
sar -c
SunOS fullerton 5.4 Generic_101945-46 sun4m     09/23/97

00:00:01 scall/s sread/s swrit/s  fork/s  exec/s rchar/s wchar/s
01:00:01    3       0       0      0.01    0.01      98     108
02:00:02   58       0       0      0.02    0.02    1004    1031
03:00:03   23       7       0      0.05    0.05     250     148
04:00:01    4       0       0      0.02    0.01      61     108
05:00:01    2       0       0      0.00    0.00      34      56
06:00:01    2       0       0      0.01    0.01      70      91
07:00:01    3       0       0      0.01    0.01     349     183
08:00:01    8       2       0      0.01    0.01     274     284
09:00:00   33       7       2      0.01    0.01    1056     922
10:00:01   26       2       2      0.01    0.01     971     926
11:00:03   86      32       3      0.04    0.04    2195    1704
12:00:01   68      12       4      0.02    0.02    2988    1944
13:00:01   98      28       4      0.05    0.03    2789    2581
14:00:01   73      24       3      0.04    0.03    2016    1524
15:00:02   91      17       6      0.06    0.05    5328    2475
16:00:02  194      98       7      0.11    0.13    5535    2039
17:00:01  306     180      11      0.12    0.22    4208    2416
18:00:01  110      40       9      0.03    0.05    2882    2285
19:00:01   43      12       4      0.01    0.02    1216    1136
20:00:00   42       3       6      0.01    0.01    1525    1486
21:00:01   88      13      12      0.03    0.02    2723    2462
22:00:01   45      16       4      0.01    0.02    1000     863
23:00:01   11       1       1      0.01    0.01     547     444

Average    62      21       3      0.03    0.03    1701    1183
```

- scall/s—all system calls

- sread/s—read system calls

- swrit/s—write system calls

- fork/s—fork system calls

- exec/s—exec system calls

- rchar/s—characters transferred by read system calls

- wchar/s—characters transferred by write system calls

Each call activity type is reported in calls per second.

The message and semaphore report (option -m) is very straightforward (Fig. 16-6). Two columns are displayed:

- msg/s—the number of messages per second

- sema/s—the number of semaphores per second

In both of these reports, the statistics are useful only for determining what the average or typical activity of the system is. None of the values is an indicator of a performance problem, in and of itself.

Figure 16-6

sar -m command output.

```
sar -m
SunOS fullerton 5.4 Generic_101945-46 sun4m     09/23/97

00:00:01    msg/s    sema/s
01:00:01    0.00      0.00
02:00:02    0.00      0.00
03:00:03    0.00      0.00
04:00:01    0.00      0.00
05:00:01    0.00      0.00
06:00:01    0.00      0.00
07:00:01    0.00      0.00
08:00:01    0.00      0.00
09:00:00    0.00      0.00
10:00:01    0.00      0.00
11:00:03    0.00      0.00
12:00:01    0.00      0.00
13:00:01    0.00      0.00
14:00:01    0.00      0.00
15:00:02    0.00      0.00
16:00:02    0.00      0.00
17:00:01    0.00      0.00
18:00:01    0.00      0.00
19:00:01    0.00      0.00
20:00:00    0.00      0.00
21:00:01    0.00      0.00
22:00:01    0.00      0.00
23:00:01    0.00      0.00

Average     0.00      0.00
```

Processes and CPU Utilization

There are three reports related to processes and CPU utilization. The first report is the `sar` default report: the report on CPU utilization. It is the report displayed if no report option is specified. It can be explicitly requested by using the `-u` option. The information in the CPU utilization report breaks down the total amount of time on the system into four percentage categories (Fig. 16-7):

- %usr—amount of time in user mode
- %sys—amount of time in system mode
- %wio—amount of time spent with at least one process waiting for block I/O
- %idle—amount of time spent idle

In general, if a system sustains an idle percentage of less than 20 percent for extended periods of time, it is very likely that overall performance is suffering during those periods. The ratio of times (%usr, %sys, and %wio) varies greatly depending on the workload of the system. In general, a system that supports a number of users in timesharing mode

Figure 16-7

sar -u command
output.

```
sar -u
SunOS fullerton 5.4 Generic_101945-46 sun4m      09/23/97

00:00:01    %usr    %sys    %wio    %idle
01:00:01      0       1       0       99
02:00:02      0       3       2       96
03:00:03      0       1       0       99
04:00:01      0       1       0       99
05:00:01      0       1       0       99
06:00:01      0       1       0       99
07:00:01      0       1       0       99
08:00:01      0       1       0       99
09:00:00      0       1       0       98
10:00:01      0       1       0       98
11:00:03      1       2       0       97
12:00:01      1       2       0       97
13:00:01      1       2       0       96
14:00:01      1       2       0       97
15:00:02      1       3       1       95
16:00:02      2       3       0       95
17:00:01      2       5       0       93
18:00:01      1       3       0       96
19:00:01      0       2       0       98
20:00:00      1       2       0       98
21:00:01      1       2       0       96
22:00:01      0       2       0       98
23:00:01      0       1       0       98

Average       1       2       0       97
```

would expect to see equal amounts of time in user and system mode. A high amount of time spent waiting on I/O indicates disk performance problems. And, a high idle time, with degraded response times, is very often an indication of network service performance problems—time spent on a client system waiting for an NFS or NIS + server to satisfy a request is attributed to %idle on the client.*

The second report (-q) is used for displaying data on the average run queue length and occupancy rate. The information reported includes four fields, only two of which are useful (Fig. 16-8):

- runq-sz—the number of processes in the run queue.

- %runocc—occupancy rate, the lower the value the better processes are being serviced.

The other two fields listed in the report header, swpq-sz and %swpocc, are not supported by sar.† If the runq-sz and %runocc rates are high

---

*This is not documented anywhere; this statement is based on the observed behavior of several systems that were having significant NIS 1 and NFS performance problems.

†Why the header continues to display these is not clear.

Figure 16-8

sar -q command output.

```
sar -q
SunOS fullerton 5.4 Generic_101945-46 sun4m      09/23/97

00:00:01 runq-sz %runocc swpq-sz %swpocc
01:00:01    1.7       0
02:00:02    1.7       1
03:00:03    1.3       0
04:00:01    1.0       0
05:00:01    1.5       0
06:00:01    2.0       0
07:00:01    1.0       0
08:00:01    1.3       0
09:00:00    1.1       1
10:00:01    1.2       0
11:00:03    1.4       1
12:00:01    1.1       1
13:00:01    1.3       1
14:00:01    1.7       1
15:00:02    1.3       2
16:00:02    1.5       2
17:00:01    1.9       3
18:00:01    1.1       1
19:00:01    1.2       0
20:00:00    1.3       0
21:00:01    1.2       1
22:00:01    1.2       0
23:00:01    1.4       0

Average     1.5       1
```

Figure 16-9

sar -v command
output.

```
sar -v
SunOS fullerton 5.4 Generic_101945-46 sun4m     09/23/97

00:00:01  proc-sz   ov  inod-sz    ov  file-sz   ov  lock-sz
01:00:01   84/1002    0  2327/2327   0  324/324    0   0/0
02:00:02   81/1002    0  2735/2735   0  312/312    0   0/0
03:00:03   82/1002    0  2735/2735   0  312/312    0   0/0
04:00:01   84/1002    0  2735/2735   0  316/316    0   0/0
05:00:01   82/1002    0  2735/2735   0  313/313    0   0/0
06:00:01   82/1002    0  2735/2735   0  312/312    0   0/0
07:00:01   80/1002    0  2735/2735   0  312/312    0   0/0
08:00:01   80/1002    0  2735/2735   0  339/339    0   0/0
09:00:00   80/1002    0  2735/2735   0  315/315    0   0/0
10:00:01   82/1002    0  2735/2735   0  321/321    0   0/0
11:00:03   83/1002    0  2735/2735   0  319/319    0   0/0
12:00:01   83/1002    0  2735/2735   0  325/325    0   0/0
13:00:01  109/1002    0  2735/2735   0  404/404    0   0/0
14:00:01   93/1002    0  2735/2735   0  340/340    0   0/0
15:00:02   99/1002    0  2735/2735   0  356/356    0   0/0
16:00:02   72/1002    0  2735/2735   0  302/302    0   0/0
17:00:01   87/1002    0  2735/2735   0  342/342    0   0/0
18:00:01   89/1002    0  2735/2735   0  351/351    0   0/0
19:00:01   89/1002    0  2735/2735   0  348/348    0   0/0
20:00:00   87/1002    0  2735/2735   0  351/351    0   0/0
21:00:01   94/1002    0  2735/2735   0  457/457    0   0/0
22:00:01   95/1002    0  2735/2735   0  461/461    0   0/0
23:00:01   92/1002    0  2735/2735   0  450/450    0   0/0
```

(greater than 3 and 80, respectively), the processor cannot handle the workload, and a faster processor (or less work) is needed.

The third report (-v) displays information on the process (proc-sz), inode (inod-sz), file (file-sz), and lock (lock-sz) tables. For each of the first three tables, the number of entries, the total table size, and the number of table entry overflows (e.g., the table was/is too small) are given. No overflow information is displayed for the lock table. Figure 16-9 is an example of this report. It is normal for the number of entries and total table size fields in the inode and file tables to be equal. Solaris does a good job adjusting the values of these tables as circumstances warrant,* so there is little need to tinker with these via the kernel parameters.

Memory Utilization (Paging and Swapping)

There are five sar reports that are related to memory utilization, paging, and swapping.

The first report (-k) reports on kernel memory allocation (KMA) activities. There are three areas of reporting activity: small memory pool

---

*This is based on the calculations it does for maxusers.

requests (requests for less than 256 bytes), large memory pool requests (requests for 512 bytes to 4K), and the amount of memory allocated for oversized requests (requests greater than 4K). For the large and small pools (Fig. 16-10), the following are detailed:

Size of the pool

Total amount of allocated memory in the pool (alloc)

Total number of allocation failures

For the oversize requests, which are allocated from paging space, the amount of memory that is available to satisfy these requests and the number of oversize requests that could not be satisfied are displayed as well. The most interesting statistics from this report are the allocation failure columns. Any allocation failures, particularly in the oversize request pool, point to a shortage of physical memory.

The -r report displays information about free memory (Fig. 16-11):

- freemem—the average number of pages available to user processes

- freeswap—the amount of space, in kilobytes, on disk blocks available for paging/swapping

Obviously, the lower these numbers are, the less free memory that is available. As these numbers approach zero, memory allocations will fail. These numbers should never be less than 25 percent of the total memory or swap space allocated.

The final three reports are all about paging and swapping activity. The -g report (Fig. 16-12) details some aspects of the paging subsystem:

- pgout/s—page-out requests per second

- ppgout/s—actual number of pages paged out per second

- pgfree/s—pages placed on the free list by the page stealing daemon (per second)

- pgscan/s—pages scanned by the page stealing daemon (per second)

- %ufs_ipf—the percentage of UFS inodes taken off the freelist (e.g., flushed pages)

Large numbers of page free or page scan operations tend to indicate a shortage of physical memory. A major indicator of a performance problem is when both pgfree/s and pgscan/s are high and both values are relatively equal; that is, pages are being stolen as fast as they are being freed. This could easily lead to thrashing.

Figure 16-10

sar -k command
output.

```
sar -k
SunOS fullerton 5.4 Generic_101945-46 sun4m      09/23/97

00:00:01 sml_mem    alloc  fail  lg_mem    alloc  fail  ovsz_alloc  fail
01:00:01 1269760 1037448     0 3358720 3041152     0     2551808     0
02:00:02 1269760 1017260     0 3526656 3158432     0     2568192     0
03:00:03 1269760 1005444     0 3526656 3168272     0     2568192     0
04:00:01 1269760 1023976     0 3543040 3173456     0     2568192     0
05:00:01 1269760 1019012     0 3543040 3163856     0     2568192     0
06:00:01 1269760 1020388     0 3543040 3165904     0     2568192     0
07:00:01 1269760 1018568     0 3543040 3162640     0     2568192     0
08:00:01 1294336 1098944     0 3567616 3190800     0     2568192     0
09:00:00 1314816 1058836     0 3579904 3173360     0     2568192     0
10:00:01 1314816 1066644     0 3608576 3174288     0     2568192     0
11:00:03 1323008 1049360     0 3620864 3179968     0     2568192     0
12:00:01 1351680 1111240     0 3645440 3204800     0     2568192     0
13:00:01 1572864 1418172     0 3645440 3438064     0     2568192     0
14:00:01 1613824 1206072     0 3727360 3267408     0     2568192     0
15:00:02 1622016 1257600     0 3637248 3289904     0     2580480     0
16:00:02 1695744 1030580     0 3702784 3119824     0     2580480     0
17:00:01 1785856 1238408     0 3776512 3261600     0     2580480     0
18:00:01 1785856 1240784     0 3829760 3259872     0     2580480     0
19:00:01 1785856 1243804     0 3874816 3249120     0     2580480     0
20:00:00 1785856 1257384     0 3874816 3254016     0     2580480     0
21:00:01 1769472 1465752     0 3579904 3275600     0     2580480     0
22:00:01 1773568 1469736     0 3624960 3287152     0     2580480     0
23:00:01 1757184 1439472     0 3559424 3269552     0     2580480     0

Average  1497177 1164999     0 3627809 3214306     0     2572288     0
```

Figure 16-11

sar -r command
output.

```
sar -r
SunOS fullerton 5.4 Generic_101945-46 sun4m      09/23/97

00:00:01 freemem freeswap
01:00:01     609   212337
02:00:02    2234   211958
03:00:03    4101   213021
04:00:01    4084   212873
05:00:01    3852   212000
06:00:01    3708   211298
07:00:01    3439   211035
08:00:01    3170   210933
09:00:00    2759   210602
10:00:01    2390   210345
11:00:03    2122   211656
12:00:01    1508   207665
13:00:01     893   201361
14:00:01    1331   179643
15:00:02    1337   177554
16:00:02    3434   212850
17:00:01    1794   194561
18:00:01    1094   186234
19:00:01     754   186144
20:00:00     638   185888
21:00:01     699   173591
22:00:01     492   171442
23:00:01     449   171125

Average     2039   198963
```

Figure 16-12

sar -g command
output.

```
SunOS fullerton 5.4 Generic_101945-46 sun4m    10/26/97

00:00:01  pgout/s ppgout/s pgfree/s pgscan/s %ufs_ipf
01:00:01    0.00    0.00     0.00     0.00     0.00
02:00:02    0.00    0.00     0.00     0.02     5.01
03:00:01    0.00    0.00     0.00     0.00     0.00
04:00:01    0.00    0.00     0.00     0.00    10.20
05:00:01    0.00    0.00     0.00     0.00     0.00
06:00:02    0.00    0.00     0.00     0.00     0.00
07:00:03    0.00    0.00     0.00     0.00     0.00
08:00:01    0.00    0.00     0.00     0.00     0.00
09:00:01    0.00    0.00     0.00     0.00     5.24
10:00:01    0.00    0.00     0.00     0.00     0.00
11:00:01    0.00    0.00     0.00     0.00     0.00
12:00:01    0.00    0.00     0.00     0.00    41.26
13:00:01    0.00    0.00     0.00     0.00     0.00
14:00:01    0.00    0.00     0.00     0.00    72.20
15:00:01    0.00    0.00     0.00     0.00     0.00
16:00:02    0.01    0.11     0.26     2.02     0.00
17:00:01    0.00    0.00     0.00     0.00     0.00
18:00:01    0.00    0.00     0.00     0.00     0.00
19:00:01    0.00    0.00     0.00     0.00     0.00

Average     0.00    0.01     0.01     0.11     5.78
```

A complementary report is displayed with the -p option. This report details (Fig. 16-13) the following:

- atch/s—page faults that are satisfied by reclaiming a page currently in memory (attaches per second)

- pgin/s—page-in requests per second

- ppgin/s—actual number of pages paged-in per second

- pflt/s—page faults caused by protection errors (illegal access to page) or copy-on-writes

- vflt/s—address translation page faults per second (valid page not in memory)

- slock/s—page faults per second caused by software lock requests that require physical I/O

If the number of pages in requests becomes much greater than the actual number of pages paged in (a less than 2-to-1 ratio), performance will suffer dramatically. Furthermore, if the number of address translation page faults is great (greater than 12 pages per second as a rough rule), it is likely that the system needs more physical memory.

The -w report reports on swapping activity (Fig. 16-14):

- swpin/s—number of swapin requests

Figure 16-13
sar -p command
output.

```
sar -p
SunOS fullerton 5.4 Generic_101945-46 sun4m    09/23/97

00:00:01 atch/s  pgin/s ppgin/s  pflt/s  vflt/s slock/s
01:00:01  0.00    0.00    0.00    0.37    0.52    0.00
02:00:02  0.00    1.07    1.13    0.86    1.33    0.00
03:00:03  0.00    0.03    0.05    2.39    3.70    0.00
04:00:01  0.00    0.04    0.04    0.79    1.30    0.00
05:00:01  0.00    0.00    0.00    0.26    0.38    0.00
06:00:01  0.00    0.01    0.02    0.35    0.52    0.00
07:00:01  0.00    0.04    0.12    0.33    0.52    0.00
08:00:01  0.00    0.02    0.04    0.52    0.73    0.00
09:00:00  0.00    0.05    0.08    1.21    1.78    0.00
10:00:01  0.00    0.05    0.11    1.05    1.63    0.00
11:00:03  0.00    0.05    0.09    4.71    6.97    0.00
12:00:01  0.00    0.07    0.12    2.77    4.86    0.00
13:00:01  0.01    0.01    0.02    5.34    7.54    0.00
14:00:01  0.02    0.04    0.05    4.63    6.99    0.00
15:00:02  0.07    0.55    0.83    6.26    9.12    0.00
16:00:02  0.03    0.14    0.17   13.78   19.45    0.00
17:00:01  0.01    0.07    0.11   20.21   24.36    0.00
18:00:01  0.00    0.04    0.07    5.30    6.84    0.00
19:00:01  0.00    0.02    0.02    1.39    1.70    0.00
20:00:00  0.00    0.02    0.03    0.73    1.20    0.00
21:00:01  0.05    0.04    0.05    3.66    4.43    0.00
22:00:01  0.01    0.01    0.01    1.71    2.22    0.00
23:00:01  0.01    0.01    0.02    0.52    0.80    0.00

Average   0.01    0.10    0.14    3.44    4.74    0.00
```

Figure 16-14
sar -w command
output.

```
sar -w
SunOS fullerton 5.4 Generic_101945-46 sun4m    09/23/97

00:00:01 swpin/s bswin/s swpot/s bswot/s pswch/s
01:00:01  0.00    0.0    0.00    0.0     13
02:00:02  0.00    0.0    0.00    0.0     19
03:00:03  0.00    0.0    0.00    0.0     13
04:00:01  0.00    0.0    0.00    0.0     13
05:00:01  0.00    0.0    0.00    0.0     12
06:00:01  0.00    0.0    0.00    0.0     12
07:00:01  0.00    0.0    0.00    0.0     13
08:00:01  0.00    0.0    0.00    0.0     13
09:00:00  0.00    0.0    0.00    0.0     16
10:00:01  0.00    0.0    0.00    0.0     16
11:00:03  0.00    0.0    0.00    0.0     20
12:00:01  0.00    0.0    0.00    0.0     20
13:00:01  0.00    0.0    0.00    0.0     23
14:00:01  0.00    0.0    0.00    0.0     20
15:00:02  0.00    0.0    0.00    0.0     28
16:00:02  0.00    0.0    0.00    0.0     30
17:00:01  0.00    0.0    0.00    0.0     33
18:00:01  0.00    0.0    0.00    0.0     23
19:00:01  0.00    0.0    0.00    0.0     17
20:00:00  0.00    0.0    0.00    0.0     18
21:00:01  0.00    0.0    0.00    0.0     22
22:00:01  0.00    0.0    0.00    0.0     17
23:00:01  0.00    0.0    0.00    0.0     13

Average   0.00    0.0    0.00    0.0     18
```

- bswin/s—number of 512-byte blocks transferred to satisfy swapin requests
- swpot/s—number of swapout requests
- bswot/s—number of 512-byte blocks transferred to satisfy swapout requests
- pswch/s—number of process switches

Swapping, any amount, is bad. If this report indicates extended periods of even minimal amounts of swapping, consult the other sar reports to determine where the bottleneck is. Most likely, more physical memory is needed, but the problem could also be that the processor is too slow.

sag—The System Activity Reports Graphical Interface

sag displays the sadc data graphically. Any of the sar reports may be plotted, either singly or in combination, as cross plots or versus time.

The syntax of the sag command is

```
sag [ -e time ] [ -f file ] [ -i sec ] [ -s time ] [ -T term ]
[ -x spec ] [ -y spec ]
```

where

-e time   Sets the end time bound, in hh:mm:ss format; the default is 18:00.

-f file   Use *file* as the data source; the default is the current daily data file, /usr/adm/sa/sa*dd*.

-i sec   Reports data at the *sec* interval value.

-s time   Sets the beginning time bound, in hh:mm:ss format; the default is 08:00.

-T term   Produces output suitable for display on terminal type *term*. The default is $TERM.

-x spec   The *x* axis specification; in the form *name [operation name] low high* (see below).

-y spec   The *y* axis specification; in the form *name [operation name] low high* (see below).

For both the -x *spec* and -y *spec* operands, the *spec* operand is specified as a string value. The *name* is a string that will match a column header in the applicable `sar` report, with an optional device name in square brackets, for example, $r + w/s[dsk\text{-}1]$, or an integer value. The *operation* value is an arithmetic operator (+ − * or /) surrounded by blank spaces. Up to five names (or *name operation name* combinations) may be specified on either axis. Parenthetical expression are not allowed, however. In addition, contrary to common convention, addition and subtraction take precedence over multiplication and division. Therefore,

```
A + B / C + D
```

is evaluated as

```
(A + B)/(C + D).
```

The *low* and *high* values are optional number scale limits for the axis. If not explicitly specified, the limits of the axis are derived from the data. An example specification for a report based on the `sar -u` report might have the following operand as a *y* axis:

```
sag -y "%usr 0 100; %usr + %sys 0 100; %usr + %sys + %wio 0 100"
```

Summary

This chapter has focused on using the system activity data collector and reporter for gathering and interpreting system performance data. This tool, along with the accounting data discussed in the next chapter, is one of the most useful tools in analyzing the activity of the system.

17

System Accounting

The second major tool for long-term reporting and logging of system data is system accounting.

The system accounting software is a set of tools that can be used to report on performance information and/or build resource accounting systems.

Accounting is turned on at system start-up time. Process accounting is handled by various programs, all of which write records in the master collection file `/var/adm/wtmp`. In addition, when a process terminates, various statistics the kernel tracked about the process are written to `/var/adm/pacct`.

On a daily basis, programs in the `acctcon` group convert the `/var/adm/wtmp` file into session and charging records, which are in turn summarized by `acctmerg`. The programs in the `acctprc` group summarize the data in `/var/adm/pacct` for charging purposes for the `acctcms` program, which summarizes individual command usage.

Current process data may be examined with the `acctcom`.

On the backend, several commands such as `prtacct` and `prdaily` are used to print information reports from the accounting data.

Setting Up Accounting

Setting up system accounting involves four steps. The first two enable the accounting to start up when the system enters run level 2 (multiuser mode) and to shut down when the system enters run level 0 (single-user mode).

If it has not already been done, the performance administrator must create a symbolic link from the base initialization shell scripts to the applicable run-level shell scripts. This is accomplished with the following commands:

```
ln -s /etc/init.d/acct /etc/rc0.d/K22acct
ln -s /etc/init.d/acct /etc/rc2.d/S22acct
```

The first statement links the accounting shell script to the run level 0 directory as a script to invoke during shutdown. The second statement links the accounting shell script to the run level 2 directory as a script to invoke during system start-up.

Step 3 involves adding `crontab` entries to the adm user table to enable daily accounting functions. Examples of the required entries in the `/var/spool/cron/crontabs/adm` table are given in Fig. 17-1. The three entries run the accounting file monitoring program (`ckpacct`), the daily accounting procedure (`runacct`), and the monthly procedure (`monacct`). Note, the adm `crontab` must be owned by root, have sys as the group, and have permissions of 644 in order to work correctly.

Step 4 also involves adding an entry to the `crontab`, but for the root user, not adm. This entry in the `/var/spool/cron/crontabs/root`

```
#ident      "@(#)adm    1.5    92/07/14 SMI"      /* SVr4.0 1.2      */
#
# The adm crontab file should contain startup of performance collection if
# the profiling and performance feature has been installed.
#
0 * * * * /usr/lib/acct/ckpacct
30 2 * * * /usr/lib/acct/runacct 2> /var/adm/acct/nite/fd2log
30 3 31 * *  /usr/lib/acct/monacct
```

Figure 17-1
Example adm `crontab`.

```
#ident      "@(#)root   1.12   94/03/24 SMI"      /* SVr4.0 1.1.3.1 */
#
# The root crontab should be used to perform accounting data collection.
#
# The rtc command is run to adjust the real time clock if and when
# daylight savings time changes.
#
0 2 * * 0,4 /etc/cron.d/logchecker
5 4 * * 6   /usr/lib/newsyslog
15 3 * * * /usr/lib/fs/nfs/nfsfind
30 3 * * * chgrp -R devlpmnt /opt/library
1 2 * * * [ -x /usr/sbin/rtc ] && /usr/sbin/rtc -c > /dev/null 2>&1
15 * * * * /data/www/library/accesswatch/accesswatch.pl > /dev/null 2>&1
1 0 1 * * /opt/scripts/wwwrpt 2>&1
1 0 1 * * /opt/momspider/runspider.cron 2>&1 > /dev/null
30 1 * * * /usr/lib/acct/dodisk
0 3 1,15 * * /opt/www/httpd_1.5.1/cgi-bin/htdig/bin/rundig
```

Figure 17-2
Example root crontab.

table will run the program that gathers and records the disk accounting information (dodisk, Fig. 17-2).

With these steps completed, accounting should run on a regular schedule, collecting data on a daily basis and producing reports for further study.

runacct—Run Daily Accounting

runacct is the main daily accounting shell procedure. Normally, it is invoked from a crontab entry. It runs several programs to process the connect, fee, disk, and process accounting files. In addition, summary files are created by the acctmerg program for use by prdaily or for billing purposes.

The runacct command can process a maximum of

- 6000 distinct sessions
- 1000 distinct terminal lines
- 2000 distinct login names

during a single run. If the number of any one of these items exceeds the maximum, the command will not succeed.

Because of the multifaced nature of runacct,* extra precautions are taken to ensure that accounting data is not lost in the event of errors. The progress of the daily accounting procedure is tracked by diagnostic messages written to the /var/adm/acct/nite/active file. When an error is detected during processing, a message is written to /dev/console, and mail is sent to the root and adm accounts.

Furthermore, runacct uses a series of lock files to protect against multiple invocations or re-invocation. The files /var/adm/acct/nite/lock and /var/adm/acct/nite/lock1 are used to prevent simultaneous invocation, and /var/adm/acct/nite/lastdate is used to prevent more than one invocation per day.

Because process accounting is not a monolithic process, runacct breaks processing into discrete, restartable components, referred to as *states*. The /var/adm/acct/nite/statefile is used by runacct to keep track of the state of the daily accounting processes. The statefile contains the name of the last state successfully completed. Because of this, runacct can always check the statefile to see what it has done and to determine what should be processed next.

The states of daily process accounting are, in order, as follows:

- SETUP—moves active accounting files into working files
- WTMPFIX—verifies the integrity of the wtmp file, correcting date changes if necessary
- CONNECT—produces connect session records in total accounting record (tacct.h; see acct(4m)) format
- PROCESS—converts process accounting records into total accounting record format
- MERGE—merges the connect and process accounting records
- FEES—converts the output of chargefee into total accounting record format and merges it with the connect and process accounting records
- DISK—merges the disk accounting records with the connect, process, and fee accounting records
- MERGEACCT—merges the daily total accounting records in /var/adm/acct/nite/daytacct with the summary total accounting records in /var/adm/acct/sum/tacct
- CMS—produces the command summaries

---

*It is not necessarily used just for performance data, it is also used for cost recovery purposes.

- USEREXIT—executes any installation-dependent accounting programs
- CLEANUP—cleans up the temporary files and exits

Restarting runacct after a failure involves several steps. First, the /var/adm/acct/nite/active file must be checked for error diagnostic information. If any data files have been corrupted, such as /var/adm/wtmp or /var/adm/pacct*, they must be fixed. Third, the /var/adm/acct/nite/lock, /var/adm/acct/nite/lock1, and /var/adm/acct/nite/lastdate files must be deleted. Finally, runacct is restarted; however, it is mandatory that the date argument *mmdd* be specified because this indicates to runacct which month and day are to be rerun. The restart point is based on the contents of /var/adm/acct/nite/statefile. This can be overridden by including the desired *state* on the command line. The following restarts processing for June 24 at the FEES state:

```
runacct 0624 FEES 2>>/var/adm/acct/nite/fd2log &
```

The formats of the reports that are generated as a result of running runacct are discussed under the individual reporting commands. The reports are saved in the /var/adm/acct/sum (for daily reports) and /var/adm/acct/fiscal (for monthly reports) directories.

Although the runacct script can be modified to meet local needs, it is better to copy runacct to a new local file, such as runacct.local. This will eliminate problems of incompatibility or lost configuration data during system upgrades. Of course, the applicable crontab must also be modified to reflect the use of a localized procedure.

Accounting Control Commands

Normally, the accounting control commands are not directly invoked for a command prompt. If the correct crontab entries have been made, system accounting should take care of itself.

accton is the base program used for starting and stopping process accounting. It is rarely called directly but instead is called by startup, shutacct, and turnacct.

shutacct is invoked during a system shutdown to turn process accounting off.

startup is invoked when the system is brought to a multiuser state, typically run level 2, to turn process accounting on.

turnacct is an interface (used by startup, shutacct, and ckpacct) to the accton command. It turns process accounting on or off.

When process accounting is turned on, the current /var/adm/pacct file is moved to the next free name in the /var/adm/pacctincr (where *incr* is a number starting with 1 and incrementing by 1 for each additional pacct file) before process accounting is started.

accton, when invoked without any arguments, turns process accounting off. If a file name is specified, process accounting is turned on and new accounting records are appended to the referenced file. The syntax of the command is

```
/usr/lib/acct/accton [ filename ]
```

If a file name is specified, the file must already exist.

Accounting File Processing Commands

A number of programs are part of the system accounting package. Many are never directly used but instead are called from the scripts that implement the major functions of accounting. The purpose of this section is to briefly describe the function of these programs.

acctdisk

acctdisk is used during the DISK phase of runacct to read the incoming disk accounting files for records that contain user id, login name, and number of disk blocks. It converts these records into total accounting records that can be merged with other accounting records

acctdusg

acctdusg computes disk resource consumption, including indirect blocks by user id. The input may come from standard input, in which case it is usually the redirected output of the following command:

```
find / -print
```

dodisk

dodisk is run before runacct to perform the disk accounting functions. Typically, this program is scheduled by a crontab entry.

acctwtmp, closewtmp, and utmp2wtmp

acctwtmp is used to write a utmp record to a file (typically, /var/adm/wtmp) to indicate an accounting event. The record (an ACCOUNTING record type*) contains the current time and a string of characters† that describe the event. The event is a string of 11 characters or less that describes the accounting event. The default system procedures use this to insert indicators for system start-up and shutdown. The corresponding commands are

```
acctwtmp "acctg on" /var/adm/wtmp
```

to indicate that system accounting has restarted and

```
acctwtmp "acctg off" /var/adm/wtmp
```

to indicate that system accounting has been stopped.

The closewtmp command is used to put a false DEAD_PROCESS record in the /var/adm/wtmp file for each user currently logged on. This is necessary for runacct, which uses this false DEAD_PROCESS record to track the time used by processes that were started before runacct was invoked but are not complete when runacct starts its daily processing.

Correspondingly, runacct uses the utmp2wtmp command to create an entry in /var/adm/wtmp for each user logged on when it starts. These records enable subsequent runs of runacct to account for the connect times of users currently logged in.

---

*For more information on utmp/wtmp records, see utmp(4).

†Eleven characters or less. Valid characters are the alphabetic characters, numbers, spaces, and the dollar sign.

nulladm

The `nulladm` command is called by various process accounting procedures to create new files. These files are created with mode 664, and `nulladm` ensures that that owner and group ids are adm.

ckpacct

`ckpacct` is typically set up as a `crontab` entry. It should be run at least once a day to control the size of the `/var/adm/pacct` file.

When the total number of free disk blocks in the `/var` file system falls below 500 (or the amount specified as an option to `ckpacct`), `ckpacct` will call `turnacct` and the collection of process accounting records will be turned off.

When at least 500 blocks are restored (or the amount specified as an option to `ckpacct`), accounting will be activated again on the next invocation of `ckpacct`.

If the amount of space in `/var` varies greatly during the course of the day, `ckpacct` should be scheduled to run more frequently than once a day to ensure that the `/var` file system does not fill up and that accounting runs uninterrupted.

lastlogin

`lastlogin` is called by `runacct` to update the `/var/adm/acct/sum/loginlog` file. This file is used to determine the last time each user on the system logged in.

monacct

`monacct` is used to process monthly accounting files. It should be invoked once each month or once each accounting period if months are not used as the accounting period.

Unless explicitly overridden, the default is to assume processing is for the current month. This is useful if `monacct` is from a `crontab` entry on the first day of the month.

The execution of `monacct` creates the process accounting summary files in `/var/adm/acct/fiscal` and restarts the current period summary files in `/var/adm/acct/sum`.

acctmerg

acctmerg is used to merge total accounting record format files. It reads input from standard input and up to nine additional files, The input files are merged by summing records whose keys (typically, user id and name) are identical. All input files must be sorted on these two keys.

The syntax of the command is

```
/usr/lib/acct/acctmerg [ -a ] [ -i ] [ -p ] [ -t ] [ -u ] [ -v ]
[ _filename ] …
```

where

-a Produces an ASCII output file.

-i Reads ASCII versions of tacct formatted files.

-p Prints the contents of the file; no other processing is performed.

-t Produces a single record that totals all input.

-u Summarizes by user id, instead of user id and name.

-v Produces output in verbose ASCII format using floating-point numbers.

acctprc, acctprc1, acctprc2

acctprc reads process accounting records from standard input and converts them into total accounting records. The activities of acctprc include

- Divides CPU time into prime time and nonprime time
- Determines mean memory size (in memory segment units)
- Summarizes records according to user ids and adds login names to the corresponding user ids

These summarized records are then written to standard output.

This processing is performed by two separate commands that are called by acctprc. These functions can be invoked individually, if desired. acctprc1 does the following:

- Reads the raw accounting input records
- Adds login names that correspond to the user ids on the records
- Writes a record to standard output for each process with the following information:
  - User id

- Login name
- Prime CPU time (tics)
- Nonprime CPU time (tics)
- Mean memory size (in memory segment units)

`acctprc2` reads `acctprc1` format records from standard input, summarizes them according to user id and name, and writes the sorted summaries to standard output as total accounting records.

acctcon, acctcon1, acctcon2

`acctcon` is used to convert connect accounting records, login/logoff record sequences (from `/var/adm/wtmp`), into total accounting records. In most cases, these records have been reprocessed with `wtmpfix` to remove inconsistencies and errors in the individual records.

`acctcon` is a script that calls the `acctcon1` and `acctcon2` commands. `acctcon1` converts login/logoff records from `/var/adm/wtmp` to ASCII output. `acctcon2` reads the ASCII records from `acctcon1` and converts them to total accounting records.

Both `acctcon` and `acctcon1` use two processing options that modify the default actions of the programs. The `-l lineuse` flag creates a summary of line usage showing

Line name

Number of minutes used

Percentage of total elapsed time used

Number of sessions charged

Number of logins

Number of logoffs

This helps track line usage, identify bad lines, and find software and hardware oddities. Hangup, termination of login(1), and termination of the login shell all generate logoff records; therefore, the number of logoffs is typically much greater than the number of sessions.

The `-o reboot` option is used to generate a REBOOT record that contains an overall record for the accounting period detailing starting time, ending time, number of reboots, and number of date changes.

The `acctcon1` command has two addition options:

-p Print report showing line name, login name, and time.

-t Use the last ending time in the file for sessions on lines that are currently active. Normally the current time is used as the ending time for each session still in progress.

fwtmp and wtmpfix

fwtmp is used to convert binary format records in /var/adm/wtmp for ASCII format. This allows bad records to be edited and fixed. Input is read from standard input, and output is written to standard output. When editing is finished, the -ic flag is used to read in the ASCII file and write it out in binary format. Again, the input is read from standard input, and output is written to standard output.

wtmpfix examines records to correct some common errors. One check performed is to ensure that date and timestamps in the records are consistent. This process is necessary because acctcon will fault if it encounters date change records that are out of synchronization.

In addition to correcting time- and date stamps, wtmpfix checks the validity of the login name field to ensure that it consists solely of alphanumeric characters or spaces. If it encounters a name that is considered invalid, it changes the login name to INVALID and writes a diagnostic to standard error.

chargefee

chargefee is invoked by user-written procedures to charge a user for some activity. Chargefee writes a record to /var/adm/fee for each invocation. The records in this file are merged with other accounting records during daily processing by runacct.

The syntax of the command is

```
/usr/lib/acct/chargefee login-name number
```

where *number* indicates the number of accounting units to be charged to *login-name*.

Reporting Commands

There are several commands in the accounting group that are used for printing reports, from simple file dumps to summary reports to detail transaction reports.

prtacct

`prtacct` is used to dump the contents of a file that contains total accounting records. The syntax of the command is

```
/usr/lib/acct/prtacct input_file [ "report header" ]
```

prctmp

`prctmp` is used to print the session record file (`/var/adm/acct/nite/ctmp`) that is output by `acctcon1`.

prdaily

`prdaily` is called by `runacct` to print a report of the daily accounting data. The report is stored in the `/var/adm/acct/sum/rprt` directory under a numeric file name, where the first two digits indicate the month and the second two digits indicate the day of the report.

The syntax of the `prdaily` command is

```
/usr/lib/acct/prdaily [ -c ] [ -l ] [ mmdd ]
```

When invoked with no *mmdd* operand, the current daily accounting reports are printed (Fig. 17-3). Previous reports are printed by specifying the exact report date desired.

Two option flags are used with the command. The `-c` flag is used to print a report of exceptional resource usage by command. This flag may only be used on the current accounting data.

The `-l` flag also prints an exception resource usage report, but this report is ordered by login id. It may be used on any accounting data, not just the current period. However, invoking this option causes the previous daily to be cleaned up; thereafter, they are inaccessible after each invocation of `monacct`.

acctcms

The `acctcms` command is used to generate a command summary report. Reading one or more accounting files as input, it summarizes all

Figure 17-3
Example acctcms
-a -o -p report.

```
Oct  5 13:27 1997  DAILY REPORT FOR fullerton Page 1


from Sat Oct   4 02:30:03 1997
to   Sun Oct   5 02:30:02 1997
1      runacct
1      acctcon

TOTAL DURATION IS 1440 MINUTES
LINE         MINUTES   PERCENT  # SESS  # ON  # OFF
console      1440      100      1       1     1
TOTALS       1440      --       1       1     1
```

the records for each command, sorts them, and writes them to the standard output. If the -a option is used, this output is in the form of a report; otherwise the output is an internal summary format that can be used for storing long-term statistics.

When the -a option is used, the output report details the following :

Command name

Number of times the command was executed

Total number of kcore-minutes

Total number of CPU minutes

Total real minutes

Mean size (in kilobytes)

Mean CPU minutes per invocation

"Hog factor"

Total characters transferred

Total blocks read and written

The report is sorted by default by total kcore-minutes. This can be overridden by the -n flag, which will sort the report by the number of command invocations, or by the -c flag which will sort the report by total CPU time.

When producing a printed report (-a), the report time frame can be bound with the -o flag to limit the report to an offshift-time-only command summary or with -p to limit the report to prime time only. When -o and -p are used together, a combination report is produced (Fig. 17-3). The output summaries will be total usage except number of times executed, CPU minutes, and real minutes, which will be split into prime and nonprime.

Oct 5 13:27 1997   DAILY USAGE REPORT FOR fullerton Page 1

OF UID	LOGIN NAME	# OF PROCS	SESS	# DISK SAMPLES	CPU (MINS) PRIME	CPU (MINS) NPRIME	KCORE-MINS PRIME	KCORE-MINS NPRIME	CONNECT (MINS) PRIME	CONNECT (MINS) NPRIME	DISK # BLOCKS	FEE
0	TOTAL	1	5	2	138	0	1440	1548514	1122	1	33	0
0	root	0	1	0	26	0	0	1044532	238	0	1	0
2	bin	0	0	0	0	0	0	422674	0	0	1	0
3	sys	0	0	0	5	0	0	2050	72	0	1	0
4	adm	0	0	0	32	0	0	1778	462	0	1	0
5	uucp	0	0	0	0	0	0	1666	0	0	1	0
25	ftp	0	0	0	0	0	0	946	0	0	1	0
71	lp	0	0	0	0	0	0	5440	4	0	1	0
100	fcervone	0	0	0	0	0	0	63990	0	0	1	0
200	aelms	0	0	0	0	0	0	4	0	0	1	0
202	choeppne	0	0	0	0	0	0	12	0	0	1	0
205	kdegraff	0	0	0	0	0	0	2	0	0	1	0
206	kkirklan	0	0	0	0	0	0	96	0	0	1	0
207	lbailey	0	0	0	0	0	0	4	0	0	1	0
208	lmurphy	0	0	0	0	0	0	10	0	0	1	0
209	mbrownin	0	0	0	0	0	0	12	0	0	1	0
211	mpower	0	0	0	0	0	0	72	0	0	1	0
213	racker	0	0	0	0	0	0	2	0	0	1	0
214	rbean	0	0	0	0	0	0	16	0	0	1	0
215	rcooper	0	0	0	0	0	0	2	0	0	1	0
216	sclarke	0	0	0	0	0	0	12	0	0	1	0
218	ttaylor	0	0	0	0	0	0	26	0	0	1	0
219	dbrown	0	0	0	0	0	0	2	0	0	1	0
229	asims	0	0	0	0	0	0	2	0	0	1	0
252	bdehart	0	0	0	0	0	0	2	0	0	1	0
253	sasaria	0	0	0	0	0	0	4	0	0	1	0
254	tseneca	0	0	0	0	0	0	2	0	0	1	0
255	lmorriss	0	0	0	0	0	0	4	0	0	1	0
256	eaddlesp	0	0	0	0	0	0	4	0	0	1	0
257	mchorazy	0	0	0	0	0	1440	64	0	1	1	0
258	mtrevvet	0	0	0	0	0	0	2	0	0	1	0
259	jdeal	0	0	0	0	0	0	2	0	0	1	0
260	jkosokof	0	0	0	0	0	0	18	0	0	1	0
60001	nobody	1	4	2	74	0	0	5062	346	0	1	0

Figure 17-3
(Continued) Example `acctcms -a -o -p` report.

The `-j` flag is used to combine all commands invoked only once under a common group of " * * * other."

The `-s` flag is used to input a file previously processed and output by `acctcms` in internal summary format.

A typical sequence for performing daily command accounting and for maintaining a running total is as follows:

Oct 5 02:30 1997 DAILY COMMAND SUMMARY Page 1

				TOTAL COMMAND SUMMARY			
COMMAND CHARS NAME TRNSFD	NUMBER BLOCKS CMDS READ	TOTAL KCOREMIN	TOTAL CPU-MIN	TOTAL TOTAL REAL-MIN	MEAN SIZE-K	MEAN CPU-MIN	HOG FACTO
TOTALS 74925379	1122 4931	127.30	5.68	32925.03	22.43	0.01	0.00
fs.scr 3994081	216 1	33.67	1.11	31.44	30.31	0.01	0.04
htsearch 9361128	93 13	23.28	0.49	0.65	47.27	0.01	0.76
sendmail 532789	102 29	13.19	0.04	0.24	336.75	0.00	0.17
httpd 48501679	23 85	8.35	2.40	32869.99	3.48	0.10	0.00
sh 112274	109 1	7.54	0.20	3.25	37.53	0.00	0.06
sed 42994	79 2	5.54	0.06	0.17	94.18	0.00	0.35
df 36575	50 2	4.03	0.04	0.05	105.17	0.00	0.84
cp 16900	45 48	3.07	0.03	0.06	98.37	0.00	0.56
awk 4006	27 4	2.66	0.02	0.03	119.91	0.00	0.63
date 27202	33 4	2.25	0.02	0.03	100.18	0.00	0.65
chmod 0	39 0	2.06	0.02	0.03	88.89	0.00	0.74

Figure 17-3

(Continued) Example acctcms -a -o -p report.

```
acctcms filename … > today
cp total previoustotal
acctcms -s today previoustotal > total
acctcms -a -s today
```

acctcom

acctcom is used to produce process accounting reports based on the records in /var/adm/pacct. Each record in the file represents the execution of one process. The acctcms report produces a summary line for

COMMAND NAME	NUMBER CMDS	TOTAL KCOREMIN	TOTAL CPU-MIN	TOTAL REAL-MIN	MEAN SIZE-K	MEAN CPU-MIN	HOG FACTOR	CHARS TRNSFD	BLOCKS READ
rm	32	2.03	0.02	0.04	94.48	0.00	0.57	0	16
sadc	24	1.76	0.03	0.11	53.39	0.00	0.31	46032	8
find	25	1.70	0.62	6.80	2.73	0.02	0.09	3271588	4255
ln	25	1.67	0.02	0.03	102.00	0.00	0.55	0	25
du	24	1.52	0.02	0.02	98.06	0.00	0.89	216	0
expr	23	1.39	0.02	0.08	72.31	0.00	0.25	5492	0
chgrp	13	1.20	0.01	0.03	89.65	0.00	0.49	20545	26
chown	13	1.08	0.01	0.01	101.69	0.00	0.93	19487	0
Isearch	3	0.94	0.04	0.10	23.60	0.01	0.40	5188096	76
acctdusg	5	0.90	0.29	6.77	3.06	0.06	0.04	3309342	281
cat	16	0.83	0.01	0.01	84.61	0.00	0.75	810	0
ckpacct	24	0.80	0.02	0.30	46.94	0.00	0.06	50592	6
diss.scr	5	0.78	0.02	0.42	31.49	0.00	0.06	62688	0
mv	9	0.62	0.01	0.01	95.79	0.00	0.49	1716	13
acctcms	4	0.51	0.02	0.02	24.81	0.01	0.84	137960	1
sort	5	0.41	0.01	0.03	80.13	0.00	0.19	7628	6
egrep	5	0.40	0.00	0.01	88.89	0.00	0.31	3310	0
pr	5	0.40	0.00	0.01	94.88	0.00	0.52	29869	0
acctmerg	6	0.34	0.00	0.01	106.95	0.00	0.46	14489	3
vidlistq	3	0.27	0.00	0.11	72.73	0.00	0.03	2488	1
nulladm	8	0.26	0.00	0.05	78.80	0.00	0.07	4056	0
acctprc	1	0.19	0.02	0.02	10.39	0.02	0.86	64368	0
acctcon	1	0.19	0.00	0.01	79.43	0.00	0.41	5250	0
getent	1	0.18	0.00	0.01	45.67	0.00	0.45	10168	0
uniq	3	0.18	0.00	0.02	107.60	0.00	0.09	4015	1
ls	1	0.10	0.00	0.00	96.00	0.00	0.38	3601	0
dodisk	3	0.09	0.00	3.72	46.67	0.00	0.00	4230	1
newsyslo	1	0.09	0.00	0.01	74.29	0.00	0.11	704	0

Figure 17-3

(Continued) Example acctcms -a -o -p report.

COMMAND NAME	NUMBER CMDS	TOTAL KCOREMIN	TOTAL CPU-MIN	TOTAL REAL-MIN	MEAN SIZE-K	MEAN CPU-MIN	HOG FACTOR	CHARS TRNSFD	BLOCKS READ
nfsfind	1	0.09	0.00	0.07	57.78	0.00	0.02	1030	1
uname	1	0.08	0.00	0.00	122.00	0.00	0.67	10	0
accton	1	0.08	0.00	0.00	95.20	0.00	0.71	1499	0
m4	1	0.07	0.00	0.00	145.33	0.00	0.17	2795	1
closewtm	1	0.06	0.00	0.00	121.33	0.00	0.43	576	0
phf	1	0.05	0.00	0.00	64.00	0.00	0.28	118	0
utmp2wtm	1	0.05	0.00	0.00	154.00	0.00	0.33	576	0
wtmpfix	1	0.04	0.00	0.00	118.00	0.00	0.25	1249	0
acctwtmp	1	0.04	0.00	0.00	77.33	0.00	0.60	36	0
getopt	1	0.04	0.00	0.00	77.33	0.00	0.60	4	0
acctdisk	1	0.04	0.00	0.00	77.33	0.00	0.11	2181	2

Oct 5 02:30 1997   MONTHLY TOTAL COMMAND SUMMARY Page 1

TOTAL COMMAND SUMMARY

COMMAND NAME	NUMBER CMDS	TOTAL KCOREMIN	TOTAL CPU-MIN	TOTAL REAL-MIN	MEAN SIZE-K	MEAN CPU-MIN	HOG FACTOR	CHARS TRNSFD	BLOCKS READ
TOTALS	52323	6745.03	499.60	2845828.62	13.50	0.01	0.00	21024088064	235761
fs.scr	10070	1582.91	50.07	2803.71	31.61	0.00	0.02	165748312	83
httpd	5011	1096.80	234.76	2386276.56	4.67	0.05	0.00	4425640576	10643
htsearch	3720	913.79	19.27	26.74	47.41	0.01	0.72	352438624	597
sendmail	3923	579.36	2.89	41.71	200.45	0.00	0.07	80291784	3313
sh	3744	261.68	7.31	32793.25	35.80	0.00	0.00	5781366	196
sed	2786	202.58	1.99	5.59	102.02	0.00	0.36	1368555	70
df	1750	140.99	1.25	1.53	112.55	0.00	0.82	1188397	68
ls	840	131.61	2.23	4.01	59.02	0.00	0.56	5180067	778

Figure 17-3

(Continued) Example `acctcms -a -o -p` report.

```
cp            1615    111.85    9.23      32.22   12.12   0.01   0.29
142717204        28344
awk            952     93.78    0.76       1.42  123.34   0.00   0.53
146011          254
date          1203     82.23    0.82       1.29  100.22   0.00   0.63
992652          117
rm            1232     77.89    1.79       7.86   43.63   0.00   0.23
949      14413
accesswa       246     76.93   19.18      20.10    4.01   0.08   0.95
94099136         780
chmod         1348     70.85    0.78       0.91   91.36   0.00   0.85
730              0
find           901     63.56   21.18     236.21    3.00   0.02   0.09
108932880        147486
sadc           840     62.32    1.12       4.02   55.79   0.00   0.28
1611120          271
ln             875     57.11    0.57       0.96  100.63   0.00   0.59
0          875
vi             410     55.66    1.66     402.57   33.56   0.00   0.00
9295806          1851
diss.scr       340     53.43    1.61      49.58   33.21   0.00   0.03
3896312           6
du             840     51.46    0.53       0.57   97.38   0.00   0.92
7700             0
expr           837     49.54    0.68       2.21   72.63   0.00   0.31
194111           0
lsearch        157     48.24    1.57       3.44   30.74   0.01   0.46
205227520        1848
chgrp          467     44.42    0.48       0.94   93.47   0.00   0.50
734177          863
formmail       183     43.01    0.79       2.50   54.25   0.00   0.32
4643992          73
chown          476     42.66    0.38       0.45  112.20   0.00   0.85
738337           10
cat            670     38.28    0.43   75541.79   89.30   0.00   0.00
241756           5
imagemap       557     36.63    0.54       0.62   67.81   0.00   0.87
518726           18
acctdusg       175     31.68   10.16     235.25    3.12   0.06   0.04
110230680        8823
admind         186     29.86    0.23     286.16  128.44   0.00   0.00
556982           27
ufsdump         48     28.23    9.69     326.08    2.91   0.20   0.03
4613831680       172
ckpacct        840     27.88    0.61      10.17   45.85   0.00   0.06
1770860          186
rpc.nisd       133     26.42    0.24      22.18  110.94   0.00   0.01
1670884           1
admintoo        84     23.86    0.95     195.43   25.02   0.01   0.00
4472385          45
mail           133     23.81    0.30       0.99   78.86   0.00   0.31
1117639          104
rquotad        165     21.04    0.24     330.28   86.16   0.00   0.00
546287           28
in.ftpd         84     19.54    0.87     226.00   22.45   0.01   0.00
14394472         419
```

Figure 17-3

(Continued) Example acctcms -a -o -p report.

```
gopherd     108      19.26    0.40    139989.52    48.26    0.00   0.00
254146     1019
acctcms     141      18.09    0.76         0.87    23.85    0.01   0.88
4581152      36
quota        99      17.29    0.24         0.53    72.85    0.00   0.44
493920       44
mv          237      16.22    0.17         0.39    95.23    0.00   0.44
2097928     328
pr          178      15.32    0.15         0.28    99.94    0.00   0.54
1110749       0
sort        179      15.08    2.24        25.27     6.73    0.01   0.09
80430128    460
in.telne     89      15.07    0.41      2529.52    36.50    0.00   0.00
1605208      73
vidlistq    139      14.45    0.36         3.58    40.46    0.00   0.10
543980       61
egrep       179      13.42    0.13         0.47   104.32    0.00   0.28
112625        0
ksh         111      13.28    0.81     39584.25    16.42    0.01   0.00
3873521     177
acctmerg    212      12.55    0.12         0.24   102.86    0.00   0.51
509499      104
pwd         126       9.43    0.11         0.12    89.07    0.00   0.89
86355         6
view_dir     61       9.05    0.14         0.16    66.04    0.00   0.86
1037         10
pt_chmod    114       8.90    0.09         0.12   102.84    0.00   0.74
138282       12
```

```
Oct  5 02:30 1997  LAST LOGIN Page 1

00-00-00   adm              00-00-00   sasaria   97-09-06   rbean
00-00-00   bin              00-00-00   smtp                 97-09-06   rcooper
00-00-00   daemon   00-00-00   sys                          97-09-06   sclarke
00-00-00   dbrown   00-00-00   uucp                         97-09-09   asims
00-00-00   jdeal            97-06-05   mbrownin            97-09-09   kkirklan
00-00-00   kdegraff         97-07-17   aelms               97-09-10   mpower
00-00-00   lbailey   97-08-06   ftp                         97-09-24   jkosokof
00-00-00   ldavis   97-08-15   choeppne            97-09-24   root
00-00-00   listen   97-08-19   ttaylor   97-09-24   tseneca
00-00-00   lp               97-08-20   eaddlesp            97-09-25   lmorriss
00-00-00   noaccess         97-08-20   racker   97-09-30   lmurphy
00-00-00   nobody   97-08-30   bdehart   97-10-02   fcervone
00-00-00   nuucp            97-09-06   mtrevvet            97-10-05   mchorazy
```

Figure 17-3

(Continued) Example acctcms -a -o -p report.

each command, whereas `acctcom` produces a detail line for each record. Each of these detail lines (Fig. 17-4) contains

Command name

User

TTY name

Starting time

Ending time

Real time (wall clock time) in seconds

CPU time in seconds

Mean size in kilobytes

When optional flags are used, the following fields may also be displayed:

State of the fork/exec flag—1 for `fork()` without `exec()`

System exit status

Hog factor

Total kcore-minutes

CPU factor

Characters transferred

Blocks read (total blocks read and written)

If the command was executed with superuser privileges, a # is prefixed to the command name. When a is not associated with a known terminal, a ? is printed in the TTY name field.

Multiple `/var/adm/pacct` files may be used as input; each is processed in the order specified.

The syntax of the command and the meaning of the various flags are discussed in Table 17-1.

Summary

System accounting is a complementary function to the system activity data collector. Both tools should be used in conjunction to gain an accurate picture of the activity on the system.

```
ACCOUNTING RECORDS FROM:  Sun Oct 19 02:30:03 1997
COMMAND                           START     END       REAL     CPU     MEAN
NAME        USER     TTYNAME      TIME      TIME     (SECS)  (SECS)  SIZE(K)
#accton     root     ?            02:30:03 02:30:03   0.07    0.05    93.60
turnacct    adm      ?            02:30:02 02:30:02   0.43    0.02   100.00
mv          adm      ?            02:30:03 02:30:03   0.08    0.04   121.00
closewtm    adm      ?            02:30:03 02:30:03   0.06    0.03    77.33
cp          adm      ?            02:30:03 02:30:03   0.07    0.04   115.00
acctwtmp    adm      ?            02:30:03 02:30:03   0.05    0.03    77.33
cp          adm      ?            02:30:03 02:30:03   0.04    0.04    97.00
chmod       adm      ?            02:30:03 02:30:03   0.03    0.03    94.67
chgrp       adm      ?            02:30:03 02:30:03   0.04    0.04   127.00
chown       adm      ?            02:30:03 02:30:03   0.04    0.03    94.67
nulladm     adm      ?            02:30:03 02:30:03   0.21    0.04    50.00
utmp2wtm    adm      ?            02:30:03 02:30:03   0.04    0.04    62.00
cat         adm      ?            02:30:03 02:30:03   0.04    0.04   108.00
cp          adm      ?            02:30:03 02:30:03   0.06    0.04   117.00
chmod       adm      ?            02:30:03 02:30:03   0.04    0.04    71.00
chgrp       adm      ?            02:30:04 02:30:04   0.05    0.04   132.00
chown       adm      ?            02:30:04 02:30:04   0.04    0.04   127.00
cp          adm      ?            02:30:04 02:30:04   0.05    0.04   111.00
chmod       adm      ?            02:30:04 02:30:04   0.03    0.03    94.67
chgrp       adm      ?            02:30:04 02:30:04   0.04    0.03   169.33
chown       adm      ?            02:30:04 02:30:04   0.05    0.04   117.00
nulladm     adm      ?            02:30:03 02:30:03   0.43    0.03    66.67
wtmpfix     adm      ?            02:30:04 02:30:04   0.07    0.04   109.00
cat         adm      ?            02:30:04 02:30:04   0.04    0.04    71.00
cp          adm      ?            02:30:04 02:30:04   0.06    0.04    73.00
chmod       adm      ?            02:30:04 02:30:04   0.04    0.04   104.00
chgrp       adm      ?            02:30:04 02:30:04   0.05    0.05   109.60
chown       adm      ?            02:30:04 02:30:04   0.05    0.05   107.20
cp          adm      ?            02:30:04 02:30:04   0.05    0.05    96.80
chmod       adm      ?            02:30:04 02:30:04   0.04    0.04   107.00
chgrp       adm      ?            02:30:04 02:30:04   0.05    0.05   108.80
chown       adm      ?            02:30:04 02:30:04   0.05    0.04   137.00
cp          adm      ?            02:30:04 02:30:04   0.05    0.04   126.00
chmod       adm      ?            02:30:04 02:30:04   0.03    0.03    94.67
chgrp       adm      ?            02:30:04 02:30:04   0.05    0.05   108.80
chown       adm      ?            02:30:05 02:30:05   0.05    0.05   109.60
cp          adm      ?            02:30:05 02:30:05   0.06    0.04    73.00
chmod       adm      ?            02:30:05 02:30:05   0.03    0.03    94.67
chgrp       adm      ?            02:30:05 02:30:05   0.05    0.05   109.60
chown       adm      ?            02:30:05 02:30:05   0.05    0.05   109.60
nulladm     adm      ?            02:30:04 02:30:04   0.81    0.03    66.67
acctcon     adm      ?            02:30:05 02:30:05   0.08    0.04   130.00
cat         adm      ?            02:30:05 02:30:05   0.04    0.04    75.00
expr        adm      ?            02:30:05 02:30:05   0.12    0.09    32.89
sed         adm      ?            02:30:05 02:30:05   0.13    0.03   104.00
cp          adm      ?            02:30:05 02:30:05   0.08    0.04   117.00
chmod       adm      ?            02:30:05 02:30:05   0.04    0.04    74.00
chgrp       adm      ?            02:30:05 02:30:05   0.05    0.05   106.40
chown       adm      ?            02:30:05 02:30:05   0.04    0.04   127.00
nulladm     adm      ?            02:30:05 02:30:05   0.25    0.03    66.67
acctprc     adm      ?            02:30:05 02:30:06   1.01    0.87     6.67
cat         adm      ?            02:30:06 02:30:06   0.04    0.04   112.00
acctmerg    adm      ?            02:30:06 02:30:06   0.08    0.04   116.00
```

Figure 17-4
Abbreviated acctcom report output.

```
ls          root      pts/1       21:30:53 21:30:53    0.12    0.08     75.00
more        root      pts/1       21:31:05 21:32:06   61.79    0.07     82.29
sh          root      pts/1       21:31:05 21:32:06   61.82    0.04    133.00
man         root      pts/1       21:31:05 21:32:06   61.89    0.06     94.67
cat         root      pts/1       21:32:26 21:32:26    0.04    0.04    108.00
acctmerg    root      pts/1       21:32:26 21:32:26    0.05    0.03     89.33
acctmerg    root      pts/1       21:32:26 21:32:33    7.11    0.29     18.62
#pr         root      pts/1       21:32:26 21:32:33    7.79    0.63      8.57
prtacct     root      pts/1       21:32:26 21:32:33    7.85    0.03     66.67
cat         root      pts/1       21:33:14 21:33:14    0.04    0.03     94.67
acctmerg    root      pts/1       21:33:14 21:33:14    0.03    0.03    109.33
acctmerg    root      pts/1       21:33:14 21:33:14    0.67    0.29     18.62
pr          root      pts/1       21:33:14 21:33:14    0.68    0.29     19.03
prtacct     root      pts/1       21:33:13 21:33:13    0.74    0.02     82.00
fs.scr      nobody    ?           21:33:31 21:33:39    8.86    0.31     30.97
sh          root      pts/1       21:34:27 21:34:27    0.01    0.01    168.00
more        root      pts/1       21:34:40 21:34:45    5.17    0.06     98.67
sh          root      pts/1       21:34:40 21:34:45    5.22    0.04    131.00
man         root      pts/1       21:34:40 21:34:45    5.51    0.07     81.71
acctcom     root      pts/1       21:34:48 21:34:54    6.07    2.86      4.18
```

Figure 17-4

(Continued) Abbreviated `acctcom` report output.

TABLE 17-1 `acctcom`—Search and Print Process Accounting Files

```
acctcom [ -abfhikmqrtv ] [ -C sec ] [ -e time] [ -E time] [ -g group] [ -H factor ] [ -I
chars] [ -l line] [ -n pattern ] [ -o output] [ -O sec][ -s time] [ -S time] [ -u user ]
[filename…]
```

Options	Meaning
-a	Show some average statistics about the processes selected. The statistics will be printed after the output records.
-b	Read backward, showing latest commands first. This option has no effect when standard input is read.
-f	Print the fork/exec flag and system exit status columns in the output. The numeric output for this option will be in octal.
-h	Instead of mean memory size, show the fraction of total available CPU time consumed by the process during its execution. This "hog factor" is computed as (total CPU time)/(elapsed time).
-i	Print columns containing the I/O counts in the output.
-k	Instead of memory size, show total kcore-minutes.
-m	Show mean core size (the default).
-q	Do not print any output records; just print the average statistics as with the -a option.
-r	Show CPU factor [user-time/(system-time + user-time)].
-t	Show separate system and user CPU times.
-v	Exclude column headings from the output.

TABLE 17-1 (Continued) `acctcom`—Search and Print Process Accounting Files

```
acctcom [ -abfhikmqrtv ] [ -C sec ] [ -e time] [ -E time] [ -g group] [ -H factor ] [ -I
chars] [ -l line] [ -n pattern ] [ -o output] [ -O sec][ -s time] [ -S time] [ -u user ]
[filename…]
```

Option	Meaning
-C sec	Show only processes with total CPU time (system-time + user-time) exceeding sec seconds. -e time Select processes existing at or before time.
-E time	Select processes ending at or before time. Using the same time for both -S and -E shows the processes that existed at time.
-g group	Show only processes belonging to group. The group may be designated by either the group id or group name.
-H factor	Show only processes that exceed factor, where factor is the "hog factor" as explained in option -h above.
-I chars	Show only processes transferring more characters than the cutoff number given by chars.
-l line	Show only processes belonging to terminal /dev/term/line.
-n pattern	Show only commands matching pattern, which is a regular expression.
-o output	Copy selected process records in the input data format to output; suppress printing to standard output.
-O sec	Show only processes with CPU system time exceeding sec seconds.
-s time	Select processes existing at or after time; the format is hours[:minutes:sec].
-S time	Select processes starting at or after time.
-u user	Show only processes belonging to user. The user may be specified by a user id, a login name, # (which designates only those processes executed with superuser privileges), or ? (which designates only those processes associated with unknown user ids).

The first part of the chapter focused on the data gathering aspects of the accounting subsystem. The concluding part focused on the data reporting aspects through such commands as `prtacct`, `prctmp`, `prdaily`, `acctcms`, and `acctcom`.

The next, and concluding, chapter discusses the general aspects of capacity planning management.

18

Capacity Planning Management

All computer installations perform capacity planning in some way. When this function is performed regularly and well, both the information technology (IT) department and the overall organization benefit. These benefits can include

- Cost saving through better use of equipment, thus prolonging its useful life
- More effective business processes because system availability is known and consistent
- Higher morale because few people want to work in an environment of confusion and uncertainty

The purpose of this chapter is to discuss what some of the important nontechnical aspects of managing a capacity planning project are. In this chapter, the discussion will focus on predicting capacity requirements, reporting issues, and developing a structure for continuing capacity planning.

Predicting Capacity Requirements

Capacity planning uses performance tuning efforts as a component of the overall plan but is not concerned with predicting device utilization levels or other such measures of computing power as an end in itself. Instead, these are used as factors in maintaining desired levels of service.

Capacity planning is a predictive activity. The primary concern is to determine what the effect of changes in the system workload, whether abrupt or gradual, will have on the overall system and the level of service delivered. Four steps (Fig. 18-1) are typically involved in this predictive activity:

1. Characterization of the workload

2. Development of a workload model

3. Forecasts of expected needs

4. Recommendations for action

Characterization of the Workload

In Chap. 3, the various types of workload and their characteristics were discussed. Understanding the types of workloads and their occurrence

Figure 18-1
Capacity planning as a predictive activity.

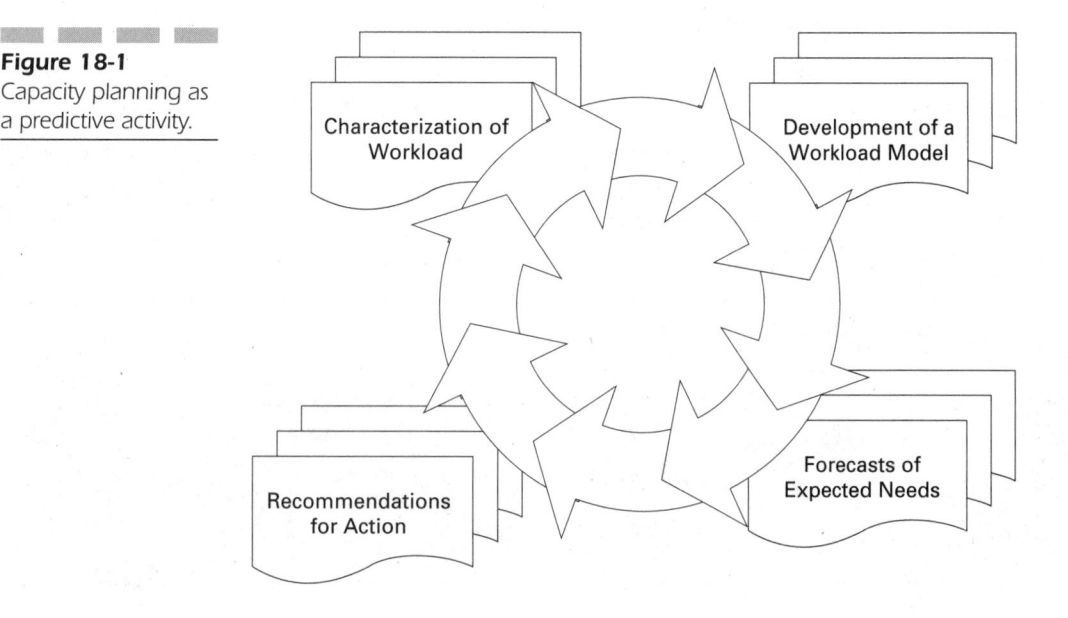

on the system is essential for effective capacity planning management (Fig. 18-2).

Characterization of the workload of a system consists of the following components:

- Identifying the units of work in the system based on workload type and business function; these are known as the units of functionality (UFF).
- Determining the relative frequency of each UFF.
- Identifying the interactions among UFFs.
- Determining the relative frequency of each UFF interaction type.
- Determining the amount and type of system resources consumed by each UFF and UFF interaction type.

Development of a Workload Model

The five components of the workload characterization form the basis for developing the workload model. The model takes the components and uses them to determine the average and peak number of transactions in any given period of time. This provides a baseline against which to measure.

An important factor in the development of the workload model is that in many cases it may not be possible to identify or know a significant amount of the workload. This can be for several reasons. General system overhead is one factor. Although this can and should be measured, it cannot be accurately identified in some cases; therefore, it is difficult to predict with accuracy.

However, the more common problems in developing an accurate workload model are related to the definition of the UFFs. If a business unit cannot adequately describe a business function, the UFF for that function will be, at best, incomplete. At worse, it may be totally off base.

Particularly difficult is when the interactions between UFFs are unknown or not completely understood by the business unit. It is very possible that a detailed analysis of how various activities influence and modify other business activities has never been performed.

Development of an accurate workload model requires that these areas be explored. When accurate measurements cannot be taken, estimates based on a "best guess" must be made. But the performance analyst

Figure 18-2
The steps in activity
forecasting.

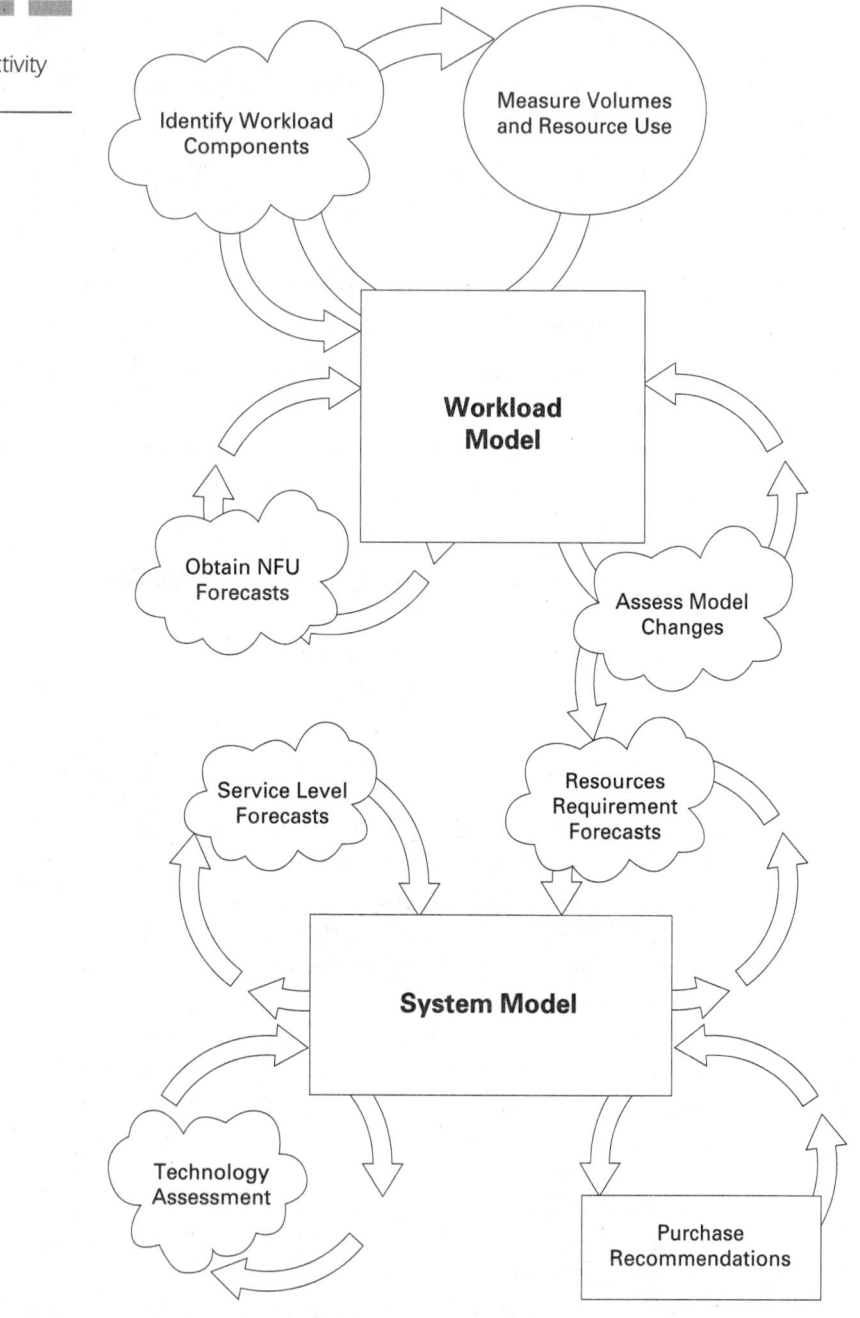

must be careful to note, for future reference, that guesses were made because data was incomplete or inconclusive.

Forecasts of Expected Needs

Forecasts of expected needs come from a wide variety of sources, most of which are found outside of the information technology organization. Business units are the best judge of what changes are likely to take place in their realm within a fixed period of time, so they must be consulted in order to determine future needs.

However, these estimates or projections cannot be used in isolation from other factors and considerations. Business units may not be aware of all of the events occurring within the larger organization. Business units may also have inaccurate evaluations of events occurring within their own unit. This can be for any number of reasons: naiveté, lack of or incomplete functional analysis, holding beliefs that are no longer true, denial of current reality, etc.

The easiest and most common source of data used for forecasting is existing system performance data. Using historical data, statistical projections can be made to determine what the expected needs will be at a particular point in the future. For simple analysis, this may be all that is required. But one needs to be cautious in relying too much on this method; trends can be grossly misleading. Although an increase in system use may foreshadow increasing amounts of business, an increase in system use will also occur just before the shutdown of a business or business unit.

Other sources of information for forecasting expected needs include

- Corporate strategic plan
- User interviews and questionnaires
- Current application development projects
- Economic trends
- Anticipated changes in business legal requirements, required practices, or regulations
- Actions of competitors or others in similar business environments

The corporate strategic plan should give the capacity planner insight into the future direction and focus of the organization overall. However, this needs to be supplemented with interviews with or questionnaires to those in the business units implementing the plan. The business units can provide details regarding the implementation of the strategic plan and also provide information on deviations from the plan that are occurring.

Bear in mind that in most cases it is not possible to interview all user groups nor is it necessary. As with many things in life, typically 80 percent of the workload of a system will be generated by 20 percent (or less) of the organization. Obviously, the capacity planner will want to focus on the 20 percent of the organization that is generating the majority of the work.

When conducting the interviews, the capacity planner needs to ensure that all user interviews and/or questionnaires are designed such that consistent information is derived from the business units; that is, ask everyone the same questions.

Current applications development projects will assuredly have an impact on capacity planning efforts. In addition to the increased workload that will result due to moving completed projects into production, the capacity planner should not forget to include the changes in system utilization that the development and testing functions will impose on the system.

The last group of factors that were outlined above are more esoteric and traditionally have been considered less important if considered at all, by capacity planners. Economic trends, changes in business legal requirements, required practices or regulations, and the actions of competitors or others in similar business environments all have an impact on what will occur on the system in the future. If the capacity planner is able to factor these into the forecast, this will make the forecast all the more accurate.

Recommendations for Action

Once the forecast has been developed, it can be applied to the working model to predict what resources will be required at a particular point in the future. Based on this, recommendations can be made on actions to be taken.

An important point to consider is that a recommendation for action may be that no action should be taken at the present time. If the system is performing adequately and appears that it will continue to do so indefinitely, there is no reason for not stating this and recommending that ongoing actions simply continue to monitor the performance of the system.

■ ■ Reporting Issues

Capacity planning or performance analysis reports should strive to meet certain goals. All of these are related to the effective and relevant communication of information. The goals of every report should be to

- Enhance the management process, whether this is in IT or in a business unit
- Provide meaningful information
- Objectively depict performance information
- Be in understandable and consistent units
- Relate to corporate goals
- Be direct and uncluttered
- Encourage productive dialog
- Strengthen control over automated systems

There are cases where individual reports will not meet all of the criteria. This is understandable and expected. However, these goals should be used as a basis for developing the reporting structure used in a capacity planning project.

Basic Issues in Reporting

It is important for the capacity planner to realize that as information moves up the organizational hierarchy, less emphasis (and interest) is placed on the details of a matter. Instead, the focus increasingly centers on the underlying issues and what needs to be done to facilitate the resolution of the issues.

Furthermore, each level of the hierarchy has different information needs. The final report of a capacity planning project is typically the only document from the project that will receive the attention of the highest levels of management. Managers of business units may receive more specific and continuing analysis and reporting. And, of course, in the information technology department, the level of analysis will vary from the daily statistics the capacity planner receives to detailed analyses of trends the manager receives.

At all levels and positions within the organization, though, the primary question asked about capacity planning data is What are the trends: Are things worse, better, the same? How this information is conveyed is of great importance to the success of the capacity planning project. Information of this type is often displayed as numeric tabulations of statistics, that is, as text directly from a listing from the performance analysis tool. This is a big mistake. Trends are best understood when displayed in graphical format. The use of graphical representations allows variations to be more easily and readily determined. Figure 18-3 demonstrates this principle.

There are multiple formats for graphical data. Line graphs are useful when two variables are to be compared over a period of time. An example is the number of visits to a Web site per hour over the course of a day (Fig. 18-4).

When more than two variables are involved, bar charts are useful. These allow for the comparison of several different variables over a peri-

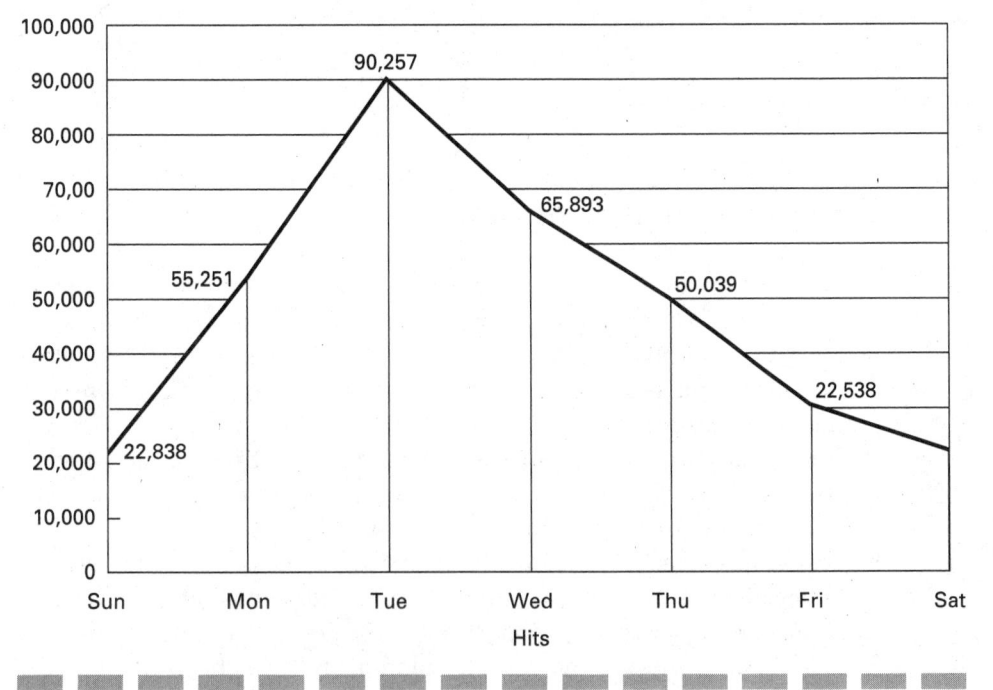

Figure 18-3
The graphical display of information has more impact than simple numeric reporting.

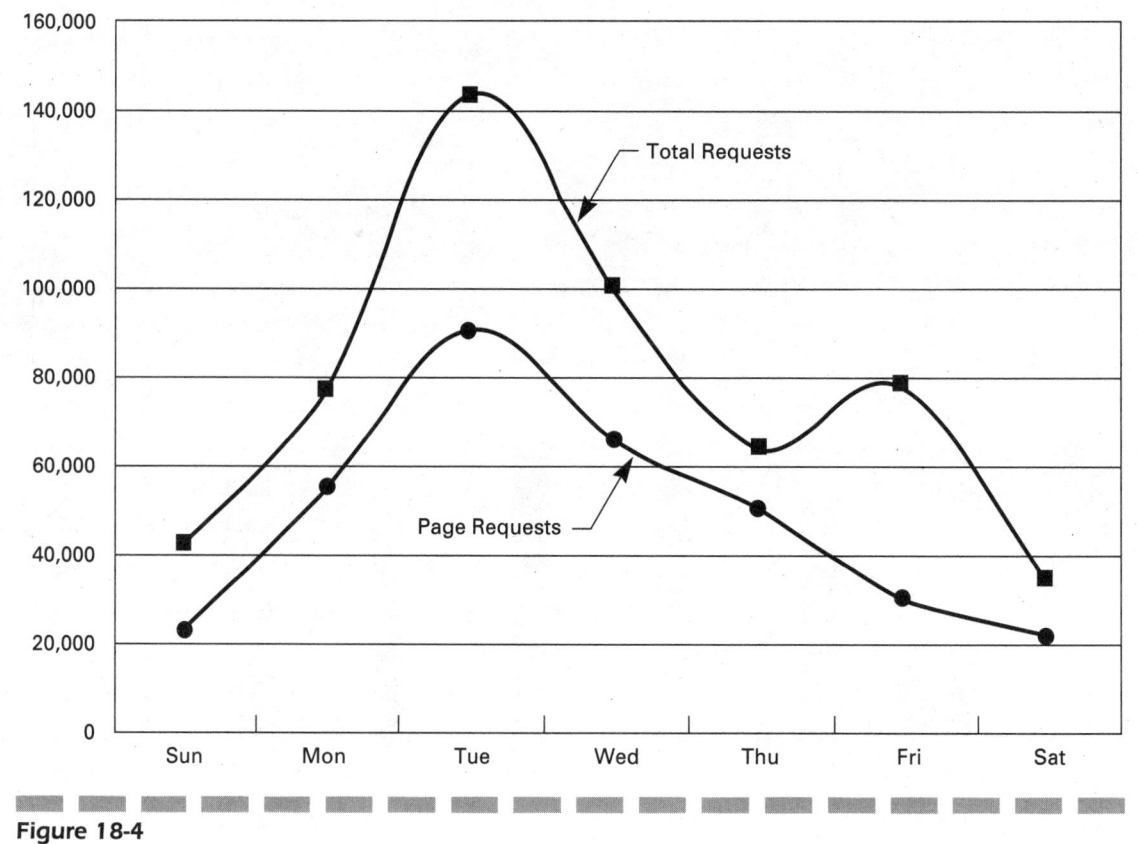

**Web Page Hits for the Week of
September 28, 1997**

Figure 18-4
Line charts are useful for tracking multiple data items.

od of time (Fig. 18-5) and for contrasting changes in a few number of variables over a period of time (Fig. 18-6).

Although other types of charts may be used in reporting, such as Gantt, Kiviat, and Schumacher charts, these are not as commonly used in most business functions and therefore lead to the potential for misunderstanding and miscommunication. A capacity planner who decides to use one of these other formats must be sure to put a method in place for ensuring that people viewing the report will be able to understand what the report is trying to communicate.

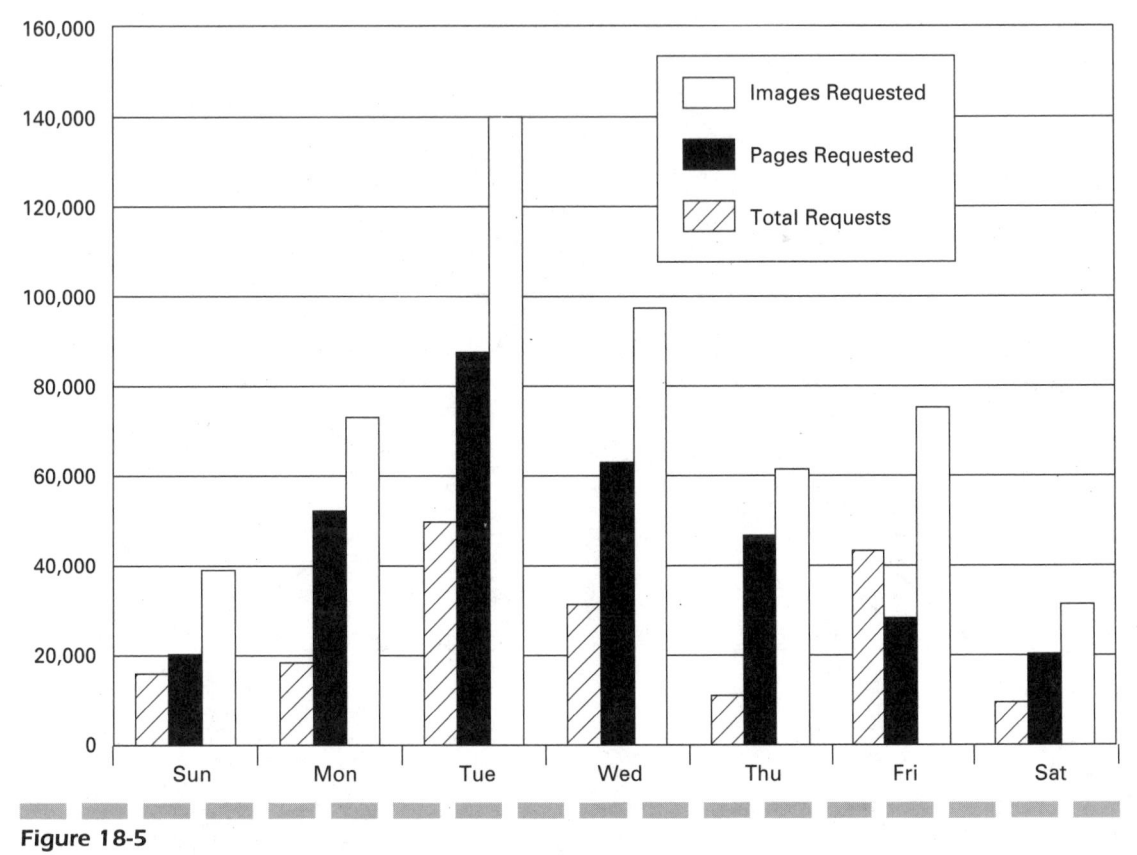

**Web Server Activity for the Week of
September 28, 1997**

Figure 18-5
Bar charts enable graphic representation of comparisons among multiple data items.

Additional Considerations

Terminology is very important when constructing a report. Although the capacity planner may be interested in *mbuf* usage or the number of commands queued for a SCSI device, no one outside of the capacity planning function cares. Very few managers outside of IT have the time or interest to understand the technical terminology of performance management. Jargon is a hindrance to communication outside of the capacity planning function; it should be avoided, and common terms should be used whenever possible.

Relevancy of information is critical to understanding. Returning to the immediately preceding example, if a report of *mbuf* usage is to be

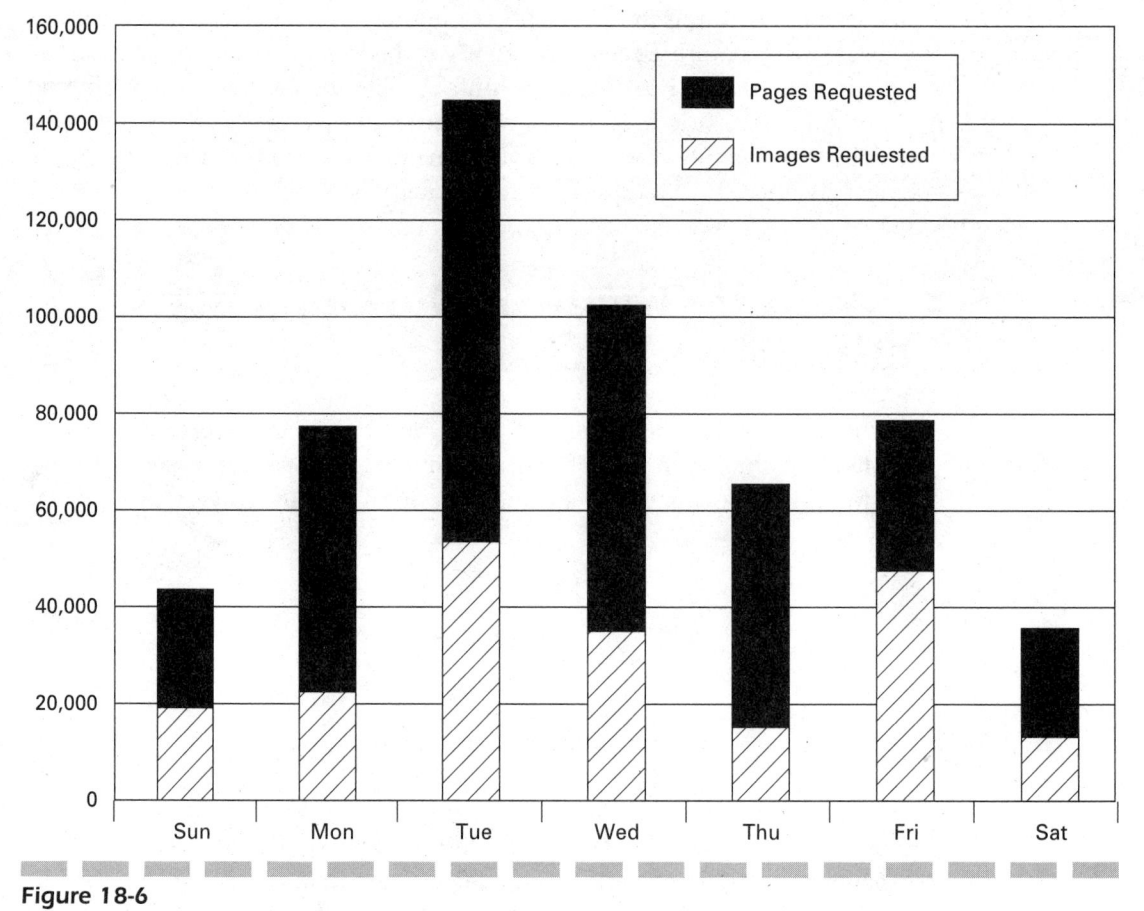

**Pages and Images requested for the
September 28, 1997**

Figure 18-6
Modified bar charts allow for individual items to be combined into a total representation.

relevant to anyone outside of the capacity planning group, the relevancy of *mbuf*s must be explained in common and understandable terms. If this cannot be done, the item should not be put on the report. This is a fundamental rule—if an item cannot be related to a business function or made relevant to the viewer, do not report on it outside of the immediate capacity planning group. Reporting on items that appear to be irrelevant (or are not understood) can raise doubts about the relevancy and veracity of the report.

Reporting procedures should be consistent. That is, a particular report should always contain the same functional points of measurement, and it should be delivered on a consistent schedule. Short, periodic reports that contain the same reporting parameters and trends for comparison are the best format for reports outside of the immediate capacity planning group. Reports should not overwhelm nontechnical users with detail. Excessive detail can be misconstrued as an effort to hide something. Furthermore, unfavorable variations in performance should not result in skipped reports or alterations of data reporting points to deemphasize unfavorable variations. Actions of this type significantly affect the credibility of the capacity planner.

The Life Cycle of the Capacity Planning Function

The performance management and capacity planning functions have a life cycle similar to that of other technical development projects. In this life cycle, the capacity planning function typically moves through five stages:*

- Vendor
- Special studies
- Technician
- Organizational development
- Mature

In the first stage, *vendor*, the organization does no capacity planning on its own. In this stage, it completely relies on the assessment of the original equipment vendor and their recommendations. At this stage, the performance management function is tuned into the need of the information technology department, but the needs of the larger organization are not taken into account.

Reliance on the vendor cannot continue indefinitely, however. A number of factors (vendor objectivity, introduction of additional equipment vendors, professional self-respect of the IT function) cause the capacity planning function to enter the second stage—*special studies*. In this phase, an ad hoc team is set up as problems occur to analyze the situation and recommend solutions. In this stage, there is no continuity of experience in the capacity planning projects. Insights into system performance that may have been gained are typically lost. This occurs

---

*This life cycle was first discussed by H. Pat Artis.

because the team is disbanded after the recommended solution has been implemented.

When a permanent team is established, the capacity planning function enters stage 3—*technician.* In this phase, more complex tools are used for performance measurement and monitoring, and a great deal of emphasis is placed on methods for tracking performance. Reports issued during this phase tend to concentrate heavily on technology and methodology issues. Because of this, they are of limited use outside of the immediate capacity planning group. Furthermore, higher levels of management are not able to discern the benefits of capacity planning during this stage because of this high reliance on technology and methodology reporting.

Stage 3 cannot last for very long. Either the capacity planning function moves into stage 4—*organizational development*—or the capacity planning function is abandoned. This abandonment occurs due to the refusal of upper management to continue to support something for which they cannot see a benefit.

In stage 4, the capacity planners become more aware of external issues and start focusing more on the external perspectives of business units and less on technology and methodology. Essentially, the capacity planners take on more of a management-oriented view, which in turn results in better acceptance of the capacity planning function and the reports and recommendations that come from the group.

The final stage, *mature,* is the natural outgrowth of stage 4. As the capacity planner becomes more aware of the organization and its requirements and peculiarities, the responsibilities of the capacity planning function increase. In this stage, the capacity planning function should be an integral part of the organizational planning and decision-making processes.

It is neither inevitable nor desirable that every organization will go through each distinct phase. Neither is it inevitable that each phase will last for a predetermined period of time. Depending on the level of commitment and level of expertise in the capacity planning function, it is possible to move quickly (or even directly) into the last two stages of the capacity planning function.

Developing a Continuing Structure

A critical component of the continuing capacity planning function is visibility throughout the organization. A performance and workload measurement system should be established (if not already in place). This system should cover all elements of information technology equipment and networks.

A performance reporting system should be established. Wide distribution to middle- and senior-level management should be implemented.

Once the performance reporting system has been established, business units must be more intimately involved in the capacity planning process. Business units must be involved in defining the units of functionality and should be consulted to determine what interactions occur among them. Business units will also be able to supply information about workload forecasts.

It is also at this point that *service level agreements* (SLAs) may be worked out with business units. Typically an SLA will include

- Predictions by the business unit of workload volumes
- *Response time* rates for transactional workload
- *Turn-around* times for batch workloads
- System reliability and availability targets
- Discussion of the mechanisms for the transfer of information, such as
  - System outage notification
  - Submission of change requests
  - Notification of unusual system situations, extremely high transaction volume, for example
  - Communication of problems (bad response time, broken equipment, etc.)
- Disaster recovery mechanisms

Other items may be included in the SLA as well. A common item included is an application development agreement. In the agreement, both parties outline and define the procedures for requesting, developing, and testing new applications.

Defining the Planning Cycle

Although all aspects of the system must be monitored on a continuing basis, in most installations it is not possible to focus on all aspects all of the time. When there is no particular area of the system that is troublesome, it may be difficult to focus on monitoring one particular aspect of the system.

To mitigate this problem, a capacity planning cycle should be defined. The cycle should not be designed as a rigid set of procedures but instead as a guide to coordinate the review of the site.

Figure 18-7 demonstrates a sample guide of a continuous review cycle. In this cycle, the areas of attention are divided into four aspects:

- Operating system tuning
- Scheduling improvements
- Application tuning
- Configuration upgrades

This cycle works through each aspect in order of increasing difficulty and expense. It is easier to tune Solaris than it may be to reschedule workloads. Rescheduling workloads is usually easier than redesigning

Figure 18-7

The continuous cycle of computer performance evaluation.

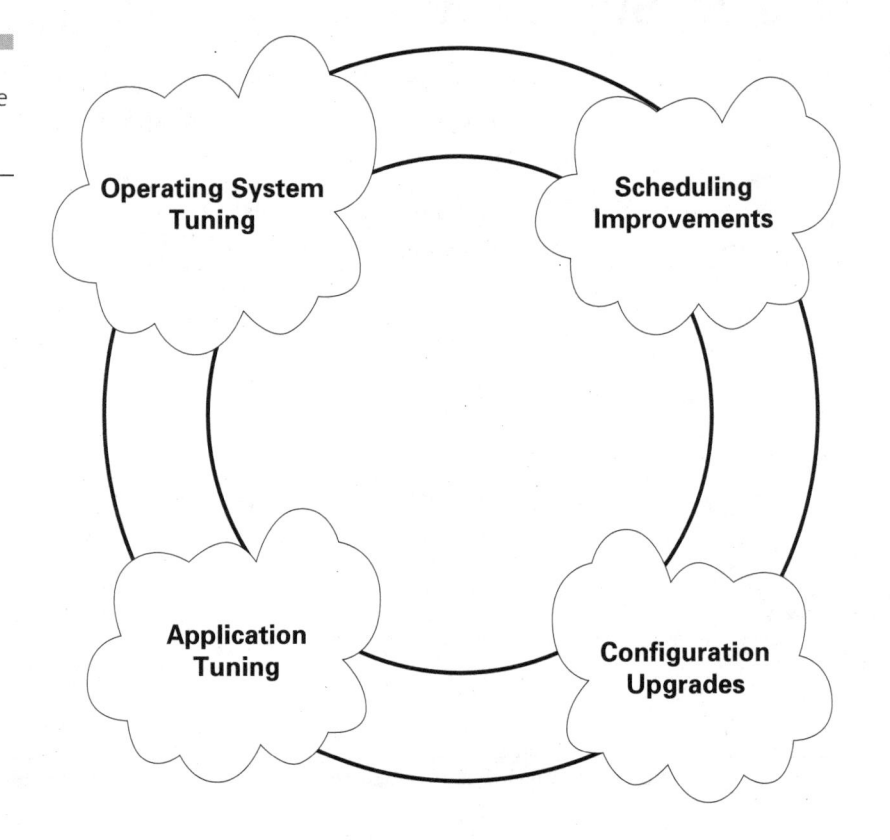

applications, and redesigning applications is sometimes cheaper than upgrading equipment.*

This cycle is not all inclusive. Many capacity planning projects may not conveniently fit into this structure. However, this cycle can be used as a basis for developing other cycles that work better within a particular organization.

The cycle has applicability outside of its use as a decision assistance tool. The cycle can also be used as a mechanism for time and resource accounting. Analysis of where the most time or money is being spent within the cycle can provide the capacity planning manager with an understanding of some of the underlying issues related to capacity planning at a particular organization. This type of analysis also provides the manager with a basis for reallocation of resources and expenditures related to the capacity planning function.

Summary

Capacity planning management has been focus of this, the concluding, chapter. In this chapter, the major aspects of capacity planning management were discussed:

- Predicting capacity requirements
- Characterization of the workload
- Development of a workload model
- Forecasting expected needs
- Developing recommendations for action

Following this, recommendations for developing a reporting structure, life cycle, and continuing structure for capacity planning were explored.

With this, the book draws to a close. It is my hope that this has been a useful and meaningful experience for the reader.

---

*But sometimes this is not the case. That is why a cycle should not be followed with rigidity.

INDEX

About the Author

Frank Cervone is the Assistant Director for Systems at the DePaul University Libraries in Chicago where he supervises a heterogeneous network of Solaris (SPARC and Intel based), Windows NT, and Novell Netware servers. He is the author of *VSE/ESA JCL: Utilities, POWER,* and *VSAM and ALX/6000 System Guide,* both published by McGraw-Hill.